JONI EARECKSON TADA

Her Story

JONI

~

A STEP FURTHER

~

CHOICES ... CHANGES

Complete in One Volume

Inspirational Press • New York

First Inspirational Press edition published in 1994.

Inspirational Press
A division of BBS Publishing Corporation
386 Park Avenue South
New York, NY 10016

Inspirational Press is a registered trademark of BBS Publishing Corporation.
Published by arrangement with Zondervan Publishing House.

Library of Congress Catalog Card Number: 94-77192

ISBN: 0-88486-103-1

Text design by Hannah Lerner.
Printed in the United States of America.

Contents

JONI

Preface

ISOLATED, BY ITSELF, what is a minute? Merely a measurement of time. There are 60 in an hour, 1,440 in a day. At seventeen, I had already ticked off more than 9,000,000 of them in my life.

Yet, in some cosmic plan, this single minute was isolated. Into these particular sixty seconds was compressed *more significance than all the millions of minutes marking my life prior to this instant.*

So many actions, sensations, thoughts, and feelings were crowded into that fragment of time. How can I describe them? How can I begin to catalog them?

I recall so clearly the details of those few dozen seconds—seconds destined to change my life forever. And there was no warning or premonition.

What happened on July 30, 1967, was the beginning of an incredible adventure which I feel compelled to share because of what I have learned.

Oscar Wilde wrote: "In this world there are only two tragedies. One is not getting what one wants, and the other is getting it." To rephrase his thought, I suggest there are likewise only two joys. One is having God answer all your prayers; the other is not receiving the answer to all your prayers. I believe this because I have found that God knows my needs infinitely better than I know them. And He is utterly dependable, no matter which direction our circumstances take us.

JONI EARECKSON

"We are handicapped on all sides, but we are never frustrated; we are puzzled, but never in despair. We are persecuted, but we never have to stand it alone: we may be knocked down but we are never knocked out! Every day we experience something of the death of Jesus, so that we may also know the power of the life of Jesus in these bodies of ours. . . . We wish you could see how all this is working out for your benefit, and how the more grace God gives, the more thanksgiving will redound to his glory. This is the reason we never collapse."

—2 Cor. 4:8–10, 15, 16, Phillips

One

THE HOT JULY sun was setting low in the west and gave the waters of Chesapeake Bay a warm red glow. The water was murky, and as my body broke the surface in a dive, its cold cleanness doused my skin.

In a jumble of actions and feelings, many things happened simultaneously. I felt my head strike something hard and unyielding. At the same time, clumsily and crazily, my body sprawled out of control. I heard or felt a loud electric buzzing, an unexplainable inner sensation. It was something like an electrical shock, combined with a vibration—like a heavy metal spring being suddenly and sharply uncoiled, its "sprong" perhaps muffled by the water. Yet it wasn't really a sound or even a feeling—just a sensation. I felt no pain.

I heard the underwater sound of crunching, grinding sand. I was lying face down on the bottom. *Where? How did I get here? Why are my arms tied to my chest?* My thoughts screamed. *Hey! I'm caught!*

I felt a small tidal undercurrent lift me slightly and let me settle once more on the bottom. Out of the corner of my eye, I saw light above me. Some of the confusion left. I remembered diving into the bay. *Then what? Am I caught in a fishnet or something? I need to get out!* I tried to kick. *My feet must be tied or caught, too!*

Panic seized me. With all my will power and strength, I tried to break free. Nothing happened. Another tidal swell lifted and rolled.

What's wrong? I hit my head. Am I unconscious?. Trying to move is like trying to move in a dream. Impossible. But I'll drown! Will I wake up in time? Will someone see me? I can't be unconscious, or I wouldn't be aware of what's happening. No, I'm alive.

I felt the pressure of holding my breath begin to build. I'd have to breathe soon.

Another tidal swell gently lifted me. Fragments of faces, thoughts, and memories spun crazily across my consciousness. My friends. My parents. Things I was ashamed of. Maybe God was calling me to come and explain these actions.

"Joni!" A somber voice echoed down some eerie corridor, almost as a summons. God? Death?

I'm going to die! I don't want to die! Help me, please.

"Joni!"

Doesn't anyone care that I'm here? I've got to breathe!

"Joni!" That voice! Muffled through the waters, it sounded far off. Now it was closer. "Joni, are you all right?"

Kathy! My sister sees me. Help me, Kathy! I'm stuck!

The next tidal swell was a little stronger than the rest and lifted me a bit higher. I fell back on the bottom, with broken shells, stones, and sand grating into my shoulders and face.

"Joni, are you looking for shells?"

No! I'm caught down here—grab me! I can't hold my breath any longer.

"Did you dive in here? It's so shallow," I heard Kathy clearly now.

Her shadow indicated she was now above me. I struggled inwardly against panic, but I knew I had no more air. Everything was going dark.

I felt Kathy's arms around my shoulders, lifting.

Oh, please, dear God. Don't let me die!

Kathy struggled, stumbled, then lifted again. *Oh, God, how much longer!* Everything was black, and I felt I was falling while being lifted. Just before fainting, my head broke the water's surface. *Air!* Beautiful, life-giving, salt-tinged air. I choked in oxygen so quickly, I almost gagged. Gasping, I gulped in mouthfuls.

"Oh, thank You, God—thank You!" I managed.

"Hey, are you okay?" Kathy asked. I blinked to clear my mind and dissolve the confusion. It didn't seem to work because I saw my arm slung lifelessly over Kathy's shoulder, yet I felt it was still tied to my chest.

I looked down at my chest. My arms were not tied. I realized with a growing horror that my limbs were dangling motionlessly. I couldn't move them!

In the confusion, Kathy took charge. She called a nearby swimmer on an inflated raft. Together they wrestled me onto it and pushed it toward shore. I heard the raft beneath me slide against the sandy beach.

I tried to get up but felt pinned against the raft. People began to hurry over to see what had happened. Soon there was a crowd hovering above me, faces looking down in curiosity. Their stares and whispers made me feel embarrassed, uncomfortable, and even more confused.

"Kathy, please make them leave."

"Yes, everyone stand back! Someone call an ambulance. Move away, please. She needs air," Kathy instructed.

Kathy's boyfriend, Butch, knelt beside me. His lean frame shielded me from the crowd, now moving back. "You okay, kid?" he asked. His large dark eyes, usually smiling and full of good-natured fun, were clouded with concern.

"Kathy—I can't move!" I was frightened. I could see they were, too.

Kathy nodded.

"Hold me!"

"I am, Joni." She lifted my hands to show that she was grasping them firmly.

"But I can't feel it. Squeeze me."

Kathy bent over and held me close. I couldn't feel her hug.

"Can you feel this?" She touched my leg.

"No," I said.

"This?" She squeezed my forearm.

"No!" I cried. "I can't feel it!"

"How about this?" Her hand slid from my arm to rest on my shoulder.

"Yes! Yes, I can feel that!"

Relief and joy suddenly came over us. At last, somewhere on my body, I could feel something. As I lay there on the sand, I began to piece things together. I had hit my head diving; I must have injured something to cause this numbness. I wondered how long it would last.

"Don't worry," I reassured Butch and Kathy—and myself. "The Lord won't let anything happen to me. I'll be all right."

I heard the wail of a siren. Soon the ambulance pulled up and doors opened. In less than a minute, attendants efficiently lifted me onto a stretcher. Somehow their starched white uniforms were comforting as they carefully placed me in the back of the ambulance. The crowd of curious onlookers followed.

Kathy started to climb up into the ambulance.

Butch took her hand and said softly, "I'll follow in the car." Then he nodded sternly to the driver. "Be careful with her," he instructed.

The siren began to wail, and we headed away from the beach.

I looked up at the attendant riding beside me and said, "I hate to put you to all this trouble. I think once I catch my breath I'll be okay. I'm sure the numbness will wear off shortly."

He didn't say anything but reached over and brushed sand off my face, smiled, and looked away. *I wish he'd say something to let me know I'll be all right—that I'll be going home as soon as the doctors at the hospital check me over*, I thought.

But no comforting words were offered. I was left to my own thoughts and prayers as the siren wailed. I looked through the window at the city speeding by outside.

The Lord is my shepherd . . .

People on curbs stared curiously.

I shall not want . . .

Cars pulled over to let us pass.

He maketh me to lie down in green pastures . . .

The ambulance slowed and turned down a busy boulevard.

He restoreth my soul . . .

I could not collect my thoughts enough to pray. I clung to memorized promises from the Bible.

Yea, though I walk through the valley of the shadow of death, I will fear no evil: for thou art with me. . . .

Suddenly the ambulance siren growled into silence. The driver backed up to the doors of the hospital, and the attendants quickly began to ease my stretcher out. As they swung me smoothly through the doors, I saw the sign:

EMERGENCY ENTRANCE
NO PARKING
Emergency Vehicles Only

By now the city sky was dark; the sun had set. I was cold and longed to be home.

Inside, the emergency area was alive with activity. I was taken into a room and placed on a hospital table with wheels. The light hurt my eyes. As I turned my face to avoid its glare, I could see all the equipment and supplies arranged in ready rows. Bottles, gauze, bandages, trays, scissors, scalpels, jars, packets with long, medical-sounding names, and unfamiliar shapes were all about. The antiseptic smells and pungent odors made me slightly queasy.

A nurse strapped me to the table and wheeled me into one of the many small cubicles. She pulled privacy curtains around me. Again I struggled desperately to move my arms and legs. They were still numb and motionless. *I feel so helpless. I'm getting sick. I'm scared.* Tears welled up in my eyes.

"Can't you tell me what's happened to me?" I begged.

The nurse merely shrugged and began to take off my rings. "The doctor will be here soon. Now, I'm going to put your jewelry in this envelope. Regulations."

"How long do I have to stay here? Can I go home tonight?"

"I'm sorry. You'll have to ask the doctor. Regulations." Her answer was emotionless and reminded me of a telephone recording.

Another nurse came into the cubicle with forms to fill out.

"Name, please."

"Joni Eareckson."

"Johnny? J-o-h-n-n-y?"

"No. It's pronounced Johnny—after my father—but it's spelled J-o-n-i. Last name is E-a-r-e-c-k-s-o-n." Then I gave her my address, my folks' name and number and asked her to call them.

"Do you have Blue Cross?"

"I don't know. Ask my folks—or my sister. She's probably outside. She was with me at the beach. Her name is Kathy. Ask her."

The nurse with the clipboard left. The other put the envelope with my belongings in it on a nearby table. Then she opened a drawer and pulled out a big pair of shears.

"W-what are you going to do?" I stammered.

"I've got to remove your swimming suit."

"But don't cut it! It's brand-new. I just got it—and it's my fav—"

"Sorry. Regulations," She repeated. The heavy *ch-cluk, ch-cluk, ch-cluk* of the shears echoed off the plaster walls. She pulled the ruined scraps of material off and dropped them in a waste can. She didn't even care. The suit didn't mean a thing to her. I wanted to cry.

She put a sheet over me and left. I felt embarrassed and uncomfortable. The sheet slipped down, exposing part of my breasts, and I couldn't move to pull it back up. Frustration and fear finally brought a flood of hot tears as I began to sense the seriousness of the situation.

Yea, though I walk through the valley of the shadow of death, I will fear no evil; for thou art with me. . . .

I fought back the tears and tried to think of other things. *I wonder if Kathy called mom and dad. I wonder if Dick knows yet.*

A man in dark tweed slacks and white lab coat pulled the curtains and stepped into the cubicle.

"I'm Dr. Sherrill," he said pleasantly while flipping through pages on a clipboard. "And your name is Joanie?"

"It's pronounced Johnny. I'm named after my father." *Must I go through this explanation with everyone?*

"Okay, Joni, let's see what's happened to you."

"Dr. Sherrill, when can I go home?"

"Tell me, do you feel this?" He had a long pin and was apparently pricking my feet and legs.

"N-no—I can't feel that."

"How about this?"

Gritting my teeth, I shut my eyes to concentrate, hoping to feel something—anything.

"Nothing."

He was holding my arm and pressing the pin against my limp fingers, wrist, and forearm. *Why can't I feel anything?* He touched the upper arm. Finally I felt a small sting in my shoulder.

"Yes, I feel that. I had feeling there at the beach."

Dr. Sherrill took out his pen and began to write on the clipboard.

Other medical staff people began to appear. Amidst the clatter and clutter of tubes, bottles, and trays, I heard Dr. Sherrill ask another doctor to come over. He went through the pin routine with the other doctor, and the two of them conferred in subdued voices near the head of my table. The language of medical terms and jargon was unfamiliar to me.

"Looks like a fracture-dislocation."

"Uh-huh. I'd say at the fourth and fifth cervical level judging from her areas of feeling."

"We'll need to get to it. X-rays won't tell if there's continuity or not."

"Shall I order O-R prepped?"

"Yes. Stat. And try again to reach her parents."

Dr. Sherrill's associate left quickly, followed by one of the nurses. Dr. Sherrill whispered instructions to the brusque nurse who had destroyed my swimsuit, and she left, too.

I watched someone wipe my arm with a cotton ball and stick a needle into the vein. I felt nothing.

Out of the corner of my eye, I saw Dr. Sherrill holding a pair of electric hair clippers. There was a loud click and buzzing sound as they were turned on. *What on earth are those for!* I wondered. With growing terror, I realized they were moving toward my head.

"No," I cried. "Please! Not my hair! Please," I sobbed. I felt the clippers sliding across my scalp and saw chunks of damp blond hair fall beside my head and onto the floor. An attendant was preparing a soapy lather. She picked up a razor and walked toward me. *She's going to shave my head! Oh, dear God, no! Don't let them!*

The room began to spin. My stomach churned, and I felt faint.

Then I heard a high-pitched noise, something between a buzz and a squeal. *It's a drill!* Someone held my head, and the drill began grinding into the side of my skull.

I began to feel drowsy—*probably the shot they gave me.* I was falling asleep. More panic. *What if I don't wake up! Won't I ever see Dick again! Kathy! Mom and dad! Oh, God, I'm afraid!*

I saw faces. I heard voices. But nothing made sense. The room began to grow dark and the noise faded.

For the first time since the dive I felt relaxed, even peaceful. It no longer mattered that I was paralyzed, lying naked on a table with a shaved head. The drill no longer seemed threatening either. I drifted into a deep sleep.

Coming out of the blackness, I thought I heard the drill and tried to wake up enough to shout at them to stop. I didn't want them drilling when I was awake. But no words came. I tried to open my eyes. The room was spinning.

The noise in the background became more distinct, too. It wasn't the drill; it was only an air conditioner.

My head and vision began to clear, and for a moment I couldn't remember where I was or why I was afraid of a drill. Then memory returned.

I looked up at a ventilator grill above my head, at the high, ancient, cracked plaster ceiling. I tried to turn my head to see the rest of my surroundings, but I couldn't move at all. Sharp pains on each side of my head resisted my attempt to move. I sensed that the holes they had drilled in my skull had something to do with this. Out of the corner of my eyes, I could see large metal tongs attached to a spring-cable device pulling my head away from the rest of my body. It took an unusual amount of strength—both mental and physical—just to learn this much about my new surroundings.

During those first days I drifted in and out of consciousness. The drugs sent me off into a dream world, a nightmare devoid of reality. Hallucinations were common and often frightening. Dreams, impressions, and memories blurred together in confusion so that I often thought I was losing my mind.

A recurring nightmare came to me out of the surrealistic world induced by the drugs. In this dream, I was with Jason Leverton, my steady all through high school. We were in some unusual setting waited to be judged. I was naked and tried to cover myself in shame. In the nightmare, I was on my feet, standing before a figure dressed in robes. I knew him as an "apostle." He didn't say anything, but I knew somehow that I was being judged. Suddenly he pulled out a long sword and swung it in my direction, striking me square on the neck and cutting off my head. Then I'd wake up crying and afraid. This same dream haunted me again and again.

Other hallucinagenic experiences from the drugs turned even the crazy world of dreams inside out. Vivid colors, shapes, and figures swelled and contracted into strange and unusual patterns. I saw "frightening" colors, "peaceful" patterns— shapes and colors that represented feelings, moods and emotions.

Someone's loud moaning woke me from my nightmare. I didn't know how much time had elapsed since my last period of consciousness, but this time I was face down! How had I gotten in that position? The tongs were still in place. Their pressure against the sides of my head caused more mental and psychological pain than physical discomfort.

I discovered I was encased in some kind of a canvas frame. There was an opening for my face, and I could see only an area immediately beneath my bed. A pair of legs with white shoes and nylon hose stood within this narrow field of vision.

"Nurse," I called out weakly.

"Yes. I'm here."

"W-hat—where—uh—" I stammered, trying to phrase my question.

"Sh-h-h. Don't try to talk. You'll tire yourself," she said. From her pleasant voice and reassuring manner, I knew she wasn't the nurse who had cut off my bathing suit or the one who had shaved my head. I felt her hand on the back of my shoulder.

"Just try and rest. Go back to sleep if you can. You're in ICU. You've had surgery, and we'll take good care of you. So, don't worry. Okay?" She patted my shoulder. It was such a pleasant sensation to have feeling somewhere—except in my head, where the tongs bit into the flesh and bone.

Gradually I became aware of my surroundings. I learned that the device I called a bed was really a Stryker Frame. It looked like I was in a canvas sandwich held tightly by straps. Two nurses or orderlies would come every two hours to turn me over. They'd place a canvas frame on top of me, and while a nurse held the weights attached to the "ice tong" calipers (and my head), they would deftly flip me 180 degrees. Then they would remove the frame I had been lying on and make sure I was ready for my two-hour shift in this new position. I had two views—the floor and the ceiling.

Eventually I learned that my Stryker Frame was in an eight-bed ICU ward and that ICU was short for *intensive care unit*. I'd never heard the phrase used before but figured out it must be for serious cases. Patients were only allowed visitors for five minutes per hour—and then just by family members.

As the hours blurred into days, I got to know my roommates better. Through snatches of conversation, instructions of doctors, and other sounds, I pieced together quite a bit.

The man in a bed next to mine groaned constantly. On the change of nurses for the morning shift, I heard a night nurse explain to her replacement in a whisper, "He shot his wife and then tried to kill himself. He probably won't make it. He's to be restrained."

That explained the sound of chains rattling—he had been handcuffed to his bed!

A woman in one of the other beds moaned through the night. She was begging the nurses to give her a cigarette or ice cream.

Judy was a young girl like myself. But she was in a coma as the result of injuries sustained in a car accident.

Tom was a young man who was there because of a diving accident. It's funny. I knew Tom had broken his neck but didn't understand that *I* had. No one told me.

Tom could not even breathe on his own. I learned this when I asked a nurse what a certain sound was. She explained it was Tom's resuscitation equipment.

When we learned of the similarity of our accidents, we began to send notes back and forth. "Hi, I'm Tom," his first note said by way of introduction. Nurses and visitors wrote our notes and were our couriers.

At night, when the flurry of activity was less intense, I'd hear the moaning and groaning of others in my ICU ward. Then I'd listen for the reassuring sound of Tom's resuscitation equipment. Since I couldn't turn to see him, the sound was comforting. I felt a kinship with him and wondered what he looked like. *Tomorrow*, I thought, *I'll ask for his photo.*

Later that night, the resuscitator stopped. The silence was as loud as an explosion. Panic seized me, and my voice choked as I tried to call out for help. I heard nurses as they rushed to Tom's bedside.

"His resuscitator is down! Get a new one, stat!" someone ordered.

I could hear footsteps running down the tile hallway and the metallic sounds of the oxygen unit being removed. Another person was on the telephone at the nurses' station calling for emergency help. Within minutes, the room, hallway, and nurses' station were busy with urgent, whispered instructions and the confused commotion of crisis.

"Tom! Can you hear me, Tom?" a doctor called. Then snapped. "Where's that other resuscitator?"

"Shall we try artificial respiration, doctor?" asked a woman's voice.

My mind was spinning with the frustration of my paralysis. I was helpless—and even if I could move, there was nothing I could do. Wide-eyed, I lay there staring past the ceiling into darkness.

"The orderly had to go downstairs for another unit. He's on his way."

"Keep up the mouth-to-mouth. We've got to keep him alive until—" the man's voice broke off.

I heard the doors of the elevator down the hall open and close and urgent running footsteps along with the rattle of equipment. The sounds were aimed toward the ICU ward and, with a sense of relief, I heard someone say, "I've got a unit. You want to make room?"

Then, with horror, I heard the chilling reply. "Never mind. We've lost him. He's dead."

I felt the flesh on the back of my neck crawl. With mounting terror, I realized they were not talking about some unknown patient, some impersonal statistic. They were talking about Tom. *Tom was dead!*

I wanted to scream but was unable to. I was afraid of falling asleep that night, afraid that I, too, would not wake up.

The next day, my terror was no less intense. I grieved for a man I knew only through notes, and I began to think about my own situation. I was not dependent on a machine in order to breathe. But I was dependent on the IV—intravenous solutions—that put sustenance into my body and the catheter in my bladder that drained body wastes and poisons.

What if one of these fails? What if the tongs come loose from my head? What if—my brain was a frightened jumble.

A day or two later, a man was brought in with a similar injury. They put him on a Stryker Frame and put an oxygen tent around him.

Out of the corner of my eye, I could see what the frame was like. I could not see my own, but could now understand what happened each time they flipped me—two hours up, two hours down. Looking at him, I had the feeling that we were like steers being turned regularly on some huge barbecue spit. I was terrified each time they came to flip me.

The new patient was just as apprehensive. As the orderlies prepared to flip him one day, he cried out, "No, please don't flip me. I couldn't breathe when I was turned before! Don't flip me!"

"That's all right, mister. You'll be okay. We have to turn you. Doctor's orders. Ready, Mike? On three. One. Two. Three!"

"No! Please! I can't breathe! I'll pass out—I know it!"

"You'll be fine. Just relax."

They fixed the plastic tent for his oxygen and left. I could hear the man's labored, gasping breathing and prayed the two hours would pass quickly—for his sake as well as my own peace of mind.

Then, suddenly, the breathing stopped. Again there was commotion and activity as nurses and orderlies responded to the crisis. It was too late. Again.

Hot tears flowed from my eyes. Frustration and fear, my twin companions during those early hospital days, overtook me again. With a growing sense of horror and shock, I learned that the ICU ward was a room for the *dying*. I felt my own life was a fragile thing—not something I could take for granted.

Shortly thereafter, during one of the flipping sessions, I fainted and stopped breathing. But within minutes they had revived me, and I felt reassured by their efficiency and deep concern.

"We're going to take good care of you, Joni," comforted one doctor. After that, while every turn was still a frightening experience for me, I was conscious of the fact that the nurses and orderlies were more careful than before. Or so it seemed.

I began to notice how cold the ICU ward was. Nearly every patient was unconscious most of the time, so they were probably unaware of the coldness, but it began to bother me. I was afraid of catching cold. One of the orderlies had let it slip one day that a cold could be dangerous for me. Also dangerous was blood poisoning, which was somehow frequent in such cases. There was so much to be frightened about. Nothing seemed positive or hopeful.

Everyday doctors came to see me. Sometimes they came in pairs and discussed my case.

"She has total quadriplegia," one doctor explained to an associate, "the result of a diagonal fracture between the fourth and fifth cervical levels."

I knew I was paralyzed but didn't know why. Or for how long. No one ever explained anything to me about my injury.

Nurses said, "Ask the doctors."

Doctors said, "Oh, you're doing fine—just fine."

I suspected the worst—that I had a broken neck. That thought alone frightened me. A vivid childhood memory came to me. It was the only "real" instance I knew of anyone breaking his neck. A man in the story *Black Beauty* fell from a horse and broke his neck. He *died*.

So, inwardly, I didn't want to hear about my accident, and mentally I began to tune out the medical staff's discussions.

I knew that I was in a room of dying people because *I was going to die*, just like Tom and the other man. They both had had injuries like mine. *I'm going to die, too*, I thought. *They're just afraid to tell me!*

$\mathcal{Y}\!\mathfrak{d}$

Two

THE DAYS PASSED, marked only by recurring nightmares and the strain and discomfort of my canvas prison and metal tongs. I had finally decided that I probably wasn't going to die. While others in the ICU ward either died or got better and were transferred to regular hospital rooms, I stayed. I got no better, but no worse.

To take my mind off the anguish of the nightmares, from which I woke terrified and drenched with perspiration, I began to daydream, recalling all the events in my life before the accident.

I had had a happy life with my family and friends. We had never known tragedy firsthand. As far back as I could remember, there had been nothing but happiness surrounding our lives and home.

Daddy was probably the reason—the man I was named for, Johnny Eareckson. Born in 1900, dad took the best of both the nineteenth and twentieth centuries. He is an incurable romantic and creative artist but is also in tune with technology. His father had a coal (fuel) business, and during his childhood, dad cared for the horses before and after school. He drew much knowledge from what he calls the "school of hard knocks," too. He had been attracted to unusual and difficult work because of what he felt it could teach him. His values are personal character, individual happiness, and spiritual development. If a man has these and can pass these qualities on to his children, only then does dad consider him successful.

Dad had done almost everything—from being a sailor to owning and managing his own rodeo! His life was filled with hobbies—horses, sculpture, painting, and building things—his handiwork literally covering the walls and shelves of our home.

I asked dad once, "How do you find time, with your work, to do all the things you do?"

He looked at me, his clear blue eyes sparkling, and replied, "Honey, it began during the Depression. Nobody had work. Most people sat around and felt sorry about themselves and complained. Me? Why, I could use my hands. Carving didn't cost anything. So, I built things from stuff others threw away. I kept busy with my hands all through the Depression. Guess the habit stuck."

It was also during those lean years that dad was an Olympic wrestler. He was National AAU Wrestling Champion, a five-time winner of national YMCA championship wrestling honors, and earned a berth on the U.S. Olympic team of 1932. During his days as a wrestler, he received an injury which makes him walk with a slight limp today.

As a young man, he was active in church youth work. In his twenties and early thirties, dad was "Cap'n John" to the church young people. He took the kids camping, on overnight trips, hiking, and on retreats. He had an old flat-bed truck and would pile kids, sleeping bags, cookstove, and supplies on board and leave for one of "Cap'n John's Tours." They were memorable times and often made an impression on many of the young people. One young woman was especially impressed by "Cap'n John." She was the energetic and vivacious Margaret "Lindy" Landwehr who took a natural interest in athletics and the outdoors and thus gained the attention of "Cap'n John."

Soon "Lindy" fell in love with "Cap'n John" and he with her. Many of their dates were crowded, however, for "Cap'n John" brought the entire youth group along!

As an expression of his love, dad worked night and day and built a house for mom as a wedding present. It was toward the end of the Depression and money was still scarce, so he scoured the area with his truck. From an old sailing ship, he salvaged huge beams for the foundation and rafters.

While driving one day, he saw some men demolishing a rock wall.

"What are you going to do with those rocks?" he asked.

"Why?"

"I'll be glad to haul them away," dad replied.

"Okay," the foreman grunted, "just make sure they're gone by Friday. We've got a job to do here."

"Yessir!" shouted dad. He began the remarkable job of single-handedly moving boulders—most weighing more than a hundred pounds. He did it by himself, somehow maneuvering them onto his truck. After many trips, he had enough for his house. Today two beautiful, huge stone fireplaces are the result of that labor.

The same kind of thing happened when he needed lumber, bricks, and other building supplies. Finally his dream house was completed. He and his bride moved in and have lived there since.

Daddy had the same active interest in business and civic affairs. Years ago, he started his own flooring business.

He said, "I guess I'm too independent to work for somebody else. I love my family too much to be tied down to someone else's schedule and interests. By being my own boss, if I want to take off a day and drive my family to the ocean or take 'em horseback riding, I don't have to ask anyone. I just put a sign on the door, lock up, and go."

And we did. We took many trips and vacations, and they were so much fun that it's difficult to believe they were also part of our education. Dad taught us geography and geology during "survival" backpack outings in the desert or mountains. He showed us how to distinguish between the tracks of various animals, their calls, their ways—things we could never learn in the city.

He introduced us to horseback riding almost as soon as we could sit up. I was in the saddle at age two. In fact, daddy often bragged, "Do you remember the time our whole family rode a hundred miles on horseback? It was from Laramie to Cheyenne, Wyoming. Remember, Joni? You were only four years old! Youngest ever to ride in the Cheyenne Ride." When we were a bit older, he took us pack-riding in the wilderness of the Medicine Bow range where we acquired a deep appreciation for God and His creation.

Dad taught us all to ride gracefully balanced and gave us lessons in show horsemanship. "Just ride in a rolling motion with the horse," he'd say, "not like the beginners—bouncing on the horse. It's almost impossible to synchronize your up and down bounces to the horse's movements. You've got to roll with him, not bounce."

Dad was always even-tempered and amiable. Nothing or no one ever ruffled him. Not once during all our growing-up years did I see him lose his temper. Our behavior then was based on "not hurting daddy." We didn't do certain things because of "what it would do to daddy," not because it was simply questionable or wrong.

When dad came to the hospital for the brief visits allowed in the ICU ward, he tried to communicate the same genial, positive spirit I'd always known. But no matter how much he tried to appear relaxed and hopeful, his clouded blue eyes, usually so clear and sparkling, betrayed his nervousness. His weathered, gnarled hands shook as they revealed his true feelings. He was afraid and hurt. The daughter he loved and named after himself was lying helpless in a sandwich of canvas and a tangle of IV and catheter tubes.

The hospital was no place for this man who had spent a lifetime outdoors as an active athlete. His pain and restlessness were difficult to hide.

It hurt me to see what my accident had done to him. *"Why, God?"* I asked. *"Why are you doing this?"*

There was an unusually strong bond of love which tied us together as a family. Mom was a source of that strength. She, too, loved the outdoors and athletic competition and shared dad's interests. In fact, it was she who taught us girls to play tennis. Swimming and hiking were also things we did as a family.

Mom, with her strong character and loving personality, worked as hard as daddy to see that we had a happy home. There was seldom any disagreement between my parents, and their obvious love for one another was reflected in our lives and made us feel wanted and secure.

After the accident, mom was the one who took charge at the hospital. She stayed there around the clock the first four days, catching short naps on a sofa in the lounge. She did not leave until she was absolutely certain I was out of danger.

Since we were such a close family, my sisters shared my parents' concern. Kathy, twenty, dark-haired, pretty, and shy, was the one who had pulled me from the water and saved my life.

Jay, twenty-three at the time of the accident, was the sister I was closest to. She was quiet and graceful, her long, blond hair lightened by constant exposure to sun and swimming.

Jay was married and the mother of a little girl named Kay. In spite of her family responsibilities, she found time to come to the hospital and be with me, and I looked forward to her visits. If my Stryker Frame had me facing down, she'd lie down on the floor. There she'd spread out *Seventeen* magazines for us to read together. And she tried to brighten my corner of the room with plants and posters, although "regulations" soon required that they be removed.

Linda, my oldest sister, was married and had three small children. Because she was about ten years older than I was, I was not as close to her as to Kathy and Jay.

The memories of our good times as a family did help to take my mind off the pain and nightmares. I also recalled the good experiences of my high school years and the friends I had made then.

Woodlawn Senior High School was located in a scenic part of our suburban Baltimore area. The two-story brick complex was situated in the midst of a campus that made full use of the outdoors. Sidewalks were lined with trees, and a small stream wound through the grassy grounds. Art students were often scattered around the picturesque, landscaped campus, sketching or painting.

Out back, on the athletic field, were ball diamonds, track courses, tennis courts, and lacrosse courts. Lacrosse was the sport I loved most. In fact, being named captain of our girls' lacrosse team in my senior year meant more to me than my nomination to the Honor Society.

As a sophomore at Woodlawn, I had come into contact with an organization called *Young Life*, a religious-oriented youth work that ministers primarily to high school kids. I had noticed that lots of the "neat" kids, the achievers, the popular ones, were Christian kids from *Young Life*, so when I heard about a "fantastic retreat" *Young Life* was sponsoring, I wanted to go.

"Mom," I begged, "you've simply got to let me go. Please?" I was fifteen, a young girl searching for identity and meaning to life.

The *Young Life* weekend was held in Natural Bridge, Virginia. Crowds of kids from Baltimore area high schools converged on this tiny community for a weekend crammed with fun and challenges to consider what the Bible had to say about our relationship to God.

Carl Nelson, the *Young Life* camp speaker, shared how the gospel begins with God's glory and His righteousness. "That standard of righteousness was expressed through the Ten Commandments," he told us.

Carl opened his Bible and read "and by the law comes knowledge of sin."

"And so, gang," he went on, "it's impossible to reach heaven by trying to stick to a list of moral do's and don'ts. There's just no way any one of us can live up to those commandments God has lain down."

The meeting broke up, and I wandered out into the fall night air. *Me, a sinner?* I'd never really understood what the word meant. However, now I saw my rebellion in the light of God's perfection. I knew *I* was a lost *sinner*, no matter how strange it sounded.

Well, I obviously can't save myself, so who. . . .

Then everything that Carl had shared thus far that weekend began to make sense. *That's why Jesus, God's Son, had come!*

"He being God in the flesh fulfilled the law and lived the perfect life. And when He died, He was paying the penalty of your sin." I recalled Carl's words.

I sat down and leaned back against a tree and looked up at the silent expanse of stars, half-expecting to see something—I don't know what. Only flickering specs blinked back. Yet, as I looked, I was overwhelmed by the love of God. I closed my eyes. "Oh, God, I see my sin; yet I also see Your mercy. Thank You for sending Your Son, Jesus, to die for me. I've decided in my heart not to do those things which will grieve You anymore. Instead of doing things my way, I want Christ to sit on the throne of my life and lead me. Thank You for saving me from sin and giving me eternal life." I got up and ran back to the room, anxious to tell my friend Jackie how God had saved me.

I had always heard how much God loved me as I was growing up. Mom and dad were Christians and members of the Bishop Cummings Reformed Episcopal Church in Catonsville.

But in my early teens I was looking for my own way and life style, and I didn't have time for God. I had experimented with many things to find out where I fit into life. At first I thought popularity and dates were the answer. Then I thought the discipline of athletics was where I would find it. But now my searching ended. All the pieces of the puzzle fit together, and it all made sense! *Jesus, God's Son, had come to save me and make me a whole person.*

A great flood of personal joy came to me that night, and I made a decision to invite Jesus Christ into my heart and life. I didn't fully understand it all, but I was to learn that God is patient, loving, forgiving, and tolerant of our mistakes.

I heard two concepts presented that weekend which I had never clearly understood before. I learned that I was a sinner because I wasn't able, nor was anyone able, to live up to God's standards for behavior. That's why He allowed His Son, the Lord Jesus Christ, to die for *me*. It was an emotional, meaningful moment when I realized Jesus died for me, personally.

Then I heard about an exciting concept called "the abundant life." Our counselor explained that Jesus came to die for our sins, but that He also came to give us "abundant life" (John 10:10). In my immature mind, the abundant life meant I'd lose weight or have new popularity and dates at school, lots of friends, and good grades.

My concept of what was meant by the abundant life was completely wrong, of course, and by the time I was a junior in high school, things had slipped for me. I had expected, as a new Christian, to find security and purpose in *things*—the things I'd based my spiritual life on—going to church, singing in choir, serving as a *Young Life* club officer. My whole focus was on these things, not on God. My life revolved around temporal values, my own ego and desires.

About this time, I met Jason Leverton. Jason was a handsome, muscular, and personable guy. With his broad shoulders, serious brown eyes, and thick light-colored hair, he was called the "Blond Flash" by his wrestling teammates for his speed and ability in state champion competition. Jason and I dated regularly and were always together at school and social functions.

Dad was especially fond of Jason because of his own keen interest in wrestling. It was not surprising for me to play second fiddle to dad when Jason came to visit. Frequently they would good-naturedly "take on" one another, demonstrating unusual wrestling holds or pins.

Jason was lots of fun. He and I shared secrets and our plans for the future. We planned to go to college together, probably even get married one day.

We had a favorite place—a nearby park—where we'd take walks and talk. Jason was also active in *Young Life* so these times were often used for sharing spiritual thoughts and praying together. Sometimes I'd even climb down the drain pipe outside my bedroom window and meet him after curfew—until mom caught me one night! She made certain I obeyed curfew rules after that.

It was about the time Jason and I started to get romantically serious that real conflicts started. We both were seniors in high school and knew there were stated limits in expressing our affection for one another. But neither of us had the inner resources capable of dealing with problems of temptation.

We would often go driving or horseback riding. Many times we'd ride out to an open meadow surrounded by beautiful woods, deep blue skies, and magnificent summer clouds. The sights, sounds, and smells of the country were terribly romantic and erotic. Before we realized what was happening, innocent, youthful expressions of love for one another—hand-holding, hugging, kissing—gave way to caressing, touching, and passions neither of us could control. We wanted to stop, but often when we found ourselves in a secluded spot, we fell into each other's arms. Our mutual lack of self-restraint bothered us tremendously.

"Jason—why can't we stop! What's wrong with us?" I asked one night.

"I don't know. I know we shouldn't mess around, but—"

"Jason, we've got to stop seeing each other for awhile. It's the only way. I can't stop. You can't either. Every time we get alone, we—uh—we sin. If we're really serious about repenting of all this, then we're just going to have to stay away from each other for awhile so we can avoid temptation."

Jason was silent for awhile. Then he agreed. "Maybe we should."

He suggested that I might enjoy dating his friend Dick Filbert, a sensitive, mature Christian. I guess he thought if I was dating someone else, it might as well be a friend. That way we'd still have an indirect contact.

Dick was tall, lean, and good-looking—like Jason—but there the similarity ended. Dick was quiet, shy, but more expressive. An aura of casualness surrounded him right down to his worn jeans and moccasins, and his soft voice reflected a peace and serenity. Dick's eyes, bright and blue, could quiet any storm in my soul, and his presence was a strong, unmoving rock that I could cling to in times of confusion.

During my senior year, my time was divided between Jason and Dick. I tried to avoid romantic interest in either of them and to treat each as just a good friend. I relaxed by horseback riding, playing records and guitar, and I tried to learn more about the Christian life through *Young Life* Bible studies. Even my prayer times began to reflect more serious goals.

I was accepted for the fall term at Western Maryland College on academic recommendations. My life seemed to be falling in place, going somewhere—and yet it wasn't.

I remember lying in bed one morning shortly after graduation and thinking about all these things.

The summer sunlight flooded into my window. Filtered through leaves in the trees outside, it splattered into flickering points of dancing light across my bed and along the pink, rose-print wallpaper. I yawned and rolled over to look outside. When daddy built his dream house, he included these unique touches like the small "porthole" window near the floor beside my bed. I'd just turn over in bed and look down outside.

It was still early but I got up quickly and fished out a pair of Levi's and a pullover shirt from my dresser. As I dressed, my eyes turned once more to the black leather diploma folder on the dressing table. I ran my fingers over its grain and the embossed Old English lettering of my name and school crest. Just a few days earlier, I had walked down the aisle in cap and gown to receive that diploma.

"Breakfast!" Mom's voice downstairs punctuated my reverie.

"Coming, mom," I called. Bounding down the stairs, I pulled a chair up to the table.

"Are you going out to the ranch after church, Joni?" asked mom.

"Uh-huh. I know Tumbleweed's going to be ready for the summer horse show circuit but I want to spend more time with her, anyway."

The "ranch" was our family farm some twenty miles west of town. It was situated on a panoramic ridge in the rolling, picturesque river valley and was surrounded by state park land.

By the time I got there, the sun had already climbed high in the sky and the fragrance of new-mown hay was blown toward me. The breeze also caressed the tall wildflowers and grasses of the sloping meadows and gently tossed the uppermost branches in the sweet-smelling apple trees nearby. Humming softly and happily, I saddled Tumbleweed and swung up to mount her.

It was refreshing to be so far away from the dirt, noise and noxious smells of the city. In summer, Baltimore suffers from the industrial air pollution and swelter-ing humidity that rolls in from Chesapeake Bay. Here, in our own little paradise, we're free to enjoy the summer sun and air.

I pressed my thighs against Tumbleweed's sides and nudged her with my heels. The chestnut mare headed up the dusty dirt road at a walk. When we came to the pasture, I dug my heels again. Tumbleweed really didn't need the silent com-mand. She knew there was room to run here without concern for potholes or rocks. Scattered across the field were several log-rail fence jumps. We cantered toward this first jump, a broad, four-foot solid rail fence. As I tightened my knees against Tumbleweed, I felt the smooth, precision strides of the big horse.

The experienced rider instinctively knows the right "feel" of a horse preparing to jump. Tumbleweed was experienced and so was I. We had won all kinds of ribbons and horse show awards. I knew the sound of hoofs—the proper cadence, pounding across the earthen course.

Smoothly, the horse lifted up and over the fence. Suspended for an instant, it was like flying. Nearly ten feet off the ground aboard Tumbleweed, I was exhilarated each time the mare jumped. After several runs, Tumbleweed was wet with sweaty lather.

I reined her to a slow trot and turned back toward the barn.

"Joni!"

Looking up, I saw dad astride his gray gelding galloping across the field toward me. Smiling, dad pulled his horse up.

"I saw her jump, Joni. She's in excellent shape. I think you'll both run away with the ribbons at next week's show!"

"Well, if we do, it'll be because you taught me everything I know about riding," I reminded dad.

By the time dad and I returned to the barn, unsaddled the horses and slapped them toward the corral, it was 4:30. "We'd better head for home. We don't want to be late for dinner," I said.

I recalled the pleasure of the previous perfect day, riding on my horse Tumbleweed under a beautiful summer sky. But inwardly I knew it was an elaborate form of escape. I didn't want to face the real issues. I wondered—*Lord, what am I going to do? I'm happy and content, grateful for the good things You supply—but deep down, I know something is wrong. I think I'm at the place where I need You to really work in my life.*

As I traced my spiritual progress over the last couple years, I realized I had not come far. Jason and I had broken up, true; and Dick was better for me in that regard. But I was still enslaved. Instead of "sins of the flesh," I was trapped by my "sins of the emotions"—anger, jealousy, resentment, and possessiveness. I had drifted through my last years of school. My grades dropped and, as a result, I began to fight with my parents. I lacked goals or the motivation to do well. It was obvious to me that I had not made much spiritual progress in the two years I'd been a Christian. It seemed no matter how hard I tried to improve, I was always a slave of my desires.

Now I was insistent with God. "Lord, if You're really there, do something in my life that will change me and turn me around. You know how weak I was with Jason. You know how possessive and jealous I am with Dick. I'm sick of the hypocrisy! I want You to work in my life for real. I don't know how—I don't even know, at this point, if You can. But I'm begging You—please do something in my life to turn it around!"

I had prayed that prayer just a short time before my accident. Now, lying encased in my Stryker Frame, I wondered if somehow God was answering my prayer.

Three

"THE BIBLE SAYS, 'Everything works together for good,' even your accident, Joni." Dick was trying to comfort me, but I wasn't listening too intently.

"I've already been in this stupid hospital a month," I complained, "and I haven't seen very much good!

"I can't sleep at night because of nightmares and hallucinations caused by the drugs. I can't move—I'm stuck in this dumb Stryker Frame! What's good? Tell me, Dickie, what's good about that?"

"I—I don't know, Joni. But I think we should claim God's promise. Let's trust Him that it will work out for good," Dick said quietly, patiently. "Want me to read something else?"

"No. I'm sorry. I didn't mean to jump on you like that. I guess I'm not really trusting the Lord, am I?"

"It's all right—" Dick was on the floor beneath my Stryker Frame looking up into my eyes. Incredible sadness and pity made his expressive eyes well with tears. He blinked and looked away. "Well," he said finally, "I gotta go now. See ya later, okay?"

Dick's faithfulness in visiting was one thing I clung to during those first grim weeks, along with mom, dad, Jackie, and Jay. Others, like Jason, came when they could, too. The hospital personnel joked about all my "cousins," and the "five minutes per hour for family members" regulation was bent many times.

When mom and dad came, I always asked to be flipped if I was facing the floor. While they joked and got down on the floor if I was face down, I was deeply hurt that they had to go through the indignity of crawling around on the floor in order to visit with me.

I tried hard to kindle their hope and faith, too. As I thought about my problems, it was easy to find others around me in the hospital who were worse off than I. With that in mind, I tried to cheer my folks and others who came to visit. I even began to be pleasant to the hospital staff.

It wasn't that my personality had become sweeter. Rather, I was afraid people would stop coming to see me if I got bitter and complained, so I worked at cheerfulness.

"My, you're in a good mood today," observed Anita, one of the nurses from the day shift.

"Sure, why not? It's a gorgeous day."

"It's raining!"

"Not on me. I'm snug as a bug," I teased.

"Want me to come by later?"

"Would you? Yes—I'd like that, Anita." Although she was assigned to duty elsewhere in the hospital, Anita took a special interest in me. She often spent her lunch hour with me, reading Robert Frost's poetry or just chatting. Since I'd already spent so much time in the intensive care ward, many of the nurses were becoming my friends. By now I was more accustomed to the routine and regulations. And just as they sometimes bent some of the rules when visitors came, so I began to overlook the hospital's shortcomings as well.

Anita patted my shoulder and waved. "I'll see you later, Joni." I heard her light footsteps click away down the tiled hallway.

When she left, Jason came to visit. "Hi, kid," he grinned, "you look terrible. When do you get to leave here?"

"Not for awhile, I guess. I think I'm supposed to be learning something through all this," I answered. "Dickie says God is working in my life."

"God doesn't have anything to do with it! You got a busted neck, that's all. You can't lay back and say 'it's God's will' and let it go at that! You gotta fight it, Joni. And get better," Jason said sharply.

He looked at me, not knowing what else to say. Our relationship had been sort of "tabled" when we agreed to a cooling-off period. Now he was suggesting—if not by words, by the expression in his eyes and squeeze of his hands on my shoulder—that he still cared deeply.

"We gotta fight this thing, Joni. You gotta get better, y'hear?" His voice broke and he began to cry. "Forget the business about it being God's will that you're hurt. Fight it! Y'hear?"

He swore softly for added emphasis and said, "It doesn't make any sense. How could God—if there is a God—let it happen?"

"I know it seems that way, Jason. But Dickie says God must have some kind of reason for it."

"I dunno. Maybe I'm just bitter—cynical. But I don't feel God is interested any more. I don't think He's there."

This admission by Jason was the first step in his drifting away from trust in a loving God—his resignation that what happened was the result of blind, random forces.

I stared at the ceiling after he left. It had been a month, and I was still here. *What's wrong with me?* I wondered.

"Hello, lassie. How's m' favorite lass today?" I couldn't see him yet, but the voice was that of Dr. Harris. As his tall, redheaded frame came into my field of vision, I smiled and greeted him. Dr. Harris had been in the shock trauma unit of the hospital the night of my accident. He had taken a personal interest in me and followed my case. I was charmed by his Scottish brogue and the fact that he always referred to me as "lassie."

He picked up my charts and looked them over. "Hm-m. You're lookin' good, lassie. Feeling better?"

"I—I don't know. What's wrong with me, Dr. Harris? The nurses won't tell me, and Dr. Sherrill just gives me a lot of medical jargon. Please. Won't you tell me—when can I go home? How much longer do I have to be in here?"

"Well, hon, I can't say. That is, I'm not really on top of your case like Dr. Sherrill. I'm just—"

"Dr. Harris," I interrupted, "you're lying. You know. Tell me."

He replaced the charts, looked serious for a moment, then concentrated on bringing forth his best bedside cheerfulness. "Tell y' what, lass. I'll talk with Dr. Sherrill. I'll have him give y' the whole story in plain English. How's that?"

I smiled. "Better. I mean, I have a right to know, don't I?"

Dr. Harris nodded and pursed his lips as if to say something; then, as if thinking better of it, he merely smiled.

Dick came bursting into the ward later that day. He was wearing a jacket, which was unusual for August.

"I—I've just run up all nine floors!" he gasped.

"Why?" I laughed. "Why didn't you use the elevator?"

"This is why," he replied, opening his jacket. He pulled out a small, lively puppy. It began to climb all over Dick, lying on the floor under my Stryker Frame, licking his face, and barking quietly with a *yip–yip–yip* we thought would alert the entire hospital.

"Sh-h! Quiet, pooch—you want us to get kicked out?" Dick begged.

He put the puppy up by my face. I felt its fuzzy warmth and the wetness of his tongue licking my cheek.

"Oh, Dickie—he's beautiful. I'm glad you brought him."

"I thought I heard something!" a nurse exclaimed in mock seriousness. "How did you get him past the Gestapo in the lobby?" she grinned.

"I came up the back stairs. You aren't going to turn us in, are you?"

"Who, me?" She bent down and cuddled the puppy, then put him down. "I don't see anything," she said simply and left for other duties.

Dick and I played with the puppy for nearly an hour before being discovered again. He picked up the small dog. "I'll take the stairs again," he said as he got up to leave. "Otherwise they may frisk me every time I come up here!"

We laughed, and Dick left with the puppy hidden beneath his jacket.

The next day I was taken down to the laboratory for a bone scan and myelogram. The bone scan was done quickly and smoothly, for it consisted basically of "taking a picture" of my spine. However, the myelogram was not so simple or painless. It meant tapping my spinal cord of its fluid and replacing it with a special dye, using two giant six-inch hypodermic needles. My spinal fluid was drained, pushed out by the dye going in. When the transfer was complete, I was turned upside down and placed in various positions under the fluoroscope while the medics ran their tests. When done, the dye was removed by injecting the spinal fluid back. One side effect of this treatment was a severe headache if some of the fluid was lost or nerve endings (which need the fluid as a lubricant) dried out. There was no medication for this, so I was sedated for several days.

When Dr. Sherrill, the physician in charge of my case, came by later, I accosted him. "Dr. Sherrill, what's wrong with me?"

His reply was even, without inflection, so I had no way of measuring the seriousness of what he said. "Don't you remember, Joni? You have a lesion of the spinal cord at the fourth and fifth cervical levels caused by a fracture-dislocation."

"I broke my neck?"

"Yes."

"But that means I'll die."

"No. Not necessarily," Dr. Sherrill replied. "It means only that it is a very serious accident. The fact that you've survived about four weeks now means you've more than likely passed that crisis."

"You mean you thought I was going to die? Before?"

"You were a badly injured girl. Many people don't survive accidents of this nature."

I thought of Tom and the other man who had died undergoing the same treatment as I was. "I guess I'm lucky," I offered.

"Lucky, indeed. And strong. You have a tremendous will. Now that we've passed this crisis, I want you to concentrate all your will power on getting better. You see, when you're strong enough, I want to perform fusion surgery on you."

"What's that? In plain English, please, Dr. Sherrill."

"Well, it's sort of a repair process. Your spinal cord is severed. We have to fuse the bones back together."

Back together! My mind grabbed at the simple statement and raced with it.

That means I'll get my arms and legs back! That's what Romans 8:28 meant. Dickie was right—things do work together for good. Before long I'll be back on my feet!

"When do you want to do the surgery?" I asked.

"As soon as possible."

"Great. Let's do it!"

I didn't know all that was involved in fusion surgery. I thought that by fusing the bones back together and having the spinal cord healed everything would be the same as before—no more paralysis. But I wasn't really listening carefully.

Following surgery, I was elated to leave the ICU ward and be wheeled into a regular room. *It's a sign I'm getting better*, I thought. *If I wasn't, they'd keep me in ICU.*

Mom and dad, smiling and happy to see me return from the surgery, were in my room, and Dr. Sherrill came by.

"Everything went fine," he said, anticipating our question. "The surgery was a complete success."

There was a collective sigh of relief.

"Now I want you to concentrate on the next steps of recovery. There is much progress to be made yet. There will be difficult days ahead, Joni. I want you to know it and brace yourself for them. The toughest part of the battle is the psychological aspect. You're fine now. You've been angry, frustrated, afraid. However, you haven't really been depressed. But wait until your friends go off to college. Wait until the novelty of all this wears off. Wait until your friends get other interests and stop coming. Are you ready for that, Joni? If not, better get ready. Because it'll come. Believe me, it'll come."

"I know it'll take time, but I'll get better," I gamely replied. "These things take time—you said so yourself, doctor."

"Yes," dad said. "How much time are we talking about, Dr. Sherrill?"

Mother added her concern, too. "You're talking about Joni's friends going off to college this fall. But I sense you're saying Joni won't be able to. We made a deposit on her tuition for the fall term at Western Maryland University. Should we postpone her entrance until next semester?"

"Uh—at least."

"Really?"

"Mrs. Eareckson, you might as well have them return your deposit. I'm afraid college will be out of the question for Joni."

"Y-you mean—that you don't know how soon Joni will walk again?"

"Walk? I'm afraid you don't understand, Mrs. Eareckson. Joni's injury is permanent. The fusion surgery didn't change that."

The word *permanent* slammed into my consciousness like a bullet.

I could tell that this was also the first time mom and dad had been confronted with the fact of a permanent injury. Either we had all been too naive or the medical people had been too vague in their explanations. Perhaps both.

Silence hung over the room for a few moments. None of us dared react for fear of upsetting and worrying the others.

Dr. Sherrill tried to be encouraging, however. "Joni will never walk again, but we're hoping she'll regain the use of her hands one day. Many people lead useful and constructive lives without being able to walk. Why, they can drive, work, clean house—it's really not a hopeless thing, you know. We're confident she'll be able to get her hands back in time."

Mom had turned her face away, but I knew she was crying.

"Don't worry, mom—dad. There have been lots of times people with broken necks have recovered and walked again. I've heard lots of success stories while I've been here. I'm going to walk again! I know it. I believe God wants me to walk again. He'll help me. Really! I'm going to walk out of here!"

Dr. Sherrill didn't say anything. He put his hand on mom's shoulder, shook hands with daddy, and left. For a long while none of us said anything. Then we began to chat about inconsequential things. Finally my parents left.

I lay in the dim light of the room. I should have been happy—the surgery was successful, I was getting better, and I was now in my own room. But I wasn't happy. Grief, remorse, and depression swept over me like a thick, choking blanket. For the first time since the accident, I wished and prayed I might die.

After nearly an hour, a nurse, Alice, came by. She emptied my catheter bag and rearranged things in my room. Then she went over to the window to adjust the drapes.

"Looks like you'll be getting some visitors," she said.

"Oh?"

"Uh-huh. I see your mom and dad sitting together down in the courtyard outside. They'll probably be up here in a minute."

"No—they've already been here," I replied. I felt tears, hot and salty, spill out of my eyes and roll down my cheeks. My nose became stuffy. I couldn't even cry because I couldn't blow my own nose. I began to sob anyway.

"Hey, what's wrong, Joni?" Alice wiped my face with a tissue. She pulled another from the box. "Here. Blow. Feel better now?"

I smiled. "I'm sorry. Guess I was just thinking of mom and dad down there. Dr. Sherrill just told us that my injury is permanent—that I'll never walk again. I know they're down there talking about it. And crying. And I'm up here crying. It's just too much to handle, I guess."

Alice ran the back of her hand along the side of my face. Her concern, her gesture, felt good. It was reassuring and comforting to feel something.

"I'm going to walk out of here, Alice. God will help me. You'll see."

Alice nodded and smiled.

During the weeks following surgery, I didn't get stronger as I had vowed. Still fed intravenously or by liquids, my weight began to drop. The thought of solid food made me nauseous, and I just couldn't eat food brought on trays to my room. I could only drink grape juice. The nurses stocked up on it and brought me glasses to sip.

One day a stranger in a hospital uniform came into my room. "I'm Willie, the chef," he explained. "I came to see why you don't like my food," he added.

"Oh, it's not your food. I just get sick thinking about food in general," I apologized.

"What did you like best? Before the accident, I mean?"

"Before? Well, my favorite foods were steak—baked potatoes—"

"Vegetable?"

"Oh, I don't know. Corn, I guess."

"Salad?"

"I liked Caesar salads."

"Well, let's see what we can do." Then he left.

That evening a nurses' aide brought my tray as usual. As she lifted the cover, I saw a big steak, huge baked potato with butter and sour cream, sweet corn, and magnificent Caesar salad. But when she put the tray down in front of me, somehow the smell made me nauseous again.

"Please. Take it away. I'm sorry—I just can't eat it."

She shook her head and took the tray back, and I turned away in frustration and sadness.

I never knew whether the nausea was typical or just a side effect of some medication. I was used to the hallucinations by now, and I believe even some of my dreams, or nightmares, were drug-induced. Lately I had sensed ugly "beings" standing around my hospital bed, waiting to carry me away, and this daydream or nightmare or hallucination, whatever it was, depressed me further. I couldn't really see them, but I knew they were there—terrible and fierce, waiting for me to die—or maybe just fall asleep. I fought sleep for fear of being carried off by them.

I was glad when visitors came, for to some extent, their presence kept me in touch with reality and gave me something to look forward to. But I never really knew how difficult it was for them to come back day after day.

When friends came to visit for the first time, they were awkward and uncertain of how to act in a hospital room. As they began to be somewhat at ease, they all asked the same questions.

"What does it feel like?"

"Does it hurt?"

"How do you go to the bathroom?"

Many visitors were squeamish and uncomfortable; some were particularly upset to see the tongs pressing into my skull. It often seemed they had more difficulty coping with my situation than I did.

One day two girl friends from high school came to visit. They had not seen me since before the accident, and I was as unprepared for their reaction as they were. They came into the room and slowly looked around at the Stryker Frame and other paraphernalia. Then they stopped hesitantly beside me. I watched out of the corner of my eye as they came toward me.

"Hi," I smiled. "I'm sorry I can't turn my head to see you, but if you'll—"

"Oh, Joni!" choked one of the girls.

"Oh, my God—" whispered the other.

There was an awkward silence for a moment—then I heard them run for the door. Outside the door, I heard one girl retch and vomit while her friend began to sob loudly.

I felt a twinge of horror sweep over me. No one else had acted that unusual. Were they particularly squeamish around hospitals—or was there something else?

For awhile I didn't want to know. Then a few days later when Jackie came to visit, I looked up at her and said, "Jackie, bring me a mirror."

She had been reading some cards and other mail and looked up abruptly. "Why?" she asked.

"I want you to get me a mirror."

"Uh—okay. I'll bring one next time I come."

"No. I mean now. Get one from the nurse."

"Why don't we wait. I'll bring you your pretty dresser set from home."

"Jackie!" I was getting angry at her. "Bring me a mirror! Now!"

She slowly edged toward the door and was back shortly with a mirror. Her hands were shaking, and her eyes blinked nervously as she held it up before me.

I screamed and Jackie jumped, nearly dropping the mirror. "It's ghastly!

"Oh, God, how can You do this to me?" I prayed through tears. "What have You done to me?"

The figure in the mirror seemed scarcely human. As I stared at my own reflection, I saw two eyes, darkened and sunk into the sockets, bloodshot and glassy. My weight had dropped from 125 to 80, so that I appeared to be little more than a skeleton covered by yellow, jaundiced skin. My shaved head only accented my grotesque skeletal appearance. As I talked, I saw my teeth, black from the effects of medication.

I, too, felt like vomiting.

Jackie took away the mirror and began to cry with me. "I'm sorry, Joni," she sobbed, "I didn't want you to see."

"Please take it away. I never want to look in a mirror again!

"Jackie—I can't take it any more. I'm dying, Jackie. Look at me. I'm almost dead now. Why do they let me suffer like this?"

"I—I don't know, Joni."

"Jackie, you've got to help me. They're keeping me alive. It's not right. I'm dying anyway. Why can't they just let me die? Jackie—please—you've got to help," I pleaded.

"But how, Joni?"

"I don't know. Give me something—you know—an overdose of pills?"

"You mean you want me to kill you?" Jackie asked wide-eyed.

"Yes—I mean no—you won't be killing me. You'll just be helping me die sooner. Look, I'm already dying. I'm suffering. Can't you help me end the suffering? If I could move, I'd do it myself!" I was angry and frustrated. "Please—cut my wrists—there's no feeling. I'd have no pain. I'll die peaceful, Jackie. Please! Do something."

Jackie began to sob. "I can't, Joni. I just can't!"

I begged her, "Jackie, if you care for me at all, you've got to help. I'm dying anyway—can't you see? Look at me! Just look at me."

"Joni, you don't know what you're asking. I just can't. Maybe you *would* be better off, I don't know. I'm so mixed up! I want to help. I love you more than I love anyone, and it kills me to see you suffer like this. But—but I can't do it!"

I didn't say anything more then. Several other times, though, in similar spells of depression and frustration, I begged Jackie to help me commit suicide. I was angry because I couldn't do it by myself.

I fantasized about how it could be done. Pills would be easiest, but the nurses would find me and pump my stomach. I could have Jackie slash my wrists. Since I had no feeling there, I'd have no pain. I could hide them under the sheets and—no, that wouldn't work either. All I could do was wait and hope for some hospital accident to kill me.

Jackie became more conscious of my appearance after these bouts with depression. She tried to help me "look good" to people and to interest me in things that might take my mind off my situation.

"You'll be better soon, Joni," she promised. "Remember, the Lord says He will never allow us to suffer more than we can humanly bear."

"Oh, yeah?" I grunted.

The medication and paralysis also left me with an acute sensitivity to light and sound. I made Jackie and the nurses keep the shades and blinds drawn and the door shut to keep out light and noise. Dr. Harris said it was evidence of nerves beginning to heal, but I was dreadfully discomforted by it. I could even hear conversations clearly from adjoining rooms. The usual hospital routine turned into a harsh, discordant cacophony.

One hot summer day, Jackie was moving a fan for me, and she accidentally dropped it. It sounded like a painful explosion going off inside my head as it clattered on the tile floor.

"Jackie!" I screamed and cursed at her. The ugly words which came out of my mouth were strange and obscene, dredged up from some dark recess of my mind. I called her awful names.

Then guilt washed over me. "I'm sorry, Jackie. It's so easy to cave in." I cried softly. "I know God must have some purpose in all this. Please call Dickie before you go. I need him. Tell him to come up tonight."

Jackie nodded and started to leave.

"Jackie—wait. There's something I have to say before you go."

She stood near me. "Jackie, you're such a close friend—I'm taking you for granted. I yell at you all the time—especially since I can't scream at anyone else! I feel like being mad at God, at mom and dad, at Dickie. Y'know? It kinda gets to me sometimes, and I have to let off steam. But you're the only one I can safely scream at. Mom and dad are already suffering so much—I have to make a special effort to be pleasant when they come. It isn't fair for me to be critical, demanding, and mean to them. And I can't take a chance on losing Dick by taking things out on him. I need him; I don't want to lose him, maybe forever, by hurting him now. So, Jackie, I'm sorry. You've been my scapegoat. You get the brunt of every ugly emotion I let go."

Jackie smiled warmly and shrugged. "That's okay, Joni. I know you don't really mean it. Besides," she grinned, "what are friends for?"

She came over, smoothed my hospital gown, and kissed me on the forehead. "I'll call Dick for you."

Dick came by the hospital later. Quietly I lay there listening to the comforting words of Scripture he read to me from a J. B. Phillips New Testament paraphrase. Many of the verses were alive with contemporary meaning.

"Listen to this, Joni," Dick said excitedly. "'When all kinds of trials and temptations crowd into your lives, my brothers, don't resent them as intruders, but welcome them as friends! Realize that they come to test your faith and to produce in you the quality of endurance'" (James 1:2-4).

"What do you suppose it means, Dickie?"

"I think it means just what it says—that God has allowed your accident to happen for a purpose, not as an intrusion in your life, but to test your faith and spiritual endurance."

"Oh, wow! Have I ever been letting the Lord down."

"Listen to the rest of it, Joni. 'And if, in the process, any of you does not know how to meet any particular problem he has only to ask God—who gives generously to all men without making them feel foolish or guilty.'"

"My problem is one *I* can't meet. Let's ask God to heal me. Just like it says."

Dick put the book down and began. "Father, we thank You for Your care and concern. We thank You for Your Word, the Bible, and the promises You have there for us. Your Word says, 'If any of you does not know how to meet any particular problem, he has only to ask God.' Well, Lord, we're asking—please hear our prayers, in Jesus' name, amen."

I prayed next. "Lord Jesus, I'm sorry I haven't been looking more to You for help. I've never thought of my accident before as something for testing my faith. But I can see how that's happened. Lord, just like Your Word says, I believe my accident came to test my faith and endurance, but I also feel that You really want me healed. Thank You for this lesson. With Your help, I'm going to trust You. Thank You that even this accident 'works' together for good. I pray that others around me will see You through me. In Your name I pray, amen."

After that, I began to see more positive aspects about my accident. During the following days I shared with nurses, doctors, and visitors the thought that God had allowed my accident merely to test my faith and endurance. "Now, with that lesson learned, I can trust Him to get me back on my feet. You'll see!"

I took this attitude with everything.

The doctor told dad, "You should know that your insurance probably won't begin to cover the expenses of Joni's accident. Her hospital bills will likely be $30,000 or more before she leaves."

I said simply, "Don't worry, God will provide us with what we need."

When Dr. Sherrill explained, "Joni, paralysis is generally a lot harder on an athletic person than ordinary people. I want you to know that when depression sets in, you'll really have a struggle with it."

"God will help me," I replied glibly.

When a nurse commented, "I was reading about your accident. You know, if your break had occurred an inch or less lower, you'd still have the use of your arms. Sad, isn't it?"

I answered, "Yes. But if the break was an inch higher, I'd be dead. God knows best, doesn't He?"

Just after Labor Day, Dick stopped by with a present. My room was overflowing with stuffed animals, posters, pictures, cards, and other get-well mementos. One of them was a green and white plush bear which I doused with British Sterling shaving lotion and named after Dick. The familiar scent reminded and reassured me of Dick when he was absent.

This time, Dick gave me a huge study Bible—one with print large enough to read when it was laid on the floor below my Stryker Frame. I could read it by myself if someone turned the pages. In the front, he wrote:

"To my dearest Joni, with hopes that Christ will always remain in our relationship, and that Christ might give us the patience to wait for each other. With all kinds of love,

Dick

Sept. 9, 1967   Romans 8:28"

Not long after Labor Day, Dick, Jackie, and all my friends went away to college. Dick hitchhiked back as often as possible to be with me. I didn't know how difficult this was for him—or that his grades suffered as a result of his concern for me. I just took it for granted that he should be there. In my selfish little world, I didn't care how he managed it; I just wanted him to be there with me. After all, I needed him. Without knowing it, I began to use my accident as a device to keep him interested. I even resorted to blackmail one evening.

"Hi, Joni," Dick grinned as he bent over to kiss me.

"Where have you been? It's nearly eight o'clock."

"Sorry. I couldn't get away. How was your day?"

"You said you'd be here by six, and it's now eight. You can only stay here a half-hour now before you have to leave. What kind of visit is that?" I fumed.

"Joni, I said I'm sorry. I couldn't get away." Dick was getting defensive, and I didn't want him to get angry.

"Dickie, my day is absolutely miserable without you. Last night I dreamed you left me for another girl."

"I'd never do that—"

"Oh, promise me, Dickie. Tell me you love me and that you'll never leave me."

"You know how much I care for you, hon."

"Tell me. Tell me."

"I love you." Dick said simply. I could tell he didn't want to say it. Not because he didn't care for me deeply—I know he did. Rather, he resented my telling him to say it. He wanted to tell me in his own way, in his own time. But he smiled and added, as if to make the statement spontaneous, "I've loved you for a long time, Joni. If you'd waited five minutes, I'd have told you again—without prompting."

"But I needed to hear you say it now, Dickie."

"All right. I love you. I love you. I love you." Each time he said it, he bent over and kissed me.

"Oh, Dickie. I love you, too. Won't it be great when I'm able to leave here?"

"I'm praying it'll be soon. Boy, this hitchhiking sure wrecks my study habits."

"It may be a long time."

"Oh? Did you hear something today?"

"It'll be several months of rehabilitation. Maybe a year."

"Oh, wow."

"Dickie, I'm scared. I can take it if you're with me. You have to help me. But I can't do it without you. If you leave me, I'll die. I know it. I won't be able to live without you. Promise me you won't leave me."

"Of course."

"If you really love me, promise you'll be with me forever—"

"Sure," he said, glancing down.

"First I'll get my hands back. Then I'll walk. Then we can go to college together," I promised.

"Right," whispered Dick.

"How is college? Is it really neat?"

"Oh, it's fine. Really a lot tougher than high school, though," said Dick. "A lot tougher."

"Maybe because you're doing so much. How's the team doing?" I asked.

"The team? Oh, just fine, I guess. First game is Friday."

"Are you all ready for it?" I asked excitedly.

"I'm not playing," said Dick simply.

"Not playing? Why?"

"I lost my football scholarship."

"But why?"

"Look, it doesn't matter."

"Oh, Dickie, I'm sorry." *It's because he has to visit me so much—he has no time to study*, I told myself.

"It's all right. We've still got time for that. Want me to read something from the Bible?"

"Not tonight, Dickie. I'm tired. And you'll have to go in a minute. Just hug me and kiss me before you go."

He bent over me and held my chin in his hand. He kissed me softly, lingeringly. "I love you," he whispered. "I'll wait forever for you—you know that. Remember that always. I'll always be here."

When he left, I cried bitterly. I felt cheap and selfish. I had put Dick over a barrel. What choice did he have? Could he say how he really felt: "Joni, we're still too young to know if we should get married. We don't know God's will for the future. Let's just play it by ear. You know you can always count on me. I care for you deeply." I'm sure that's what he would have said. But that wasn't strong enough for my frayed emotions. And Dick was too sensitive to hurt my feelings—especially after the accident—so he said what I wanted to hear.

Now I had driven a wedge into our relationship. I had forced feelings and commitments before they were ripe. I began to mistrust all my own motives.

"I'll make it right," I promised the Lord in my prayers that night. "I'll do everything I can to be worthy of Dick's love. I'll do everything possible to walk again. Then he won't have to love me because of the accident but because he wants to. Things will be better. That's what I want, Lord. Please—please. . . ."

When the hospital therapist came by the next day, I remembered Jason's instructions: "You gotta fight." PT—physical therapy was the first step in actual rehabilitation. I decided to give it everything I had.

The therapist fastened my arms in slings and began to explain the process.

"Your fracture was at the fourth and fifth cervical level, as you know. At the first level are nerves for vital organs—heart and lungs. People who have breaks at this first level seldom live.

"The second and third levels control neck muscles and head movement," she continued. "At the fourth and fifth levels, quadriplegia—like your case—

generally results. The sixth level controls the pectoral and arm muscles. Now, you have feelings in your shoulders, upper arm, and chest just above your breasts. That means that maybe you can train other muscles—muscles in the back and shoulders—to compensate for certain arm muscles you've lost."

"Is that what the doctors mean about getting the use of my hands back?" I asked her.

"Partly. Your chart indicates you've got about 50 percent use of your biceps—those are the upper arm muscles that move the arm in its fullest range of movements. We won't know until we get into therapy just how much you'll be able to do. We'll have to train new muscles to do motor movements for the ones you've lost."

"All right, let's try it," I said.

"First, try to lift your arm by using the muscles of your back, neck, and shoulders. Just move it to begin with," she instructed.

I tried. Nothing happened. I closed my eyes to concentrate more intensely. I felt the muscles tense and vibrate, but they seemed independent of my will. I could not get them to move.

"Keep trying. You'll get it," the therapist urged.

I gritted my teeth and tried again. Nothing.

"C'mon, Joni. Try again," she insisted.

"Don't you think I'm trying?" I snapped and swore for emphasis.

"It's a matter of directing new muscles to do the work of the old ones. Don't try to lift your arm with the old movements. Think of how the muscles in the arm are hooked up to the ligaments and bones—here." She showed me diagrams in a book and traced the lines on my own arm. "Try to get movement from these muscles. Just twist or flex your back and try to move your arm in the process."

I tried once more as she pointed to the spot. For more than ten minutes I exerted all my will power and strength. Finally my arm rose less than an inch and flopped back limply.

"Beautiful! Great! Once more," she instructed. "Put all your energy and concentration into lifting that arm and holding it up."

Using all the strength I could gather, I tried again. After several tense moments of agonizing effort, my arm raised once more—this time about an inch off the table—and strained against the slings fastened to it.

"Again!" she ordered.

"I can't. It hurts. It's too tiring. I have to rest first," I begged. Nearly a half-hour had gone by, and all I had done was move my arm about an inch two times.

"All right, Joni. You can see it is going to be hard work. We have a lot to do before you can really begin rehabilitation. But soon we'll have you strong enough to leave here for Greenoaks," she smiled.

"Greenoaks?"

"Yes. Greenoaks Rehabilitation Center," she explained. "Dr. Sherrill will tell you all about it. That's the next step. It's a hospital specializing in motor-damaged cases."

"A rehabilitation center? Oh, yeah—I remember now. That's where I'll learn to walk!"

The therapist smiled, unfastened the slings, and stood up. "Good luck, Joni. I'll work with you again tomorrow. Let's get you ready for Greenoaks!"

❦

Four

For nearly a month, I concentrated on getting prepared for Greenoaks. That was where I would learn to walk and begin life again. When word came that they had a place for me, everyone was excited. The nurses and doctors all came by to wish me well on this step toward rehabilitation.

"Well, lassie, y'behave yourself now. No wild parties and carryin' on," Dr. Harris teased, "or we'll have to come and get you and bring you back here."

"Oh, no you won't!" I exclaimed, "you'll never get me back here—you guys have plenty of sick people to work with. Well, one of these days, I might come back," I amended, "but it'll be on my own two feet—and I'll take you to MaDonald's for lunch."

"It's a date, lassie," Dr. Harris grinned. He squeezed my shoulder, winked, and left.

Two nurses—Anita (my favorite) and Alice—helped take down the pictures and posters and pack away all the things I had accumulated—several boxes—during my three-and-a-half month stay at the hospital.

Finally the orderlies came in to transfer me to the ambulance waiting downstairs to take me to Greenoaks. As they wheeled me through the outside double doors at the ground level, a slight rush of beautiful, sweet-smelling, outdoor air tickled my nostrils and the bright sunlight was everywhere.

"Oh, wow! Wait just a minute, please," I asked the two orderlies. "Do you smell that air?" I said excitedly.

"Polluted!" Snorted one of the guys good-naturedly.

"Oh, it's beautiful!" I breathed deeply of its rich and, to me, heady fragrance.

"Hey, you're gonna get high on oxygen," teased one of the men. They eased my stretcher into the ambulance, shut the doors, and we began the drive to Greenoaks.

I couldn't help contrasting this ambulance drive with my last one. Then the trees had been green, the grass and flowers lush and gorgeous. The air had been hot and humid, the people dressed in summer clothes.

Today, the air was crisp and cool. The stores were decorated for Halloween and fall sales. The trees were gold, red, and orange—the landscape reflected the full variety of autumn colors and textures.

An entire season had passed by while I was in the hospital! It was a strange feeling, but it did not stay to disturb me. The excitement and beauty of the ride was much too thrilling to waste worrying about a lost summer. I let the warm sun bathe my face through the window, and the driver kept his window rolled down so the fresh air could come in and sweep over me. It was such a pleasurable experience that I almost cried with joy.

As we approached Greenoaks, I became even more excited. Greenoaks. Even the name had a pleasant ring to it. In my mind I pictured a big, colonial structure with tall, white pillars overlooking sweeping green lawns shaded by huge green oak trees.

When we pulled into the driveway, however, I could see that it looked nothing like this. It was a sprawling, low brick building, more like an industrial park, office complex, or factory.

"Well, here we are," said the driver.

"Yeah," I said slowly.

"Anything wrong?"

"Uh—no. I guess not," I said sheepishly. "I suppose any place you build up in your mind doesn't live up to your expectations. Y'know?"

He nodded, then added, "Don't worry—they do good work here. I think you'll like it. Quite a few girls your age here. You should hit it off swell."

"I hope so," I replied apprehensively. As he wheeled me down the corridor to my assigned ward, I looked around and into open doors of various rooms. It was quiet, like the hospital. No one was "cured"—*walking.*

I saw people slouched in wheelchairs, encased in Stryker Frames, or lying in beds. The halls seemed dark and depressing, with people lined up in wheelchairs. It was an old institution, badly in need of decorating.

By the time we got to my room, I was discouraged.

Mom and dad were there to meet me. They had signed me in and cared for the billing details and other business. They tried to cheer me up, but as soon as I was as comfortable as possible, they excused themselves. I had seen this reaction before—at City Hospital when they were told of the permanence of my injury. I knew they were again on the verge of breaking down and didn't want me to see their tears and disappointment. They left, promising, "We'll be back soon as possible, darling."

I looked around at my room when they left. Four other girls shared the small ward with me. I decided to introduce myself. "Hi, I'm Joni Eareckson," I began.

"Joni Eareckson!" I heard my name repeated contemptuously, followed by a string of obscenities. "That's all I heard at City Hospital—Joni this, Joni that. I could puke!"

Stunned by the bitter voice, I recovered enough to smile and say, "Oh, I didn't know I had a fan club here."

The ice was broken. The others laughed. "You'll have to excuse Ann," explained one girl. "She's new here, too. She came to City Hospital after you, and I guess she wasn't quite the model patient you were. They did an awful lot of comparing her with you. I'm Betty—Betty Jackson. The girl in the bed over there is Denise Walters."

"Hi. Pardon me if I don't get up."

"Yeah, I know the *un*-feeling," I wisecracked, adding, "Nice to meet you, Denise."

"And this is Betty, too," said Betty Jackson, pointing with a flop of a useless arm, "Betty Glover. They call me B.J. to tell us apart." Betty Glover was a pretty, petite black girl who looked much younger than the rest of us.

"Hi, Betty," I smiled.

Betty looked up and nodded slightly.

"I'm here because of a broken neck—like you," B.J. explained. "Betty has a blood clot on her spine. They're working on her to see why she's paralyzed. And Denise is here because she has M.S"

"M.S.?" I asked ignorantly.

"Multiple sclerosis."

I regretted asking. I recalled hearing about M.S. in the hospital. *It's a fatal disease. Denise will probably be dead before she reaches her twentieth birthday,* I thought, shivering inwardly, and wondered how she maintained her gracious and open attitude.

"And in this cor-nah," clowned B.J., "is Ann Wilson, whose mouth you've already met. Ann is in charge of b ————————."

"Aw, go—" Ann cursed. She took a cigarette from her lips and threw it at Denise. It landed harmlessly on the tile floor.

"Well, now you've met us. You ready for this marriage?" asked B.J.

"I—I guess so, yeah," I stammered. *Except for Ann and that smoke,* I thought to myself.

Ann had lit up another cigarette. In the hospital, I had discouraged people from smoking around me. In Greenoaks, many of the patients smoked. To me, smoking was ugly, smelly, and something I wanted other people to do only in their own homes or rooms—not around me. I hated the choking smoke and acrid smell. But now I could claim only one-fifth of this room. There wasn't anything to do but get used to the smoke and make the best of the situation.

I tried the one ploy I knew and said to Ann, "You know, that stuff causes lung cancer. It'll kill you."

She looked squarely at me and replied in even tones, "Why do you think I'm doing it?"

But Ann wasn't nearly as difficult and contrary as my first impressions of her. I could see a lot of my own attitudes of bitterness and resentment in her. *A few weeks ago, I was going through the same depression and despondency*, I remembered. I wanted to kill myself, too. Ann was more confused than anything else. She used anger to lash out because she didn't know what else to do. I decided to try and get to know her better.

During the next few days, I got an even closer look at Greenoaks. Patients from every age, economic, occupational, and racial background were housed in the four wings of the institution. They consisted of amputees, paraplegics, quadriplegics, polio victims, and those suffering from muscular dystrophy, multiple sclerosis, and other diseases affecting the motor and nervous systems.

"How come there are so many new people—mostly guys our age?" I asked B.J.

"Broken necks. Most broken necks happen in summer with swimming and diving accidents. They usually spend a couple months in city hospital and then come here for rehab," B.J. explained.

I made a mental note of the way she abbreviated the word *rehabilitation*. I listened for other such "inside" or slang terms used by the girls so I would not sound so much like a greenhorn.

"How many broken neck cases are new?" I asked.

"Oh, maybe ten, fifteen."

"How long have you been here, B.J.?"

"Two years," she answered.

Two years! I recoiled inwardly at the thought. *Two years—and she's still paralyzed and in bed like me!* The fact that *I* might be here that long really depressed me. I was silent for a long while.

That night as I lay in my Stryker Frame trying to sleep, I was troubled by the old attitudes and bitterness that had made me so despondent at the hospital. I tried to pray and couldn't. I tried to think of some promises from God's Word to encourage me. Nothing seemed reassuring.

Seemingly the other girls had adjusted. They were chatting quietly, waiting for "lights out." Except for Ann. She was complaining loudly, punctuating her objections with salty language. I decided that even if I had to be in an institution the rest of my life, I'd be pleasant—at least on the surface—and not like Ann. She had absolutely no friends on the outside. And inside, people treated her in kind. No one tried to understand her or make friends with her.

I need to have my friends, or I'll lose my mind, I said to myself, so I promised myself never to lose my cool with mom, dad, Jackie, or the others when they came to visit. No matter how bitter I was, I wouldn't let it show.

"That's a good idea," observed B.J. when I told her about my thoughts the next day. "In here, everyone's the same. So you won't find much sympathy here. In fact, you'd be smart not to make many friends here."

"Why?" I wondered.

"It's an ivory tower. Everyone here is the same—give or take an arm or two—so it's comfortable. You get out for visits home when you have enough sitting-up time, but you can't wait to get back. It's easier to be here with people like us. No hassling about braces, wheelchairs, and stuff. It's hard to leave here. The people on the street think because your legs are paralyzed, your brain must be, too. They treat 'cha like a dummy. So everybody always comes back here complaining and comparing injuries, but content to stay because they feel at home here. You'll be the same if you make all your friends here. Just because it's *easier* to be in an ivory tower doesn't mean it's better. It isn't. I know. I've been here two years. Whatever you do, keep your friends on the outside!"

Jay seemed to sense my emotional needs in that regard. She not only came often herself, but often rounded up old school chums to visit. I especially remember Jay and several friends dressing up in costumes and coming over on Halloween night. There was no bending of rules here, though. Unlike City Hospital nurses, Greenoaks' staff rigidly enforced visiting hours. Promptly at eight o'clock, Jay and our friends were asked to leave.

My days became dull routine, brightened only by my visitors. I was confined to bed because of bedsores. A nurse would feed me in the morning and empty my catheter bag. Then she'd check the round mirror above my head to see that it was focused for me to watch TV.

About noon, I'd be fed and "emptied" again. And more TV in the afternoon. Mornings were the game shows. Afternoons, the soap operas. At evening, another meal and catheter emptying followed by more television watching until "lights out." Each new day was a boring and monotonous extension of the previous day—eat, watch TV, sleep—in an unbreaking, sickening cycle.

I had to learn to eat and drink my food quickly. The staff people were always busy, too busy to linger with those who dawdled with their meals. They were also too busy to really do more than care for our immediate physical needs. If my nose itched, I'd have to wait until Jay or a staff person was nearby. My hair was growing back and became tangled, matted, dirty, and snowing dandruff because no one had time to wash it.

One day when Jay came for a visit, she asked, "What's that horrible smell?"

"What smell?" I asked.

"Ugh! It's your hair. When did they wash it last?" Jay demanded.

"Over a month ago. At City Hospital," I replied.

"It's awful! It stinks, it's so bad! I've got to do something about that!" she exclaimed. Jay checked, got a basin and soap, and improvised a means for shampooing my hair.

"Oh, it feels so good!" I exclaimed.

"Me next!" called out Denise. "Wash my hair, please, Jay."

"Then me," echoed B.J. and Betty together. So, a regular hair wash and set, along with brushing, became Jay's duty to the five of us every week until "regulations" put an end to her efforts.

With my hair now growing out and sometimes even combed, I began to take a little interest in my appearance. The side effects of the medication had slackened somewhat by now, too, and I didn't seem quite so grotesque. However, I was still thin and underweight, and my bones bulged through my skin causing open, ugly bedsores.

Diana White, a friend from high school and *Young Life*, began to visit me regularly. She was a sensitive, caring Christian girl, with a positive, out-going personality. She always seemed happy and cheerful. Yet, she was practical as well as optimistic. Her attitude was not glib, happy-go-lucky naiveté. Rather, she encountered difficulty and pessimism with her own strong personality. She had an innate spirit of helpfulness and won instant acceptance with people. Diana's wide face, dark hair, and eyes lighted up when she talked, and the corners of her mouth curled up in a smile, making me feel brighter, better.

I appreciated her visits more and more because Jackie—now facing some inner turmoil of her own—no longer came as frequently to see me. Diana's encouragement and reading from God's Word also filled the void created by the fact that Dick's studies prevented him from coming as often. Jason began to drift out of my life, too. From others, I heard that he was dating a girl he had met at college and seemed serious about her.

I was grateful when P.T.—physical therapy—became a part of the daily routine, for it offered an additional element of variety to my life.

At first the physical therapist, Barbara Marshall, came to my room to exercise my paralyzed limbs. After a few weeks, I was taken to the P.T. center for two hours of therapy every day. My first impression of this big room was that it resembled a strange torture chamber. There were bizarre machines and devices for stretching, pulling, and bending useless arms, legs, and bodies. But as strange as this room appeared, it had positive overtones for me—I was going to learn to walk like the others I saw moving with crutches and walkers.

Joe Leroy, a brawny therapy aide with great patience, took me to the P.T. room to show me what would happen when the therapist put my limbs through the full range of potential movement to keep them from becoming atrophied.

"Look," he encouraged, "all this flat-on-your-back ballet really does have a purpose." Joe then proceeded to explain how twisting, bending, and stretching my legs, arms and limp body in arcs, circles, and all kinds of angles would help me.

"It keeps your muscles elastic," Joe explained.

"But I can't feel anything. Why does it matter if they get stiff?" I asked.

"Makes problems for the blood—circulation gets bad. Also, when your muscles go, your body gets stiff, your limbs shrivel up, and your body gets all twisted up," Joe said as he pointed to other patients being pulled, pushed, and lifted.

The physical therapists worked with me twenty minutes each day, putting elasticity back into my muscles, even though they would never function again. Next, they began to work with me in order to get me out of my Stryker Frame and into a regular bed.

Then came grueling exercises to try to enable me to sit up. They fastened me to a tilt-board and lifted my head and lowered my legs. As they slowly raised me past the horizontal position, I felt blood rush from my head and waves of nausea sweep over me.

"Wait. Don't go any higher. I can't take it," I cried.

Even just a few seconds with my head elevated was too much after nearly six months in a horizontal position.

"Oh, Joe," I sobbed. "I thought I was going to faint! Won't I ever be able to sit up?"

"Sure, Joni. Just takes time. We only had you elevated about 45 degrees. We'll try again for a little bit longer. When you can take it for several minutes, we'll increase the angle of the tilt-board. By Thanksgiving you should be sitting up in a chair," Joe said brightly.

Earl, another aide, nodded and said, "You see, your body is so used to lyin' flat that your circulation has adapted to this position." Earl punctuated his explanation with wide, sweeping arm gestures. "When we raise your head, the blood leaves your head, and you feel like you're gonna black out. But if we do it slow 'n easy, your heart will 'remember' and begin to do its job again. Your circulation will pick up and blood will be pumped to your brain again."

So we worked out longer and longer each day until I could "sit up" on the tilt-board without blacking out or getting nauseous.

We took inventory of my muscle capability and feeling. Doctors and therapists determined I had full feelings in my head, neck, and shoulders to the collarbones. There was a slight tingling sensation in my upper arms and chest, making it feel as if these parts of my body were asleep.

Diana came by after I was making progress in P.T. and offered her encouragement. Her optimism was contagious. Each time she came to visit, she'd have new encouragement from the Bible. "Listen," she exclaimed, "it's from John 16:24: 'I assure you that whatever you ask the Father he will give you in my name. Up to now you have asked nothing in my name; ask now, and you will receive, that your joy may be overflowing.' Isn't that great?"

"Yeah, it really is. Hey, maybe God is doing something special. Did you hear about our church?" I asked.

"Church?" Diana asked. "No. What's happening?"

"Our church is having an all-night prayer service for me. They're going to pray for my healing and recovery," I explained.

"Oh, wow. That's neat! 'Ask now, and you will receive,'" Diana repeated.

I was further encouraged because my P.T. had by now brought a tingling feeling to my fingers. While they were still numb and paralyzed, I could feel a remote sensation in them. I knew God was beginning to heal me.

On the night of the prayer service at church, friends from high school, teachers, parents of friends, and friends of friends crowded into the Bishop Cummings Reformed Episcopal Church. And I went to sleep that night expecting to awake the next morning fully healed.

It didn't happen that way of course. So I rationalized that the Lord was testing our faith and that the healing process and full recovery would come slowly and not in some sudden, supernatural way.

When Diana, Jay, my parents and *Young Life* friends came by for a visit, I gave the outward impression that everything was under control, hiding my disappointment and impatience.

"The Lord's going to heal me," I promised them. "Let's keep praying and trusting."

"Oh, Joni," someone would gush, "you sure are brave. I wish I had your faith."

I'd smile sweetly and pray under my breath for God to hurry up and heal me.

✌ᴈ

Five

BY DECEMBER I was still weak, thin, and covered with bedsores, but my physical therapy gave me enough sitting-up time so I could go home for one day. I chose Christmas day and began to get excited planning for it. The night after they told me I could go home for a day, I was too thrilled to sleep. I lay in the darkness of my room and tried to recall all the memories of my last Christmas before the accident—walking in the snow with Dick, Christmas Eve at the cathedral, making angels in the snow, drinking hot chocolate beside the fireplace, singing carols as I played my guitar. What would it be like this year?

Christmas Day finally came! Jay helped the nurse dress me for the trip home. I wore the pretty dark suit I had bought on the trip our family had taken out West just weeks before my accident; it hung on me like a sack. Jay also brought me a lovely blond wig to wear over my own hair which was still not long enough to style.

Dad drove up to the door and waited while Joe and Earl carried me to the car. They instructed my family on how a quadriplegic should ride in a car.

"It never occurred to me that just riding in a car is dangerous," I said, adding, "unless, of course, we crash."

"You don't have to be in a wreck to get hurt," Joe cautioned. "You see, a quad can't sit up alone. If the car swerves, stops suddenly, or just turns a corner, you'll be carried by momentum. You'll spill—maybe crack your head on the door or smash your face on the dashboard or windshield, if you're sitting up front." He explained how to use the car's shoulder-harness to strap me in but also cautioned to be aware of holding on to me, especially on turns, starts, and stops.

Nothing happened on the way home, although the drive seemed exciting and full of interesting little pleasures. *It's winter now*, I thought. *Two whole seasons have slipped by since I was home.*

"Well, we're almost there now," observed Jay as the car turned at the familiar triangle intersection. I looked up the street—the high school, the house of my piano teacher, the drugstore—everything as I remembered it. A twinge of homesickness swept over me.

In a few minutes, we had driven up the steep avenue in front of my folks' home and pulled into the driveway in back. Dad and Jay gingerly lifted me from the car and carried me inside.

The feelings of homesickness were real by now. The house was decorated for the holidays, and a big, fragrant pine tree had been set up in the dining room where I was to stay.

Mom had somehow obtained a hospital bed and set it up in the dining room. I thought of my old room, just above this one, keeper of so many of my secret thoughts, prayers, and hopes. Of course, my family couldn't carry me up the narrow, twisting staircase to my old room so, for this one day, the dining room would be my room.

Mom had pushed the huge dining room table alongside the wall to make the room more comfortable. Dad must have known when he built the house that we'd entertain a lot, for the room was huge—two or three times the usual dining room size, about eighteen by twenty-five feet—with a large table able to seat fourteen with ease.

A crackling fire in the stone fireplace, beautiful and fragrant Christmas decorations, candles, and lights filled the room with happiness. It was almost too much for my senses. The smells, sights, and sounds were intoxicating. During my hospital stay and confinement at Greenoaks, my spirit had suffered as well as my body, for my spirit had suffered sensory deprivation. Now the room reeled as all of these sweet sensations assaulted my brain in a feast of pleasure.

I was able to sit up only a little while before tiring, so the hospital bed proved useful. I half-sat and half-lay on the bed. Dressed in the suit and blond wig, I looked "almost human," but I was still self-conscious about my appearance. Especially my legs. It seemed to me they were sticking out awkwardly, disgustingly.

"Please, will you cover me, mom?" I asked.

"Are you cold, dear?"

"No. I just want to be covered. I look awful."

"Nonsense," she replied. "You look lovely. Doesn't she, Jay?"

"Of course," answered my sister.

"But I still want to be covered. Bring that brown blanket and put it over my legs. I don't want people coming over to stare. Please!" I was insistent.

"All right, Joni. As you wish," sighed mom, as she spread the blanket over my legs and tucked it in. The real reason I wanted my legs covered wasn't because others would be offended by my useless limbs. Rather, it was because they were a constant reminder to me of how different this Christmas was. I couldn't bear to look at them.

Dick, along with friends and family, came to visit that day, and the time rushed by. At first, I resented this swift passage of time. Then I was grateful, because as my mind recalled former Christamases, I was saddened and depressed at the changes in my life.

No more could I spontaneously run out in the snow or sing carols for the neighbors; these and other pleasures were gone forever, and everyone seemed to sense it. There were no tears, at least not now, but the air of sadness was awful.

It wasn't until I was back in my bed at Greenoaks that I allowed myself to cry. Then there was no stopping. B.J., Betty, Denise, and Ann had also gone home for a one-day Christmas visit. But for those who went and for those who had nowhere to go, Christmas was the same: a sad, depressing reminder of better times and happier places when we had been whole.

I tried to evaluate my feelings about what had happened at Christmas. I was happy and thrilled about going home; but, I was sobered by the experience of having to relate to familiar people and old surroundings in strange, new ways.

When the nurse came by the next day, she examined me and said, "Joni, I'm sorry, but that will have to be your last visit home for quite awhile."

"Why?"

"Because it opened all the sores on your back and hips! Your bone protrusions are rubbing the skin away. They won't heal at all unless we put you back in the Stryker Frame," she said simply.

"But can't I sit up at all?" I begged.

"I'm sorry, no. Sitting up is what stretches the skin of the wounds and breaks open the sores. Let's wait until they heal."

Dick came by as often as he could, hitchhiking the sixty-mile round trip from the University of Maryland. I could tell that my accident was really taking a toll on him; his emotions were as frayed as mine.

"Dickie," I told him one day, "we're holding onto the past. We can't do that. We can't go back to high school times."

He looked at me sadly and nodded. "But things will get better. Soon you'll be—"

"No!" I cried. "They won't get better. Don't you understand? I'm not going to get better! Don't you see that?"

Once again, I desperately wanted to kill myself. Here I was, trapped in this canvas cocoon. I couldn't move anything except my head. Physically, I was little more than a corpse. I had no hope of ever walking again. I could never lead a normal life and marry Dick. *In fact, he might even be walking out of my life forever*, I concluded. I had absolutely no idea of how I could find purpose or meaning in just existing day after day—waking, eating, watching TV, sleeping.

Why on earth should a person be forced to live out such a dreary existence? How I prayed for some accident or miracle to kill me. The mental and spiritual anguish was as unbearable as the physical torture.

But once again, there was no way for me to commit suicide. This frustration was also unbearable. I was despondent, but I was also angry because of my helplessness. How I wished for strength and control enough in my fingers to do something, anything, *to end my life*. Tears or rage, fear, and frustration only added to my despondency.

There was an added complication to my lack of well-being. The sores, caused by my protruding bones, did not heal. In fact, the doctors insisted surgery was the only way to correct the problem. So, on June 1, 1968, I was driven back to City Hospital for bone operations, further confirmation that my injury was permanent. The doctors would not shave the boney protuberances from my hip and tailbone if there was any hope of my using my legs again.

The surgeon, Dr. Southfield, explained the operation.

"Since you have no feeling, it will not be necessary to anesthetize you. But if you're squeamish about the sight of blood and tissue—."

"Never mind," I said curtly. "I've been through it all. I've been here almost a year, remember. There isn't much I haven't seen. And there's precious little they haven't already done to me. Carve away!"

I listened as Dr. Southfield's hands guided the scalpel through the flesh on my hip. Blood spurted behind the blade as he laid back the skin and muscle tissue. Assistants gave him various surgical tools as he called for them.

In a few minutes, I could hear a strange rasping, scraping sound as he chiseled away on my hip bone, filing down the sharp, jutting joints that caused my bed sores.

In spite of my earlier bluster, I didn't like the sights and sounds of the surgery. I felt queasy, so I began to sing, taking my mind off the operation. I sang loud and long, going through a terribly depressing assortment of pessimistic songs.

"Can't you sing something else—something brighter?" asked Dr. Southfield.

"No!" I snapped and kept up my "concert."

After awhile, I was turned over, and the surgeon began to operate on my tailbone. He shaved and chiseled more bony protuberances. Finally, he sutured all the incisions. Then I was bandaged, examined, and driven back to Greenoaks for recuperation.

When the sutures and bedsores healed, I was allowed to sit up slowly. Earl carefully placed me in bed and tried to help me sit up.

"Here we go, Joni," he said. "Take it nice and slow. Don't want 'cha to get dizzy and pass out. Right?"

"Right," I echoed.

"Easy now."

"How'm I doing, Earl? I'm sitting up! How about that!"

Earl did not reply. Soon he quietly carried me back to the Stryker Frame.

"Hey. Leave me in bed, Earl," I commanded. "I've waited to sit up again. If you're worried about me passing out—."

"Sorry, Joni. I gotta put you back. The operation didn't take. Your backbone just busted the incision open again. You're bleeding."

As I lay in the Stryker through the following long weeks, I finally gave up ever hoping to walk. But I began to strain every atom of will power into getting back the use of my hands. If I had my hands, I wouldn't be so helpless. I wouldn't have to depend on Jay or Diana to wash or brush my hair. Or put on make-up. Or just feed myself. If I could only do something—anything at all—I wouldn't feel so helpless.

"You can use your mouth to do some of the things you'd normally do with hands," suggested therapist Chris Brown one day after learning of my feelings. She added, "You've seen people in O.T. (occupational therapy) learn to write or type by holding a pencil or stick with their teeth. You can learn, too."

"No," I said. "It's disgusting. Degrading. I won't do it!"

Chris did not press me. "Maybe some other day," she said.

Later, Jay came to see me. Although she smiled and seemed in control, she'd been crying again.

"Hi, sis," she said.

"You've been crying, Jay."

Jay nodded. She never wanted to worry me with her own problems and often hid her feelings from me, but I had eventually learned of the difficulties she was having with her marriage. Now her divorce had become final.

She said evenly, "It's over. And it'll be all right, Joni. Don't worry."

"But—"

"Really. Don't worry." Jay changed the subject. "Here, I've brought you some goodies." She opened a bag of doughnuts and held one up. "Your favorites, see?"

We spent an hour or so chatting and reading through a *Seventeen* magazine she spread out beneath the frame.

Then, as she prepared to leave, she looked soberly into my eyes and said, "Joni, I want—I want you to come and live with little Kay and me when you get out of the hospital."

"Let's think about it, Jay," I replied. "We'll see, okay?"

She kissed me on the cheek and ran the back of her hand across my forehead. Smiling, she left.

The significance of Jay's visit slowly sank into my consciousness, and I pondered her comments and offer. I promised myself not to make any plans, although the thought of living with Jay was reassuring.

When Dick came by later, he wheeled my Stryker to the game room and sat on the floor under me so we could talk. We were trying out a new relationship—being friends only. While neither of us had really discussed such a change, we each had assumed that we had no immediate future together as husband and wife. First, I'd have to get my hands back. Then I'd have to be rehabilitated, and that would probably take a long time. So neither of us talked about things like love and marriage.

His visits consisted mostly of friendly encouragement—and reading to me, usually from a modern New Testament translation. The message was there, loud and clear: faith, hope, trust. But I dismissed this as being too superficial. Fine for the ordinary person on his feet dealing with life, temptation, and doubt. But what was God saying to me, encased immobile in my Stryker?

Diana read to me from the Old Testament, and I began to identify with many of the prophets. Like Jeremiah, I thought perhaps God's wrath was being poured out on me in judgment.

I read the poetry of the Book of Lamentations and identified fully with the sorrows about which Jeremiah had written:

> "She weeps bitterly at night,
>   the tears flow always on her cheeks;
> no one of all her lovers
>   now seeks to bring her comfort."

> > *Oh, God, how*
> > *true. And I can't*
> > *even wipe my own*
> > *tears away!*

> "For the Lord has afflicted her
>   because of the greatness of her
>   transgressions."

> > *Yes! I broke His moral*
> > *commandments.*
> > *Now punishment.*

> "Look and see if there is any sorrow
>   like my sorrow,
>   which is being dealt out to me,
> which the Lord has inflicted
>   in the day of His fiery anger.

> > *No one else is being*
> > *punished like this. Why*
> > *did God do this to me?*

"From on high He sent fire into my
    bones,
and it has subdued them."

> *Diving accident . . .*
>   *paralysis . . .*

"He has given me over to frustration
and faintness all day long."

> *rage . . .*
> *weakness and fear.*

"He has made my strength to fail.
The Lord has delivered me into hands
which I am unable to withstand."

> *In bed for a year,*
> *completely dependent*
> *on orderlies and nurses.*

"My eyes are exhausted with weeping;
    my emotions are deeply disturbed;
my grief is poured out on the earth."

> *How much more can*
> *I take? I'm at the*
> *end of my rope!*

"Surely He has turned away from me;
He has turned His hand against me
    all the day."

> *Why God . . .*
>   *why?*
>   *why?*

"He has made my skin and my flesh
    turn old:
He has crushed my bones."

> *The bedsores, stitches,*
> *bone surgery . . .*

"He has piled up against me, and
    surrounded me
with bitterness and distress."

> *and I'm still*
> *surrounded by canvas,*

> *catheter tubes,*
> *and urine bags.*

"He has caused me to dwell in dark
    places,
as the dead of former times."

> *I'm trapped in this*
> *gloomy hospital where*
> *we sit like zombies*
> *waiting to die.*

"He has built a wall around me, I
    cannot go forth;
He has weighted me down with
    chains."

> *I'm trapped!*
> *Stryker, straps,*
> *and Crutchfield tongs . . .*

"Even when I cry aloud and call for
    help,
He shuts out my prayer."

> *and God doesn't care.*

"I have forgotten what enjoyment is."

> *He doesn't even care.*

(Jeremiah 1:2, 5, 12–14; 2:11; 3:3–8, 17, Berkeley)

Who, or What, is God? *Certainly not a personal Being who cares for individuals,* I reasoned. *What's the use of believing when you prayers fall on deaf ears?*

My doubts began to be as deep-seated as my resentment. When Diana or Dick read a promise from the Bible concerning hope or trust, I shut them off.

"That's too pat," I told them. "Those verses are too glib to have anything but surface meaning. Try to apply those promises to me. You tell me how my being here for over a year 'works together for good.' What good? Where? When? I don't want to hear any more!"

And there were people at Greenoaks who added to my feelings of helplessness and depression. Mrs. Barber, attendant on the midnight shift, was as angry and bitter as I was for reasons of her own. She'd often make obscene or insensitive comments designed to hurt and demean those of us who got in her way. To Mrs.

Barber, we were not patients in need of care, but hindrances to her routine of chores which had to be done.

One night, she came into our room and angrily swept my pictures off the window air conditioner near my Stryker. "How the ____ do you think I can turn on this ____ air conditioner with all this ____ on it?" she hissed. The pictures had been there for weeks and in no way interfered with its operation.

She picked out a photo of Dick and said terrible things—including that Dick was involved in all kinds of lewd and vulgar conduct. Her perversity sickened me, and I snapped back at her.

She came over to my Stryker and snarled, "I ought to leave you like this until morning and not flip you. But to show you what a nice person I am, I'll turn you." With that, she flipped me violently. She had not taken the usual precaution of checking to see that my arms were tucked in first. One arm was loose, and when she spun me, my hand stuck violently against the Stryker.

Although my hand was paralyzed and I could feel no pain, it began to swell and was badly bruised. She left the injured arm dangling and rushed out of the room to other duties.

Shaken, angry and afraid, I began to sob quietly.

"I saw what she did, Joni," said B.J. "You ought to report her to the supervisor."

"Yeah. I heard everything. You oughtta turn her in," added Denise.

"But I can't report her. She'll do something else—worse," I sobbed.

The next day, however, mom came to visit and asked about my swollen and bruised hand. I tried to dismiss it lightly as an accident, but the girls told mom what had happened. Incensed, mom went directly to the supervisor and complained in the most vocal terms.

Late that night, Mrs. Barber came into our darkened room, approached me quietly, and put her face next to mine. With a voice that was both whisper and evil menace, she said, "If you ever say anything against me again, you ____ , I'll see that you pay for it dearly! Do you understand, you ____ ?"

It was no idle threat. I was terrified, frightened that something horrible would happen to me if I did complain.

In addition to the few who were like Mrs. Barber, who hated patients and having to care for them, there were others who did care, but only a few had time. Nurses seemed to have time only to fill out medication and defecation charts. Most attendants were overworked and poorly paid, and—as a result—some just didn't care.

These episodes only added to my depression. Jim Pollard was a bright, young quadriplegic who was asking many of the same questions I was. His muscles wouldn't quite support his head, so it dropped slightly to the left. But his voice, mind, and spirit were strong.

"If there isn't a personal God who cares about me, then what's the use?" I asked him.

"That's the whole point," he explained. "I've done a lot of reading and studying. I've looked at religion, philosophy, everything. Life has absolutely no meaning. It's pointless. Absurd."

"Then why bother?" I countered. "Why not just commit suicide? In fact, why doesn't the whole human race commit suicide if life has no meaning?"

"Oh, it can have meaning. Some people believe in God, and that gives them meaning. But when the chips are down—like for us here—you see just how shallow religion is," he said earnestly.

"But do you think life makes sense?"

"Probably not for us. People on their feet can eat, work, and make love—all kinds of things. 'Pursuit of happiness' and all that, y'know?"

I nodded.

"But here. Well, that's a different story. We've reduced life to its barest elements. And, for the most part, there's no reason to live."

"Then why are you still alive?"

Jim shrugged. "Guess I'm just not gutsy enough to do myself in. Besides, life does have meaning if you find it for yourself."

"How?"

"Your mind. Intelligence. I get a kick out of developing my mind. To h ____ with my body. Maybe I can find something in being intelligent."

"Maybe," I offered. "But what about everyone else? Everyone on their feet. They're born. They live and die with existence as their only goal. Why bother?"

"You've got me, Joni," he answered. "Why not read some of my books and tracts. I've got some stuff here by Sartre, Marx, and other great minds."

I read it all, and it all pointed me further and further from God and hope—the meaning of life was that *it had no meaning.* Life without an eternal focus, without God, led to despair. I could see this but didn't know what else to believe. Had not God, if there was a God, turned His back on me?

Jim continued to counsel me in agnosticism. "You see, Joni, nothing will ever make sense. Accept it. Life is capricious as well as temporal. Jobs, success, friends, family—these only have meaning as a means to that end. You're only here for the moment, so if you want anything out of life, get it now. Don't get the idea you're putting something away for an afterlife."

"But the trouble is, Jim," I interrupted, "I found out in high school that temporal things don't satisfy me. There has to be something permanent."

"What about your accident? That sure isn't temporary," he reminded me. "You've told me the Bible says even your paralysis works out for good. How? What's the purpose of your paralysis?"

"I—I don't know. That's what's making me doubt God. If He was real, wouldn't He show me? Wouldn't I have some sense of purpose with it all?"

Jim said, "You're just outgrowing your need for religion and God, Joni. Did you read any of the other books I gave you?"

"Yes. I read *Siddhartha* and Kafka's *The Trial, Bio-Ethics*—uh—*Man's Search for Meaning*. All of them. I've read every existentialist author you've given me," I told him.

"Well, I'm impressed. Then you ought to know by now that the idea of a personal God is ridiculous."

"I'm not there yet, Jim. I don't know. I've read everything you've given me. These books build a pretty strong case for your point of view. But—"

"But you're afraid. You think God is sitting up there in heaven waiting to zap you if you have doubts. Well, tell me, Joni. If there is a God, what can He do to you that hasn't been done already? That's the way I look at it. I'm crippled. For good. I'll never be on my feet again. What's God going to do if I don't believe? Damn me to hell? I'm already in hell! No—there's no God, Joni. No God—" His voice trailed off wistfully, as though he had once held out hope that somehow God did exist. Yet now, convinced in his unbelief, Jim was resigned. "There's no God."

I prayed desperately: "God I have just two choices: either You exist or You don't. If You don't exist, then I don't see any logical reason for living. If people who believe are only going through motions that mean nothing, I want to know. Why should we go on fooling ourselves? Life is absurd most of the time. And it seems man's only end is despair. What can I do, Lord? I want to believe, but I have nothing to hang on to. God, You've got to prove Your existence to me!"

My mind was a jumble of thoughts and philosophies. Logical, rational, intellectual positions were posed and just as quickly disposed of by opposing concepts, apparently just as valid. What was right? What was wrong? Truth? Oh, what a maze of confusion. *Am I losing my mind as well as my body?*

Weary from thinking, my eyelids fell shut. Then, from somewhere, a calmness took over. A thought—or memory—"a still, small voice"—reminded my troubled brain, *Thou wilt keep him in perfect peace whose mind is stayed on thee.*

And I slept.

Six

Diana came by more and more now. She came so often, in fact, that some visitors thought she was one of the staff. One day she put down the Bible she'd been reading from and said, "Joni, I've decided to be a volunteer worker here so I can take better care of you."

"But, Diana, you can't drop out of school," I protested.

"I've prayed about it a lot, Joni. I believe it's what God wants me to do. You see, I don't know what the Lord has planned for me in the future. I'm going to drop out for a semester or so and ask God for specific guidance for the future," she explained.

"Yes, but—"

Diana interrupted, "But nothing. While I'm seeking God's will on this, I'll be a volunteer—at least until next fall."

"Diana, I appreciate what you want to do. But are you sure it's the right thing?" I asked.

She nodded. Her eyes were bright with determination. "Yes. I've made up my mind, and I have real peace about it."

It was good to have Diana around as a hospital volunteer. She busied herself with other patients as well as me. And she watched the nurses and therapists so she could help in even more areas.

Meanwhile, my spiritual confusion was leading me down blind alleys. In my attempts to be open-minded about other concepts, as opposed to belief in God, I became even more confused and frustrated. The more I read, the more tangled my beliefs became. Was there no such thing as truth and meaning? All my reading of Sartre, Hesse, Marx, and others brought me no light.

It seemed the further I opened my mind to these philosophies which denied God, the further I went away from Him. Finally, I became convinced there was little to be learned or understood from these confusing writings. My search had led me back to the Bible.

I began to sense that God was real and that He was dealing with me.

"My thoughts are not your thoughts. My ways are not your ways," He reminded me from His Word. I needed to understand that—that I could not comprehend my own purpose or meaning without taking God's deity into consideration.

"What do you mean?" asked Diana when we were discussing this subject one day.

"Well, I've been trying to have the world make sense by having things to relate to me. I want to see my life have meaning and purpose. But the Bible says our purpose is to glorify God. My life has meaning when I glorify God," I explained.

"Yes, I understand," said Diana. "But how do you get that concept to work?"

"I'm not sure. But I know until now I've been looking for a way to make the world revolve around me. Now I'm convinced that I need to plug in some other way."

"Well, the answers to all questions are in the Bible," offered Diana. "Maybe if you look for them, you'll find God's will."

"Yeah," I replied. "I think I get impatient because I don't see life as God does. A year in a Stryker seems like a century to me—but a year isn't much time to God. His frame of reference is eternity. Maybe things just take a little longer than I expect."

"What's next then, Joni?"

"I don't know. I— I guess I'll have to take things one at a time. One, I'm paralyzed and don't know why God allowed it to happen to me. But maybe I'll never know why. Maybe I shouldn't let it hang me up."

"Then concentrate on getting out of here," urged Diana.

"Yeah, well, I suppose so. I'm scared, Di. I'm scared, I guess, because I don't know what'll happen when I do go home."

"But that's the whole point of trusting the Lord, Joni," she was smiling, her eyes wide in the enjoyment of a new truth which had just come to her. "You don't have to know why God let you be hurt. The fact is, God knows—and that's all that counts. Just trust Him to work things out for good, eventually, if not right now."

"What do you mean?"

"Would you be any happier if you did know why God wants you paralyzed? I doubt it. So don't get worked up about trying to find meaning to the accident," she scolded.

"Then what do you think I should do?"

"Well, therapy, for one thing. You know how you've avoided occupational therapy—you've said 'what's the use of learning to write with a stick in my mouth?' Well, if God knows the ultimate purpose and meaning of things, then He can find or give meaning to a paralyzed life, too. But you can't fight Him on it."

"But I'm making progress in physical therapy. Why should I learn how to write with my mouth? I expect to get the use of my hands back!"

"But," Diana paused carefully, "but what if you don't get your hands back?"

I didn't answer right away. The possibility was not even an option as far as I was concerned. I thought, *I can give up a year or more of my life to lie here paralyzed. I can even sacrifice my legs and spend the rest of my life in a wheelchair. I won't complain. But, God, You wouldn't keep me from getting my hands back and leading a fairly normal life! You wouldn't leave me like this forever, would You?*

"Joni—"

"Yes."

"Maybe we shouldn't think about the future just now," said Diana softly, as if reading my mind. "Let's just take it one step at a time, like you said."

"I guess I haven't been setting my mind toward getting out of here. After all, this is a rehab hospital. I should be concentrating on being rehabilitated, huh?"

The next day, I told Chris Brown, my occupational therapist, that I wanted to learn how to do things using my mouth.

Chris was every bit as pleasant, cheerful, helpful, and encouraging as Joe and Earl, my two physical therapy aides.

"My job," she explained simply, "is to help you learn how to function out there, in the world."

"That's all, huh?" I kidded.

"Well, you'll be doing all the work. So my job is easy."

"What are you going to teach me?"

"Well, first, how about learning how to write?"

"Okay, Chris, what do I do?" I asked.

"Hold this pencil in your mouth. Grip it with your teeth, like this," Chris explained. She held a pencil in her own mouth to demonstrate and placed one in my mouth.

"Okay. Good. See, it's easy. Uh—not so tight. Don't clench it in your teeth, or you'll get writer's cramp in your jaw," she joked. "Just hold it firmly so you won't drop it—tight enough to control it. See?"

"Mm-mff," I mumbled, meaning I understood.

Chris taught me how to make lines, circles, and other marks. At first these were squiggly and wobbly. But after many hours of practice, I began to have more control.

Finally, I was able to make letters. With determination and concentration, I wrote a letter to mom and dad. It was brief, and the letters were still big, awkward squiggles, but it was writing!

This sense of accomplishment gave me a more positive attitude, and I began to enjoy my therapy, reinforced by the encouragement of a staff and patients who cheered every fragment of progress.

In September, I was taken to Kernans Hospital for a second back operation. I didn't really want to go, but my protruding backbone was still making it impossible for bedsores on my back and bottom to heal. This hospital was only a mile away from our house in Woodlawn, so it was difficult for me to deal with the emotions of being so close to home, yet knowing I couldn't return there.

This time, the operation was successful, for which I thanked God. However, I still faced fifteen days of lying face down in my Stryker. During this time of recuperation, I had a bout with the flu and did a lot of reading. To balance all the negative, agnostic, and atheistic books I had read earlier, I now turned to the Bible and helpful Christian literature.

Mom patiently held the books for me for hours as I read. *Mere Christianity* by C. S. Lewis was a refreshing change and gave a beautiful balance to all that I'd been reading before. It helped my spiritual outlook tremendously.

On October 15, my birthday, I received a most welcome and appreciated gift—I was finally turned face up! It was a grand occasion. Diana, mom and dad, Jay, and Dick all visited me. While there had been a transition in our relationship from sweethearts to intimate friends, Dick was just as faithful as ever in coming to see me.

Back at Greenoaks, things began to look brighter for me. Because the operation was a success, I would eventually begin to use a wheelchair, and I was having an easier time in my various forms of therapy.

It was also encouraging to see people leaving Greenoaks. Some of my paraplegic friends had been rehabilitated and were free to go home and find their way back into the world. This seemed exciting to me—so much so that I plunged into my own rehab with renewed determination.

Chris Brown was eager to tap this new energy and enthusiasm. "Why not do something artistic now, since you can write pretty well using your mouth?"

"Artistic?" I asked.

"Yes. You've shown me drawings you did in the past. You enjoy creative things. You can paint these ceramic discs. They make nice gifts," she explained.

I watched as another quadriplegic held a paint brush in her mouth and slopped paint on one of the clay pieces. It seemed useless—like a kindergarten game.

"I don't know—" I said quietly.

"Oh, come on, try it," Chris urged.

"All right."

I tried the painting, spilling globs of color and splashing clumsy designs on the clay discs. It was discouraging and frustrating. At first, I hated every minute of it.

But when the discs came out of the kiln, they looked half-way acceptable. And as I practiced—as with writing—I improved.

After a few weeks, I had created several Christmas gifts for my family and friends. I didn't know what they'd think of the nut or candy dishes, but I thought they were pretty good—considering. And it gave me satisfaction to know that I had done them myself.

One day, Chris brought me some moist clay.

"What's that for?" I asked.

"I want you to draw a picture on it."

"How? With a pencil in my mouth?"

"Try this stylus."

"What should I make? Should I write something?"

"Why not do something to express yourself? Make something that you like," she suggested.

Carefully I gauged the distance from my mouth to the soft clay, tested the consistency of it with the pointed stick, then tried to etch something.

I told Chris, "The last time I drew something was on our trip out West before my accident. All during my childhood daddy encouraged me to draw. He's a self-taught artist." I also recalled that I had particularly enjoyed making charcoal sketches of scenes. Out West, I had filled my sketch pad with drawings of mountains, horses, people, and animals.

I remembered these scenes now and tried to remember the unconscious process of drawing—how the mental image was communicated to my hands, which moved to transfer the scene to paper. My hands held the key to my talent as an artist. Or did they?

I looked down at the simple sketch I had just done. It was a line drawing of a cowboy and horse etched in the soft clay. It wasn't terribly creative or impressive, but it was a beginning.

Chris seemed amazed at my first attempt. "Joni, that's great! You've got real talent." She grinned and said, "You should have done this before. You need to get back to your art."

"But that was when I had hands," I protested.

She shook her head. "Doesn't matter. Hands are tools. That's all. The skill, the talent, is in the brain. Once you've practiced, you can do as well with your mouth as you did with your hands!"

"Wow—really?" I asked.

"Yeah! Want to try?"

"Sure! Let's do it."

It was an enormously satisfying day for me. For the first time in almost a year and a half, I was able to express myself in a productive, creative way. It was exciting and gave me renewed hope.

My spiritual temperature was improving, too. Earlier, my anger and confusion had turned to resentment. I thought, *How can a loving God—if such exists—allow this desperate situation?* My search into other areas didn't turn up a reasonable answer, so when I turned back to the Bible, my bitterness was softened.

I was angry that my life had been reduced to the basics of eating, breathing, and sleeping—day in and day out. But what I discovered was that the rest of the human race was in the same boat. Their lives revolved around the same meaningless cycle—except with them, it wasn't as obvious. Peripheral things distracted them from the fact that they were caught on the same treadmill. Their jobs, school, families, and recreation occupied them enough so they never consciously recognized that their lives were the same as mine—eating, breathing, sleeping.

And slowly I became aware of God's interest in me. I was some sort of "cosmic guinea pig"—a representative of the human race on whom truth could be tested. All the distractions, trappings, and things were gone. God had taken them away and had placed me here without distractions. My life was reduced to absolute basics. So now what? *What am I to do with my life?* I wondered. *I have no body, but I am still someone.* I had to find meaning, purpose, and direction, not just some measure of temporary satisfaction.

Even the clean, sterile sheets in the austere ward were symbolic. Eating, breathing, sleeping. Eating, breathing, sleeping. *For what purpose? How can I glorify God? What can I do?*

Yes, there has to be a personal God, I reasoned. He may choose not to reveal Himself to me in some spectacular way—but then, why should He? Why was I any more important than the next person who had to find God and purpose by faith, not sight? Why should I be different?

I told Diana of my thoughts. "Nothing is really making any sense yet, Diana. I don't know what God is doing—but I believe He is real and that somehow He knows—and understands. There's a positive aspect to my thoughts now. I'm still confused, but before, my confusion leaned toward doubt. Now it leans toward trust."

"Maybe it has something to do with your prayer before the accident," Diana suggested.

"What prayer?"

"Remember? You told me that shortly before your accident, you prayed, 'Lord, do something in my life to change me and turn me around.' Maybe this is God's way of answering that prayer."

"I've wondered about that myself. It could be. But it's sure not what I expected. And He certainly has His own timetable!" I said, adding, "I don't know His purpose in this. I probably won't ever walk again. And I don't see how I can ever be happy again. I guess that's what really bothers me."

"Not being happy?"

"Yeah. I mean, if there's one thing I learned from those existentialist writers, it's 'man cannot live with despair.' Do you think I can ever be happy, Diana?"

"I don't know, Joni—I don't know."

My studies in the Scriptures began in earnest now, along with other Christian literature. Writings by Francis Schaeffer and C. S. Lewis seemed like a breath of fresh air compared with Marx, Hesse, and the non-Christian books I'd read. I began to sense a direct application of and appreciation for the Word of God in my life. For the first time, I saw meaning for me in the Bible. My own "fiery trials" were now a little easier to cope with as I saw how I fit in with God's scheme of things, especially through reading the Psalms. "The Lord will sustain him (me) upon his (my) sickbed" (Ps. 41:3 NAS).

Pressures seemed greatest at night. Perhaps therapy had gone badly that day. Or no one came to visit. Or maybe Mrs. Barber was being mean to me again. Whatever the problem, I'd want to cry. I felt even more frustrated because I couldn't cry, for there was no one to wipe my eyes and help me blow my nose. The Scriptures were encouraging, and I'd apply the reality and truth of them to my own special needs. During these difficult midnight hours, I'd visualize Jesus standing beside my Stryker. I imagined Him as a strong, comforting person with a deep, reassuring voice, saying specifically to me, "Lo, I am with you always. If I loved you enough to die for you, don't you think I ought to know best how to run your life even if it means your being paralyzed?" The reality of this Scripture was that He was with me, now. Beside me in my own room! That was the comfort I needed.

I discovered that the Lord Jesus Christ could indeed empathize with my situation. On the cross for those agonizing, horrible hours, waiting for death, He was immobilized, helpless, paralyzed.

Jesus did know what it was like not to be able to move—not to be able to scratch your nose, shift your weight, wipe your eyes. *He was paralyzed on the cross.* He could not move His arms or legs. Christ knew exactly how I felt! "Therefore, since we have a great high priest who has gone into heaven, Jesus the Son of God, let us hold firmly to the faith we profess. For we do not have a high priest who is unable to sympathize with our weaknesses, but we have one who has been tempted in every way, just as we are" (Heb. 4:14, 15, NIV).

Before my accident, I didn't "need" Christ. Now I needed Him desperately. When I had been on my feet, it never seemed important that He be part of my decision making—what party to go to, whether to go to a friend's house or a football game, etc. It didn't seem that He would even be interested in such insignificant things. But, now that my life was reduced to the basic life routines, He was a part of it because He cared for me. He was, in fact, my only dependable reality.

These new and reassuring concepts had a quieting effect on my spirit, and I think they were even helpful as I shared them with Jay during her personal troubles.

My drawing, still self-expression in style and simple in approach, was more of a therapy than I had anticipated. As a reflection of my new mood, I began to sign "PTL" on my drawings—for "praise the Lord"—an expression of my belief that God cared for me. It was a simple expression, giving Him the glory for His direct help in restoring this one aspect of my individuality.

I also began to take more of an interest in my personal grooming. Before, I had avoided all mirrors. Now, Jay and Diana helped me fix my hair, brighten my face, find and wear attractive clothes, and discover ways to improve my overall appearance.

In therapy, I was able to try sitting up. I was bothered by dizziness and nausea again as they lifted me to a siting position in my new bed, with my legs dangling over the edge. It was a slow process, but soon I was almost upright. Then I used the slant-board to get used to the vertical position again, while muscles, long unused, had to get accustomed to holding up my head. When my inner ear and neck muscles adjusted to the vertical once more, I was allowed to sit in a wheelchair. My legs were wrapped in elastic bandages to avoid circulation problems because by blood settling in the arteries of my legs and thighs, and I was fitted with a tight corset that supported my upper torso. This enabled me to sit up and breathe comfortably.

I was excited about my progress and looked forward to going home for the Christmas holidays again. Christmas, 1968—a whole year had passed since I was last home! But this time I could go home for several days.

Just before Christmas, dad and mom brought me some interesting news.

"Joni, we've heard about a new hospital in California," said dad. "It's called Rancho Los Amigos, it's in Los Angeles, and they are making some pretty remarkable advancements in therapy."

"Their approach to rehabilitation is very progressive," mom added. "They've been able to teach people to regain the use of their arms and legs. Even so-called impossible cases."

"Oh, wow!" I exclaimed. "Yeah! Let's go there. Can we?"

"We're checking now. We expect to hear soon. But I think it looks good," said dad. "We can't go with you, but we've talked with Jay, and she wants to go. She could fly out and rent an apartment nearby to be with you."

"That sounds marvelous!" I shrieked. "Let's pray that God will make it possible. Wow—wouldn't that be some Christmas present?"

It was an exciting Christmas. I was strong enough to stay at home for several days, and it was good to be in normal surroundings once more. And when Dick asked me to go with him to a movie, I was really thrilled.

But as much as I dearly wanted to be normal again, it was impossible. Dick put his arm around me, and I didn't even know it. He squeezed me affectionately, lovingly—but I couldn't feel a thing. I kept watching the movie. Finally he asked, "Don't you feel that?"

"What?"

"This." He squeezed me again.

"No," I said softly, embarrassed. "I—I'm sorry." I really wanted to feel his arm, his touch.

Driving home, Dick was forced to stop the car suddenly, and I flew forward and hit my head on the dash. I couldn't help myself—couldn't even pick myself up. I was not hurt. Only my pride and ego were damaged.

Dick berated himself for letting this happen. "Why didn't I remember to hold on to you?" he scolded himself.

"Dick, please don't blame yourself. It takes getting used to. And I'm not hurt. Let's not allow it to spoil our evening."

We drove home without further incident. As Dick wheeled me into the house, I said, "Dickie, thank you. Oh, wow, did I have fun! It—it was almost like the exciting things we used to do. This is the first time I've done anything normal in a year and a half. Thank you, Dickie."

"It was a lot of fun," he said simply and leaned across to kiss me on the forehead. "Glad you enjoyed yourself." His ever-sensitive eyes smiled lovingly into mine.

It was fun. But it wasn't really like the "old times." We were both still uncomfortable and awkward with my chair, and I wondered, *Will things ever be normal again?*

I promised myself to do everything I could to make it happen, at least with my attitude. What a contrast with last Christmas! A year before, I had had only a day at home, and I had been so ashamed of my appearance and handicap that I had cringed in the background and covered my legs with the old brown blanket.

This year, I wore new hose and a bright orange sweater with stylishly short corduroy skirt to match. My hair, although still short, was done in a casual, feminine style, and I felt like a woman again, not just a body stuffed in hospital pajamas!

This time I did not want to go back to Greenoaks.

"You won't have to, Joni," said dad.

"What?"

"You won't have to go back to Greenoaks. We've just received word from California. Rancho Los Amigos has room for you. We'll be leaving next week, after New Year's."

I began to cry. "Oh, daddy, I'm so happy. The Lord is real. He does answer prayer."

"Mother and I will fly out there with you, and Jay will drive out and meet us there."

"I can't believe I'm really going."

Ranchos Los Amigos—that's where I'll get back my hands, I thought.

Seven

THE FLIGHT TO California was a memorable experience. After all, it was my first flight, and I was flying toward *hope*. I'd soon regain the use of my hands—Dick and I could resume our relationship and get married. At last I could see what I thought was God's pattern "for good" for my life.

When we arrived in Los Angeles—some 3, 018 miles from the freezing cold and icy streets of Baltimore—the weather was balmy and sunny. I knew immediately that I was going to enjoy my stay.

Remembering my disappointment at my first sight of Greenoaks, I purposely avoided making a mental picture of Rancho Los Amigos. To my surprise, Rancho was beautiful and well-staffed. Many of the orderlies and staff people were college students working their way through school. Several were girls, and I was glad to have people of my own age and background to whom I could relate.

I was impressed by the order and controlled activity of this place. At Greenoaks, the staff people were always busy, but it was the kind of chaotic busyness of those who are overworked. Here, there was no lost motion. Though everyone had plenty to do, it was for the benefit of the patient, not at his expense. I'm sure that this was due to the fact that Rancho was well-staffed and the people well-paid.

Mom and dad stayed long enough to get me comfortably settled; then they returned to Baltimore, leaving Jay and Kay in a rented apartment near Rancho Los Amigos. One night, about a week later, I heard a commotion in the hall. I strained to hear the voices—there was no mistaking them. Exploding into my room were Diana, Dick, and Jackie!

"Ta da!" sang Diana, gesturing and bowing outlandishly.

"I can't believe it!" I shrieked.

"We got lonesome," grinned Dick.

"Glad to see us?" asked Jackie.

"Oh, you guys! How did you get here?"

"We drove all the way," said Diana.

"Non-stop," added Dick. "That's why we're so grubby."

"Yeah," smiled Jackie, "we came directly to the hospital. We gassed up in Nevada and haven't made any stops since then—we wanted to get here tonight before visiting hours ended."

"I think we drove the last fifty miles on gas fumes," laughed Dick.

"You guys are too much!" I said. It was a wild, exuberant reunion, and a few rules regarding visitors were "bent" that night as they shared the details of their trip with me. They all talked excitedly and at once, alternately flopping on my bed and punctuating their conversation with wild gestures and contagious laughter.

Jay and Kay arrived before they left and promptly invited them to bring their sleeping bags and camp out at the apartment during their visit.

Therapy at Rancho began immediately and consisted of trying to get me to become as independent as possible. I was fitted with braces for my forearms and taught how to use shoulder and back muscles to get my arms to respond. By "throwing" certain muscles, I found that I could raise and lower my arms to some extent, but I could not move my fingers or bend my wrists, limiting the movements and use of my arms, as well as control of these movements. I could not pick up or grasp even the easiest item or utensil.

However, I did learn to feed myself. A spoon was bent at a 45-degree angle and attached to my arm brace. By moving my arm, I could swing it into a plate of food, scoop up a bite, and lift it back toward my mouth. The movement—smooth, easy, and unconscious for seventeen years of my life—was now awkward and difficult and required supreme concentration. By raising and lowering the spoon into the food on the plate, I was able to feed myself. The movement was like that of a steam shovel, and often I spilled more than I got in my mouth. But it was an exciting experience—feeding myself for the first time in a year and a half!

Gradually my movements became smoother, and I tried a fork, bent in the same way, with moderate success. It's a small thing to be able to lift a bite of mashed potatoes to your mouth, but the sense of accomplishment for me was thrilling.

My doctor at Rancho was a bright young specialist whose methods were new and, perhaps, a bit unorthodox.

"Thanks for not sending my friends away when they burst in here, doctor," I said.

"I don't want anyone chasing your friends away," he responded. "In fact, I want them to come—as often as they can."

"Really?"

"Yes. I want them to observe you in all your therapy, to learn as much as possible about you and your handicap."

"You mean you want them to watch me doing P.T. and O.T.?"

"Everything. You see, Joni, I want your friends and family to know your procedures, your needs, and your problems as we know them."

"Why, doctor?"

"To help you become less dependent on a hospital for care," he said.

"You want them to learn how to take care of me?"

"That's right. And I want you to set a realistic goal for yourself regarding getting out of here and going home for good."

"H-home?" I stammered.

"I think you should plan to finish here by April 15," he announced.

"April 15! But that's only three months away. Will I be ready?"

"That's up to you. Are you willing to work toward it?"

"Oh, wow, am I?"

This seemed incredible. I was not used to dealing with my rehabilitation in this way. At Greenoaks, I never knew what was happening, if anything. I was forced to be reactionary in my hopes, so I made no plans at all. I simply took things a day at a time. But now I had something to look forward to, and it was only three months away. My head was swimming with thoughts and dreams of going home for good.

Judy, a Christian college student who worked at Rancho part-time as an attendant, became a friend. Her spiritual maturity seemed much greater than mine, so I often talked with her about the Lord, hoping some of her faith might brush off on me. Judy was attending a Bible college nearby and was delighted to share her new-found knowledge of scriptural truth with me. I felt I was making progress now in every area of my life.

Judy came in early one morning, pushing an empty wheelchair, and said, "You have enough sitting up time to be able to use a wheelchair."

"Really? I can make it go? How?"

"You see these eight rubber knobs on the outside of the wheels?"

I nodded.

"Well, you let your arms hang down beside the wheels and get your hands up against these knobs. See?"

"Yeah—but then what?"

She said, "Remember; we've been working on your shoulder muscles. By throwing your shoulders and biceps into the movement, you can make your arms move against the wheel knob. It'll be slow and tedious until you get the hang of it."

"Okay. When do I start?"

"Now. You can drive to P.T.," said Judy.

"But I don't have P.T. until nine o'clock. It's only seven now," I told her.

Judy just grinned. "Right."

It sure is a slow, tedious process, I thought. I was strapped in to keep me from throwing myself to the floor, and it was a good thing. I tried every exercise I could remember to make back and shoulder muscles substitute for the muscles in my arms. And it took me all of those two hours to coax the wheelchair just the thirty feet or so down the corridor to the P.T. area. By then, I was so exhausted and winded, I had no strength left for P.T. exercises!

However, Judy was waiting there to see my progress and grinned widely at my efforts.

"Beautiful!" she said excitedly.

"Really? Does everyone take this long?"

"The first time," Judy nodded. "A lot of them just give up completely—and a few even fall out of the chair."

I felt proud and exhilarated by the accomplishment—the first time in over a year and a half that I had moved myself through my own efforts.

With practice, I was able to improve my wheelchair ability and speed. There were some minor setbacks, though. A few times I veered into a wall and was stuck for thirty or forty minutes until rescued by someone. Finally, I was given an electric-powered chair to use. What a sense of freedom and adventure this gave me. My chair was controlled electrically by a box which I operated by using my arm brace, and I got so good at it that I practically lived in my chair.

The California community surrounding the hospital had built its sidewalks to accommodate wheelchairs; even the curbs were gently sloped for easy wheelchair traffic. It gave me a sense of independence and satisfaction to be able to go to the nearby Taco Bell for other patients with less freedom to get around. However, it was still humiliating to have people on the street stare or make comments. It was also humbling to "drive" all the way to the Taco Bell only to be stymied there, unable to get the money out to pay the man for my order. He was accustomed to waiting on handicapped people, however, and handled the situation easily and with good humor. He'd place the order securely on my lap, make change from my purse, and joke about entering me in the Ontario Raceway 500.

I didn't enter the stock car competition at Ontario, but I did do some racing. Rick, another quadriplegic, and I each had electric wheelchairs as well as similar backgrounds in competitive sports, and that could only lead to contests.

"I can make my chair go faster than yours," I bragged one day.

"Oh, yeah? That's what you think. Y'wanna race?"

There was a whirring sound as our chairs raced down the corridor in a "50-yard dash." It was a tie.

"We've got to go farther in order to build up speed," Rick grinned. "Let's race from this corner of the building all the way to the other end of the corridor, around the corner, to the front doors. Okay?"

"You're on!" I said.

Judy and another attendant pretended not to notice our high jinks and walked the other way.

"On your mark!" I called to Rick. "Get set! Go!"

We were off side by side, veering crazily and noisily down the hall.

"Don't crowd me, Eareckson," chuckled Rick. "Get over to your own side of the street!"

As we noisily raced by the rooms, patients inside stared or smiled at our game. First Rick's chair pulled into the lead, then mine, then his again.

Neck and neck, we went into the "far turn"—the right angle turn down the next corridor. I swung into the corridor without even slowing. As I whipped around the corner, I came face to face with a nurse carrying a tray full of bottles and medicines. She froze. I screamed, "Look out!"

Too late. The tray went flying, crashing on the tile floor, and my chair pinned the nurse, screaming, against the wall. I tried to stop the motor by striking at my control box, but I was clumsy and couldn't shut it off. The wheels were spinning, the nurse was shrieking, and Rick was laughing hysterically.

As punishment for my reckless driving, they took away my driving privileges for a while and confined me to low gear when I took to the road again.

Diana, Dick, and Jackie teased me about that for several days. Their "few days" visit now had stretched into three weeks, but finally, they had to go back East. It was a sad but hopeful good-by. I told them to expect me home soon after April 15.

Before he left with the others, Dick held me tight. "I want you to know that I love you very much. I'll be waiting to see you in April." A great sense of security and reassurance came over me as Dick held me in his arms, and I began to be more optimistic about our future together when we could be more than friends again, when I'd get my hands back. Dick and I still hoped and prayed for nothing else. Perhaps we still had a future together.

By April 15, 1969, I had reached my goal in rehabilitation and was told I could go home. But a serious question was still unanswered.

"Doctor, I've been working hard to get my hands back. Now I'm beginning to wonder if I ever will."

"No, Joni. You won't ever get your hands back," he said bluntly. "You might as well stop hoping and get used to the idea."

The words were exactly the opposite of what I wanted to hear—what I'd been praying to hear. I wasn't prepared to accept the fact that I'd always be a quadriplegic. Forever dependent, forever helpless.

It was not terribly surprising news. I suppose I'd always suspected it. Yet, I continually hoped that I'd find some miracle cure at Rancho Los Amigos.

Tearfully, I wrote Dick a letter explaining what the doctor had said.

For some reason, God has chosen not to answer our prayers. Dickie, I'll never be able to use my hands. That means I'll always be dependent and helpless. I can never be a wife. I know you love me as I love you. Yet, God must have something else in mind for us. Let's continue to be friends, Dickie. But I want you to be free to choose other relationships. Date other girls and look for God to lead you to the right one for you for marriage. I can never be that woman. I'm sorry, Dickie, but I can never ask you to be part of such a hopeless relationship. Let's continue our relationship based on friendship.

I didn't sign it "your Joni" as I had done on my other letters to him. This time, I simply signed it, "Joni."

It wasn't easy for me to end that special relationship with Dick; in fact, I was frightened to end it. I loved him, didn't want to lose him, but knew I couldn't marry him—not now. My paralysis was too great a burden to place on his shoulders. And a commitment without marriage was unfair to him. Heavy waves of grief swept over me when I realized that I would never marry Dick, and I knew I had to quit thinking about past promises which couldn't, or shouldn't, be kept.

I had accepted the fate that I'd never walk again. But I had believed I could still join the ranks of those handicapped persons who drive cars, make meals, work with their hands, and put their arms around someone in love. That I'd be able to drink a glass of water, bathe myself, brush my hair, and put on my own make-up. Little things, to be sure, but things important enough to make the difference between one who is merely handicapped and one who is totally dependent.

Now, ever so slowly, the reality of my injury began to sink in—I was to be a quadriplegic *as long as I lived.*

Eight

WHEN I RETURNED from California, I stoically and glibly thanked God for whatever purpose He had in the fact that I wouldn't get the use of my hands back, that I couldn't ever marry Dick. But I was becoming cynical again and doubting the reality of Romans 8:28.

Mom and dad were glad to have me at home, and I was happy to be there. But inwardly I was bitter and resentful that God had not answered my prayers, had not given me my hands back.

Diana spent a lot of time at our house, taking care of my needs and trying to keep me encouraged.

"I know they told you at Rancho Los Amigos that you'd never be able to walk or use your hands again, but you can't give up," she urged.

"Why not?" I replied dully.

"You've got to work with what you have left."

"I have nothing left."

"Don't give me that," scolded Diana. "I saw people at Greenoaks and Rancho who were really bad off—blind, mute, deaf. Some even lost their minds—they were almost vegetables. *They* have nothing left, Joni. But you have your mind, your voice, your eyes, and your ears. You have everything you need. And you're going to make them work for you if I have anything to say!" she said.

"We'll see—we'll see," I told her.

Dick came to visit, and our conversations seemed awkward and strained. He had never really replied to my letter directly—he never said, "Yeah, Joni, you're right. We can never get married because I can't handle the problems and emotions involved with your handicap."

Finally, one night, he broached the subject. "Joni, I don't care if you get healed or not. If you aren't healed and I'm fortunate enough to marry you, I'll be the only person in the world to whom God gave the gift of a woman in a chair for a wife."

"How can you say such a thing? The gift?"

"Sure. I look at you and your handicap as a special blessing."

"A blessing?!" I interrupted.

"Yes, blessing—because God gives only good gifts," Dick replied simply.

"No, Dickie. It'd never work. My paralysis—that's a lot to handle. It's almost too much for me, let alone you."

"But sharing the burden would make it lighter for each of us."

"That's romantic, but unrealistic," I told him.

Dick was silent. He did not want to accept what I was saying. He was envisioning what he wanted the outcome to be, not what would be. Finally, his eyes ready to spill tears, he smiled and nodded. "You're right, I guess. Maybe—I can't deal with it. Maybe—I'm not up to it—" His voice trailed off.

Eventually Dick did start dating again. But often he'd bring his new girl friends over to the house to meet me. In fact, some of his dates consisted of nothing more than trips to visit me.

I withdrew into myself and the solitude of home. After being away so long, I appreciated the old house with all its pleasant memories. Yet for some reason, I couldn't really feel at home there any more; I felt awkward in my own home.

This left me with eerie, anxious feelings—like the depression I felt trying to adjust during those nightmarish months after my accident.

"What's the matter, honey?" dad finally asked.

"I—I don't know, daddy. I'm just sad—depressed."

Dad nodded.

"I don't know if I can ever really adjust to being paralyzed," I told him. "Just when I think I've got things under control, I go into a tailspin."

"Well, you just take your time, Joni. We'll do anything—anything at all to help, you know that." His sparkling blue eyes and smiling face radiated love and encouragement.

I sighed deeply, then said, "I guess the thing that affects me most is that I'm so helpless. I look around the house here, and everywhere I look I see the things you've built and created. It's really sad to think that I can't leave a legacy like you. When you're gone, you will have left us with beautiful buildings, paintings, sculpture, art. Even the furniture you've made. I can never do any of that. I can never leave a legacy—"

Dad wrinkled his forehead for a moment, then grinned again. "You've got it all wrong. These things I've done with my hands don't mean anything. It's more important that you build character. Leave something of yourself behind. Y'see? You don't build character with your hands."

"Maybe you're right, daddy."

"Of course I am."

"But why does God allow all this? Look at our family. We've had more than our share of heartbreak—first my accident, then Jay's divorce, now—now little Kelly (my niece dying of brain cancer). It's so unfair," I cried.

Daddy put his hands on my shoulders and looked straight into my eyes. "Maybe we'll never know the 'why' of our troubles, Joni. Look—I'm not a minister or a writer—I don't know exactly how to describe what's happening to us. But, Joni, I have to believe God knows what He's doing."

"I don't know," I offered.

"Look, how many times have you heard somebody—we've done it ourselves many times—pray piously: 'Lord, I'm such a sinner. I deserve hell and Your worst condemnation. Thank You for saving me.' We tell God in one breath that we aren't worthy of His goodness. Then, if we happen to run into some trouble or suffering, we get bitter and cry out against God: 'Lord, what are You doing to me?!' Y'see? I think that if we admit we deserve the worst—hell—and then only get a taste of it by having to suffer, we ought to try somehow and live with it, don't you?"

"Do you think I deserved to be paralyzed—that God is punishing me?"

"Of course not, honey. That was taken care of on the cross. I can't say why He allowed this to happen. But I have to believe He knows what He's doing. Trust Him, Joni. Trust Him."

"I'll try," I said half-heartedly.

As spring turned into summer, my emotions got no better. I'd expected a miracle from God at Rancho Los Amigos. I was convinced He'd give me back the use of my hands. When I didn't regain my hands, I felt betrayed. God had let me down.

So I was angry at God. In order to get back at Him, I discovered a way to shut Him out along with the rest of the world. I went into moody, depressive, fantasy "trips." I'd sleep late in order to dream, or I'd take naps most of the day to daydream and fantasize. By concentrating hard, I was able to completely shut out the present and reality.

I tried to recall each vivid detail of every pleasant experience stored in my memory. I focused all my mental energy on living these experiences again and again.

In these fantasies, I recalled every physical pleasure I had had—what it felt like to wear a soft pair of worn Levis, the warm splash of a shower, the caress of wind on my face, the feel of summer sun on skin. Swimming. Riding. The squeaky feel of saddle leather between my thighs. None of these simple pleasures was wrong in itself. But I used them to shut God from my mind.

One day, I was sitting in my wheelchair outside at the ranch, our family's farm, in Sykesville. The friends who had come to visit me had saddled horses and gone on a trail ride. I was feeling sorry for myself, comparing my lot to theirs. Warm summer sunlight glimmered through the branches of big oak trees and danced in bright patterns on the lush grass underneath. I closed my eyes and visualized a similar day a couple years earlier. In my daydream, I was again with Jason, riding horseback together toward the forest, across the fragrant meadows, stopping in a deserted place. I relished memories of unrestrained pleasure, excitement and sensual satisfaction—feelings I knew I had no right to enjoy then or relive now.

When the Holy Spirit convicted me, I rebelled even more. "What right have You to tell me I can't think of these things? You're the One who put me here! I have a right to think about them. I'll never enjoy sensual feelings and pleasure again. You can't take away my memories!"

But the more I thought of these and other experiences, the more withdrawn I became. I was frustrated and bitter and blamed God that these feelings meant so much to me.

I tried to savor and experience other pleasures and memories. When at a friend's house beside their swimming pool, I treasured the experiences I used to have in the water. The liquid pleasure of wetness all around me, of slicing through the clear waters. Of bobbing up from the bottom and feeling the rush of fresh air pouring into my lungs and on my face. Of wet, stringy hair under my head as I lay sunbathing on the warm concrete apron. Of the warm tiny beads of water making small tickly lines while dripping down my drying arms and legs.

I was angry at God. I'd retrieve every tiny physical pleasure from my mind and throw it up to Him in bitterness. I couldn't accept the fact—God's will, they said—that I'd never do or feel these things again. Outwardly, I maintained a facade of cheerfulness. Inwardly, I rebelled.

My fantasy trips became longer and more frequent. And when I ran out of memories which I felt would anger God, I created new ones. I developed wild, lustful, sexual fantasies which I believed would displease Him.

Diana came to live with us that summer. At first, she wasn't aware of my "trips." Then she sensed that my fits of depression were getting out of control, as if I were in a trance.

"Joni! Stop it! Wake up!" Diana screamed one day. She shook my shoulders violently. Slowly, I regained my sense of reality.

"W-what?"

"Joni! What's wrong? I was talking to you, and you were just staring past me into space! Are you sick?"

"No. Leave me alone. Just leave me alone!"

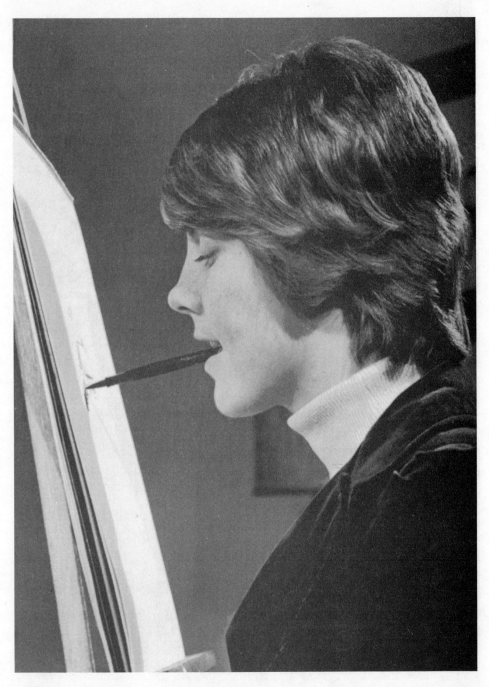

The house Joni's father built for his wife and family in Baltimore.

Joni's parents, Lindy and John Eareckson.

76

Joni and her father do acrobatics
at the beach, 1965.

Joni and her father on their trip west,
just prior to the accident, 1967.

Joni and two of her sisters on a recent trip to Toronto. Left to right: Kathy, Joni, Jay.

Joni doing trick riding and show riding, 1966.

Her drawing opposite indicates
her remaining interest in horses.

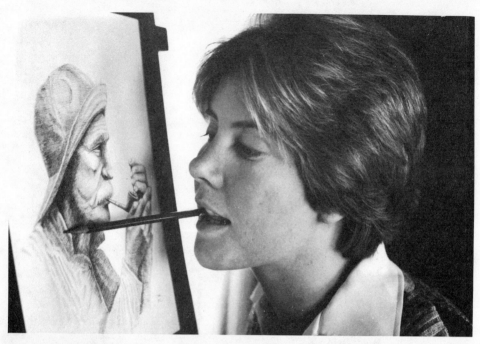

Joni at her easel,
drawing with her mouth.

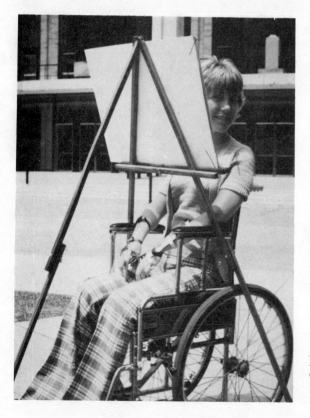

Joni at Lincoln Center Plaza, N.Y.,
exhibiting her artwork, 1975.

Jay and Joni.

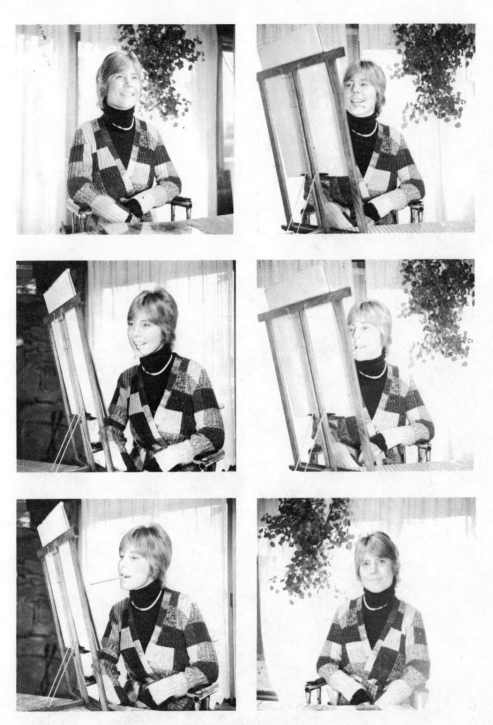

Above: Joni at home.

Dick Filbert, 1971.

Joni in the chair with overhead arm support attachment, aided by neighbors.

Friends gathered for dinner at Joni and Jay's home—the farm in Sykesville.

Diana and Joni in Central Park, N.Y., 1975.

Right: Steve Estes, 1975.

Above right and below: Views of the Sykesville farm.
Above left: Joni tells stories to nieces and nephews outside her home.

Diana, Joni, and Jay and outside views of the farm and horses.

87

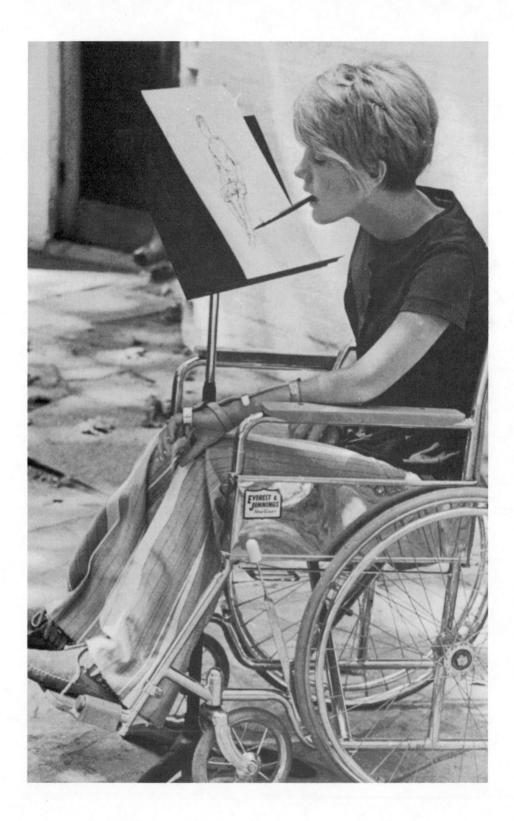

It is important to remember that the promise "...God causes all things to work together for good.." only applies to those who love God, those who have been born into His family. However, due to our sin and rebellion we are alienated from God and subject to His judgment. Praise God though, that He sent His Son, Jesus to be judged on the cross — paying the death penalty for my sin and your sin! If we truly trust that our punishment was borne by Christ and obey Him as our LORD, we can be assured of eternal life and the promise of Romans 8:28.

It is my hope that in the course of reading this book, the Holy Spirit has enlightened your heart and mind to these truths. Jesus is alive and His power is available to you...He proves Himself daily in my life, and what more couldn't He do in your life! Are you a part of God's heavenly family? For indeed, I hope one day we shall meet in glory

Joni
PTL

"It's not going to help you to avoid reality," Diana said. "You've got to face up to the truth. Don't shut it out. The past is dead, Joni. You're alive."

"Am I?" I replied cynically. "This isn't living."

Periodically she scolded me back from my fantasy trips, but, just as often, I'd leave again. I learned that taking a nap in a darkened room with a window air conditioner was my best "transportation." The hum of the air conditioner was a hypnotic sound which shut out the world; soon I'd be in my trance, capturing past feelings and pleasures.

Finally, I realized I wasn't getting anywhere with my rebellious temper tantrums against God. I began to see it was my way of sinning. Before my accident, sin consisted of the things one did. But now, there was no opportunity for me to give action to sinful thoughts. I began to see that sin was an attitude as much as an act. Before the action, the mind frames the thoughts and attitudes which become the basis for our rebellion against God. I saw that anger, lust, and rebellion, although "merely" attitudes, were sinful. Sin wasn't just all the bad things I did, but was an integral part of my makeup. Although there was no opportunity for me to physically rebel against God, I sinned nonetheless. It was a part of my nature.

I knew that I was being what Paul the apostle described as carnal as opposed to spiritual. I was in an impossible condition—unhappy and unable to please myself or God. "For the carnal attitude is inevitably opposed to the purpose of God, and neither can nor will follow his laws for living. Men who hold this attitude cannot possibly please God" (Rom. 8:7,8).

Or themselves, I reminded myself. I saw that my fits of depression and flights into fantasy were doing nothing except confusing and frustrating me.

I did not understand what God was trying to show me, so I prayed: "Lord, I know now that You have something planned for my life. But I need help understanding Your will. I need help in knowing Your Word. Please, God, do something in my life to help me serve You and know Your Word."

Nine

IT WAS SUMMER, 1969, two years after my diving accident. I thought of the many things which had happened to me during those two incredible years. In taking inventory of my spiritual life, I found it consisted mainly of fantastic highs and lows—but mostly lows. In fact, I'd recently climbed out of the worst depression I'd experienced since the accident. If I didn't receive some help, some mature guidance, I knew I'd sink again. It was only a matter of time.

I made as much progress in rehabilitation as was physically possible. It was evident now I'd never walk again; I'd never get the use of my hands again; I'd forever be paralyzed from the neck down, unable to even care for my own personal needs. It was certain now that I'd be forever dependent on others for every physical comfort or function.

This dependency was enough, in itself, to trigger another bout with depression and self-pity, and I talked about my concerns with Diana.

"I have this tremendous feeling of hopelessness and worthlessness, Di," I told her. "I'm praying that the Lord will do something in my life to show me that it has meaning."

"I've been praying, too, Joni," she replied, adding, "you know, I'm going to bring a friend over to meet you."

"Who? Why?"

"Steve Estes. You don't know him, but he's at just the opposite side of things spiritually. He has a love for the Lord and knowledge of the Scriptures that really ought to help."

"Sure," I volunteered without much enthusiasm.

"He's a young guy. In fact, he's still in high school."

"High school?! Diana! He's a kid?"

"No—don't judge. Wait 'til you meet him."

Steve Estes came over to the house that evening, and the minute he walked through the door, he shattered all my preconceived notions about him.

Steve loomed tall above my wheelchair, and his piercing green eyes immediately communicated an attitude of warmth and openness. In the introductory conversation which followed, he made me completely at ease. He evidenced maturity and comfortable self-assurance, and one of the first things I noticed was his attitude toward me.

Many people who meet me for the first time seem awkward and uncomfortable with the chair. It intimidates them or causes them to pity me. It usually takes several visits and conversations for us to move past the chair and deal on an ordinary level. Unfortunately, some people never get to that point, and consequently, I usually feel self-conscious.

Yet Steve was completely at ease, making me comfortable, too. He talked fast, expressing himself with animated gestures, and seemed enthusiastic about everything. As we conversed, he began to share biblical concepts—ideas that were exciting to him and stimulating to me.

"Joni," he said earnestly, "isn't it great what God is doing in different people's lives today?"

What? Who? Where? I was too embarrassed to ask the questions as they popped in my mind. It didn't matter. Steve answered them for me.

"Kids are experiencing fantastic things in *Young Life* at Woodlawn. And in our church, we've seen God's Spirit make a lot of people really come alive. One couple was on the verge of divorce—God brought 'em back together. One guy was heavy into dope, and Christ saved him. A girl I know was really messed up inside, and the Lord straightened her out. Man, you should see her today!" The stories came rapid-fire, and I began to see a new reality to God's power. The Lord had worked in people's lives, and the truth and meaning of it spilled over into Steve's experience and then into mine through Steve's recounting.

Steve himself had seen God demonstrate His love and power. Steve's faith, energy, and spiritual maturity were evidently the qualities that made him so different from me. He radiated trust, a love for Christ, and self-assured success. It was amazing to me that a sixteen-year-old could offer so much spiritual insight and wisdom. As a young adult of twenty, I had not come as far. There was something about him, a quality in his life, that I wanted. He radiated confidence, poise, and authority. He spoke convincingly of the Lord and the simple, quiet strength that faith in Christ brings to a life.

"Steve, what you say is like fresh new truth," I said to him excitedly. "Please come back and tell me more."

"Sure, I'd like that."

"Can you help me get what you have? I'm a Christian. But there's so much I don't know about the Lord. You have so much more spiritual knowledge than I do."

"Joni, what would you say if I came over every Wednesday and had a Bible study with you?" he suggested.

"Great," I answered.

Diana was smiling and nodding. "I'm going to be there, too, and maybe Jay and others would like to come. Is that all right?"

"Sure," Steve smiled. It was strange. Here was a boy, just sixteen, planning to teach a group of young adults about the Christian faith. Yet no one questioned his authority or ability to do so. Even then, he had the eloquence and charisma of a spiritual teacher, a minister. Everyone respected him and responded to his qualities of leadership.

Steve enjoyed the challenge. He said, "Joni, your house really makes me feel comfortable. It's like a retreat—the atmosphere makes me feel like we're at L'Abri with Francis Schaeffer."

He sensed that I—and some of the others—had not really mastered some of the basic Christian doctrines—the character of God, deity of Christ, sin, repentance and salvation—and these became the focus of our weekly Bible studies.

"In Ephesians," he explained, "Paul tells us that we have a fantastic heritage: Christ *chose us* even before He made the world. He created us, in His image, for a particular purpose. God wants us to grow and excel, to be successful. A lot of people are confused about what true spirituality is. If a guy knows a lot of Bible verses, he's often thought of as spiritual. But having head knowledge of Bible truth isn't spirituality. True spirituality is putting God's Word into practice—making His truth valid by actually doing what He says and not just pointing to it as a nice standard."

As Steve shared basic Bible doctrine with us, I began to see the shallowness of my own faith and spirituality. My spiritual ups and downs could be charted as easily and accurately as my physical progress. This became something I wanted to overcome, something I wanted to deal with in a positive way. I began to look to the spiritual principles and revolve my life around them for a change.

Alone with God, I recalled how I'd withdrawn from reality and turned my back on Him so often. I confessed, "Lord, I've been wrong—wrong to try and shut You out. Forgive me, God. Thank You for this new understanding of Your Word which Steve has shared. Please forgive me and bring me back to You—back into fellowship with You once more." The Holy Spirit began to convict, then teach me. With each succeeding week, spiritual truth became more real, and I began to see life from God's perspective.

I learned that God's Word is a handbook for sensible living; He doesn't give us instructions without reason.

I saw, in fact, that God tries to warn us in Scripture; for example, sex before marriage is wrong.

There seem to be so many more warnings in the Bible about illicit sex as compared to warnings about other sinful conduct or behavior, such as gossip, envy, lying, and anger. The Bible says of these, "Resist the devil" (James 4:7)—stand and fight and overcome these faults. But as for sexual sin and sensuality, the Bible says, "flee" (1 Cor. 6:18). If I had been obedient and not given in to temptations, I would not have been tormented by longings and desires which now could never be satisfied. They were like an unquenched thirst. No matter how much I shut out reality and lived the experiences in fantasy, it could never be the same. The feelings were shadow substance and unsatisfying.

I had learned some painful lessons from my relationship with Jason. Now I reaped the consequences. I was tortured, but not because I had done something ugly and repulsive. On the contrary, physical love is beautiful and exciting. Yet God knows how it frustrates and torments without the context of marriage. I was lusting after memories. I know other girls who have cried bitter tears over the same thing. They have found that guilt and remorse over sex outside of marriage can cloud and ruin otherwise happy lives and handicap otherwise successful marriages.

But now, with God's help and forgiveness, I repented and put all that behind me. I prayed for His direction and the mental will power to think His thoughts and not wallow in self-pity and lustful memories and fantasies.

I concentrated on the fact that, once and for all, I had to forget the past and concentrate on the present, trusting God, claiming the promise of Scripture that God separates our sins from us forever (Psalm 103:12).

I decided to rid myself of as many reminders of the past as I could. I gave away my cherished hockey and lacrosse sticks, sold my horse, Tumbleweed, and got rid of all the other *things* that tied me to the old memories.

Now I was forced to trust God. I had no alternative but to thank Him for what He was going to do with my future.

As I began to pray and depend on Him, He did not disappoint me. Before, I'd say, "Lord, I want to do Your will—and Your will is for me to get back on my feet or, at least, get my hands back." I was deciding His will for me and rebelling when things didn't turn out as I planned.

Now I wept for all those lost months filled with bitterness and sinful attitudes. I prayed for an understanding of His will for my life. What was God's will for my life? To find out, I had to believe that all that had happened to me was an important part of that plan. I read, "In everything, give thanks, for this is the will of God concerning you." God's will was for me to be thankful in everything? Okay. I blindly trusted that this was truth. I thanked God for what He did and what He was going to do.

As I concentrated on His positive instruction from the Bible, it was no longer necessary to retreat from reality. Feelings no longer seemed important. Fantasies of having physical feeling and touch were no longer necessary because I learned that I was only temporarily deprived of these sensations. The Bible indicates that our bodies are temporal. Therefore, my paralysis was temporal. When my focus shifted to this eternal perspective, all my concerns about being in a wheelchair became trivial.

Steve showed me other evidence in the Bible that God's perspective is different than ours. In Hebrews 12:1, we are encouraged to endure life with patience. Second Corinthians 5:1–5 reminds us that our bodies are the temporary dwellings of our spirits and personalities. Philippians 1:29 says some are called to suffer for Him—maybe even suffer "fiery ordeals," as the author of 1 Peter expressed it: "And now, dear friends of mine, I beg you not to be unduly alarmed at the fiery ordeals which come to test your faith, as though this were some abnormal experience. You should be glad, because it means that you are called to share Christ's sufferings. One day, when he shows himself in full splendour to men, you will be filled with the most tremendous joy" (1 Peter 4:12, 13, PHILLIPS.) Steve took me through the Scriptures and helped me fit my pain and suffering into this perspective.

"Those who suffer," explained Steve, "should concentrate on doing right and commit their lives and souls to His care. We should all do that, but the Bible makes a point of telling those who suffer fiery trials to especially live for Christ."

In my fantasies and daydreams, I had sought the reality of past experiences because I wanted to avoid the truth of the present. Yet, even the present isn't true reality. There will, one day, be an existence for us that will be the ultimate in reality and experience, and we can understand this truth only by faith. What we see by faith is true reality.

We were all learning and growing through Steve's late night sessions at our home. Diana continued to live with us and went back to college in the fall to study psychology. One of the "games" she learned in this course was role-playing to achieve better understanding of people and various situations.

One night after our study time, we all switched roles and "walked in each other's shoes" for awhile. Diana and I changed places. Someone carried me to the sofa while Diana sat in the wheelchair.

"You know, this is strange," remarked Diana, as she played me. "You people seem afraid of the wheelchair. Everyone seems to keep his distance. There seems to be a space around the chair that no one is willing to intrude on."

"That's interesting," I added. "I was just thinking how people seem less awkward to me when I'm sitting on the couch."

We discussed the chair and what it meant to different people. The typical reaction from strangers was condescension toward one who, to them, was somehow inferior. I suppose, as I've said before, some people think that if you are physically handicapped, you are mentally deficient, too.

Diana, Jay, and Dick were so used to the chair that they took a casual attitude toward it. So casual, in fact, that walking with me was often a game. They'd push me one-handed or give me a shove and walk beside the chair. They often did this to puncture the stuffy, provincial attitudes some people have about wheelchairs. For example, the chair is only about two feet wide, but on sidewalks people clear a path wide enough for a car to drive through. Their subtle awkwardness only adds to the confusion and frustration of the person in the chair. It makes them feel clumsy and fat.

People often stare without meaning to, especially when the chair is being wheeled too fast (at least in their opinion). Apparently, popular opinion dictates that a person in a wheelchair should be treated like a load of priceless antiques.

Older women often came up to me in a department store or on the street, clucked their tongues, and said something like, "Oh, you poor, dear, brave, brave girl." I'd smile politely but often felt like telling them my real feelings—which weren't always charming!

However, I came to terms with myself. If others had a problem with the chair, I tried to do everything I could to make them feel at ease. At the Bible studies, I had Dick carry me to the sofa. Out of sight, the chair no longer intimidated people. Sitting, with my legs propped up on an ottoman, I looked like a "normal" person.

What began as a simple experiment in practical psychology became a regular habit for me. I enjoyed being one of the crowd in this way and was glad it made all more comfortable.

Diana tried another experiment in role-playing. This time, I saw my situation as others do. She sat in the chair, and I was on the sofa. "Joni, I'd like a glass of water," Diana said, pretending to be helpless.

Taking her role, I saw something I'd never noticed from my chair. I was annoyed.

"Gee—I'm really engrossed in this TV program. Can you wait until the commercial?" I asked.

"Well—I guess so," sighed Diana.

Everyone smiled knowingly. I said, "Is that the way I really am? Oh, good grief—I'm sorry. I see how selfish I can be without even knowing. I'll try to be more considerate of you guys from now on."

Being out of the wheelchair was also good for my self-confidence as a woman. In the chair, sometimes I felt stiff and awkward, but sitting here on the couch, I felt relaxed and at ease. One evening when we were watching TV, Dick stretched out and put his head in my lap. I managed to take off my arm brace and began to stroke his hair with my hand. Of course, I couldn't feel anything, but Dick could. He relaxed and enjoyed the normal attention of a girl running her fingers through his hair.

These were pleasant moments of growing and learning, offset only by the fact of Kelly's sickness. She was growing weaker almost daily. But her situation, as well as my own, were made easier as I began to grow in faith and understanding.

Steve continued to come, sometimes several times a week. His Bible-based teaching of simple doctrinal truth was becoming a part of my life. Before, I had accepted doctrine pretty much without question. But it was not real in my experience. Its truth had not been tested. In my earlier depression at Greenoaks, I had examined other philosophical and theological points of view. It was no longer possible for me to accept doctrine without question, but even as I questioned, answers were provided. Steve explained Bible truth in such a way that it was as if the Lord spoke directly to me.

I saw Steve's coming into my life as a specific answer to the desperate prayer I had prayed just before I met him.

We discussed the second coming of Jesus Christ. I learned that one day Jesus would return to earth and I'd get a brand-new body. Christ would give me a glorified body that could do everything I could do before—probably even more. Some day I would have feelings again! *I won't be paralyzed forever.*

This new perspective made it unnecessary for me to retreat into fantasy trips or daydreams any more.

Steve helped me end my cycle of peaks and valleys of spiritual progress. "Set your heart on things above," he read from Colossians 3, "and not the passing things of earth." Since I could see that one day I'd have a renewed body, it became easy for me to focus my desires on heavenly, eternal things. I had already lost temporal things, the use of my earthly body, so it was easy to accept this truth. Although "condemned" to a wheelchair, I knew one day I'd be free of it.

"Steve," I said to him, "I'm beginning to see the chair more as a tool than a tragedy. I believe God is going to teach me something more about this!"

Steve introduced me to the process of putting God's Word into practice, of acting on His promises and commands. I would read something in the Bible and consciously say, "This is God's will." Intellectually, I understood the meaning of it. Emotionally, I had to put this new truth to the test, to prove it by my own will. "Yes, this is God's will," adding, "for me."

"Lord, I'm trusting You to bring me through all this victoriously," I reminded Him. Scripture took on personal meaning. Job had suffered, so he could speak convincingly to my needs. Jeremiah had suffered, and I learned from him, too. Since Paul had endured beatings, shipwrecks, imprisonment, and ill health, I related to his sufferings as well. I began to see what the Bible called a "fellowship of suffering."

I memorized Scripture portions that had great meaning to me. Understanding these passages that spoke to my needs enabled me to better trust God with my will as well as my life. Even when distressing or despondent times came along, I could depend on the fact that "He knows what He is doing," as daddy frequently said.

Through memorizing God's promises, I learned that the Lord would take me out of training in this school of suffering—but in His own good time. The apostle Paul wrote that the key was to keep forever striving. Even he, at the peak of his life and commitment to Christ, admitted that he had not arrived spiritually.

Probably, I thought, *my suffering and training is a life-long process. It will end only when I go to be with Christ.*

There was a lot of catching up for me to do. If life was going to mean anything, I'd have to learn everything I could—not just spiritual truth, but academic understanding as well. I'd have to find a way to make some kind of contribution to society.

Diana and Jay were eager to help me get back into circulation, up-to-date with the outside world. Seeing people and going places was refreshing and stimulating. By now, I was even comfortable in my chair, used to the stares and awkwardness of others. Being outside that summer was a pleasant experience to my senses. Shut in various hospitals for two years, I'd almost forgotten all there was to see, hear, and smell in the outdoors. These experiences saturated my starved senses. But as a result of such sensory shock, I tired easily and was forced to rest after these outdoor trips.

Steve tried to encourage me to verbalize my new understanding—to put this new truth into practice. He asked me to share my faith, the testimony of my Christian experience, with the youth group at his church. The thought of speaking to fifteen teen-agers terrified me. My natural tendency then was to be shy, so when the time came, I was really nervous. I looked out at those polished, self-assured faces and was almost too petrified to speak.

"I . . . uh . . . I'm Joni Eareckson . . . and . . . uh . . . uh. . . ." My mind went blank. *What was I supposed to say?* The teens were polite and didn't break into snickers or mocking. "I . . . I . . . uh . . . I want to tell you . . . uh . . . what Christ means to me. Uh . . . you see . . . He is very . . . uh . . . real to me. I've . . . uh . . . had . . . uh . . . lots of troubles . . . uh . . . but I . . . I mean *He* . . . He's been faithful. And uh . . . I hope you know Him as I do."

My throat was dry, my face was flushed, and I couldn't think of any way to continue, so I merely dropped my gaze and said nothing.

After an awkward, terrifying pause, Steve picked up on what I said. Somehow, he put the pieces together and made sense of it. I was both relieved and impressed that he could salvage the situation.

Later I said firmly, "I never want to do that again as long as I live!"

"Nonsense," Steve countered. "You just need experience. I was the same way the first time a friend asked me to give my testimony at one of his street-corner evangelism meetings."

"Really?"

"I stammered all over the place. I thought my tongue was swollen."

"But I don't have your gift for speaking—your presence of mind. I just can't."

"You should go to college," he said, slapping my knee good-naturedly. "You could attend classes in your wheelchair at the University of Maryland. They have quite a few handicapped people there. You shouldn't have any trouble," Steve suggested.

"Hm-m. Maybe you're right."

He grinned and nodded.

"All right," I conceded, "if Jay and Diana will help, I'll go to college this fall."

In September, I began attending a few classes at the university. Jay or Diana went with me and took notes for me. I signed up for *Oral Interpretation, Voice Diction* and *Public Speaking.* My speeches were related to things I knew about and could discuss easily: relating to people with handicaps, accepting the wheelchair, and my Christian experience.

Slowly, I developed confidence, especially as I saw that people were interested in what I was saying. Deep inside, I sensed that God was preparing me; that somehow, someday, I'd be able to use what I was learning.

At the same time, I began to understand spiritual truth in meaningful ways. This new understanding gave me victory over past sin, temptation, and depression. God had given me the means to control my sinful nature when I realized the importance of His reality and the present.

The fantasies ended. Forever. With God's complete fulfillment. I didn't need to relive memories from the past. I had come to the place where my body no longer needed the sensations I once thought so terribly important. God had taken me beyond the need for feeling and touching. Yet, He saw to it that, whenever possible, I could enjoy such things as the feel of a cashmere sweater on my cheek, a hug from someone I care about, the reassuring movement of a rocking chair, and the sensations He brought everytime I went outside—wind, sun, even rain on my face. And I was grateful for all He gave.

꧁

Ten

IN FEBRUARY, 1970, my niece Kelly died of the brain tumor that had kept her in constant pain for a year. Her death underscored to me the importance of each individual soul.

I was just beginning to get a handle on a positive spiritual frame of reference myself, so Kelly's progress in faith, though she was only five, was encouraging and helpful to me as I saw the reality of Gods's love and power in her tiny life. Her tragedy brought us closer as a family and closer to the Lord.

We had all accepted the inevitability of Kelly's death, and we had peace about it; yet, this did not mean that the agony of losing her did not take its toll on us or that we did not ever ask "Why, God?"

Kelly's mother, my sister Linda, suffered the most. Soon after Kelly became ill, Linda's husband left and divorced her. This left her with two sons and Kelly to support, along with facing Kelly's death. Her world seemed to be collapsing around her, and for a long time she didn't want to face it.

Through Kelly's death and my own paralysis, I was learning that there was nothing but unhappy frustration in trying to second-guess God's purposes. *Why God? Why did Kelly die? Why was I paralyzed? Why was someone else alive and healthy?* There was no reason apart from the overall purposes of God.

We aren't always responsible for the circumstances in which we find ourselves. However, we *are* responsible for the way we respond to them. We can give up in depression and suicidal despair. Or, we can look to a sovereign God who has everything under control, who can use the experiences for our ultimate good by transforming us to the image of Christ (2 Cor. 3:18).

God engineered circumstances. He used them to prove Himself as well as my loyalty. Not everyone had this privilege. I felt there were only a few people God cared for in such a special way that He would trust them with this kind of experience. This understanding left me relaxed and comfortable as I relied on His love, exercising newly learned trust. I saw that my injury was not a tragedy but a gift God was using to help me conform to the image of Christ, something that would mean my ultimate satisfaction, happiness—even joy.

Steve, in one of our fellowship study sessions, compared my life to the experience of the apostle Paul: "I want you to know, my brothers, that what has happened to me has, in effect, turned out to the advantage of the gospel" (Phil. 1:12).

I reflected over this concept one evening as Steve crossed the room to stir the fire in the fireplace. He reminded me, "Joni, what is happening to you will advance God's cause! Paul had his prison chains; you have your chair. You can rejoice in suffering because He is allowing you to suffer on His behalf." Steve then sat down and stretched his frame into the overstuffed chair, thumbing through his Bible. "'You are given, in this battle,'" he read, "'the privilege not merely of believing in Christ but also suffering for his sake' (Phil. 1:29)."

It was exciting to think that what had happened to me could indeed "turn out to the advantage of the gospel." I began to share my faith with more people in a positive context, and I saw that the Word of God could not be bound and chained, even if I was (2 Tim. 2:10).

Now, as each successive problem arose, it came in a context I understood. I merely trusted God. I reminded myself that all things came into my life according to Andrew Murray's formula: by God's appointment, in His keeping, under His training, for His time. And I had His promise that He would not heap upon me more than I could bear.

As I began to see that circumstances are ordained of God, I discovered that truth could be learned only through application.

In 1 Thessalonians, I read, "In everything give thanks." But sometimes I didn't want to give thanks. Emotionally, it was something I just didn't feel like doing. Yet, I could give thanks with my will, if not my feelings.

"After all," I reasoned one day to Steve, "for two years, I woke up every morning in a hospital. If for no other reason than that, I can give thanks that I'm no longer there."

So I began a habit of giving thanks, even when I didn't feel thankful. After awhile, a curious thing happened. I began to feel thankful!

"Your paralysis could even be a blessing," observed Steve during one of our times together.

"A blessing?"

"Sure."

"I don't know about that," I admitted. "I've come a long way just to accept my accident as something God has allowed for my ultimate good. But I don't really feel it's a blessing yet."

During the weeks ahead, I read more and more on the subject of God's sovereignty. It truly was a reassuring doctrine. As its light flooded my intellect and mind, it brightened my spirit and self-image. I felt secure, safe. God had control of everything in my life.

That spring, Steve and his parents went to a seminar where the value of "self" was explained in biblical terms. Steve shared these concepts with me one afternoon when he stopped by with some books he wanted me to read.

"Joni, you must know by now the value God places on you," he said as he plopped them on the table.

"Yes, I suppose so. Why?"

"Well, I think you're still hung up on your self-image."

"Hung up on my self-image? What do you mean?"

"You're always putting yourself down—always on the defensive," he replied.

Steve was right, of course. I'd still look at healthy, active people—attractive people—enjoying themselves around me. Everyone I compared myself to came out best. I'd even lose out when I compared myself to a mannequin!

"But that's the same for everyone if we let society determine our value," Steve explained as he sat down on the piano bench. "We always lose when we evaluate ourselves according to someone else's ideas or standards. And there are as many standards as there are people. A jock measures you by your athletic ability; a student by your brains; a steady by your looks. It's a losing battle," he said, striking a sour piano chord for added emphasis. "We have to forget about what people say or think and recognize that God's values are the only important ones."

It was true. God knew that I had hands and feet and arms and legs that did not work. He knew what I looked like. And none of these things really mattered. What counted was that I was His workmanship created in His image. And He wasn't finished with me (Eph. 2:10).

In the days that followed, I thanked Him for "me"—whatever I was in terms of mind, spirit, personality—and even body. I thanked Him for the way I looked and for what I could and could not do. As I did, the doctrine of His sovereignty helped everything fall into place, like a jigsaw puzzle.

Not only was there purpose to my life at this point, but there was an iceberg of potential as well—10 percent above the surface, 90 percent below. It was an exciting thought—an entire new area of my life and personality not even developed yet!

"Joni, I learned this concept from an illustration Bill Gothard (Institute in Basic Youth Conflicts) uses. He says our lives are like paintings which God is making. Often we jump off the easel, grab a brush, and want to do things ourselves. But when we do this, we only get a bad copy of the masterpiece He intended for our lives."

Steve added to this thought. "Joni, your body—in the chair—is only the frame for God's portrait of you. Y'know, people don't go to an art gallery to admire frames. Their focus is on the quality and character of the painting."

This made sense. I could relax and not worry so much about my appearance. God was "painting" me in just the perfect way so I could enhance the character of Christ within. This gave a whole new perspective to the chair. Once it had been a terrible burden, a trial for me. Then, as I saw God working in my life, it became only a tool. Now, I could see it as a blessing. *For the first time in my paralyzed life, it was indeed possible for the wheelchair to be an instrument of joy in my life.*

❦

Eleven

WITH NEW UNDERSTANDING and a more positive self-image came a concern for my appearance. Jay and Diana helped me fix my hair and make-up, and we learned how to buy clothes that fit me better. For example, Jay discovered that by buying my slacks three inches too long, they hung properly and didn't hitch up above my ankles when I sat in the chair.

I was at the point of my life where I was actually satisfied with my situation. I had begun by thanking God with my will. Now I could do it with my emotions. My wheelchair was now a comfortable part of my life.

In the summer of 1970, Diana, Jay, Sheri Pendergrass (a thirteen-year-old neighbor), and I drove to Philadelphia to attend the Gothard seminar which Steve recommended highly. The sessions further helped to crystallize my thinking on all that had been happening to me. One seminar section dealt with "Sources of Irritation," and I learned that God allows certain circumstances to come into our lives almost as a rasp to file down the rough edges, to smooth us into gems.

"Irritations come through circumstances and people," Diana reminded us after one of the sessions. "That's why it's important not only to endure, but to respond with a godly attitude."

"Yeah," I said quietly. "I guess I've really been slow to see this truth. It's not enough for me to put up with all that God permits by way of suffering. I need to use my situation for His glory—to let these situations make me more Christ-like."

"That's not easy," Jay observed.

"Boy, that's for sure," Sheri added. " 'Respond with a godly attitude.' That's what it says. But it sure isn't all that easy!"

"Well, let's put it to the test," Diana suggested. "When sources of irritation come along, let's not give in to them and let Satan get a victory over our emotions and feelings."

During the next intermission, it seemed God gave me an excellent opportunity to test this principle concerning sources of irritation. Since I'm confined to a wheelchair, I have to drink a lot of liquids to force my kidneys to function properly in removing body wastes. Consequently, I have a catheter attached to a leg bag which collects urine and has to be emptied periodically. Sheri was taking care of me that day, and she emptied the bag but forgot to clamp it again. Soon after that a man seated in front of us looked down, then turned around.

"Miss, I think something is wrong—" he said.

"Oh, no!" I looked down and saw a puddle running down the aisle. I flushed with embarrassment and a sick, sinking feeling. I began to feel irritation developing—irritation at Sheri, at the whole routine of my chair, at many things. Then I remembered the lesson just learned. It seemed we all saw in this humiliating incident an object lesson which proved we really did learn the truth of that point.

Other seminar truths also made a significant impact on my life. I saw anew the importance of my family in my life.

The fact that I am single and handicapped makes me especially aware of my dependence upon my folks and my sisters. Yet the principles are the same for everyone. It is no mistake that our lives and experiences are what they are—even the number of brothers and sisters we have and who our parents are. They are all part of God's purposes and plans.

That is certainly true in my life. Each of my sisters is special to me, but each is different, with varied skills, abilities, and personalities.

"If I can't learn to love each one of my sisters for themselves alone, how can I ever hope to love someone else with their traits?" I wondered with my friends.

"That sure makes sense," said Diana.

"Yeah," added Jay.

"Jay—" I said slowly, "I'm just beginning now to see how little I've loved and appreciated you, Kathy, and Linda. I've really taken your love for granted. You pick up after my friends, cook, clean, and never complain. I'm sorry I've been so thick. Maybe I can have my friends clean up after themselves when they visit—I mean like put the dirty dishes and glasses in the dishwasher after we have snacks."

Jay smiled and hugged me. I had touched a sensitive spot, and she seemed appreciative.

"And I've really been kind of insensitive to Kathy and Butch since their recent marriage. I mean, well, she's a schoolteacher, and I guess I don't know enough about her work and problems to really relate to her. I'm going to make an effort to change. Will you guys pray for me?"

"Sure, Joni. We need to pray for each other 'cause we all want to change," said Sheri.

My greatest insight from these seminar sessions was learning that solid relationships have to be worked at. I promised the Lord (and myself) to be generally more considerate of my family and more thoughtful of their needs. It became clear to me that what happened with my family was, in a sense, a proving ground for the consistency of my dealings with others out there in the world. It was harder to be real, to be consistent, at home—but if it worked there, it would work anywhere!

Working things out through love is the standard by which God measures the success of relationships. The principle is the same whether we're talking about a husband-wife relationship, a roommate relationship, a mother-daughter relationship, a father-son relationship, or any relationship in which God has placed us.

Before, because of my injury and unique handicap, my world revolved around me. I enjoyed the attention and things people did for me. But now I could see the selfishness in such a situation, and I consciously tried to change—to make my world revolve around others.

In so doing, I learned not to take my friends and family for granted, not to expect them to always do things for me, but to be genuinely appreciative for all that they did, for all their favors. As a result of this conscious effort to be consistent in all my relationships, especially with my family, my friends who came to visit saw I was the same Joni Eareckson to both.

One friend said once, "Well, I think you can let your hair down with your family and be yourself and not worry about what others think."

I disagreed. "Uh-uh. That's the same as giving us freedom to sin. We both know guys who are pious on Sunday but live like the devil the rest of the week. It's like saying, 'I don't really care enough about my family to show them love and patience. They're not worth it.' I think that if Christ is to be real in my life as I relate to others, He first has to be real in my attitudes with my family."

I saw God continually "working out my salvation." He helped me deal with my past, for which He had forgiven me through Christ's death and resurrection. Then I saw Him effectively at work in the present. Although still apprehensive, I knew God was working in my life to save me not only from the past penalty of sin, but from its present power. Finally, I knew His Spirit was busy within me, trying to create a Christlike character in my life. Therefore, I could trust Him for the future and the full expression of His redemption which I would realize in the life to come.

My art had no special place in my life during this period of growth. Although I often relaxed by drawing or dabbling in creative things, art didn't really fit into the overall scheme of things. It was just a simple pleasure I pursued for fun, as was my interest in music.

During the summer of 1970, I met Dick Rohlfs and brothers Chuck and Craig Garriott. After we got to know one another during Steve's Bible studies, Dickie, Dick, Craig, Diana, and I formed a singing group. Often our house was filled with music and people. Craig's bass guitar resounded off the cathedral ceilings of our living room, and the music got so loud we had to open the windows. Many times, mom and dad sat on the steps at the edge of the room, clapping and singing along with us, often until after midnight when we were all too hoarse to continue. We were pretty good—good enough to sing for *Young Life* and *Youth for Christ* clubs, churches, and other functions.

About this same time, I was asked to work as a counselor with a *Young Life* club in nearby Randallstown. I agreed and began to share with the high school kids the excitement and enthusiasm of the wonderful things God was now doing in and through my life. The spiritual lessons and values I'd learned were of importance to every Christian, and I was concerned that these eager, bright, young teen-agers might learn the lessons God had taught me without having to go through the same suffering I had.

I understood their lives and experiences. Just a few years earlier, I, too, had been restless, uncertain, searching. I could relate to them on many levels, and I understood them from the perspective of their own "handicaps"—shyness, being overweight, not having a date, braces on their teeth, divorced parents, and many other "handicaps."

"God's Word is true," I told a group of the girls. "I know it's true because I've experienced it. I've found it to be so." They listened attentively as I shared my emotional failures and spiritual successes. Many of them came to the Bible studies we'd hold out at the ranch in Sykesville. To break the ice, we dreamed up all kinds of fun projects for the girls who came, ranging from simple pajama parties to ridiculous games designed to bring the girls together not only for the fun, but for the spiritual lessons which followed.

That summer, Jay and I went to the *Young Life* camp in Colorado as counselors. The camp, named *Frontier Ranch*, was situated in the central Rocky Mountains. It was exciting to be there—the first time back in the crisp mountain air since before my accident. I basked in the sun and Rocky Mountain beauty, with fragrant pine-laden breezes. Of course, I couldn't participate in the hikes, horseback riding, running or mountain climbing, and the kids felt badly about this. But when they saw I wasn't unhappy and was content to watch them, they seemed more relaxed.

"Don't you wish you could do these things with us?" one young girl asked me.

"Well, not really. I'm just happy to be out here—out in God's outdoors where I can meditate on His goodness and greatness and pray. I'm not upset because I can't keep up with you girls. After all, some of the other counselors can't keep up in everything you want to do either!"

Gradually the girls accepted me and my chair and tried to involve me as much as possible in their activities. And although they knew I couldn't check on them after curfew, they never took advantage of my handicap and always treated me as a normal human being.

In the club meetings, outings, and Bible studies, we challenged the kids to live for Christ. We also helped them envision success—to relate their God-given gifts and abilities to service for Christ and His kingdom.

One girl, for example, took an interest in helping me. Debbie (who has since married Chuck Garriott) became a physical therapist. I don't think I necessarily planted that idea in her mind, but I did provide an experience for her in which she felt needed and important by using her talent to help someone.

Towards the end of summer, we had a going-away party for Steve. It was a time of mixed emotions. I was happy for him that he was going off to Bible college, but I was sad to think that our spiritual sharing would end.

"It's not going to end," Steve reassured me. "Look, I read somewhere that 'nothing of God dies when a man of God dies.' You can also interpret that to mean 'no one is indispensable.' God doesn't leave when His children move away. Joni, you just keep your focus on Christ, not me."

"But, Steve, I've learned so much from you this past year. You've introduced me to Paul, to the great Christian writers. I'm excited for you—and I'll pray for you at Columbia Bible College—but I'm going to miss you. God has used you to turn my life completely around. I've grown dependent on you as my spiritual leader this year."

"Listen—that's not true, Joni. God just used me. The Holy Spirit was your real instructor. Keep on with Christ. Keep memorizing the Word. He'll be faithful, Joni."

Steve left for college and, in spite of his reassurances and many letters, I still missed him. Yet, he was right in that I could still grow and learn by looking to the Holy Spirit for direction and understanding.

✤

Twelve

THAT FALL OF 1970, my life began to take on interesting dimensions. With Steve away at Bible college and other friends at college or getting married, I became aware once more that there were no prospects for my own marriage. I began to deal realistically with the concept that God's plan for me was singleness. It was a disappointment to read Christian books on the subject, since most of them assume that the single woman must prepare to one day be a married woman. Few, if any, gave realistic, practical advice for a woman confronting singlehood as a life-long reality.

I still had deep-seated and highly emotional reservations about giving up Dick. I felt I was doing the proper thing. I had no right to marry—unless God returned that right as a special grace. That seemed remote and highly unlikely.

So I tried to accept my single role without bitterness or bad attitudes.

I often sang or was a bridesmaid at the weddings of my friends—and even caught the bridal bouquet several times. These occasions brought forth feelings and emotions long forgotten—or so I thought until they surfaced.

I suppose, deep down, I was secretly wishing for the right man to come along—the man who could handle my handicap and the chair. *Lord, You know I'm content in my present state, but I suppose I'll always wonder if You have a man planned for me.*

Many of my friends were married now, and I often found it difficult to relate to them. Their interests were different; they were caught up in establishing a home and family—too busy with their own lives taking on new directions to be involved in the interests we once had together. By now I was mature enough to accept this as a natural development in our friendships, so I wasn't resentful or bitter. But I did feel separate, alone.

I wondered whether God would ever bring into my life a man capable of loving me for myself and willing to spend his life with me. Could I ever be happy single? Hadn't I gone through enough? Would God try me further by allowing me to remain single all my life?

These questions fed my emotional insecurity, and loneliness swept over me.

"God," I prayed, "please bring someone into my life to bridge this emptiness."

Why? Isn't My grace sufficient for you?

I knew I was asking for my desires and not God's will. But, after all, didn't Jesus say, "Ask whatever you will in my name and I'll give it to you"?

Shortly after that, at a *Young Life* leadership meeting, I met Donald Bertolli, a friend of Dick's.

"Don's from the tough area of town—Pimlico—and works with kids from the street," the leader said, as he introduced Don. "Our church, Arlington Presbyterian, sponsors this work among the poor minority kids there."

Donald was a handsome, rugged man of Assyrian-Italian descent, with large, dark brown eyes. He seemed wound like a spring—full of energy and strength. Although he was older than most of us—twenty-seven to my twenty-one, for example—he seemed to enjoy the time together with us.

When he spoke, it was often with a question. His voice had cracks and a roughness that reflected a streetwise background. He distrusted pat answers and persisted to get at the real core of truth. His voice was also hesitant, somewhat shy, almost as if he was afraid to share his inner thoughts aloud.

As he questioned, he'd stop to reflect. He gave intense concentration to what was said, but didn't seem easily swayed or convinced.

When someone acknowledged, "But that's the way it is," Donald interrupted with, "That's a cop-out! Nothing has to be just because that's the way it's always been before."

I was impressed not only with his good looks and intelligence, but with his mature Christian testimony and strong character.

Donald came over to me after the meeting ended and chatted briefly. In those few moments, I learned we had a great deal in common. He talked about his interests—athletics, God, and Christian service.

"Joni, let's talk some more. Can I see you again?"

"Sure—come on over any time."

It was a standard invitation. I'd extended it to many others who asked to talk with me, so I didn't really expect him to be at our door first thing the next morning. But he was.

"Someone's here to see you. I don't know who he is, but he sure is good looking!" said Jay in hushed tones, waking me.

"Who? What time is it?" I yawned.

"Nine o'clock. He says his name is Don."

"Tell him I'll be out in awhile. Just give me a minute to wake up." Being a late riser, this was the time I usually woke in the morning.

Jay went into the other room and chatted pleasantly for a moment or two, then excused herself to come and help me get up, dress, and ready for the new day.

"Good morning!" I said cheerfully a half-hour later when Jay wheeled me into the other room.

"Hi!" Donald said. He bounded out of the chair and came toward me. "Hope I'm not intruding—but you did invite me, didn't you?"

"Of course I invited you. My day usually starts around this time, so you're not intruding."

Donald began to talk. When he stopped for breath, it was noon. I hadn't had breakfast and was hungry, but he showed no signs of ending the visit.

"Donald, would you like to stay for lunch?" I asked.

"Hey, I'd love to—if it's no bother."

Jay prepared a lunch and listened while we talked. Actually, I did most of the listening, too. I learned about Donald, his family, how he met the Lord, all about his work among the young black kids in Pimlico, and his ideas for Christian service.

"Donald, would you like to stay for dinner?" asked Jay later.

"Hey, I'd love to—if it's no bother."

We talked through dinner and finally, after dinner, Donald rose to leave.

"Can I come back to see you?" he asked.

"Uh—well," I hesitated, thinking he might be at the door in the morning again. "Tomorrow I have classes at college."

"Let me take you."

"Uh—that's okay, Donald. Thanks, but Jay usually takes me. She knows my routine and needs."

"Okay. Well, I've really enjoyed this visit. Let's do it again."

"I'd like that."

The next day, he met us outside the school and spent the remainder of the day with us. At first, I was a little put off by what seemed an overbearing approach. But by the third day (when he came to the ranch again), I was beginning to like him.

At the next *Young Life* leadership session, he was there, smiling, handsome, and personable. During the course of the evening, Diana and I got into a friendly but heated discussion over some theological insignificance, and many of the younger people there chose sides and joined in. Yet, Donald seemed to withdraw. That was strange, since there were several new Christians at the study. I was sure he would speak up and end the confusion which Diana and I had raised in our debate.

Finally, the study ended. Donald rose and said to me, "Joni, before you turn in tonight, look up 2 Timothy 2:14 and read it. I think it'll really speak to your heart."

Then he left.

Excitedly, I looked for my Bible. "Hey, great! Why didn't he tell me about this verse before?" I said, thinking it was a verse to help me convince Diana that I was right. Someone found the verse and read it to me: "Remind your people of things like this, and tell them as before God not to fight wordy battles, which help no one and may undermine the faith of some who hear them."

I was stunned by the impact of that truth and convicted that we had argued about such a trifle that evening. Most of all, though, I felt badly about my own immaturity.

However, the other side of the coin immediately became clear to me. I was impressed with Donald's maturity, sensitivity, and wisdom. I saw in him a man of authority, and he became more and more attractive to me. I thought of him often during the next few days.

At our next meeting, we exchanged greetings and immediately shared how much each of us was beginning to mean to the other.

"Joni, before I became a Christian, where I come from it's every man for himself—dog eat dog, y'know? I've been in Christian circles for several years now, though. But, it's funny—I've never experienced people showing love before. I'm really attracted to you."

"I like you, too, Donald. No one's ever come to me before and started a friendship so easily. Usually they're put off by my chair. It takes a while to get past my handicap. When they get to know me, they forget the chair. But with you—well, it's like you never saw the chair in the first place."

"Joni, I don't know—I guess it's my background—but I can't cover my feelings and emotions. I won't try to hide behind some jive talk or hypocrisy. I won't ever con you," he told me.

"I'm glad you don't beat around the bush. I like it when a person isn't afraid to say what's on his mind," I replied.

We saw a great deal of each other in the weeks and months which followed. Before summer ended, Donald took me to Ocean City. He stood beside my wheelchair on the boardwalk as we inhaled the fresh, salty ocean air and soaked in the sounds of gulls and waves crashing.

Old memories returned—the feel of sand between my toes and the exhilarating wetness of the surf splashing over me in the water. I sighed and sat in my chair, prepared to watch Don swim for my vicarious enjoyment.

But suddenly, seeming to sense my mood, he began pushing me off the boardwalk into the sand. The wheels bogged down, but he was strong and virtually plowed furrows toward the wet sand near the water's edge. Here it was packed and traction was easier.

Donald didn't stop! He plunged ahead with a controlled recklessness until I was all the way out in the water—up to my legs.

"Don-ald! What are you doing?" I screamed. The wheelchair was completely into the rolling surf. I was both shocked and thrilled at the impromptu excitement.

People on the beach looked at this ridiculous sight, uncertain as to whether they should intervene and stop this "madman" who was "trying to drown the poor crippled girl." My laughter and obvious enjoyment reassured them, however, and they returned to their own preoccupations.

Donald picked me up and carried me out into the breakers. I couldn't feel it, but I knew my heart was pounding madly.

After this Ocean City experience, I was floating on air. Donald made me feel "normal" for the first time since my accident. The wheelchair was no object to get in his way—there was no pity or uncomfortable, awkward uncertainty. He treated me as he would any woman he liked. He was strong, but always gentle, giving me assurance. I knew he'd never let anything happen to me.

Donald also made me feel attractive, feminine. For the first time since my accident, I felt like a woman—appealing to someone who saw qualities of beauty in me.

As the season changed, Donald took me on picnics and trail hikes. He'd push my wheelchair as far as he could on the trail. When the path narrowed too much, he'd simply fold up the chair, pick me up, and carry me to the top of the hill. There he'd spread out a blanket, and we'd have a picnic lunch and view the scenic beauty.

We'd talk for hours, sharing God's Word and what each of us had learned through our individual Christian experiences. These were romantic, enjoyable, spiritual times. And each one brought us closer together.

I began to worry about my growing deep affection for Donald and where such feelings might lead me. I knew I had to guard against becoming too involved, too close, guard against caring too much for him. Anything more than a "platonic" relationship would be out of the question.

By the spring of 1971, we were spending a great deal of time together. He often took me with him to his work on the street. As I watched him minister to the kids, I was even more impressed with him as a person. His strengths made him a dominant individual in every situation he faced. He was confident without being domineering.

Against my better judgment, I was allowing myself to become even closer to him, allowing strong emotional ties.

One day as I was outside drawing a picture in the warm, spring sunlight, Donald leaned over and said softly, "Joni, I love you."

Caught up in the creative and spiritual expressions of my drawing, I said, "I love you, too, Donald," with the same inflection I'd use in saying, "Yes, you're a good friend, too, Donald."

"Joni, I don't think you understand—" he paused and looked intently into my eyes. "Joni—I'm falling in love with you!"

He bent down to take my face in his hands and kiss me. I was frightened. I couldn't kiss him without weighing the importance of my actions. A kiss from another woman might be just a casual display of affection. But for me, in a wheelchair, it called for mutual commitment. I didn't want to impose such a commitment on Donald without letting him think through the consequences.

"Look, Donald, this is—"

"But I love you."

"I—I don't know." I was afraid. A relationship based on anything but friendship would be out of the question. "You—uh—we're not able to handle it."

As confident and self-assured as Donald was with me, I felt deep inside that even he could not ultimately deal with the complications my paralysis presented.

Later, I mentioned the episode to Diana and Jay. As I shared my emotional feelings, they both became overprotective and guarded.

"I don't think you should get serious with Donald," urged Jay. "You'll both get hurt."

"Joni," added Diana, "I know he's sincere and doesn't take advantage of you. I know he's good to be with, and I can tell he really likes you. But love? Wow, that's something else altogether. Be careful. Please be careful."

Thirteen

THAT SAME SUMMER I had met Don, Diana had met and fallen in love
with a young man named Frank Mood. Diana and Frank were married in June,
1971, and moved into a house near our family ranch in Sykesville. About the
same time, Jay invited me to come and live with her at the family ranch. Jay lived
in a two-hundred-year-old stone and timber building that had once been slaves'
quarters well over a century ago and which dad had remodeled. It was a quaint,
two-bedroom cottage on a knoll overlooking the picturesque river valley. Living
at the ranch would mean that I could spend time with Jay, Diana and Frank, or
Kathy and Butch, and they all would share in caring for my needs.

When it was decided I would live with Jay, dad added a wing to her house. It was
a big room, planned for the same kind of traffic and entertainment of friends as
the house in Woodlawn. In the corner was a beautiful fireplace. The outside walls
had picture windows to let in light and scenic beauty. The inner walls were lined
with wood paneling he made by hand. The center of the big room was dominated
by a huge oak dining-conference table where all our activities seemed to center.

I had loved the ranch as a girl; I loved it even more now. It brought a sense of
tranquillity and beauty into my life.

Donald liked the ranch, too, and he spent more and more of his time there with
me. Together we took trips to Ocean City, went on picnics, and hiking trips in the
hills, and other outings. I never worried about going anywhere with him because
I knew he could handle any emergency. He was strong enough to carry me by
himself; he helped me eat and drink; he emptied my leg bag, and he could position
me in my chair.

I was relaxed and at ease with him. He was never put off by the physical aspects of my handicap and never bothered by the wheelchair itself. He treated me normally; he joked, played, challenged, and provoked me as he would if I were not paralyzed.

If anyone can handle the physical and psychological problems of my handicap, Donald can, I thought. The possibility of a man coming into my life, not as a brother in Christ, but as a romantic interest, both frightened and excited me.

Diana and Jay again warned me not to get romantically involved with Donald. Later, Diana told me of a similar "Dutch uncle" talk she had had with Donald on the same subject.

"Donald, I want you to know that Jay and I are concerned about what's happening with you and Joni," Diana had cautioned.

"Concerned?" he asked.

"Yes. You're getting too serious. Have you thought about what this means to Joni?"

"Yes, I have," Donald replied. "I've thought very seriously about what's happening. I wouldn't lead her on if I weren't serious. Diana, I'm falling in love with Joni."

"But—Donald—uh—usually when two people fall in love, they make plans to marry and spend the rest of their lives together."

"Yes, I know. Diana, I know all the problems. I've thought and prayed about all the problems of such a relationship. I know the consequences if we'd get married. But I can handle it. I'd marry her now if she'd have me!"

When Diana shared her conversation with me, she still wasn't sure. "Joni, I'm really happy for you—but—"

"I know, Diana," I reassured her. "I'm filled with mixed emotions, too. On one hand, I'm sure I love him, and I believe, really believe, that if anyone can handle such a marriage, Donald can. On the other hand, I think it's probably impossible for anyone to cope with it. I—I guess it's that doubt I want to protect myself from."

"Do you love him?"

"Yes, I guess I do. It's scary. But, y'know, I like it!"

As our love grew, I kept weighing the significance of such a relationship.

"We're talking about a terribly important commitment, Donald," I said one day as we were driving to a softball game.

"I know. But we're able to handle it, Joni. We're both independent and resourceful spirits. We can do it."

"But marriage—"

"Is no more out of the question than anything else. I could take care of you—bathe you, fix meals, clean the house. We could get a mobile home so everything is compact and easy to handle. When we can afford it, we could get something better—maybe even some cleaning and cooking help. Meanwhile, I could do it. I could take care of you."

We pulled into the park and stopped near the ball diamond. "But I could never really be happy not being able to serve you fully as a woman. I want to fix you meals, care for your needs. I want to be able to express my love and tenderness fully as a woman."

"Well, I'm a liberated male, I guess. My cooking and caring for you won't detract from my masculinity. And as for sex, well—I've heard it said that it's over-rated," he smiled. "Don't worry, Joni. Sex isn't that important. I can handle it."

I was unsure. I felt that sex was, indeed, an important part of marriage. But as I weighed the problem, I thought, *Perhaps Donald is right. After all, if he says he can cope with the problems, I believe him. I've learned to trust his judgment.* I also recalled the lectures given to paraplegics and quadriplegics at Rancho Los Amigos during my rehabilitation there. Doctors instructed us on the possibility of lovemaking—even the fact of being able to have children. Our bodies being paralyzed only meant we had no physical feelings; function was not impaired.

"But you know—I can't feel anything," I reminded Donald. "I don't think that I could really be free to satisfy you. I'd feel trapped by my body, not able to express love and tenderness in ways that would meet your needs. We'd both be turned off by a lifetime of mutual frustration!"

"I said it's not important." Then he took my chair out and lifted me into it, continuing, "People live with worse problems. Besides, we'll work it out."

"I—I don't know. I suppose. If you tell me that you can handle that kind of a marriage, I guess I believe you. I—I suppose I could commit myself to you."

Donald smiled tenderly and nodded. Oblivious to the players on the ball diamond, he bent his face toward me in a kiss. This time, I felt his gesture was rich with mutual commitment and meaning. And this time, I returned his kiss with the deep feelings of giving and trust. My head swam with emotion and excitement as he wheeled me toward the bleachers.

This is too good to be true! I thought. *Donald came into my life at exactly the time Diana, my best friend, is going out of my life for marriage and a family of her own.*

God had brought me someone who really cared about me; someone who sincerely believed in the idea that we could spend the rest of our lives together.

"This is God's highest plan for me," I reasoned with Jay when I returned home that evening. "It's that 'most excellent thing' He has reserved for my life! After all these years of patience, in accepting my lot as a handicapped person—and especially an unmarried person—God is now rewarding my patience and trust. Donald is the answer to my prayers!"

I was deliriously happy. Even when I was on my feet, I'd never been this happy.

We both talked excitedly about sharing our lives together, about serving Christ together.

As I thought of this and what God's will on the matter was, I looked to Scripture. Everywhere I turned, verses leaped from the pages to confirm my thoughts.

"No good thing will the Lord withhold from those who walk uprightly.

"Every good gift and every perfect gift is from above.

"Donald is my 'good thing,' my 'perfect gift' from the Lord," I told Jay.

She shook her head. "I don't know, Joni. Don't read in more than is there."

I wrote a song expressing my thoughts and gave the poem to Donald:

> I woke up this morning to the sight of light—
>   bright, yellow, mellow—
>   and I thought it only right
> To praise my God for morning—and you.
>
> Lying here, teasing my mind with sleep
>   in mist-muted colors—
>   Smiling, I keep on
> Praising my God for the evening—and you.
>
> A trail of thoughts giving way to dreams
>   of past and future—
>   that finally it seems that I
> Praise my God for the present—and you!

I was so happy. I'd never imagined anyone would love me as a woman while I was in the chair. I suppose that's why I was so thrilled and excited when it really happened.

Just before Christmas that year, Donald and I had our first argument. We'd been spending a lot of time together, and I began to become possessive. I was even upset when he had to work. I wanted to spend all my time with him; I wanted his life to center around me.

When pretty, young girls from church or youth groups came to visit, I was jealous when he laughed and chatted with them. I became envious that I wasn't on my feet to compete for his attention.

It became more and more difficult for me to concentrate on God's Word and have a devotional or prayer life. It was hard to discuss spiritual things after bickering about "why didn't you come and see me last night?" As a result, my prayer life dwindled to nothing.

My feelings for him became almost all-consuming.

Donald reacted vocally and forcefully. He reminded me that I was acting foolish—like a possessive schoolgirl. I told him I was sorry, that I wouldn't be so demanding of his time and affections; but for some reason, I'd still give in to these unreasonable fears.

Donald decided we both needed a vacation from each other, so he planned to take a trip to Europe in January, 1972. I resisted, taking his plans as a personal rebuke, as if he wanted to get away from me for some reason.

"I just think we need some time to ourselves, Joni," he explained. "Don't read anything else into it at all. Besides," he added, "I've wanted to take this trip for a long time. The guys and I will probably never have an opportunity like this again."

Dickie and Dave Filbert went to Europe with him. Inside, I had all kinds of unreasonable fears. For the first time, I was afraid for our relationship. *What if he leaves me? What if he really can't cope? What if it doesn't work out?* The trip to Europe lasted about three weeks. During that time I received letters and postcards from Switzerland, Germany, France, and other places they visited. The messages were all the same—that he missed me, loved me, and wished I was with him.

When he returned from Europe, he exploded into the house. "I missed you so much, I couldn't wait to get back," he exclaimed. He did come back—more loving and sensitive than ever.

Donald and I began talking about the possibility of my being healed. Until now, I'd accepted my situation. But my desire to be a complete woman led me to fiercely claim promises I felt the Lord had put in His Word for me. *After all,* I reasoned, *He allows us to have experiences of suffering and sickness to teach us. I've learned an enormous amount through my accident. But now that I've learned what He had for me to learn, He might heal me!* This was to be a new adventure of faith—the next phase of spiritual development for me.

Of course, physiologically, I could not be healed—my injury was permanent. Yet I knew nothing was impossible for God. Did He not, through Christ, heal all kinds of paralysis and sicknesses? He even raised the dead.

Even today there are miracles of healing. I'd heard about many cases of "permanent," "incurable," or "fatal" diseases or injuries being reversed.

Donald and I read James 5 and other passages, concentrating on the idea that it was God's will for me to be healed. The Lord seemed to speak to us through John 14 and 15 and many other passages, and we prayed with renewed enthusiasm and thankfulness.

We believed that finding God's will was a matter of circumstances, faith in God's love, the assurance of His Word, and dependence on the power of His Holy Spirit. There was new optimism in the prospect of sharing our lives together.

"We're absolutely convinced that God wants me healed!" I told Diana.

"Joni, this whole thing is getting out of hand. You're twisting God's arm—blackmailing Him. You're not being realistic about this," she replied.

"Diana, I'm surprised that you'd say that. I thought you'd have more faith than that. You must have faith that God really does want to heal me," I said by way of rebuke.

Donald and I prayed that God would bring about the circumstances for us to trust Him. I began to inform my friends that God was going to heal me soon. Each time Donald and I got together we prayed it would be soon.

"Lord, we have faith. We believe Your Word that You want us healthy and able to better serve You," prayed Donald.

"Thank You for the lessons in trust and patience that You have taught me through suffering, Lord. And thank You for what You plan to do to bring glory to Yourself by healing me according to Your promises," I added.

As we continued to pray about this matter, we planned to attend a church service where the format of the healing ministry outlined in James 5 could be followed.

Several friends drove me to the church. Elders came and laid hands upon me and anointed me with oil, according to the scriptural injunction. They read promises from the Bible and prayed for me.

With all the faith, devotion, and spiritual commitment we could discover through our own inner resources, Donald and I prayed and trusted.

I wasn't anticipating immediate healing, but expected a slow recovery, since my rehabilitation alone had taken nearly two years. It was logical to think God would restore me gradually, I reasoned.

But after several attempts and many healing services, it became obvious that I wasn't going to be healed. I was able to accept the reality of the situation, but I was frustrated—probably more for Donald than myself. Donald was quiet, yet intense. He seemed to be questioning everything, reevaluating all that had happened. It was awkward, especially for him, after pinning so much to that prayer of faith which went "unanswered." His introspection was guarded, and he began spending more time away from me. I resented this, again jealous of his time.

When Steve came home on college break, he, Diana, and I discussed the possible reasons God did not answer our prayers.

"Why do you suppose He didn't want you healed?" Diana asked.

"I don't know."

Steve broke in. "You know, I was thinking about that when I read Hebrews 11 recently. You know the passage?"

"'Yeah, it talks about the people of faith," I answered.

"Well, it also says there are two categories of people—those whose faith was rewarded and those whose faith was not. All kinds of miraculous, fantastic things happened to some. Others were 'sawn asunder,' 'saw not the promises,' or did not experience a visible reward."

"And you think I'm in the latter category?" I asked.

Steve leaned forward to make a point. "Uh-huh. I think so. For now, anyway.

But not forever. Second Corinthians 5 tells about the wonderful resurrection body you'll have some day instead of a useless, earthly body. We're living in 'tabernacles' now—temporary dwellings. But someday we'll live in temples—heavenly bodies that are perfect and permanent."

"But what about those verses we read about faith?" I protested.

Steve grabbed my knee to emphasize his words—as if I could feel it. "But that's what I'm trying to say! Remember the faith healer who told you, 'I believe it is God's will that you be healed?'"

"Yes."

"Well, I believe it, too. I believe it's God's will for everyone to be healed. But maybe we just can't agree as to timetable. I believe it is His will, but apparently it doesn't have priority over other things. You will be healed, but probably not until you receive your glorified body."

"But God does heal other people," I argued.

"Yes, I know. I don't question His sovereignty on this," he replied.

Diana added, "But when He does heal someone supernaturally, He must have reasons for it. For instance, there seems to be a lot of examples of healing miracles overseas in cultures where missionaries work. When people don't have the written Word of God, maybe they need a more obvious witness—you know, like 'signs and wonders'—to attract them to Christ."

"Yeah, could be," I answered.

Steve went on to say, "In our culture, it wouldn't be appropriate or necessary. Some hot-shot, sensation-seeking press would change the focus and distort the whole situation. God wouldn't receive the glory, and the whole purpose would be lost."

"I think maybe that's the way it works," I remarked.

Diana nodded. "It's a dangerous misunderstanding of the Bible to say categorically that it's God's will that everyone be well. It's obvious everyone is not well."

"Right. We're trying for perfection, but we haven't attained it yet. We still sin. We still catch colds. We still break legs and necks," I said, adding, "The more I think about it, the more I'm convinced that God doesn't want everyone well. He uses our problems for His glory and our good." As I thought of this, I recalled several godly families touched by tragedy and disease. Many who truly love the Lord are often afflicted the most and fall into this category.

Man's dealing with God in our day and culture is based on His Word rather than "signs and wonders."

"You know," Steve said, "there's really no difference in God's power. Maybe you have greater credibility because of your chair than if you were out of it."

"What do you mean?"

"Remember the Greek word for the power of God? I think it's *dunamos*."

"Yeah, it's where we get the word *dynamite*."

"Or *dynamo*," Steve said. "They both mean great power. One is explosive energy. The other is controlled, useful energy. A healing experience would be like an explosive release of God's energy getting you out of the chair. But staying in the chair takes power, too—controlled energy flowing through you that makes it possible to cope."

Over the next few months, Donald and I talked about this and many other things; but one thing we now avoided was talking about our future.

Then one day when Donald came, I sensed an awkward quiet, a tenseness. Finally, in a low voice, he said, "Joni, I'm going to be counseling this summer up in New York at a *Young Life* camp. I'm leaving tomorrow. I just wanted to come and say good-by."

I thought, *That's good. Things have been a bit sour in our relationship lately. We both needed a breather from each other—like the Europe trip.* But I was puzzled about the decisive inflection Donald gave to the word *good-by.*

"What do you mean good-by? You'll be gone for several weeks, but—"

"No, Joni. This is it. I'm sorry. We never should have allowed this relationship to develop the way it has. I never should have kissed you. We never should have shared the things we shared. We never should have talked and dreamed of marriage. It was all a mistake."

"A mistake! What do you mean? You were the one who encouraged me! I was the one who didn't want to get involved. You've kissed me and held me. I went from fear to hope because you told me you loved me and wanted us to build a life together! Donald—I've shared things so deeply with you—more than I've shared with my own family. And you're just going to walk away, just like that? Now you're saying it's a mistake—that you were just leading me along?" My voice faltered as I desperately tried to put words and thoughts together.

Hot tears of rage and frustration made me want to throw myself on him and beat him with my fists. All I could do was sit there and sob.

"I wasn't leading you along, I swear it," Donald said firmly. "I sincerely thought I could do it. But I was wrong. It's impossible. It's all a mistake."

"Oh, dear God, what is this? Is it really happening?" Panic swept over me as I thought of Donald standing across the room saying good-by. *What happened?* He came into my life and made me feel so attractive and useful—a *woman.* I didn't think anyone would ever care for me as much as he had. I didn't think it possible I could love anyone as deeply as I loved him.

I tried to stop crying. "Maybe you need time to reconsider—"

"No, Joni. I've thought seriously about what I'm doing. There's no turning back. It's over. I'm sorry." With that, he turned and walked to the door.

"Donald! Don't leave me! Donald, wait!"

"Good-by, Joni!" he said quietly and closed the door behind him.

"No! Oh, my God—why are You letting this happen? Why are You hurting me like this?"

Fourteen

AND SO, WITH a simple "good-by," Donald walked out of my life. My heart and mind raged. *How could he be so cruel after being so loving and tender?*

Yet, after I regained my composure, I saw that he hadn't meant to be cruel. It was simply his style—no jive, no hypocrisy, he had said.

I knew when he left that he was walking out for good. He gave me no false hopes, no wrong impressions. In the long run, it was the least painful of any method he could have used.

I learned that Dick and Donald, good friends since school days, had shared the problem with each other. Dick, who himself had had similar confusion in his relationship with me, earlier, had warned Donald not to let his feelings for me get out of hand.

"I know exactly what Don is going through," Dick told me later. "I was confused and torn up inside after you wrote me from California that you wanted to be 'just friends.' I knew what you were doing, but I felt then—and still feel—very much in love with you. But I also know you're right about what my being able to really face up to all your injury means. I just don't know. But I was willing to commit myself to making it work. Maybe you knew me better; maybe you didn't believe I could handle it. I don't know. In any event, since we've been 'just good friends' the past two years, I was happy for you both when you and Don fell in love. I prayed that he'd be able to do whatever I couldn't and that you'd really be happy together."

"Then what went wrong?" I asked.

"I don't know. I began to see Don questioning the relationship. Several times he confided to me that he wished he'd never let his feelings for you get so out of hand. I suppose he—being older and probably wiser than me—saw what you saw with me: that many guys really can't deal with the chair in the long run. Or, at least it seems Don and I can't."

My hurt was even more painful as I continued to hear about Donald second-hand. He wrote letters to kids we had both been counseling. I was angry and resentful when kids we both had prayed with and helped received letters and were still close to Donald and I wasn't.

I'd been warned not to let my feelings for Donald get out of hand. Jay and Diana had urged me many times to be careful, but I didn't listen. Now my hopes and dreams for marriage were hopelessly crushed.

Why, God? I don't understand why. My reactions included rage at Donald, self-pity for myself, and jealous anger at friends who were still close to him. A young high school girl, a new Christian whom we had both counseled, came over to read a letter she had received from Donald telling her how God was working in his life in exciting ways. She, of course, didn't know what happened between us. She merely came over to share an encouraging, newsy letter to her from Donald. My envy grew and hot tears began to run down from the corners of my eyes.

When she left and I was by myself, I felt ashamed of my attitudes. I wasn't handling this "irritation" with a godly response. I turned to a familiar Scripture passage for comfort—1 Corinthians 13, the love chapter of the Bible. But my mind played tricks with the words.

"Though I speak with the tongue of men and angels and have *lust*, I'm like sounding brass or crashing cymbals. If I have prophetic gifts, absolute faith, and lust, I amount to nothing. If I give away all I have, even allow my body to be burned, and have lust, I achieve nothing. Lust is quick to lose patience; it is possessive; it tries to impress others and has inflated ideas of its own importance. Lust has bad manners and pursues selfish aims. It is touchy. . . ."

By substituting the word "lust" for "love," I saw what had gone wrong with our relationship. I had *lusted* after Donald—after his time, his attention, his presence—because I felt I had a right to. I saw what a consuming, fiery passion lust was. It was a desire that I did not want to deny myself. In the end, I lost everything that I sought to selfishly control.

Now the truth of 1 Corinthians 13 became evident. True love is unselfish, disciplined, directed, self-controlled, patient, and kind.

I began to sob bitterly at my confusion and hurt. This time, however, my hurt drove me to the Lord instead of to self-pity and self-centered introspection. I reread Scriptures which had helped me to overcome previous disappointments.

I decided I didn't want to listen to the birds. They all reminded me of the beautiful times Donald and I had gone to the woods for quiet retreats and this was the only way I could consciously shut him out of my mind. It was difficult enough just to be outdoors with all those memories. How can I describe my feelings? For a year my mind had been working toward fulfillment of an ideal—my marriage to Donald; I had believed that our plans were part of God's perfect will for us. Then, in one brief day, my dream disintegrated before my eyes so completely that there was not a flicker of hope that it could be revived.

I recalled Steve's mention of Lamentations 3. He had once told me, "Joni, God must have His reasons. Jeremiah says that 'it is good that a young man bear the yoke in his youth.' Perhaps your life will have greater value in years to come because you're going through this experience now."

"Lord," I prayed, "what is happening to that 'excellent gift' I read about in Your Word? What are You doing?" I recalled passages from the Gospels in which Peter and John questioned Jesus as I was now doing. "What is that to thee?" was the Lord's simple, blunt reply. Jesus didn't coddle Peter or allow him to indulge in self-pity. The Lord said, in essence, "What do you care? It doesn't matter. You keep your eyes on me." I learned that God's truth is not always kind or comfortable. Sometimes His love for us involves harshness or a stern reproof.

I read other verses: "Welcome trials as friends," said the apostle James, reminding me of the lessons God had already taught me in the hospital and during the years that followed. "In everything give thanks. . . . All things work together. . . ."

I forced myself back into God's Word. There was no extensive self-pity, no wallowing in tears. God was merely providing me with yet another test—a "gut" testing of His truth, love, and purposes.

Letters from Donald to mutual friends were vibrant with his testimony of God at work in his life. He wrote of exciting spiritual growth and progress as the weeks turned into months. After the long summer, he wrote to friends telling of a lovely young woman he had met while working at the camp.

I felt the sting of hurt as I received the news that Donald had fallen in love with another woman. But the Lord seemed to say, "What is that to thee?"

I wrote to Steve, away at Bible college, and poured out my heart. He wrote back and assured me of his concern and prayers. His letter closed with a promise from Psalm 40: "His truth and lovingkindness shall continually preserve thee"—that whatever the hurt involved in this learning process, God always deals with us in love. This and other passages sustained me through this difficult period.

It was hard for me to accept the fact that Donald was not God's will, God's best for me. "But, Lord, if not Donald, I believe You have someone or something better for me. I will trust You to bring it into my life." I recalled hearing a preacher say *God never closes a door without opening a window—He always gives us something better when He takes something away.*

I took this promise at face value. It's obvious, looking back, that God did know best. I had read into circumstances, Scriptures, and everything else all the right "meaning" to make Donald a part of my life. It was easy to say "God wants us happy, doesn't He?" and then bend verses to fit my purposes. I suppose I knew all along it wasn't going to work but pursued the idea that it was God's will that Donald build his life around me.

After my accident, I had clung to Dick, then Jay, Diana, and until now, Donald. I needed their love and support to satisfy my emotional needs. Now, however, I felt free. It was as if I had finally gained emotional independence through complete dependence on God. One day, while sitting outside in my wheelchair, I was quietly reflecting over these thoughts. *Lord*, I prayed, *I wish I could have seen this earlier—I wish I'd have remembered that Your grace is sufficient for me.* As I sat there on the quiet wooded lawn, verse after verse came to mind to comfort me. *Please, Lord, make Yourself real to me just now.*

Peace of mind and inner joy flooded my mind and soul. Then I looked up. Almost as a symbol of God's love and reassurance, a butterfly from high among the trees fluttered within inches of me. It was both startling and beautiful.

"Lord, thank You for Your goodness. Sending that butterfly at precisely this instant was a creative, subtle way of testifying to Your quiet and understated presence." I promised myself to think of God's goodness every time I saw a butterfly.

I reflected over this most unusual and difficult summer during long outdoor retreats with the Lord. I sought to be outside and meditate on His purposes, so to occupy myself during these times, I devoted all my time and energy to my art; I found a renewed interest in drawing. And it seemed my art was getting better. There was a quality that hadn't been there before. I didn't know what it was, but others noticed the difference too.

It was a slow transition, but not as difficult as I had expected. I saw Donald in a new light, with greater understanding. He had done what was right and best, even if it hurt us both, for I know now that it hurt him as much as it hurt me.

We were both blind to the serious consequences of what such a relationship would mean. When we're in love, our love takes expression in actions. If there is nowhere to go, in reality, then wishful thinking and fantasy convince us that "everything will work out." People warn us, but we choose not to believe them.

Many young people ignore reality. They know something is wrong, that a relationship won't work, but they go ahead anyway, as we would have done, convinced by wishful thinking.

I look back now and thank God for our relationship. There are so many things I never would have learned if Donald had not come into my life and left me, and so I thank the Lord for this experience. I'm especially grateful God helped me deal with our separation without lingering feelings of bitterness or despair.

I even accepted Donald's new love with honest joy that he, too, had at last found God's perfect will for his life. At a Bible study one evening, a friend came up to me. Hesitantly, he said, "Uh—Joni, I want to tell you something before you hear it from someone else."

"Jimmy, you don't have to say anything more. I know."

"You do? You've already heard that Donald is engaged? How?"

"I don't know," I smiled. "I guess I just knew it, that's all."

I was shocked at how easily God helped me meet what should have been a hurtful, difficult meeting. And when Donald brought Sandy, a beautiful, young widow who had lost her husband in an accident, to Bible study three weeks later, we were seated next to one another.

She knew about me. In any other situation, this would have been awkward, to say the least. But I turned to her, a tall, lovely woman whose dark features complemented Donald's own good looks, and said, "Sandy, I'm really glad to meet you. I want you to know how genuinely happy I am for you and Donald."

She smiled and said thank you.

I told her, "I pray for you both every night. I praise God for what He's done in all three of our lives. I'm really excited about you both—especially your willingness to serve Christ." And I meant every word.

Friends and family members who knew how deeply Donald and I had cared for one another were amazed at my attitude. They had expected me to fall apart. And I probably would have gone to pieces if I had not allowed God to handle the situation.

I really began to see suffering in a new light—not as trials to avoid, but as opportunities to "grab," because God gives so much of His love, grace, and goodness to those who do.

My life changed more during the last half of 1972 than any other period of my life—even my previous five years in the chair.

When Donald walked out of my life, there was no one in whom I could put my trust—except God. And since the Lord had always proved Himself faithful before, I trusted Him now.

Fifteen

DURING THE FALL of 1972, I began to ask serious questions about my future. "Lord," I asked, "if not college, if not Donald, then what? What do You have for me?"

I believed that if God took something away from me, He would always replace it with something better. My experience had taught me this as I relied on the sovereignty of God. "Delight thyself in God," the psalmist said, "trust in His way." As I did so, it became easier to express true gratitude for what He brought into my life—good as well as suffering.

The suffering and pain of the past few years had been the ingredients that had helped me mature emotionally, mentally, and spiritually. I felt confident and independent, trusting in the Lord for my physical and emotional needs.

Pain and suffering have purpose. We don't always see this clearly. The apostle Paul suffered for Christ. His experience included imprisonment, beatings, stonings, shipwreck and some physical "thorn in the flesh." The blessing of suffering is, as J. B. Phillips interprets Romans 5:3–5, ". . . we can be full of joy here and now even in our trials and troubles. Taken in the right spirit, these very things will give us patient endurance; this in turn will develop a mature character, and a character of this sort produces a steady hope, a hope that will never disappoint us."

I believed He was working in my life to create grace and wisdom out of the chaos of pain and depression.

Now all these experiences began to find visible expression in my art. At first, I drew for fun; then, to occupy my time; finally, to express my feelings for what

God was doing in me. I sensed, somehow, that my artwork fit into the scheme of things. Perhaps it would be the "something better."

But the last thing I wanted was for people to admire my drawings simply because they were drawn by someone in a wheelchair holding a pen in her mouth. I wanted my work to be good in itself—in creativity and craftsmanship. That's why I was both pleased and proud at having my work displayed in a local art festival—for its own sake, and not because of my handicap.

For the first time, I threw myself fully into my artwork. I sketched pictures of things that had beauty rather than things that expressed emotions or hurts I'd experienced. It was a positive collection, with hope reflected in the drawings of animals, scenes, and people. As a result, people accepted them. They were attracted to sketches of youngsters, mountains, flowers, and forest animals because of the common beauty such subjects expressed.

I honestly felt God had brought me to this place and had even greater blessings in store. I never would have believed this a year or two earlier, but I had now come to the place where the "something better" was in being single. I read in 1 Corinthians 6 and 7 that there could be a calling higher than marriage for some. A single woman could devote herself to being holy with fewer distractions if she had no husband, family, or house to care for, and I was free from a house-oriented routine. True, I did not have the pleasures and privileges that went with such a role, but God had substituted other joys, and I was more than fulfilled. I had my own freedom to come and go without having to maintain a schedule involving others. I could travel, keep late work hours, read, talk, or whatever I choose. It was a great freedom.

People often said to me, "You had no choice about being single. That's why you can accept that role more easily than I can. That's why you can be joyful. But I am lonely, frustrated, and unfulfilled."

"I'm not sure it's easier for me," I told them. "Every person who is faced with the prospect of singlehood should trust God's wisdom. Because I did not trust Him for my own life but sought to engineer His will in my relationship with Donald, I was also frustrated. But when I had no choice but acceptance, trust, and surrender, this did become easy for me. If we accept this handicap from God, we are freed from the constant agony and anxiety of wondering, worrying, and desperate searching. Not knowing the future and worrying about it causes most of our bitterness and grief."

"You mean I should give up hoping to be married at all?" a girl asked me once.

"I'm saying that acceptance of the role of being single ends the frustration of not knowing," I replied. "But that's the hardest part. Surrender to the idea of being forever single, with all the sacrifices that implies, is the most difficult. But once acceptance is made, living with that role is easier."

"That sounds like just giving up," she observed.

"Maybe it is. This is not to say God will never allow us to marry someday.

Maybe He will; maybe He won't. What I'm saying is that it doesn't matter because we leave the choice and decision with Him. We trust His judgment that 'all things work together for our good' if we love God."

"But I feel I have needs to be fulfilled—that I have a right to be married!"

"Only God is capable of telling us what our rights and needs are. You have to surrender that right to Him. Begin your life as a single person, working and living according to the priorities of serving and glorifying Him. In turn, God gives a rich and satisfying life. In place of one partner, He brings many friends into our lives to meet our emotional needs and loneliness."

"That's what you've experienced, Joni?"

"Yes. And it gets better. Maybe, God will give you back that right to be married after you surrender it completely. He may bring someone into your life after all. But holding tightly onto that hope and thinking constantly about the possibility of it happening is terribly frustrating."

Young people listened respectfully when I shared these concepts with them. But I could always see the reservation and holding back in their eyes. It was difficult for them to comprehend how a handicap of being single could be better than the joys of marriage.

"Scripture says," I reminded them, "in 1 Corinthians, 'Eye hath not seen, nor ear heard, neither have entered into the heart of men, the things which God hath prepared for them that love him.' The apostle was comparing the natural man with the spiritual man in this passage, but I also think it could apply to us concerning our future."

"What do you mean?" a girl asked me one day.

"Well, we think of the greatest experiences of love, tenderness, and feelings we might have with a guy—all the beautiful things that have entered into the heart, mind, eye and ear. God is saying *These are nothing compared to what lies ahead.* I still don't know what this means. But I've found that God never places any real emphasis on the present—except as preparation for the future. We only have a limited sense of reality. This doesn't mean I'm preoccupied with heaven and the hereafter. It just helps me put things into perspective."

"But don't you think that's true for you because you're in a wheelchair?" someone usually asked.

"No, I don't think so. This is a universal truth. A lot of people who aren't in wheelchairs still have to deal with being single, just as I do. It can be a source of constant irritation and frustration, or it can be a joy."

"You mean you believe you'll never marry?"

"No. I have no feeling one way or the other. I'm not sure that I will never marry. Or that I will. I'm content, whether I marry or not."

"Well, what about those of us who haven't come to that place where we can accept that role as easily as you?"

"If you're single, with no plans or prospects, just live as though God will have you remain single until He brings someone or something better into your life."

"Sort of like that verse you quoted—'eye hath not seen, nor ear heard,' right?" someone asked.

"Yes. Sometimes I recall experiences of feeling—of running through grassy fields, swimming in a cool, clear stream, climbing up a rugged mountain, smelling flowers, riding a horse—all the sensations I'd have on my feet. But God says all of this together can't compare with the glory and future reality He has prepared for me. It's as I said before—the future is the only reality that counts. The only thing we can take to heaven with us is our character. Our character is all we have to determine what kind of a being we will be for all eternity. It's what we *are* that will be tested by fire. Only the qualities of Christ in our character will remain."

I was grateful for these opportunities to explain how God was working in my life. I began to see a mature purpose in all His dealings with me, and I was happier than I had ever been. My experiences charged me with creative energy and a maturity I didn't have before, and my art had a new quality and professionalism.

I experimented with various papers, pens, pencils, and charcoal. I tried different approaches and techniques, finally settling on the elements that seemed to work best. Using a sharp, felt-tip *Flair* pen, I sketched with precision and control. I gave drawings to friends as wedding presents and Christmas gifts. This demand for my art kept me fairly busy. However, I had still not found an outlet for my drawings which would enable me to derive income from them and become gainfully employed—and more independent.

Then one day an insurance executive called on my father at his downtown office. Neill Miller is an energetic, good-natured, successful, Christian business-man. He is Senior Field Underwriter for the Aetna Life and Casualty Company, as well as being actively involved with several Baltimore charity drives. Neill Miller sees opportunities where other people see obstacles. Through his efforts, national celebrities have become interested in the causes he represents and have volunteered their services and talents.

During his visit with dad, Mr. Miller noticed one of my drawings on the wall of the office.

"I really like that drawing, Mr. Eareckson. Is it an original?" he asked.

"Yes. As a matter of fact, my daughter drew it," dad replied.

"Really? She's quite an artist. It has a great deal of character as well as realistic detail. She has an original style—it shows unusual discipline," observed Mr. Miller.

"Thank you. I'll tell her." Then dad said, "You might be interested to know Joni—that's my daughter—is paralyzed. She has to draw holding the pen in her mouth."

"That's even more remarkable!" Mr. Miller stood up and examined the drawing more closely. "Amazing. Absolutely amazing."

"She's never had any formal training," dad explained. "I've dabbled in art most of my life, and I suppose she's inherited my interest in art. But her talent and style are her own."

"Has she exhibited her art?" Mr. Miller asked.

"No, not really—just at a couple festivals. She does it for fun. She draws for friends and family mostly."

"Well, we can't let such talent go unnoticed," exclaimed Mr. Miller. "Do you think she'd object if I arranged a small art exhibit for her?"

"Why, I'm sure she'd be delighted."

"Fine! Let me see what I can do. I'll be in touch."

Mr. Miller telephoned dad later to say that he had arranged for a small exhibition at a local restaurant. Dad took all the original drawings I'd been working on for the past several months to the Town and Country Restaurant in the center of downtown Baltimore. The Town and Country is a popular, prestigious gathering place for local businessmen and important political figures.

I expected a small, informal gathering of people to look at my drawings, chat, and go on their way, as that was the pattern I'd observed at several other art exhibits with other artists. I secretly hoped I might even be able to sell one or two drawings.

Jay, Diana, and I drove downtown the morning of the exhibit. We had been told to arrive at ten o'clock. As Jay turned onto South Street toward the restaurant, we found the avenue blocked off.

"That's strange," I remarked. "They're not working on the road or anything. Why would they block off a main street like this?"

"I don't know. I'll turn down this side street and cut over," said Jay.

"Wait. You can't get through there either. There's a policeman directing traffic."

"It must be something for the Chamber of Commerce," remarked Diana.

"Yeah. Maybe a Lincoln's birthday parade or something," added Jay.

"It must be a parade—look," I exclaimed.

"A big brass band. How exciting. Too bad we're going to the exhibit. We could watch it," Jay smiled.

"Maybe you can turn down—" I didn't finish the sentence.

We all saw it at the same time and gasped, unbelieving.

The brass band was in front of the Town and Country. And blazoned across the front of the building was a huge banner declaring "Joni Eareckson Day." A television camera crew was standing there waiting, along with a growing crowd of people.

"Oh, no! What's happening?" I cried. "Jay, quick! Turn into the alley before they see us!"

The car came to a stop between the buildings, comfortably out of sight of the commotion.

"What am I going to do?" I asked Jay. "This is incredible. What has he done?"

"Oh, wow, Joni. I've never seen anything like this. He did say 'small' exhibition, didn't he?"

We sat there several minutes trying to decide what to do. When it was obvious we had no choice but to go ahead with the event, Jay backed the car around and pulled up to the restaurant.

I prayed inwardly that Jay, in her own nervousness, would not drop me as she and Mr. Miller lifted me from the car into my wheelchair.

I said under my breath, "Mr. Miller, what have you done?" But before he could explain, I was besieged.

Reporters from the Baltimore *News-American* and local NBC television affiliate were asking questions. I blinked and sheepishly tried to collect my thoughts. A liveried, chauffeur-driven representative of FTD brought me a beautiful bouquet of roses. An official from city hall was reading a proclamation from the mayor announcing a local art appreciation week and honoring me in "Joni Eareckson Day" ceremonies. I was overwhelmed and somewhat embarrassed at all the attention.

I said to Mr. Miller, "Is all this really necessary?" I thought perhaps the entire focus of the exhibit would be lost or at least misconstrued, with everyone's attention turning to the wheelchair. Yet, as the event unfolded, that was not the case at all, and I apologized for my hasty judgment. Perhaps I'd grown too sensitive in this area, half-expecting the usual pity and put-down accorded to people in wheelchairs. I had already experienced (a fact confirmed by the National Paraplegic Foundation) the difficulty of getting people who didn't know me to accept me as an intellectual equal.

Perhaps I overreact to this type of situation, but I am intensely interested in getting people to relate to me, my art, or my Christian witness strictly on their own merits. I don't want my chair to be the overriding focus as I talk to people, whether about art or Christ.

I'm not upset about the chair, so don't you be, I want to tell people.

The ceremonies were excellent, and the focus on my art was not lost. The questions of reporters dealt primarily with my art; the chair was merely background.

Mr. Miller told me, "Joni, your sights are set too low. You don't realize just how good your art is. I'm sorry if all this embarrassed you at first. But I guess I don't believe in doing things in a small way."

The excitement peaked following the ceremonies, and the rest of the exhibit followed the standard procedures for such events.

People asked:

"Where do you get the ideas for your drawings?"

"How long does it take to complete a picture?"

"Did you study art professionally?"

When the crowd thinned at one point, Mr. Miller brought a tall, good-looking young man over and introduced him. His hands were stuffed into the pockets of his jacket, and he looked uncomfortable.

"I wanted him to talk to you, Joni," Mr. Miller said and walked away, leaving us awkwardly looking at one another.

"I'm happy to meet you," I said. "Won't you sit down?" He sat at the nearby table without speaking, and I began to feel uneasy.

Why was he here? He didn't seem to want to talk to me. My efforts at small talk were hopeless. Yet I could tell by his eyes something was bothering him.

Trying once more, I asked, "What do you do?"

"Nothing." Then, almost as a concession, he muttered, "I used to be a fireman. But I can't work now."

"Oh?" *What do I say now?* "Uh—will you tell me about it?"

"It was an accident."

"Yes?"

He shuffled nervously in his seat. "Look," he said, "I don't know why I'm here. Miller told me I ought to come and talk to you—that you had a rough time a while back with—uh—with your handicap."

"Yeah—I sure did. I guess I'd have killed myself if I'd been able to use my arms. I was really depressed. But—" I paused, letting him know I still didn't know what his problem was.

His handsome young face was contorted with anguish. He raised his arms, taking his hands from his coat pockets. But he had no hands—only scarred stumps where they had been amputated.

"Look at these ugly stumps!" he said. "My hands were burned in a fire—and they're *gone*. And I just can't cope!"

The frustration, pent-up rage, and bitterness poured out as his voice broke.

"I'm sorry," I told him, "but Mr. Miller was right. I can help you, I think."

"How?" he said sharply. "I'll never get my hands back."

"I know. I don't mean to sound glib. But I've been where you are. I know the anger, the feelings of unfairness—of being robbed, cheated of your self-respect. I had those same feelings. Maybe it's worse for a man—you know, trying to be independent and self-supporting. But I think I can identify with you."

I told him something of my own experiences at the hospital and Greenoaks. I told him that his feelings were natural.

"But how'd you get over it? How do you cope with your handicap? You're cheerful, not at all cynical today. Where do you get the power to pull it off?" he asked.

"Boy, that's quite a story. Would you like to hear it?"

He nodded. I told him how a relationship with Jesus Christ gives access to God and all His power. I shared how God had been working in my life the past few years and how He alone helped me face my fears and take on the tasks of living. Then I shared with him the simple gospel message I had heard as a fifteen-year-old at *Young Life* camp.

His face brightened as we talked. For nearly a half hour, I shared the principles God had taught me. When he left, he said, "Thanks, Joni. Neill Miller was right. You have helped me. I'll try again. Thanks."

(Today, this young man is enthusiastic about life again and is chief spokesman in the school system for the city fire department.)

Meanwhile, the exhibit at the Town and Country drew to a close, and Neill Miller's idea turned out to be the event that launched my art career. By early evening, I was stunned to learn I'd sold about a thousand dollars' worth of original drawings at fifty to seventy-five dollars each!

The event also got exposure for my work on Channel 11 in Baltimore: in addition to covering the exhibit, they invited me to be on a local talk show and feature my art.

Seymour Koph, of the Baltimore *News-American*, carried a full feature in his column.

"Why do you sign your drawings 'PTL'?" Mr. Kopf had asked. He recorded my full answer in his column:

"It stands for 'praise the Lord.' You see, Mr. Kopf, God loves us—He *does care*. For those who love God, everything—even what happened to me at age seventeen—works together for good. God has been good to me. He has ingrained the reflection of Christ into my character, developed my happiness, my patience, my purpose in life. He has given me contentment. My art is a reflection of how God can empower someone like me to rise above circumstances."

I was invited to participate in local art shows later that spring. The exhibit also opened the doors for me to address Christian women's clubs, schools, church groups, and civic functions where I not only showed my art, but shared my Christian testimony as well. I even made a special tour of the White House, where I left one of my drawings for First Lady, Pat Nixon.

Other TV and radio appearances were offered, and each new contact seemed to generate additional stories or appearances.

On the strength of growing art sales, I was thrilled to see a small measure of independence. I wouldn't have to be a financial burden on anyone but would now be able to earn my own money. I even created a line of greeting cards and prints from several of my drawings, and these began to sell well, too. We named this company *Joni PTL*, and it expanded rapidly.

About this time, a close friend, Andy Byrd, told me of his plan to buy a Christian bookstore franchise and open a store; he wondered if I would like to have a partnership. We talked to Ken Wagner who became a third partner.

Our plans were not only exciting but seemed like a solid business investment.

A Christian bookstore was something many of us had prayed for as a necessary element for Western Baltimore.

Finally, in September, 1973, after months of plans, prayer, and hard work, there was a grand opening of the Logos Bookstore, 1120 North Rolling Road, in the Rolling Road Plaza shopping mall. Just before the store opened, amid boxes of materials, books to price, and supplies, we prayed. Our prayer of dedication was for the many secular-oriented shoppers passing by—that our store would be a center of Christian concern and outreach where people could come for help.

I used the store as a center for selling original art and prints of several originals. These sold almost as quickly as I drew them. Between the bookstore, speaking engagements, and art fairs or festivals, it was difficult to keep up with the demand.

I developed a brief testimony sheet which I printed and handed out at art shows while I was drawing. It explained my unusual drawing methods and faith in Christ and became a great tool for counseling and witnessing as people who came to watch stopped to chat and discuss the power of God in my life.

Through all the activities and events, there was one overriding focus to all this: that, humanly speaking, my art would help me gain independence, and, more importantly, that it would be used to glorify God.

Sixteen

I WAS SITTING outside at the ranch at Sykesville one beautiful late summer morning in 1974 when a telephone call came for me.

"Miss Eareckson, I'm calling from the 'Today Show' in New York. We'd like you to come on the program and tell your story and show your drawings. Can you come?"

My heart was in my throat. The "Today Show"!

"Of course," I replied. "I'll be glad to come." Jay stood by the phone writing down the information. We agreed on an appearance for September 11.

Jay drove me to New York, taking our friends Sherri Pendergrass and Cindy Blubaugh to help. After getting settled at the hotel the day before the scheduled appearance, we went over to Rockefeller Center to meet with the director. He explained the procedure to me, and we discussed possible interview questions. He made me feel relaxed and comfortable, not only with the mental preparation for the show, but with the line of questioning the hostess, Barbara Walters, was likely to take.

Early the next morning I found myself sitting opposite Barbara Walters. Lights flooded the set with warmth and brightness. Miss Walters smiled and glanced quickly at her notes.

"Just relax, Joni," she said warmly. "Are you comfortable?"

"Yes. Thank you."

"Fine."

"Fifteen seconds!" someone called from behind the cameras.

I wasn't as nervous as I thought I might be—probably because I was secure in what I was planning to say and knowing that my testimony would be shared with so many millions of people. I didn't know what Miss Walters planned to ask me, but I knew of nothing she could ask that would make me uncomfortable.

"Ten seconds."

Lord, I prayed quickly, *give me confidence, wisdom, opportunity. Make this all meaningful.*

"Five." I swallowed and wet my lips, watching the floor director count down with his fingers. "Three, two, one."

A red light on top of one of the cameras went on, and Barbara Walters turned toward it.

"We want to show you a collection of drawings which we have in the studio today," she said. "And, as you'll see, they're drawings that have been obviously executed with artistic skill and what would seem to be a fine hand. But they were drawn in a manner unlike, I believe, any pictures you've ever seen before. The artist is Joni Eareckson of Baltimore, Maryland."

Then she turned to me, and the interview began. I don't recall all I said, except that Miss Walters made it natural and enjoyable. Her questions were interesting and not at all threatening. I liked her instantly and had the feeling I knew her, that she was an old friend.

The camera also took in a display of my drawings as we talked. The interview lasted ten minutes before Miss Walters broke for station identification. Then while the affiliate stations around the country cut away for local news, she interviewed me for another five minutes for New York City viewers.

I was able to say everything I wanted to say. Miss Walters thanked me and resumed her duties with other features of the show for that day.

Eleanor McGovern, wife of the senator, was also a guest that morning. She and I talked at length after the show went off the air. She told me how her husband, George, the former Democratic presidential candidate, had discovered some of the same values and concepts that I had learned. "It was when he studied for the ministry, before he became interested in politics," Mrs. McGovern explained, and we chatted about her own spiritual values and beliefs. I gave her a drawing of Christ I'd done, and we exchanged addresses to keep in touch with one another.

As the production crew began putting things away, turning off lights and putting lens caps on the cameras, I finally had time to reflect on what had happened.

"Just think," remarked Jay, "you probably talked to twenty or thirty million people this morning about your faith. That's quite an opportunity!"

Mr. Al Nagle, president, and Mr. John Preston, vice president, of the PaperMate Division of the Gillette Company were each watching that morning. Having noticed I was using a *Flair* pen, their company arranged several national exhibits.

Many other people watching the "Today Show" that morning wrote to me.

Some wanted prints of my art work, others ordered greeting cards, and still others asked questions about my experiences.

My first exhibit sponsored by PaperMate was held in Chicago at the prestigious Rubino Galleries on LaSalle Street in the shadow of the famous John Hancock Center.

I exhibited my art and demonstrated my drawing for a week. During that time, I was interviewed by the *Chicago Tribune* and *Sun-Times*. I also appeared on the CBS-TV affiliate in Chicago. "The Lee Phillip Show."

When we returned home, again a flood of mail greeted me. I began to be swamped with requests for additional interviews. Art exhibits were scheduled for Lincoln Center in New York and Atlantic Richfield Plaza in Los Angeles. Scores of churches and Christian groups contacted me to come and speak. *Women's Day, People, Teen,* and *Coronet* magazines asked for interviews. *Campus Life* did a four-page story. *Moody Monthly* and *Christian Life* also did stories. There were more radio and TV appearances.

I could see how the Lord was going to use the "Today Show" to broaden my scope of witness and open many new doors.

Epilogue

"**W**OULDN'T IT BE exciting if right now, in front of you, I could be miraculously healed, get up out of my chair and on my feet? What a miracle! We'd all be excited and praising God. It'd be something we could confirm for ourselves. We'd actually see the wonder and power of God. Wouldn't that be thrilling?" I was speaking to an audience of 1,600 young people.

I paused as they visualized that scene. Then I continued, "But far more exciting and wonderful in the long run would be the miracle of your salvation—the healing of your own soul. You see, that's more exciting because that's something that will last forever. If my body were suddenly and miraculously healed, I'd be on my feet another thirty or forty years; then my body dies. But a soul lives for eternity. From the standpoint of eternity, my body is only a flicker in the time-span of forever."

Afterwards, someone asked me, "Do you suppose you were so strong-willed and stubborn that the only way God could work in your life was to 'zap' you and put you in a wheelchair?"

I shook my head. "In the Psalms we're told that God does not deal with us according to our sins and iniquities. My accident was not a punishment for my wrongdoing—whether or not I deserved it. Only God knows *why* I was paralyzed. Maybe He knew I'd be ultimately happier serving Him. If I were still on my feet, it's hard to say how things might have gone. I probably would have drifted through life—marriage, maybe even divorce—dissatisfied and disillusioned. When I was in high school, I reacted to life selfishly and never built on any long-lasting values. I lived simply for each day and the pleasure I wanted—and almost always at the expense of others."

"But now you're happy?" a teen-age girl asked.

"I really am. I wouldn't change my life for anything. I even feel privileged. God doesn't give such special attention to everyone and intervene that way in their lives. He allows most people to go right on in their own ways. He doesn't interfere even though He knows they are ultimately destroying their lives, health, or happiness, and it must grieve Him terribly. I'm really thankful He did something to get my attention and change me. You know, you don't have to get a broken neck to be drawn to God. But the truth is, people don't always listen to the experiences of others and learn from them. I hope you'll learn from my experience, though, and not have to go through the bitter lessons of suffering which I had to face in order to learn."

In the months after the Chicago trip, I began to see the chair as a tool to create an unusual classroom situation. It was particularly gratifying to see many young people commit themselves to Christ after my sharing with them. This, too, was "something better."

I understood why Paul could "rejoice in suffering," why James could "welcome trials as friends," and why Peter did "not think it strange in the testing of your faith." All of these pressures and difficulties had ultimate positive ends and resulted in "praise, honor, and glory" to Christ.

I quietly thanked God for the progress He had helped me make. I recalled how at the hospital a few years earlier someone had told me, "Just think of all the crowns you'll receive in heaven for your suffering."

"I don't want any crowns," I had barked back. "I want to be back on my feet."

Now my thought was, "Good grief, if I'm winning crowns, I can't wait to get more because it's the other thing I can give to the Lord Jesus Christ when I meet Him."

I am actually excited at these opportunities "to suffer for His sake" if it means I can increase my capacity to praise God in the process. Maybe it sounds glib or irresponsible to say that. Yet, I really do feel my paralysis is unimportant.

Circumstances have been placed in my life for the purpose of cultivating my character and conforming me to reflect Christlike qualities. And there is another purpose. Second Corinthians 1:4 explains it in terms of our being able to comfort others facing the same kinds of trials.

Wisdom is *trusting* God, not asking "Why, God?" Relaxed and in God's will, I know He is in control. It is not a blind, stubborn, stoic acceptance, but getting to know God and realize He is worthy of my trust. Although I am fickle and play games, God does not; although I have been up and down, bitter and doubting. He is constant, ever-loving.

James, the apostle, wrote to people who were being torn apart by lions.

Certainly their lot was far worse than mine. If this Word was sufficient for their needs, it can definitely meet mine.

At this writing, the year 1975 is just ending. I am sitting in my chair backstage at a large auditorium in Kansas City. I've been asked to speak to nearly 2,000 kids in a Youth for Christ rally tonight.

I have had several moments to pause and reflect behind the heavy curtains that separate me from the audience. My mind has roamed back through the scenes of the past eight years. Familiar faces of family and friends come to mind. Jay, Diana, Dick, Donald, my parents, Steve—people God has brought into my life to help bend and mold me more closely to Christ's image. I can, and *do*, praise Him for it all—laughter and tears, fun and pain. All of it has been a part of "growing in grace." The girl who became emotionally distraught and wavered at each new set of circumstances is now grown up, a woman who has learned to rely on God's sovereignty.

I hear the voice of YFC director Al Metzger introducing me. Suddenly the purpose of my being here is once again brought sharply into focus. In the next thirty minutes, I will speak to 2,000 kids, telling them how God transformed an immature and headstrong teen-ager into a self-reliant young woman who is learning to rejoice in suffering. I will have a unique opportunity. What I share with them may determine where they will spend eternity, so I approach this responsibility seriously.

I will talk to them about the steps God took in my life—and explain His purposes, as I understand them, to the present. In the process, I will share the concepts of God's loving nature, His character, the purposes of Christ's coming, and the reality of sin and repentance.

Al Metzger, the YFC director, is finishing his introduction now. Chuck Garriott carries my easel on stage while his wife, Debbie, wheels my chair into the glare of the footlights. As the applause dies down, I quiet my thoughts and pray for the Holy Spirit to once again use my words and experience to speak to people. Hopefully, here—as in other meetings—scores of kids will respond to God. But I will be pleased if only one person is drawn to Christ.

Even one person would make the wheelchair worth all that the past eight years have cost.

A STEP FURTHER

To Verna

(still *laying down her life*
for God and those around her)

We love and respect you

Contents

THANKS TO

Jay—for being part of the team that put this book together.

Verna—fastest fingers in the east (on a typewriter).

Judy Markham—our editor extraordinaire, the unsung hero of many books, including this one.

Elisabeth Elliot and *Margaret Clarkson*—for what they teach through example.

Dr. Richard Gaffin and *Dr. George Schelzel*—for their suggestions and encouragement.

The *congregation of Steve's church*—for "loaning him out."

Special thanks for *all those friends* who helped pray this book into being.

A Personal Note
to You . . .

HE SAT IN a straight-backed chair in a dull gray room. Although only fifty years old, Henryk looked an easy seventy. He peered into my eyes.

"I've known you for many years, but I've never met you till today," he said in broken English. "You've been a great help to many of us here. We've passed your story around to everyone in the group." Henryk wiped his hand over the tattered, worn cover of a book I halfway recognized. *Krok Dalej*, the title read. *A Step Further* . . . I had never seen it in Polish.

"We so appreciate your visiting our country. We have, perhaps, had a few tests of faith over the years."

What do I, a paralyzed person, share with a Polish clergyman who has spent the past thirty years under an oppressive regime? What do you have in common with him? What about a ninety-year-old man spending long, meaningless days in a Florida nursing home? What do you have in common with dry-breasted mothers carrying starving infants in Ethiopia? Or with a smartly-dressed wife in Southern California driving a BMW while biting her manicured nails over her ruined marriage?

The one thing that binds the entire human family together is suffering, and the questions raised by it. That's why I felt compelled to write my first book *Joni* in 1976. It catalogs my spiritual journey to accept my suffering—my paralysis—and the life God had planned for me in a wheelchair.

But *Joni* was only the beginning. My friend and spiritual mentor Steve Estes and I wrote *A Step Further* in 1978 to help answer the myriad of follow-up questions about suffering being raised in hundreds of letters. We had no idea that

God would spread the ministry of *A Step Further* to not only thousands of individuals, hospitals, and rehab centers in America, but to scores of countries overseas. In fact, Steve and I were stunned when Zondervan Publishing House informed us that more that 2,500,000 copies of our book were in print in nearly thirty languages.

That drove us to our knees. In Steve's case, literally, and in my case, figuratively! How good of God to use our combined gifts—Steve's theological background and my years in a wheelchair—to inspire and encourage so many others who knew all forms of suffering.

And the ministry of *A Step Further* continues. When Zondervan asked Steve and me to revise what they called a "classic," we were thrilled yet hesitant. On one hand, we were anxious to roll up our sleeves, update the writing style, change the illustrations, expand the theological insights, and generally overhaul the entire book. On the other hand, we had seen God use *A Step Further* over the years just as it was.

We decided to leave well enough alone—the principles of accepting God's hand in hardship have not changed one iota over time. True, Steve has changed. He is now the father of six and pastor of a growing church in rural Pennsylvania. I too have changed. Having married Ken Tada, I now throw myself into wifely routines as well as paint, write, and direct an international ministry to people with disabilities. Yes, Steve and I have changed. But as to the content of this special book, we wouldn't change a thing.

Other things haven't changed either. The chapter about "Heaven" is still my favorite. It shines with the joy I feel about going there. I still consider "Let God Be God" the most important chapter, for only when I began to get a proper view of God was I able to come to grips with my paralysis. And when people ask me questions about miraculous healing, I still recommend the section "Healing: A Piece of the Puzzle?"

One final thing hasn't changed. Steve and I still pray that you will encounter in these pages not only satisyfing answers to your questions about pain, but the tenderness and love of God Himself. After all, He knows something about suffering. He once had a Son go through a terrible ordeal. . . .

Because of Jesus
Joni

PUTTING TOGETHER THE PUZZLE OF SUFFERING

Introduction

Once again, I desperately wanted to kill myself. Here I was, trapped in this canvas cocoon. I couldn't move anything except my head. Physically, I was little more than a corpse. I had no hope of ever walking again. I could never lead a normal life and marry Dick. *In fact, he might even be walking out of my life forever,* I concluded. I had absolutely no idea of how I could find purpose or meaning in just existing day after day—waking, eating, watching TV, sleeping.

Why on earth should a person be forced to live out such a dreary existence? How I prayed for some accident or miracle to kill me. The mental and spiritual anguish was as unbearable as the physical torture.

But once again, there was no way for me to commit suicide. This frustration was also unbearable. I was despondent, but I was also angry because of my helplessness. How I wished for strength and control enough in my fingers to do something, anything, *to end my life.*

(December 1967, from the book *Joni*)

As I sit on our porch balcony overlooking the surrounding hills of our horse farm and take in all the smells and sounds of this pretty summer day, it's hard to believe I ever had thoughts like that. In fact, I almost can't remember what feeling that way was like. Oh, I'm still paralyzed—still can't walk, still need to be bathed and dressed. But I'm no longer suicidally depressed. And to be honest, I can even say I'm actually glad for the things which have happened to me.

Glad? How can that be? What has made the difference? My artwork and my supportive family and friends helped pull me out of my depression. But the heartfelt gratitude I have for this life in a wheelchair could only have come from God and His Word. They helped me piece together some of the puzzle which was so confusing. It took some seeking and studying. But today as I look back, I am convinced that the whole ordeal of my paralysis was inspired by His love. I wasn't a rat in a maze. I wasn't the brunt of some cruel divine joke. God had *reasons* behind my suffering, and learning some of them has made all the difference in the world. He has reasons for your suffering, too.

Joni Eareckson
Sykesville, Maryland
Summer 1978

&

One

We're In This
Together

WHEN I FIRST began realizing all the adjustments that being paralyzed involves, I thought to myself, *My lot in life is harder than anyone else's. How many people have the humiliation of needing someone else to bathe them? Or empty their leg bag? What other girl can't even scratch her own shoulder or comb her own hair?*

Of course, it wasn't long before I was forced to realize that many, many people face problems just like mine—or worse. Every day thousands of people in hospitals and nursing homes all around the world need to be bathed and have their leg bags emptied. Many victims of paralysis have less movement than I do. Some have lost their limbs altogether or have been grotesquely deformed by disease. Others are terminally ill. To top it off, a good percentage of these folks have families who are either unable or unwilling to care for them at home (if they're fortunate enough to have families at all).

It's a kind of scale, I finally reasoned. *Every person alive fits somewhere onto a scale of suffering that ranges from little to much.*

And it's true. Wherever we happen to be on that scale—that is, however much suffering we have to endure—there are always those below us who suffer less, and those above who suffer more. The problem is we usually like to compare ourselves only with those who suffer less. That way we can pity ourselves and pretend we're at the top of the scale. But when we face reality and stand beside those who suffer more, our purple-heart medals don't shine so brightly.

A mile from the house in Baltimore where I grew up, a beautiful children's hospital lays nestled among several acres of grassy hills and giant elms. Sometimes after school I would ride my bicycle there or kick up leaves during an autumn afternoon walk, enjoying the beauty outside, seldom thinking of the children inside. I never compared myself with them. I only stacked myself up against so-and-so at school who was prettier than I. Caught up in my life as a high school sophomore, it didn't dawn on me that my problems were nothing compared with the problems of kids who had been confined to those buildings for years. Who cared about crippled children? Or suppertime lectures from mom about starving kids in India? I had *important* things to worry about—like dates and friends and field hockey games!

But not long after my accident I underwent several weeks of operations in that very hospital. When God moved *me* a few notches up the scale of suffering—ah, then it was a different story. *Now* the sterile smells and lonely, institutional atmosphere became more than just something I'd seen on a TV medical show. A whole new world had opened up and become real to me, an unpleasant world at that.

I was eventually to come to the conclusion that *one of God's purposes in increasing our trials is to sensitize us to people we never would have been able to relate to otherwise.*

Let me share with you one reason this is so important. I have observed how people who have known deep suffering are sometimes turned off by the glowing testimonies of Christians who have had life easy. Try to imagine yourself as a terminally ill patient watching television from your hospital bed. How do you think you'd respond if an attractive and talented young Christian, with seemingly everything going for him, suddenly appeared on the screen sharing how Christ can give a person victory over all of life's trials? It would be hard to stifle thoughts like: *What does this guy know about life? He can't even imagine what it's like to really hurt. If he had to face the problems I face, he'd drop that Colgate smile and "Jesus gives you joy" routine.*

It would be nice if the Christian message could be accepted or rejected on its merits alone. But the fact is that few of us can ever divorce a product from the person who sells it.

Now I'm not saying the answer is to go out, break your neck, and buy a wheelchair so people will listen to you! Even being paralyzed I've met people who had difficulty listening to me talk about suffering. All they could see was the contrast between my good health and their chronic disease, my traveling opportunities and their confinement, my supportive family and their dead family.

What I am saying is that to reach and comfort someone, it sometimes takes a person with a similar problem. No one person can reach everyone. I can empathize with quadriplegics. You, perhaps cannot. But you can identify with difficulties I have not experienced . . . perhaps marital problems. We as Christians can usually best reach people who have suffered less than, or the same as, we, not those who have suffered more. God has placed each of us exactly where

He pleases on the scale of suffering. But remember, He reserves the right to move us up or down that scale any time He chooses in order to open up to us new avenues of ministry.

Two years ago I was sharing my testimony at a country church in Southern Pennsylvania. After the service as I sat chatting with several members of the congregation, I kept noticing a tall and rather handsome man standing in the background with his family. Eventually he eased up to my chair. "Joni, excuse me, my name is Doug Sorzano. I just wanted to tell you that I wish I could understand and appreciate what you're going through. You see, I've never known what it means to be paralyzed or face a really traumatic accident. I have a lovely wife and beautiful kids—in fact, they're right here. Let me introduce you."

Between introductions he managed to tell me how deeply impressed and excited he felt over all that had been said and done that evening. But he was honest in that he did not pretend to know and fully grasp all I had experienced. He was one who could not say, "I know exactly how you feel."

Riding home later in our van, my traveling companions and I prayed that God might use what I had said to help some people.

Weeks passed in which I busied myself with drawing, reading, and an occasional speaking engagement.

One afternoon, perhaps a month later, I received a phone call from a neighbor of the Sorzano family who had been in church that evening in Pennsylvania. She had called to let me know about "something awful that had happened."

"It was just last Saturday, Joni. Doug has always been a motorcycle buff and spent lots of his free time riding trails. And, I'll tell you, he's good. But this time he and his buddies decided to tackle a new area of the woods."

"Go on," I added hesitantly.

"Well, from what we can gather there was a quick turn in the path. Anyway, apparently Doug came up suddenly on a hidden log. The front wheel of his bike hit it, and he was thrown some distance. . . ."

I was listening intently, but my imagination ran ahead of what my ears were hearing. Scared to ask, but wanting to know, I interrupted her with a question.

"Is he . . . uh . . . that is, has he—"

Reading my thoughts, she answered me in mid-sentence.

"His neck's broken."

There was an awkward silence.

The shock stunned me and made my ears ring. I was glad she couldn't see my eyes fill with tears and my face becoming flushed and heated. Getting hold of myself, I tried to speak, but didn't know exactly what to say. All I could do finally was assure her I would call or write this family very soon and let them know I would be praying for them in this time of real struggle.

After we hung up, my memory desperately tried to scramble back and recall my brief conversation with Doug. "I've never faced a really traumatic accident,

Joni . . . have a lovely wife and beautiful kids . . . I wish I could understand what you're going through. . . ."

I later learned that this man was paralyzed from the shoulder level down, confused, and frustrated.

My sister, Jay, grabbed a pen and some stationery and came into the room to help me write a letter to Doug and his family. But what do you say to a guy who has just broken his neck? Give advice? No, not just yet. Share some Scriptures? Okay, but it sure would be good to say something more personal. What does a person really want when he's hurting? I guess he wants love . . . and to be understood. *That's it. He wants someone to know just what it is that he's going through. And I can do that.*

I am so glad that as I wrote that letter I was able to comfort Doug with real empathy. My own paralysis enabled me to walk in his shoes and see things from his point of view. It allowed me to honestly say, "I know exactly how you feel."

There is a healing balm in those words, but only if they are made believable by our own experience of suffering. People know whether or not we really understand them. They can look into our lives and see whether or not we have experienced deep anguish. If we say "I know how you feel" glibly, our words are empty, hollow statements. But if we can say it in sincerity, it can be such a comfort.

Jesus Himself came to earth partially to answer the charges that heaven's "ivory palaces" kept Him from knowing the pains of mankind. "Because He Himself suffered when He was tested, He can help others when they're tested . . . We have a High Priest who can sympathize with our weaknesses" (Heb. 2:18, 4:15 BECK TRANSLATION). If He endured hardship in order to relate to those who suffer, we can expect to do no less. Therefore, I have learned to view the breaking of my neck as a special act of God that helps me relate to and comfort people in similar conditions.* . . .

So far I have been speaking about relating to people who must cope with difficulties that are higher on the scale of suffering than ours. These are people who face death, paralysis, and bankruptcy, to name just a few. But this is not the whole story.

Some months after my accident, I started to notice that the small, everyday difficulties my friends and relatives experienced—broken fingernails, dental bills, hay fever, and dented car fenders—were every bit as real to them as my immobility was to me. It began to strike me that there is something universal about suffering. In the first place, everyone experiences it; no one is exempt. But

---

*At the time of publication, Doug Sorzano has adjusted marvelously to his paralysis. In speaking with him over the phone, I learned that he is presently sharing his faith with others who are in his condition. The Sorzanos lives in Kennett Square, Pennsylvania, and attend church at Willowdale Chapel.

in the second place, no matter how much or how little one must endure, everyone finds suffering unpleasant. An irksome housefly can momentarily rob a person of joy every bit as much as a broken leg in a cast.

And so, because everyone knows something about problems and pain, we can be certain the Bible is speaking to *all* of us when it speaks about suffering, no matter how much or how little we have had to endure. God's grace is just as sufficient for a paralytic as it is for a boy who doesn't make the baseball team. And the same godly response is as necessary to the happiness of a housewife whose cake has flopped as it is to a patient dying of leukemia.

All this tells us something important about being a help to others who suffer. Although having the same problem as someone else helps us to feel with them, we can still be of immense encouragement to those who suffer more than we do. That's because we need the same kind of grace to handle our little problems as they do to handle the big ones. Let me give you an example of this.

I live on a beautiful farm in central Maryland where we are surrounded by rolling green hills and pastures. The countryside is dotted with time-honored barns, sheds, and springhouses built decades ago.

On our farm there was such a building, a beautiful old barn erected long ago by Pennsylvania Dutch builders who obviously knew their craft. It had weathered countless storms and had seen generations come and go. My father loved the old barn, and there he made a workshop where he fashioned many original creations out of wood, leather, and metal.

But about five years ago on a summer Friday night something happened to change all of that. My sister Kathy, her husband Butch, and I were settled down in our dining room just talking and killing time, long after dinner. While Butch lazily picked his guitar, occasionally one of us would glance up at the stars through the open picture window. Outside, the chirping of crickets and other country sounds gave no sign of any disturbance. Even the distant screeching of tires along the narrow road that winds in front of our house barely captured our attention; young people do occasionally race their cars there.

But on this night, instead of passing the house and fading in the distance, the screeching stopped at the paddock of our barn. The abrupt silence brought an inquisitive look to Butch's face, our eyes met briefly, and the guitar became quiet. Kathy walked over to the window, unsuccessfully straining to see through the darkness. The only movement came from a moth flickering around the lamp.

In a moment, the car sped off.

It wasn't long before Kathy thought she could see a flicker of light . . . then another.

"Joni! Butch!" she screamed suddenly. The barn's on fire!"

Butch raced for the phone and fumbled through the directory trying to find the number of the fire department. I, of course, couldn't help but watched as Kathy dashed out the door, then down the pasture toward the barn. Butch quickly followed.

By this time the roaring blaze illuminated the whole area. Up through the old roof curled pillars of black smoke. By the time the fire department was able to get there, it was too late. Within an hour the barn was reduced to smoking ruins.

It was so sad to see my dad, a little, seventy-two-year-old arthritic man, shuffling through the smoldering ash and rubble the next day. Overturning charred objects with slight kicks of his toe, he searched for anything he might be able to salvage from the antiques and tools he had saved over the years. His only compensation was the old stone foundation. It, at least, had withstood the fiery test.

But dad didn't complain or get depressed because his beautiful barn had burnt to the ground. Instead, he jumped right in and got to work. No pouting, no second-guessing about God's purposes. Within two months dad had erected a new barn, a real testimony to his uncomplaining spirit and persevering faith.

Unbelievable as it may seem, two years later our family was forced to relive the same ordeal. Another summer night; another fire! The cause of the flame this time was unknown, but the results were the same. Again there were the sirens and flashing lights from the fire trucks. Again neighbors had to hold the horses back from running through the fences in fear. One more the intense heat kept the surrounding crowd at a distance and singed the leaves of nearby trees. And once more dad picked up the pieces and started over again, trusting that God knew what He was doing.

My sisters and I were simply amazed at our father's faith in God's sovereignty. I, in particular, benefited from observing his strength of character.

That my dad could encourage me at that point should teach us something. The financial and sentimental loss he suffered in those fires was very real. But it was less than what I suffered when I broke my neck. (If any of you doubt that, ask yourself, "Would I rather lose some material object of great financial and sentimental value or break my neck and be paralyzed for life?") Dad has never been paralyzed and, therefore, cannot say to me, "I know what you're going through." His trials measured lower on the scale of suffering than mine. But the way he handled them taught me a lot. His uncomplaining attitude and refusal to be angry at God convinced me that *a Christian does not always have to suffer in the same manner, or to the same degree, as his fellow-Christians to be a real help to them.*

Sitting at a distance watching my dad again pick through the rubble and again rebuild his barn reminded me once more that all of us fit onto a scale of suffering, some higher and some lower. God does give some of us especially difficult burdens to carry so that we can honestly say to others in the same boat, "I know how you feel." But it's also true that by being faithful to God in our lesser frustrations, we can comfort and reach even people who suffer far more than we do.

I think the apostle Paul had this in mind when he said it all so concisely long ago:

> Praise be to the God and Father of our Lord Jesus Christ, the Father of compassion and the God of all comfort, who comforts us in all our troubles, so that we can comfort those in any trouble with the comfort we ourselves have received from God. (2 Cor. 1:3–4).

Two

Body Building

Ｈ AVE YOU EVER noticed how the things in life that have the greatest potential for good also have an unusual potential for bad? Take fire, for instance, one of man's greatest discoveries. The same flame that cooks a steak can also ruin acres of precious forest within a matter of minutes—or burn down a barn. And what about sex? It, too, can be very good and very bad. Although God meant it to bind husbands and wives together, give them pleasure, and bring them children, its misuse brings guilt, heartache, and tears.

So it is with suffering. While it is God's choicest tool to mold our character, it also has the tendency to breed self-centeredness. I've wasted hours pitying myself and getting all wrapped up in imagining that my broken neck was God's way of getting even with me for my sins, when in reality He was far from being "out to get me." In fact, though at the time it did not occur to me, the whole ordeal of my paralysis was inspired by His love. And not only love for me, but love for those around me, for one of God's goals in our trials is to help us not only feel with one another, but actually build each other up.

This particular lesson was made very real to me during the winter of 1975. The pastor of a large Baptist church in Wichita, Kansas, had asked me to come and speak during his church's annual missionary conference. I accepted eagerly. For one thing, I was just beginning to travel and so the idea of getting on a plane to go anywhere to talk to anybody was really exciting. But also, it was the first missions conference I had ever attended, let alone participated in. I didn't know a great deal about missions, nor had I sat and talked at length with any missionaries. For all I knew they spent most of their time trekking through the jungles, fighting off snakes with their machetes. My traveling companions on that trip, Sherry and Julie, didn't know any more than I did. So as the three of us sat on the back row of that large and crowded church, we eagerly soaked in all we could from the missionary speakers on the program. Who knew? They might even tell some cannibal stories!

But do you know what we learned? They were people just like us! Listening to them tell of their daily struggles and victories in such far-off places as Brazil, Japan, and the Philippines made us aware of our responsibility to them. After all, though we lived thousands of miles apart, we were one with them in what the bible calls the "body of Christ." This really hit home as Christians who had escaped from Communist Rumania told the conference just how heavily believers behind the Iron Curtain count on our prayers. I so appreciated these missionaries sharing with us that I looked forward to the closing service on Sunday evening when I would have the chance to share with them in turn.

But missionaries weren't the only ones we met that week. We had sat with a number of the church's young people each night and had become close friends. So when none of us wanted to part company after the Saturday night meeting, we decided to go to an ice cream parlor together. What fun being with that group at 11:00 P.M., joking with one another!

After finishing our milkshakes and paying the bill, Sherry helped put me in my coat, and we all stepped out into the January night air. Ever since my diving accident, my body's "thermostat" hasn't worked very well, so I'm not able to adjust easily to extremes in temperature. Since the parking lot was deserted by this time, I asked Sherry to tilt the chair back and run us across to the car in order to escape the cold.

Two shadowy figures glided in the darkness across the smooth asphalt sea, whooping and laughing, navigating a course toward the distant lighthouse that was a streetlight. The dark seemed innocent enough, without hint of anything sinister. With friendly images of laughter and ice cream still dancing in our minds, what reason had we to suppose that anything but safety lay between us and the car? Who would have guessed the blackness of the night concealed a patch of ice on the pavement just feet in front of us?

A gasp escaped from Sherry as her heel slipped beneath her, causing the chair to swerve and careen up on one wheel. Face forward, I went flying into the air. Being paralyzed, I could not even use my hands to cushion the fall. Seeing the pavement rushing toward my face gave me only a split second to grimace and tightly shut my eyes.

I felt my face strike the asphalt and discovered that getting hit solidly like that can literally cause one to see stars. My body seemed to bounce on the surface and rolled near the front of our Ford wagon.

"Oh, no!" I heard Sherry exclaim.

It's strange, but when something like this happens, everything seems to go into slow motion. You hear every sound very clearly. Everything presses indelibly on your mind.

There was muffled talking. "Come on over here, Sherry." Shoes sounded on the pavement as someone led her away. A cash box clattered . . . coins rolling . . . money from my cards and drawings we had sold that night. "Ooh, she's got blood all over her face!" screamed one girl.

The young people began to crowd around now, but I had to tightly shut my eyes to keep out the blood. I remember moving my neck slightly to make sure it hadn't been broken, running my tongue over my teeth to check if any had been knocked out, moving my jaw to confirm that it wasn't fractured.

Immediately someone knelt near me and cradled my head in her hands on her lap. It was Julie. "Are you okay?" she managed. I opened my eyes just long enough to see her brush the hair out of my face; her hands were wet with blood. She kept asking me if I was okay, and I just nodded. Stifled sobs made me aware that she was trying to hide her crying from me. In spite of her tears, she felt it her responsibility to keep calm and stable.

It was just then that I began struggling with my own responsibility. Earlier that week when several of the young people had asked me what it is like living in a wheelchair, I had tried to explain how we are to face our trials without complaining. During our times together we had looked in the Bible where it says that all things, even hard things, fit into a pattern for good. Now I was being given the chance to prove all that. How was I going to respond?

And all that week those missionaries had taught me so convincingly about my duty to others in the body of Christ. *Part of that body is standing around me right now*—the realization came so clearly to my mind—*the youth group and all the others. What about them?*

But my selfish nature didn't want to be bothered with "them." It only cared about itself, old number one. And right now, old number one was freezing cold and hurting badly.

How come it's me that has to go through this? Haven't I already suffered more than most of these people standing around? Why can't God use somebody else to be the visual aid for His object lesson?

I knew such thinking wasn't right. But it's hard to put God and others above one's self, especially when you're in pain.

Who cares what everyone thinks about how I handle this situation? It's MY face that's all banged up. And why'd I have to get hurt above my neck—the only place on my whole body I can feel?!

Almost at once the Holy Spirit began taking up the challenge in answer to my questions. I was reminded of God's Word: "Do you not know that your body is a temple of the Holy Spirit. . . ? You are not your own; you were bought at a price. Therefore, honor God with your body" (1 Cor. 6:19-20).

Who cared how I responded? *God* cared. Did I really have the right to complain about my injured face? No. My body was not my own; it was God's to do with as He pleased. He bought it with His own Son's blood.

My first responsibility was to honor God by showing these onlooking friends in practice what I had shared with them in theory—that there are no accidents in a Christian's life. If God has sent something, it must be for our ultimate good.

Or the good of those around us, I reasoned. *Wow! Sometimes as Christians we're just not given any choice in the matter. If we care at all, we have to handle things God's way.*

Lying there, I knew what I needed to do. So for what seemed to be the ten-thousandth time in my life, as an act of my will, I grimaced and then quietly thanked God for what was happening. *Dear God, thanks for what's going on right now. . . . Don't let me get angry. These kids are watching. . . . Let them learn how to handle their tough times by seeing how I handle this. And please . . . You get the glory.*

Eventually, I knew, God would get glory in some way from this incident. But I hadn't realized He would begin doing it immediately. God was evident in the love and concern each person there showed for me. Everyone selflessly piled their coats on me for protection from the cold. Realizing I was still uncomfortable, one man knelt and held me close to him for warmth, whispering, "Everything's going to be all right." Others piled into the car to pray. One called for an ambulance and another notified the pastor of the church we were visiting.

The rest of that eventful night was spent getting X-rays, having my forehead stitched, and lying awake from the pain of a concussion and a broken nose. During those painful, sleepless hours I had plenty of time to think. *Thanks for not letting me fall apart, God.*

Eventually I was released and driven back to our hotel room. In the wee hours of the morning I finally dozed off to sleep with difficulty, needing to be wakened every two hours to check on my concussion.

The next morning a bit before 11:00 I was awakened by the sound of the hair dryer in the bathroom. Peeking her head around the door, Sherry asked with a hesitant smile, "How ya doin'?"

"Well, I . . . ooh. . . ." I began to answer, but the pain immediately reminded me of the spill I had taken the night before. Physically, I wasn't doing all that great. The stitches hurt, the headache throbbed, I hadn't gotten much sleep, and my face was bruised and swollen. But internally I was in an okay frame of mind. "I'm doing pretty good I guess. What's up?"

"We thought we'd wake you up in time for a little late morning TV," Julie piped in, adjusting the antenna. "The pastor told us we could catch the church service right here since it's televised every week."

So they propped me up with pillows, and we watched eagerly. After the choir anthem, the pastor made a special announcement. "We're sorry to announce that Miss Joni Eareckson had a spill last night resulting in a broken nose and a number of stitches. Last night as we talked in the emergency room I suggested she cancel her engagement with us this evening, but she insists she'll feel up to it. We're asking all of you to join us in prayer for her."

I was glad someone was praying for me. But as I leaned back on the pillows, I couldn't help but smile. After all, the *real* crisis was over—the one inside me.

Wheeling into the packed-out assembly that evening momentarily took my breath away. Chairs filled the aisles, and people were standing up in the back and scrunched in the choir loft. I decided not to use the carefully prepared notes and illustrations I had gotten together weeks ago. Instead, I shared some Scriptures that had to do with what happened the night before.

"One of the best things we can do for our brothers and sisters in Christ is to gain victory in our own trials." The small lapel mike picked up my words and projected them to the audience.

"The Book of Ephesians makes it clear that we are to care for other Christians *because* we are one with them. Believers are never told to *become* one; we *already are* one and are expected to act like it.

"You know, First Corinthians 12 says that together we Christians are like a human body, with Christ as the head. The human body is perhaps the most amazing example of teamwork anywhere in the world. Every part needs the other. When the stomach is hungry, the eyes spot the hamburger, the feet run to the snack stand, and the hands douse it with mustard and shove it into the mouth where it goes back down to the stomach. Now that's cooperation!"

Chuckles rose from the audience.

"So we can see why passages like Ephesians 4:16 tell us that we Christians affect one another spiritually by what we are and do individually. No organ in a body can act without affecting all the rest. A sprained ankle immobilizes the entire person; and the hands that catch a winning touchdown pass bring honor to the whole body. There is something almost mystical about the intricate link between us as believers. Your failures, are my failures, and your victories, mine."

No one was moving. Everyone listened intently. It was obvious that people were getting the message.

I continued, "Therefore, if we care anything about Christ—the head of the body—and other Christians—the rest of the body—we must face our problems with them in mind. God helped Julie and me do just that last night. She was an example to me. I was an example to others. God wants to do the same thing through you."

And so the Lord used my injuries from the previous night as a grand platform from which to share His all-wise plan in allowing His children to endure pain for their good and His glory.

About a year later I received a letter from Steve, written during a time when I was traveling a lot and was a little homesick. His encouraging words were an excellent summary of what I learned the night I broke my nose in the parking lot. I was reminded again that our sufferings, far from giving us a license for self-pity, give us an excellent opportunity to teach and build up others. Here is a portion of that letter:

> So, Joni, when you've got to speak ten times in one week, when your jaw gets a little tired from smiling at well-wishers, when your back aches, when you've got a secret inner urge sometime to be on your feet but feel you can't express it 'cause the folks around you would take it wrong, when you miss your friends, when the Bible seems boring, when you feel insecure, when you find sinful thoughts and attitudes creeping into your head, when you're tempted to run mental movies of your success and glory in yourself—in short . . . when you feel like carrying a smooth cross and slipping a bit, even "just for today" . . . don't. Don't be discouraged, and don't sin. And don't feel the hassle is in vain, because you honestly have got to be one of the mainstays in my life when it comes to setting an example when I feel like quitting.

We are onstage. Others are watching. We can do our part well, building up the entire audience. Or we can ad-lib by acting out our own bitter feelings and bring dishonor to the Playwright. The choice is ours.

Three

I Wouldn't Do This For Just Anybody!

W E PEOPLE SOMETIMES like to brag about how great and wonderful we are, but when we're unexpectedly given the chance to prove it, we often have trouble making good our words. A recent cartoon illustrated this in a clever way. During a college football game a middle-aged fan seated on the front bleacher kept hurling snide remarks at the coach and players on the losing team. His wisecracks were obviously intended to impress those seated around him with his prowess and knowledge of the game. When the frustrated coach finally had his fill of abuse, he turned to the stands, pointed a finger, and barked, "You with all the advice, go in for Oblonsky!" Gulp! He sure popped that fan's balloon.

Men often have to back down when challenged to support their boastful words with actions. But God, unlike our friend in the bleachers, never has to back down. In fact, because He really *is* great and wonderful. He's always looking for an opportunity to demonstrate that greatness to mankind. Human suffering provides one of the best platforms from which to do this.

Of course, the most obvious way God uses suffering to glorify Himself is to miraculously remove that suffering. Jesus went about restoring sight to the blind, healing the lepers, raising the dead, and doing all sorts of awesome things to ease human misery. Sure enough, as a result, "When the multitudes saw it, they marvelled, and glorified God" (Matt. 9:8 KJV).

But what about today? Jesus is no longer with us in bodily form, walking the hills of Judea, doing the things He once did. Though God still can, and sometimes does, step in to do things in a miraculous way, that is no longer His usual method.

Today God has a second, less obvious but not less powerful, way of using suffering to glorify Himself.

Strange as it may seem, it appears God often not only allows, but actually insures that His children undergo and endure long periods of real difficulty.[1] Not only that, but He seems to be hurting His own cause by letting this take place within plain view of unbelievers who scoff at Christianity. Not one embarrassing detail escapes the eyes of these scorners as they jeer, "Look at how this so-called loving God treats His devoted followers!"

But wait. As we continue observing, we notice something unusual. These Christians, on whom God has sent trial after trial, refuse to complain. Rather than shake rebellious fists at heaven, and rather than curse the One who allows them such misery, they respond with praise to their Creator.

At first the world mocks. "It's only a phase," they assure themselves. "Just wait." But as the trails continue and the Christians refuse to "curse God and die," the watching world is forced to swallow its own words and eventually drop its jaw in amazed disbelief.

Thus, *God has shown one of the most effective ways in which suffering can bring glory to Himself—it demonstrates His ability to maintain the loyalty of His people even when they face difficult trials.* If being a Christian brought us nothing but ease and comfort, the world wouldn't learn anything very impressive about our God. "Big deal," men would say. "Anybody can get a following by waiting on people hand and foot." But when a Christian shows faith and love for his Maker in spite of the fact that, on the surface, it looks as if he's been forgotten, it does say something impressive. It shows the scoffers that our God is worth serving even when the going gets tough. It lets a skeptical world know that what the Christian has is real.

I can recall meeting a girl some time ago at a bookstore in California who is a perfect example of what I mean. The store was situated in an affluent neighborhood, filled that day with homemakers and nicely dressed children with polished faces—a pleasant place to be. A line had formed as people waited to meet me or have their books and prints autographed.

As I took a pen in my mouth to sign someone's book, my ears caught a sound that seemed out of place in the general chattering and bustling going on around the room. Sneaking a glance over the top of the book which was being held before me, I discovered the source.

There, in a wheelchair at the back of the line, sat a seriously deformed young woman whose inability to mouth words resulted in rather loud, distorted grunting and groaning sounds. In the various hospitals where I'd stayed I had met many people whose speech was similarly affected by disease. I guessed that she was the victim of that horrible crippler known as cerebral palsy and found out later this was the case.

As she approached, I couldn't help noticing that her hands were shaking, her feet were twisted and gnarled, and she was drooling from lack of control over her mouth. Matted hair crowned her head, and an unevenly buttoned blouse suggested she was hard to dress. Her handicap had made her unpleasant to look at, to say the least.

I recalled the time when being around such a person would have made me uncomfortable. I used to want nothing to do with anyone whose handicap seemed only to underscore and remind me of my condition. But God had long ago helped me overcome feelings like that, and I was anxious to meet her.

"Joni, I'd like you to meet Nadine," her nurse introduced us as she wheeled the young woman's chair next to mine. In the conversation that followed, during which the nurse interpreted as best she could, I learned Nadine was a Christian and the same age as I. Though her physical appearance might have given the distinct impression that Nadine was retarded, she actually was an intelligent, well-read person who enjoyed composing poetry as a hobby.

That afternoon Nadine presented me with a letter expressing appreciation for some thoughts I had shared in my book. But then she gave me a real treasure—a small plaque consisting of a poem and some angels clipped from the front of Christmas cards. Nadine had cut the angels using the toes of her "good" foot to operate a pair of scissors. That was several years ago, and I still have it hanging in my home.

As Nadine was talking, my mind flipped back through the pages of philosophy and other books I had read during my days of searching and skepticism in the hospital. "Either God has the love to remove human misery but doesn't have the power," they argued, "or He has the power but not the love. Or perhaps He has neither. But He certainly doesn't have both."

You would think an argument like that would hit right to the heart of a thinking person such as Nadine. She is institutionalized in a nursing home and will probably never enjoy the comforts of living with close friends or family who care. She will probably never marry or experience any number of things the world considers essential for happiness. Why doesn't she curse her all-powerful, all-loving God for treating her so? She should be one of the most depressed persons on earth, full of despair and purposelessness. No one would blame her. At best she should be a resigned stoic, determined to bravely bear her lot in life and to stifle all emotions.

But conversing with Nadine for almost an hour convinced me that she hadn't gotten that message! Nadine knows what it means to experience the joy of the Lord, the "peace that passes all understanding." She can identify with Paul when he says, "Though outwardly we are wasting away, yet inwardly we are being renewed day by day" (2 Cor. 4:16).

And what is most interesting, she not only tolerates God—she *loves* Him. The God she has come to know is so worth knowing, so real, that she gladly and willingly endures her condition if that's what pleases Him.

Does Nadine's suffering glorify God? It sure does. Why? Because God miraculously removes it? No, her suffering glorifies God because the people who see and know her are forced to at least consider the fact that Nadine's Lord must be somebody special to inspire such loyalty. I thought to myself, *If anybody ever wants some evidence of what God's grace and power can do in a life, then they should see this woman.*

Sometimes skeptics will look at people like Nadine and try to deny that God is the real source of that Christian's inner peace. To them, all of this talk about heaven, God, and the joy of the Lord is mere escapism, a mental cop-out, a refusal to face reality. From time to time I myself have been accused of using faith in God as a psychological crutch.

When this happens, I merely point to the facts: It's hard enough for someone who's always been an indoor bookworm sort of person to adjust to a wheelchair life style. But most people agree that it's even harder for someone, such as myself, who's been very active. As a high school student I was always on the go—riding horses, playing field hockey, driving around in my sports car, doing crazy stunts. "When I was on my feet, I couldn't sit still for a minute," I often tell people. "Now I have to sit still for the rest of my life."

No mere set of dos and don'ts, no speculative religious philosophy dreamed up in my head, no belief in a vague and all-supreme First Cause, no creed about God could sustain and give me peace in this chair. And certainly such things could not make me actually rejoice in my condition. Either I must be mad, or there is a living God behind all of this who is more than just a theological axiom. He is personal, and He works and proves Himself in my life. And this has made many people think twice about Him.

I think I know what some of you who are Christians are wondering at this point: "My, it's exciting how God is using people like Joni and Nadine to glorify Himself. But I don't have any serious handicaps. My life is pretty normal. What about me?" If that's your thinking, please don't imagine that your trials need to be as traumatic as Nadine's or mine to be of real value to God. Accepting the everyday strains of life with a joyful heart can have the same effect on a smaller scale.

I think of my sister, Jay, and my friends, Betsy and Sheryl, who often travel with me. Let me tell you, these women know something about the everyday strains of life! In the first place, they care for all my physical needs, and if you've never cared for a paralytic while traveling, you don't know how much work it can be. Many mornings, in order to have me ready for an early meeting, they need to be up out of their hotel beds at 5:00 A.M. After getting themselves ready comes the hour-and-a-half-long process of getting me up, exercising me, bathing and dressing me, brushing my teeth, washing my hair, and so on.

But that's not all. Whenever we drive, I also need to be lifted out of my chair and into the car. This involves one of the girls leaning over my back and lifting my body from the waist up while another carries me by the legs. After being squeezed into the seat I need to be readjusted, positioned, and strapped in while someone folds down my collapsible chair and fits it into the trunk of the car. I'm not about to tell you exactly how much I weigh, but since I can't move myself, I can be pretty heavy dead weight! When we arrive, the process has to be reversed as I'm taken out of the car and placed back in my chair. On a recent trip to Minneapolis, Betsy, Sheryl, and Jay had to place me in and out of the car fifteen times in one day!

And there's an emotional strain they often have to put up with when we travel together. I'm talking about the insensitivity that a few people sometimes show by treating me like a queen and almost totally ignoring my sister and friends.

Arising early to get me ready, lifting me in and out of the car, being ignored by others—perhaps you wouldn't even call these things actual "trials" like Nadine's and my handicap. But when people see the way these women endure their small but real frustrations with an uncomplaining heart of love, it points their attention to God, and He is glorified.

In a sense, people like Nadine and my sister and friends are modern-day Jobs. You remember how Job was a righteous man, blessed by God with all sorts of material comforts. The praise he gave the Lord in return disgusted Satan. "He just serves You because You bless him," Satan jeered at God. "If You'd take away his family and possessions, he'd curse You to Your face." The implication was, "It's Your blessings he loves, not You, God. You're not great enough to get someone to follow You on Your own merits."

And so God allowed Satan to test Job. Job lost his money, his health, and most of his family. "Curse God and die," his wife urged him. But he refused. With unbelievable loyalty he cried, "Though he slay me, yet will I hope in him" (Job 13:15 NIV).

What a testimony! The statement speaks highly of Job, but even more highly of God who is able to inspire His servants' loyalty despite their toughest trials. It is the Old Testament equivalent of Paul's statement in Philippians: "What is more, I consider everything a loss compared to the surpassing greatness of knowing Christ Jesus my Lord, for whose sake I have lost all things. I consider them rubbish, that I may gain Christ" (Phil. 3:8).

I really don't mind the inconvenience of being paralyzed if my faithfulness to God while in this wheelchair will bring glory to Him. Have you considered the potential glory your life can give to God if, in *your* "wheelchair," you remain faithful?

Four

Unlikely Saints!

A DREADFUL SILENCE momentarily seized the great banquet hall of the renowned Fairbairn Castle. Not the slightest puff of wind rippled the colorful banners along the massive, grey stone walls. Over the huge medieval fireplace hung the royal family's coat of arms; and, as if in symbolic defiance, on the opposite wall was mounted the standard of the neighboring Duke Einar. Tension had been building for months between these two powers, and the duke's evil intention to overthrow the prince had been verbally challenged during this annual feast held for the lords and ladies of the entire kingdom.

Poised in crouched readiness on the wooden banquet table was the strong figure of Prince Eric. In his fist was clutched the pearl-inlaid handle of his sword, the weapon his father, the king, had passed on to him during these final days of the king's life. The sleek blade reflected a ray of sunlight stretching through the window in the thick castle wall. It was the finest sword in the land.

On the floor, surrounding the prince like sharks around their prey, paced three of the duke's henchmen, swords drawn, awaiting a split second to catch Eric off his guard. The prince's eyes flashed from one to the other, watching to see who would strike first.

Suddenly, the sound of steel meeting steel! Two of the soldiers rushed the prince, but he parried their blows with his sword, deftly avoiding each stab and thrusting with plunges of his own.

A stab . . . a wound . . . blood. One of the duke's soldiers fell to the floor, his sword dropping from his hand. But the prince could not take a second to glory in this partial victory; he swerved to continue meeting the other two.

Now a man was on each side of him. As he dealt with the blows from the enemy to his right, he stole a glance over his left shoulder, checking his position. But in doing so, his grip on his sword loosened slightly and the magnificent weapon was knocked from his hand.

A gasp escaped from the crowd. Ladies lining the outer wall drew their handkerchiefs to their open mouths, and each observer lost his breath in horror.

But wait! With deer-like speed the prince leaped beyond the range of their blades, pulled his dagger out of his belt, and grabbed the brass candlestick holder that decorated the table.

With two to one odds and armed with frightfully inferior weapons, he again sprang into the battle, diverting blows with the lamp and dealing them with his dagger. Ducking as a side thrust barely missed his head, he came back up, dodging the swing of his opponent, and delivered a deathblow to the heart of the second soldier.

The stunned survivor of the duke's force looked on in wide-eyed fear. He and Eric circled one another in silence. At the peak of tension, the soldier struck.

A hair-thin line streaked Eric's sleeve and turned crimson as blood seeped from the wound. The prince retreated, step after step, until he was finally pinned against the wall. His puny tools were no match for the sophisticated sword of his opponent. The blows came quicker. Soon he must fall.

Suddenly his opponent made his thrust. Eric jumped to the left, and the lunge aimed at his heart merely grazed his side and struck the wall. But before the duke's soldier could pull in his sword and resume his stance, Eric slapped the blade downward with his lamp and sent his dagger flying forward.

The soldier gripped the knife which lay buried in the flesh of his shoulder, put up his other hand as if to say, "No more," and conceded the victory to Eric. The joyful crowd swarmed around the prince and offered loud and hearty congratulations. They began to chat a song which became a classic for generations—

"With the sword of the king, Prince Eric is strong,
But the knife and the lamp prove him mightier still!"

I love to read adventure stories like this one about Prince Eric. Do you realize that the Bible is sort of an adventure story? It is the fascinating account of how the evil villain, Satan, enslaved the citizens of the Kingdom of Earth through treachery and deceit—how he usurped the authority of the rightful Ruler (who is good and just) and set up his own rival government. Furthermore, it is the story of how the good Ruler sent His only Son to invade Satan's territory, free the captive subjects, and retake the kingdom under the family banner.

If I were God, how would I have gotten the job done? Well, first I would probably pick the smartest men and women possible to be on my strategy team—the Ph.D.'s, the college professors. Then I would draft the world's sharpest businessmen and millionaires to finance the operation. My public relations people would be the most effective communicators to be found anywhere, tops in their field. To qualify even as a mere rank-and-file member of my organization, a person would have to be young, athletic, and unusually attractive.

Weak people need not apply. Those with physical defects? Forget it. People who might slow down my progress? Never. Those to whom the world is not naturally attracted? Someone who might jeopardize my reputation? No way. A man or woman whose life is filled with problems? Not on your life. I would accept only the cream of the crop.

But thank God I'm not running the world—He is! And He opens His arms wide to the poor, the sick, the ugly, the lonely, the weak, the ungifted, the unlovely, the unlikely. That's because of His great love. It's also because what's in a person's heart matters more to Him than what's on the outside.

But there's still another reason, a very special one, why God accepts and uses those He does. And the key can be found in the story of Prince Eric. Do you remember the words the people sang about him?

"With the sword of the king, Prince Eric is strong,

But the knife and the lamp prove him mightier still!"

Any struggle between a hero and "the bad guys" is interesting enough in itself. But when the hero is suddenly disadvantaged, as when Eric lost his sword, a new element is introduced. Now the hero is far more danger than before. He has less chance of winning. But if by sheer ability he overcomes in spite of the odds, he ends up twice as much of a hero because he won using weak and inferior weapons.

All through the Bible God shows us that this is exactly the way He does things to bring maximum glory to Himself. The apostle Paul told the Corinthian Christians to look around at themselves and realize that, on the whole, God called people into their fellowship who by human standards were neither wise, nor influential, nor of noble birth. He's saying that God deliberately chooses weak, suffering, and unlikely candidates to get His work done so that when the job is accomplished, the glory goes to Him and not to us. Think of it! The very weakness and problems we find so painful are just what He uses to honor Himself. We are not a pearl-inlaid sword in His hand. We are a dagger and a candlestick holder doing a sword's job!

When I first got out of the hospital in 1969, two years after I broke my neck, I was in a state of deep depression. There I was, only nineteen years old and with nothing to look forward to but a lifetime of sitting in a wheelchair. I knew in a vague sort of way that the Bible probably contained the answers for my situation somewhere between its covers, but I desperately needed someone to show me exactly where and what some of those answers were.

Even so, not jut anybody could have approached me with religious advice and expected to win my interest and respect. You understand. I had been into the high school scene—played on Woodlawn's field hockey team, was a member of the

National Honor Society, dated the captain of the football team from a neighboring high school. For someone to get my attention back then, they usually had to be sort of intellectual, athletic, or popular.

Now you'd think God would have packaged His answers for me in some tall, tanned youth director who ran a "surfboard ministry" down at Ocean City. *He* would have caught my attention. Or maybe I would have been impressed by some brainy seminary student in an Ivy League suit. Perhaps if Billy Graham had held a "Greater Woodlawn Crusade"—maybe that would have inspired me.

But no. Do you know who God sent? A tall, lanky, sixteen-year-old boy with a paper route. An unlikely candidate, wouldn't you say? By my standards, this guy really missed the mark. I mean, here was no super youth director or intellectual seminary student. He was just a teen-ager—only with a big, black Bible. But I was listening! And God used the long hours I spent with Steve Estes, a high school junior, to lift my spirits and help me understand God's Word. It was almost as though God delighted in displaying His power through another kid rather than sending some Bible scholar trained in counseling handicapped people.

Today as Steve and I think back to those early days of our friendship, we laugh and wonder at how God used such an unlikely relationship to begin turning my life around. But when you think about it, that shouldn't surprise us. He whittled Gideon's 32,000-man army down to 300 before sending them out to fight hordes of Midianites. He sent a teen-age shepherd boy, David, to do battle with Goliath, the seasoned warrior-giant of the Philistines. He gave Abraham a barren wife, Sarah, after promising him a nation of descendants as numerous as the stars of heaven. Why? So that when the Midianites were routed, Goliath had fallen, and Sarah had given birth to a son, the world would know that God, not man, had done it.

And that's where suffering comes in. It drives us to our knees in weakness and frailty. And don't we see that that's just where God wants us? For then His strength is most obvious.

If ever there was anyone who knew the value of being weak, it was the apostle Paul. In fact, he took up most of his second letter to the Corinthians to argue the fact that *God uses weak people.*

It seems there were all kinds of phony apostles running around trying to shoot down Paul's ministry and build up their own. They droned on and on, bragging about their fantastic accomplishments, glorious visions, and successful ministries.

"What about you, Paul?" they jeered. "Can you top what we've done?"[2]

So Paul answered them. "You want me to boast? Okay, I'll boast. I feel a little foolish, but here goes." As you read Paul's letter, you can almost picture these jealous rivals pulling out their check lists to see if he would measure up. But to their surprise, all he did was point to his suffering and weaknesses.

"You guys want to see what a big hit I've made? Here, let me list a few of my illustration credentials. Let's see . . . I've been spit on. I've been beaten. Maybe you'd like to hear about how much time I've spent in jail. . . . Oh, yes, I've been shipwrecked, too. The Gentiles hate me. And the Jews—they can't stand me."

He went on to list more awards and honors. "You want to know what kind of grand entrances and exits I make? Well, I was lowered in a basket out of a side window one night. I would have used the door, but some guards were waiting there to arrest me."

The climax came when Paul started talking about his visions.

"Now I know you guys have visions every other day. Let me tell you about one of mine. But it wasn't yesterday—in fact, it must have been about fourteen years ago. It was pretty exciting up there in heaven. But you'll never catch me doing what you do—keeping people on the edge of their seats listening to all the details."

He went on. "But I *will* tell you *one* thing that happened. God was so impressed with my ability to handle all of this that He gave me something else along with my vision—a thorn in he flesh to keep me from becoming conceited!"

At this point the sarcasm stopped. Looking his opponents straight in the eye, as it were, he told them what his first reaction was to this new form of suffering God had sent him.

"Three times," he emphasized, "I pleaded with the Lord to take it from me. But He said to me, 'My grace is sufficient for you, *for my power is made perfect in weakness.*'" (2 Cor. 12:8-9, italics mine).

Did you catch that? God answered Paul by saying, as the Living Bible puts it, "I am with you; that is all you need. My power shows up best in weak people."

If God's power shows us best in weak people, then why should we complain when we suffer and hurt? Instead, why not say with Paul:

Therefore, I will boast all the more gladly about my weaknesses, so that Christ's power may rest on me. That is why, for Christ's sake, I delight in weakness, in insults, in hardships, in persecutions, in difficulties. For when I am weak, then I am strong (2 Cor. 12:9-10).

Five

God's
Showcase

OUR GOD IS a wonderful God. Just one good look at the miracle of childbirth, the beauty of nature, or the complexity of the solar system can tell us that. These awesome wonders give us a glimpse of how powerful, creative, and wise He is. But God has other qualities, too, virtues men would never see if suffering and sin didn't give them a chance to show themselves.

Take His kindness, for instance. Would we really appreciate the good health He gives if none of us were ever sick? Would God's forgiveness ever grip us if He never let us feel the piercing guilt of our sins? And what about His compassion in answering our prayers? How would we learn of it if we never had any needs to pray about? You see, the problems we face highlight the mercies of our God.

But not only that—our problems also provide a showcase for the good qualities that *people* have, too. Let me give you an example.

Picture a young man who is interested in a certain girl. He has been looking for a way to show her he likes her without being too obvious. One evening he is driving home from the office when whom should he spot but this very girl, stranded beside the road with a flat tire. Fantastic! Pulling his car onto the shoulder, he eases it up behind hers, flips on the emergency blinkers, and offers his assistance.

"That's sweet of you," she responds, "but please don't bother. You're wearing good clothes. I'll just call a garage."

"Forget it," he objects, searching her trunk for the jack. "We'll have you fixed up in no time."

A few minutes later it begins to rain. He insists she wait in his car where it's dry. After tightening the last bolt and banging on the hub cap, he joins her back in his car—dripping wet and with a bit of grease on his slacks. She apologizes for causing him such trouble, but he generously brushes aside any sympathy.

"C'mon," he says, starting the car, "we'll take this tire to a station and get it patched. I'd hate to see you get another flat and not have a spare. Your car will be all right here for a little while."

After a brief pause, trying his best to sound offhand, he adds, "Say, maybe while they're fixing it we could get a cup of coffee or something."

She smiles. "I'd like that."

There you have it. What could have been more right than for everything to go so wrong! Any other time, being late, having a flat, changing it in the rain, and soiling nice clothes would have been a frustrating nuisance. But here it gave the young man a chance to show sacrifice and kindness for the girl—something he desperately wanted to do. And it gave her the chance to feel special and cared for.

That's what problems do for us in life. Though bad in themselves, they allow people to show concern and other kindness to one another. Do you remember my sharing with you about the time I broke my nose after a tumble on an icy parking lot? Seeing me shivering with cold as I lay bleeding on that blacktop, everyone removed their coats and piled them on me for warmth. We call this selflessness, and it's something we all admire. But if I had had no need, if I had not been "suffering" at that moment, there would have been no chance for those around to demonstrate that selflessness.

Also, in order to be selfless at that point, each person offering a coat had to go cold for awhile. They needed to "suffer" in order to be kind to me. If each of them had been carrying five extra coats and had loaned one of them to keep me warm, it would have proved nothing. Able to stay warm themselves, it would have meant no real sacrifice on their part. But my suffering gave them a chance to share, and their sharing caused them to "suffer" in a small, yet real, way. Suffering was a necessary part of the selflessness shown that evening.

The same holds true for nearly good thing a person can think or do. Suffering sets the stage on which good qualities can perform. If we never had to face fear, we would know nothing about courage. If we never had to weep, we would never know what it was like to have a friend wipe tears from our eyes.

But what does all of this have to do with God? When I say that suffering is able to bring out the best in us, am I singing some sort of hymn to human goodness? Not at all! By praising human goodness I'm actually praising God's goodness. For, you see, *God* is the author of every good and noble thing in the world (James 1:17). All of the love, kindness, sharing, and forgiveness that one person has ever shown to another comes ultimately from Him. We are made in His image—even those of us who don't acknowledge Him. Of course, that image is marred and tainted by sin. But it's still there, and whenever we do something good . . . we prove it!

Of all the suffering we might go through that helps us point people to God, there is one kind which seems to do it best. I am speaking of persecution. You have probably noticed how diamond arrangements in a jewelry store are usually set off with a dark, velvety cloth as a background. That is because the soft darkness of the cloth contrasts with, and enhances, the sharp lines and brightness of the gems. In the same way, when someone hurls abuse at a Christian's faith, that abuse acts as a velvety cloth. It makes the surprising love the Christian shows in return shine all the more brightly.

In the New Testament, Christians are told to love those who treat them badly. That's because our world is starving for the taste of genuine love. I'm not talking about soap-opera love where "I love you" usually means "I love me and want what you can give." I'm not even talking about "brotherly love." For "If you love those who love you, what credit is that to you? . . . Even 'sinners' do that" (Luke 6:32-33). What I *am* talking about is love that costs, love that gives until it hurts—even when it knows it won't get anything in return. In order for the world to see that kind of love, they need to see Christians who dare to follow Christ's example. And what was the example Christ set? He loved even those who flogged Him and beat Him.

> For what credit is it to bear it patiently, if you do wrong and are beaten for it? But if you do right and patiently suffer for it, it is pleasing in the sight of God. Indeed, it was to this kind of living that you were called, because Christ also suffered for you, leaving you an example that you might follow His footsteps. He never committed a sin, and deceit was never found on His lips. Although He was abused, He never retorted; although He continued to suffer, He never threatened, but committed His case to Him who judges justly. He bore our sins in His own body on the cross. . . . By His wounds you have been healed (1 Peter 2:20-24 WILLIAMS).

If Christ had not experienced real abuse, who would have seen His forgiveness? And if His punishment had been deserved, what would have been so special about the fact that He willingly submitted to it without fighting back? But as it is, His response to suffering gave the world a long, hard look at what God is like. And the result? Like Peter said, "By His wounds you have been healed!"

Some of you reading this book are Christians whose families, friends, neighbors, and business associates may not think much of what you believe. Perhaps they don't mind letting you know that either! Let me ask you something: Have you learned to view these pressures as God's answers to your prayers? Some hearts can only be melted by the warmth of real love. And the only way they'll experience that love is for someone to be nice to them in the face of their nastiness! If they treat you nicely, and you love them in return, so what? "Even 'sinners' do that." But if they treat you badly, what an opportunity! Then you can display the gem of Christlike forgiveness against the velvety cloth of suffering. God's greatness will be displayed from the platform of your problems.

Over ten years ago my friend Diana walked into my hospital ward with her Bible and tried to explain to me the things I've shared with you in this chapter. But at the time I just couldn't believe God would stoop to give me a broken neck just so He could look good. That theory made it almost seem as if He were on some kind of an ego trip.

But think about that ego trip idea for a minute. Suppose *you*—like God—were the most true, just, pure, lovely, and praiseworthy being in existence. And what if everything else in the universe that had any of these qualities got them from you? Because they reflected, to some extent, you? For that matter, suppose that without you these qualities would never have existed?

If that were the case, then for anyone around you to improve in any way, they would have to become more like you. For you to ask men to think about these good qualities would be to ask them to think about you. Their ego trips would be wrong, for then they would be centering their thoughts around sin and imperfection. But your ego trip would be glorious. Indeed, it would be the only hope for mankind, for your so-called ego trip would revolve around perfection.

So when God asks us to think about Him, He asks us to think about everything that is true, just, pure, lovely, and praiseworthy. This often requires suffering, and we think, "How awful." But actually His packages of suffering are wrapped with mercy, because He knows how desperately we need His qualities to become ours. For what if God did "leave us alone"? Suppose He never again sent any trials specifically intended to point us and others to Him. Would all suffering cease? Not on your life! It would only abandon us to a form of suffering far worse. Left to ourselves, with our sinful natures unchecked, in our greed and hate we would destroy one another.

But as it is, He screens the suffering, filtering it through fingers of love, giving us only that which works for good and which He knows will point us to Him. And He knows something else, too. He knows that if we come to know Him as Savior and Lord, we will eventually go to heaven where we will never suffer again.

※

Six

When
Nobody's Watching

Y OU MAY HAVE noticed that so far most everything I've said about our trails has to do with how our response to them affects other people. It's exciting to know that the way we handle our own problems can encourage others and move them to glorify God.

But that doesn't apply to some of you reading this book because you have little or no contact with other people. Perhaps you are an elderly person, living alone, who seldom gets out and has few visitors. Your active social life of yesteryear has been exchanged for a quieter sort of life—maybe reading, caring for a pet, or keeping up a small garden. "How can the sufferings I endure build up those around me?" you may be asking. "There isn't anybody around me!" How can your response to trials help God's cause when there is no one around to witness and consider?

Or how about those of you who rub shoulders with plenty of people all the time but have no real and intimate contact with them? Discussion about the weather, sports, and fashions may fill your day while the real issues of life, the kind that eat at you when you lie awake thinking at night, stay harbored deep inside. The mountains you face are unknown to those at work as you pass them in the hall with a smiling "Good morning." That's because there are some problems you just can't share with anyone and everyone. But then again, if people don't know about your problems, how can they benefit from watching you handle them?

Perhaps it is even more frustrating when the few people who do observe your godly response to suffering don't seem to be affected. Your example doesn't encourage them, and the sustaining grace of your God doesn't impress them.

When that happens, you feel like a political candidate who has quit his job and spent thousands of dollars to campaign for office, only to lose the election. All of that suffering for nothing!

To suffer for nothing—what an awful thought. For out beliefs, yes. For our families, definitely. For things we want, perhaps. But for nothing? What a tragedy! It makes no difference whether we're actually alone or simply lonely—if we get the feeling that our pains and sorrows are worthless and unproductive, it can drive us to despair.

If there was any person I ever knew whose suffering seemed to be for nothing, it was Denise Walters. Those of you who read my first book will remember her as one of my four roommates in Greenoaks Rehabilitation Hospital, along with Betty Glover, B.J., and Ann. A year and a half before I arrived at Greenoaks, Denise was completing her senior year as a pretty and popular cheerleader at Western High School in Baltimore. One morning she stumbled as she and some schoolmates were bouncing up a flight of stairs between classes. No one thought much about it, and her friends helped brush off her clothes and retrieve her scattered books.

"Getting kind of clumsy in your old age, aren't you?" kidded one.

"I don't know what it was," answered Denise, tilting her head with a confused look. "My legs feel kind of weak."

"It's probably that slim-down diet you're always on," suggested her best friend. "Of all people, you sure don't need to lose any weight; you look great. You could afford to eat more than just a carrot and apple at lunch."

"I guess you're right," Denise agreed, and they all went on to class.

But by the end of the day she could hardly walk. Arriving home, she went straight to bed, and when she woke for dinner her legs were paralyzed. Within a short time her arms were paralyzed, and before long she was blind—the victim of an unusual and accelerated case of multiple sclerosis.

Lying motionless in her hospital bed at Greenoaks, Denise Williams knew what it meant to suffer. She couldn't watch TV. Neither could she gaze out the window. The only way she could enjoy a book was if someone took the time to sit and read it aloud to her. As for conversation, it took real effort to speak even a few sentences. Most difficult of all, she knew she was dying. Friends did occasionally drop by, but prolonged stays in a hospital eventually weed out all but the most committed visitors. In the end, it was mainly her mom, a wonderful Christian lady, who faithfully came every night to read the Bible and pray with her dying daughter who also loved Jesus.

The amazing thing about Denise was that she never complained. You might think this was the reason God let her suffer—so people could see her patience and be turned to Him. But that just didn't happen. In the first place, very few ever saw her. Her mom and roommates were about the only non-hospital people with whom she had any contact. And even we, her roommates, only brought up topics of conversation that were so shallow they never gave what was going on inside of Denise a chance to show. As far as she knew, nobody saw or cared about her love for God and her trust in His plan. Perhaps the saddest thing was that even on a rare day when a ray of that love and trust would manage to shine through the dense fog of our spiritual blindness, it made no difference. Nobody ever told her, "I want the kind of life you have. How do I get it?" Her suffering seemed to be for nothing, like precious rainfall pattering down upon an unappreciative ocean while desert dwellers only miles away languish from thirst.

Five years after I left Greenoaks, Denise died. The news stirred mixed emotions in me. Of course, I was joyful that her pain was over and she was now with the Lord. But those long, trying, and seemingly wasted months prior to her death bothered me. I shared my uneasy feelings with Diana and Steve one night as we sat talking around the fireplace at my house. After a moment's thought, Diana was the first to speak.

"Judging from bits and pieces of things Denise said, I don't think she saw her situation as a waste," she began.

I agreed, but confessed I didn't understand why. "You knew the girls in that room, Di. You visited me often enough. Denise never got through to us."

"Maybe not," Diana replied. "But she knew you girls weren't the only ones around."

"You know what I mean, Di. Big deal. So a nurse stopped in every now and then. They were too busy rushing around to have anything Denise ever said or did rub off on them."

"I'm not talking about the nurses," Diana said, looking me right in the eye. "I'm talking about God and the whole spiritual world—you know, angels and demons. People might not have noticed, but they sure did."

Well, of course I knew God had been watching the whole time, though I'll admit it sometimes didn't feel that way. But angels and demons? I never realized they were watching, too.

Diana continued. "Jon, the Bible makes clear that the spiritual world is intensely concerned with the thoughts and affections of every human being. Why, the mind of the lowliest and most insignificant man is a battlefield where the mightiest forces of the universe meet in warfare."

Sensing that Diana was about to "wax eloquent" as she often does, I interrupted her before she got too far. "Diana, that sounds like something straight out of science fiction. Can you show me in the Bible where you get all this?"

Well, that was all the encouragement she needed. And so by the dim light of the fire and a single lamp, Diana and Steve took me through Scripture.

"Sure angels are interested in what men do," she related excitedly. Then leafing through her Bible like a tour guide who had been there before, she pointed out a verse to me. "Take a look at this." It was Luke 15:10.

"There is rejoicing in the presence of the angels of God over one sinner who repents," I read, half to myself, half mumbled aloud.

"Can you imagine?" she exclaimed. "It says there that God's angels actually get 'emotionally excited' when men choose to do what's right!"

"Do you think they're looking at us right now?" I asked, sneaking glances around the room, half-expecting to hear wings rustling behind the curtains.

"Sure," Steve spoke up. And taking Diana's Bible, he flipped over to Ephesians 3:10. "Here's another verse that proves the spiritual world has its eye on us. Catch this—God uses the way He brings Christians together and works in their lives to teach the angels and demons about how wise and powerful He is."

"I get it!" I lit up. "We're kind of like a blackboard on which God draws lessons about Himself."

So her life wasn't a waste, I reasoned. *Denise knew that although not many people may have cared, someone was watching her in that lonely hospital room—a great many someones.*

Several years after this talk with Diana and Steve, I was speaking at a church one Sunday night in the Baltimore area. In my time of sharing I briefly mentioned Denise and her admirable faith during her illness. Two women came up to the platform after the meeting and explained that they worked with Denise's mother. They said they couldn't wait to get to work the following Monday morning and let Mrs. Walters know that I had spoken of her daughter.

This was tremendous! For a long time I had wanted to get in touch with Mrs. Walters to share with her the things Diana and Steve had shared with me from the Bible, but I hadn't known how to reach her.

"When you see her," I pleaded, "please give her a message from me. Please let her know that Denise's life was not in vain. I know it seems those eight long years in that lonely hospital bed didn't count for much or do anybody any good. But angels and demons stood amazed as they watched her uncomplaining and patient spirit rising as a sweet-smelling savor to God."

Maybe some of you are like Denise—alone . . . or just lonely. But next time you're tempted to think that your response to your trials is doing no one any good, before you give up the battle, turn to those verses my friends and I discussed that evening beside our fireplace. It might help remind you that somebody *is* watching. Somebody cares. You might even find yourself listening for the rustling of wings!

＄

Seven

Breaks Us
And Makes Us

Over the centuries God's promise in Romans 8:28 has been a Christian favorite. "Moreover we know that to those who love God, who are called according to his plan, everything that happens fits into a pattern for good" (PHILLIPS). In my first book I shared how I took the "good" toward which everything was working to mean I would regain the use of my limbs, go to college, get married, and have a family. But then a friend showed me the verse that followed, and it explained the real "good" that my trials were accomplishing. "For those God foreknew he also predestined *to be conformed to the likeness of his Son*." The great Sculptor had taken in hand the hammer of suffering and was chiseling away at my character to shape it like Christ's.

I must admit that at first this whole idea of God giving me trials "for my good" and "to make me more like Christ" didn't excite me very much. I felt like a child who's about to be spanked listening to the old "This-is-going-to-hurt-me-more-than-it's-going-to-hurt-you" speech. *Yeah, sure. Where does God get the nerve to claim that He let me break my neck because He loves me so much? Some kind of love!*

I remember coming across a book by C. S. Lewis, called *The Problem of Pain* in which he dealt with that very problem—how could a loving God allow a world with so much pain and sickness? Everything he said was right on target, but one thing especially hit home. He explained that in accusing God of not being loving, many of us have taken just one aspect of love—kindness—and blown it up as if it were the whole thing. But what about the other aspects of love . . . like constructive criticism, or correction, or pushing a person to do his best? If by "love" we mean keeping another from all suffering or discomfort, then God is not always loving—and neither is a doctor who sticks a needle into the bottom of a crying infant.

Lewis went on to say that we as humans are most exacting and demanding on the people and things we care for and love the most. I knew he was right. As an artist, sketches I care little about I just leave alone, letting the mistakes go. But when I get excited about a drawing it gets "bruised and battered" with erasures and revisions. It seems God deals with us that way. For us to ask God to leave us alone and not refine us is to ask Him to love us less, not more!

> What would really satisfy us would be a God who said of anything we happened to like doing' "What does it matter so long as they are contented?" We want, in fact, not so much a Father in Heaven as a grandfather in Heaven—a senile ["old gentleman"] who, as they say, "liked to see young people enjoying themselves," and whose plan for the universe was simply that it might be truly said at the end of each day, "A good time was had by all."[3]

Okay. So God loves us. So His motive in suffering is to make us more like Christ. But how does suffering work? Is there some mystical link between problems and piety? Does being made helpless automatically make us holy? Of course, the answer is no. Just think about some of those prison cells that would be empty today if only the men and women who filled them had learned their lesson in their younger years. For some of them, the more knife fights they lost and the more often they landed in jail, the more calloused they became. Some people are like that: their trials harden them rather than teach them. But if the Holy Spirit has gotten your heart even slightly ready—well, as the old saying goes, "The same sun that hardens clay melts wax."

But how exactly does the wax melt? Is it just that trials make us go out and initiate a positive-thinking, I-can-do-it, self-help program? No. Of course, it is true that exercising our wills to try and follow Christ's example is an important part of becoming like Him. But even our best efforts fall so far short of His life that we look like a glove trying to imitate a human hand. As the glove needs the hand, so we need Christ Himself to live out His character in us. That's what the apostle Paul meant when he said, "It is *God* who is at work within you, giving you the will and the power to achieve his purpose" (Phil. 2:13 PHILLIPS, italics mine). Now that we know who it is who makes us like Christ, let's find out how He does it.

Breaks Us

Before almost any good thing can be achieved in our lives, we need to be broken. This involves losing our pride, bowing our wills, and seeing our sinful selves for who we really are. Usually when we first enter God's family, we are full of brokenness. But like a poor man who stumbles upon sudden wealth, we soon forget the pit from which we were lifted. Bit by bit pride and self-sufficiency seep back into our lives and, unlike our first few weeks with Christ, "little" sins slip by unchecked and ignored.

To keep us from totally sliding back down the spiritual hill which we've started to climb, God chastens us. When He does, we may think it's because He's given up on us and wants to "trade us in on a newer model" which will give Him less trouble. But the fact that He disciplines us proves we are His very own children, for a parent doesn't spank a child who isn't his (Heb. 12:7-8). It also proves He loves us, for wise parents spank their children if they truly love them (Heb. 12:5-6). Someday when we stand before God's throne to receive our rewards for the lives we lived as Christians, imagine how glad we'll be that God didn't just let us get away with all our sinfulness while still on earth!

Now just as a mere stern glance from dad will send one child in a family running in tears to his room, while with another child dad must use a belt, so God must use different means to produce brokenness in His various children. Sometimes the mere pangs of a guilty conscience are enough to bring us low—hearing a convicting sermon or feeling our mediocrity in comparison with the life of a great Christian we've been reading about. Other times it may take a broken arm, financial pressure, or embarrassment.

Whatever the method, when the crunch first comes we may stubbornly think to ourselves, "I can handle this. Nobody's going to get me to bend." But as God continues to forcefully press, we begin to realize that we can't handle it, that there is no good thing within us, and that He intends to root out all of ugly Self and replace it with His character. But remember, replacing our sin with His righteous character doesn't make us robots or less than ourselves; it frees us to be all that we were really meant to be.

It took a broken neck to back me into a corner and get me thinking seriously about the lordship of Christ. But, like everyone else, I still need refining. Having to wait for someone when I'm thirsty for a glass of water, or wetting a friend's car seat when my leg bag springs a leak are two of the methods God sometimes uses to keep me in spiritual shape. But very often His tool will be a guilty conscience, one of the more effective weapons in God's arsenal of suffering.

God used this weapon on me one night about a year ago as I lay in bed talking with my sister Jay. We were commenting about how her daughter Kay was growing up to become quite a young lady for a twelve-year-old and how excited we were that she was attending a Christian school and growing in the Lord. That led us to think about the spiritual condition of our neighbor Kathy, Kay's best friend. Kathy was always popping in and out of our house—bubbly, enthusiastic, a cute girl like Kay. We had never really talked to Kathy about the Lord since it was hard to catch her either alone or sitting still! So one evening, a few weeks before, we had invited her down to watch Billy Graham on television. As we all sat around the living room eating pretzels and watching, Kathy had really listened. After the message she said to no one in particular, "Boy, if I was in that arena I'd go forward." Jay and I caught each other's eye, but before we had a chance to talk with her she had to go home.

I knew I should be the one to follow up on that evening because if she'd listen to anybody, she'd surely listen to me. Kay had told me that Kathy had read my book, and I knew she liked me. She was always quick to get me a glass of water and do little things for me. She had even confided to my sister Jay that she thought I was one of the neatest people in the world. But the next day Kathy had to visit with her relatives. The day after, I was busy with something else, and as the month wore on I didn't seem to have the chance to talk with her. My mind was filled with all the speaking responsibilities I had in the coming weeks, and Kathy got placed on the back shelf.

Well, on the evening I lay talking with Jay, I had just gotten back from one of those speaking trips. I was tired in body and mind and felt like relaxing and not discussing anything heavy. But coming out of the bathroom still combing her hair, Jay asked me in all innocence if I'd ever talked to Kathy about the Lord.

"No, I haven't talked to Kathy about the Lord," I mumbled as I tried to shut her out and continued staring at the late news on TV. But a slight stab of conscience wouldn't let me pay attention to what was on the screen.

To shift the blame, a minute later I let drop, "Why haven't you talked to her?"

"Come on, Joni," Jay replied, "you're closer to Kathy than I am. Besides, you know how she looks up to you."

By this time my pride was beginning to hurt, my defenses were up, and I quickly got stubborn. "I just haven't had time," I snapped.

"Whoa!" Jay exclaimed. "You have time to fly all over the country giving out the gospel, but no time for your niece's best friend?"

Well, that did it. "How come everybody thinks I'm supposed to be Miss Win-the-World all the time?" I sputtered in pride and anger, and then went on to huff and puff in my defense.

But as soon as I had finished my "speech," the arrow of conscience struck my heart. Not being able to get up and leave the room, I slammed my eyes shut and turned my face away to bury it in the pillow. Inside, my heart was burning as hot as the tears which stained my cheeks. I hated to admit it, but I knew Jay was right.

After the lights in the room were out for the night, a small projector inside my head began to run mental movies of all the time Kathy and I had spent together when she was adjusting my drawing easel, emptying my leg bag, or giggling to me about her boyfriends. There were plenty of times I could've talked more seriously with her. Needless to say, my spirit was crushed and my pride was broken. More than that, I got a full glimpse of how wretched I was in the light of God's glory.

God must really be angry with me right now, I thought to myself. But as I churned that idea over in my mind, I knew it wasn't true. The verse in Ephesians popped into my mind—where we're told not to *grieve* the Spirit of God (Eph. 4:30) *I guess that's it. He's not angry with me; "hurt" is more the word.*

I remember a sermon I had heard once on just how thoroughly Christ dealt with our sins at His death. "When Jesus was sweating and suffering on that dreadful cross outside the walls of Jerusalem," the pastor had said, "it was as if God accused Him with flaming eyes: 'Jesus, why did You tell that lie? Why did You hate Your neighbor? Why did You cheat, lust, and covet? I am punishing You here for all these things!' Of course, Christ had never done one of them, but we had, and every single one of your sins and mine was put on His account there."

I remembered, how unjust it had seemed for Christ to be treated so. The preacher continued: "Suffering as though our sins were His own, He underwent the indescribable horror of having to cry, 'My God, my God, why hast Thou forsaken me?' And do you know why? On that day God forsook His own Son so that our sins could be totally erased and, in contrast, He could say to us, 'I will *never* leave you or forsake you.' If you have made Jesus Christ your Lord and Savior, dear friend, all God's anger for your sins has been poured out on Christ. He has none left for you."

No anger left for me! It made me feel so ashamed I could hardly stand it. The goodness of God was, indeed, leading me to repentance (Rom. 2:4). *God,* I breathed silently, *here I am flying all over the place to tell people about You, and yet I've never really talked to my next-door neighbor, Kathy. Oh, please forgive me for being so blind and for hurting You so. Forgive me for putting my own convenience above the value of Kathy's salvation. And thank You for loving a vermin like me.*

In case you're wondering, I imagine a vermin to be any disgusting little creature that slithers along the ground, eats dirt, and deserves to be stepped on! David had the same feeling when he said in Psalm 22 that he was no man but a worm. Unlike a snake that will rear up its head and hiss and strike back, worms can't defend themselves. They know who they are and that they're about to be crushed. I felt that way that night. I understood there was no good thing within me. I was a broken person, and that's right where God wanted me.

Little did I realize it, but in making me broken, God was making me more like Christ, for Christ Himself was the prime example of a broken man. Not that Jesus ever had a stubborn, sinful character in need of remodeling. Nothing of the sort. But in leaving heaven's glories to become a man, He demonstrated the kind of submission to the Father that we can have only by becoming broken. In fact, that's what brokenness is all about—realizing what little right we have to run our own lives and, therefore, submitting ourselves to God.

Our attitude should be the same as that of Jesus Christ:

Who, being in very nature God,
   did not consider equality with God
      something to be grasped,
but *made himself nothing,* taking the very
   nature of a servant,
      being made in human likeness.
And being found in appearance as a man, he
   humbled himself
   and *became obedient* to death—
      even death on a cross! (Phil. 2:5-8, italics mine).

What character Christ has!

Andrew Murray once mentioned that as water seeks to find the lowest level and fill it, so God seeks to fill us with the character of His Son when we are emptied, broken and low. When you think about it, that in itself is enough to give us real hope that even our most difficult sufferings are worth it.

Speaking of being filled, how filled I was with a godly joy and excitement as Kathy and Kay came bounding into my bedroom the next morning. I don't think I've ever been so glad to see someone in my life. After talking with Kathy about the Lord for only a few minutes, it was obvious the Holy Spirit had already done His work as the "advance man," softening her heart and opening her mind.

As we bowed our heads and she prayed in simple words for Christ to come into her life as Savior and Lord, I couldn't resist the urge to peek up at her for a moment. *You know, God,* I smiled inside, *being broken hurts for a while, but it sure is worth it in the end.*

No discipline seems pleasant at the time, but painful. Later on, however, it produces a harvest of righteousness and peace for those who have been trained by it. (Heb. 12:11).

Gets Our Minds on Spiritual Things

Chastening is valuable, but there are other, more positive, ways God uses suffering to make us like Christ. For instance, take the way a good father deals with his nine-year-old son. Of course, whenever the son gets out of line and disobeys, dad disciplines him. But even when he's good his father assigns him certain tasks that often, to a nine-year-old, seem like punishment and are just as unpleasant. Maybe his job is to take out the garbage twice a week or cut the grass; perhaps he has to put part of his allowance into the bank. Whatever, the boy might think to himself, "Just because dad has to work all day he doesn't want me to have any fun either." But that's not it at all. The wise father is training his son to be responsible so that when he grows up he'll be ready to face the world.

At times we are like the nine-year-old boy. We imagine God is making us suffer because "He doesn't want us having any fun," when what He's really doing is getting minds off the toys and games of this world. Colossians 3:1-4 talks about this when it says we are not to set our affections on the passing things of this earth, but are to set them on heavenly glories above where Christ is seated at the right hand of God.

When I was on my feet, I found it extremely difficult to set my affections in heaven. I was far too interested in the glittering things of now, caught up with dating the right guy, driving the right car, getting into the right college, and being seen with the right crowd. But when it finally hit me that I would never again walk, dance, swim, ride, play guitar, drive a car, or score a lacrosse goal, I was *driven* to start thinking about heaven. Not because heaven suddenly became an escape or some sort of psychological cop-out. But because I began to realize that my only true hope for any permanent happiness lay there. Suddenly, Bible passages about God's purposes in suffering that had seemed so boring before held my attention; I read with greater interest than a stockbroker reads the Dow-Jones averages.

By now, living each day in the light of eternity has become such a way of life for me that I almost forget what the old way of living and thinking was like. But God gave me a reminding glimpse not long ago.

A group of friends had come over to our farm that evening, and while my sister's husband picked his guitar we all sat around talking, laughing and singing by the light of the crackling fire in the huge fieldstone fireplace. Our rustic living room is well over 150 years old, a converted slaves' quarters with ceiling beams my dad put in from an old clipper ship and two-feet-thick plastered walls spotted with dad's rugged paintings of scenes from the old West. The handwoven Indian blanket hanging opposite the driftwood which stand guard over the mantle gives the final touch of atmosphere to this cozy hideaway.

Because I feel comfortable in my wheelchair, usually I just stay in it while others settle themselves onto the couch or in an easy chair or perhaps down on the rug with their backs against the wall. But tonight one of the guys had seated me on the couch beside my friend Betsy. After she had crossed my legs for me, I look so "normal" that, except for my arm braces, anyone coming in who didn't know me would never know I was paralyzed.

For a while I just sat back and took in everything going on in the room—laughing and clapping and singing. Then Betsy turned to me and asked how I felt being on the couch.

"You know what's really interesting?" I answered, thoughtfully, scanning the room again and then glancing over at her. "In the short time I've been in this position on the couch, maybe forty-five minutes, I can see how easy it would be for me to forget God if I were on my feet."

You see, sitting on that couch looking very un-paralyzed had made it easier for me to imagine myself doing things like getting my own glass of Coke out of the fridge, putting on a record, answering the door, or any number of things a normal person can do. I could also see how easy it would be, for me at least, to again become so wrapped up in the little things of "now" that God would soon get only a token of my thoughts.

When you think about it, a lot of us would never have thought about God in the first place had He not used some problems to get our attention. "God whispers to us in our pleasures, speaks in our consciences, but shouts in our pains: it is His megaphone to rouse a deaf world."[4] We would have gone comfortably right through our lives, scarcely giving Him or our eternal destiny a passing thought— until we got there. And God mercifully puts pain and suffering in front of us as "blockades on the road to Hell."[5]

Paul and Timothy once mentioned that God had sent them some extremely difficult trials just so they would not rely on themselves but on God (2 Cor. 1:8-9). I could relate to those verses that evening. My chair, because it is visible, is a constant reminder of how much I depend upon Him. A sudden pain inside my back, a corset that breaks, or a battle with bedsores—all remind me how disabled I really am. They are the special marks of God's ownership of me. They get my thoughts and hopes on heaven. They make me more like Christ.

Forces a Decision

Do you like to have your cake and eat it too? I sometimes do, and I'm probably not alone. Like the man who enjoys the weather of Florida but has a terrific job offer in New England, all of us are at some time faced with the crisis of having to decide between two worlds when we would dearly love to live in both.

There is no one who can appreciate this difficulty of deciding between two opposing desires more than the believer in Christ. On the one hand, the Holy Spirit helps him to love God and desire what is right. But on the other hand, his Christian commitment is constantly challenged by the lure of his own sinful nature. He would love to live in both worlds, but he must decide.

When it comes to the "big" sins like murder, drunkenness, or adultery, many of us have no trouble deciding to obey Christ. But it's the so-called "little" sins we try to hang onto, sins like worrying, complaining, or bitterness, that keep us with one foot in the kingdom and one foot in the world. Because these sins aren't as obvious as others, we would probably never really deal with them if God didn't force us. But since "little" sins are big to God, He does force us, and the method He uses is—you guesses it—suffering.

As you might imagine, worrying, complaining, and bitterness were often temptations to me as I struggled with the meaning of my paralysis in my early hospital days. Deep inside I knew they were wrong. But in my mind I justified myself by saying, "Surely God won't mind if I let off a little steam every now and then. I mean, after all, I *am* paralyzed!"

To make things worse, several months into my hospital stay I learned that I had to have an operation on the lower tip of my spine. The bone had been protruding through the skin and needed to be shaved. After the surgery I was forced to lay face down in my Stryker Frame for fifteen days while the stitches healed. Unless you've experienced it, you can't imagine what it feels like to be strapped in that awful canvas sandwich, face fitted into an opening that allows you to see only what's straight ahead. And in my case, that was the floor. *Boy, it's not enough that I've got to live life from a wheelchair; now I'm strapped on this torture rack counting tiles on the floor and can't move anything at all!*

If God had let me get away with this I would have been the loser—digging myself ever deeper into that miry pit. Nor would I have been of much use to Him. So what did God do? He added still another problem! During the first day of my two-week career as a slab of baloney in a canvas sandwich, He "mayonnaised" me with the Hong Kong flu! Suddenly, not being able to move was peanuts compared to not being able to breath comfortably. And those pounding headaches!

Why? I complained angrily. *Haven't I had enough?* But as I thought about it, I knew why. God was forcing me to open my eyes to what I was doing. No longer was my bitterness a tiny trickle; it was a raging torrent that could not be ignored. It was as if He were holding my anger up before my face and saying lovingly but firmly, "Stop turning your head and looking the other way. See! This is what you're doing. It's a sin. What are you going to do about it?" He was forcing me to make a decision.

At that point, God had me backed into a corner, the kind of corner we all need to be backed into sometimes. I had to face the facts and make a decision: Was I going to follow Christ in this thing or not? The pressure had gotten so strong that I was either going to have to give the situation over to Him completely or allow myself the short-lived luxury of totally wallowing in anger and bitterness. Either route would give some immediate sense of release, but they were two different medicines which couldn't be mixed. There could no longer be any middle ground.

When I was faced with that kind of ultimatum, it helped me see clearly what an evil, wicked course the alternative to following Him was. I came to realize that *if I was to be a true disciple of Christ, it was going to cost me my sins.* Were they worth more to me than my fellowship with God? *Of course not,* I decided, and breathed a prayer of repentance toward God. And as the steamy vapors rising from the hot basin beneath the frame cleared my head, I knew in my heart that my obedience to God was rising as a sweet-smelling vapor to Him.

When God brings suffering into your life as a Christian, be it mild or drastic, He is forcing you to decide on issues you have been avoiding. He is pressing you to ask yourself some questions: Am I going to continue trying to live in two worlds, obeying Christ and my own sinful desires? Or am I going to refuse to worry? Am I going to be grateful in trials? Am I going to abandon my sins? In short, am I going to be like Christ?

He provides the suffering, but the choice is yours.

WHILE WE'RE WORKING ON THE PUZZLE

꽃

Eight

Trust
And Obey

ONE OF THE special joys I remember about being on my feet was horseback riding. And what made riding so special was Augie, an old sorrel thoroughbred who knew everything there was to know about jumping. Now Augie certainly didn't look like a Class A thoroughbred. His long legs and thin body resembled the frame of an adolescent boy whose weight hadn't yet caught up with his height. That, coupled with his large head and Roman nose, made him too ugly a candidate to ever win any beauty contest. But he certainly knew how to jump fences, and at just about every horse show we would enter, Augie came away with the blue ribbons in all the open jumping classes.

In addition to the marvelous way he could pace himself, the exciting thing about Augie was the instant obedience and absolute trust he showed toward me. Whenever we entered a show ring he would quietly dance and prance in one place, never pulling on the reins, ears flicking backward and forward in anticipation of my command. I never had to tug his head; I just held his snaffel bit firmly against his mouth, keeping the reins low and taut. Whenever I wanted him to move ahead, all it took was a slight tightening of my knees against him and—flash! Off he would go!

Augie would confidently canter to the first jump, fly swiftly over it, and then flick his ears again, awaiting my directions for the next move. Over the second fence he would fly, then the third, fourth, and fifth, leaping through a complex maze of fences. Almost never did he shy away from a jump at the last second. After we would finish, Augie would be hot and lathered, and I often felt as I patted his shoulder that he was as pleased with his performance as I was.

Maneuvering a complicated jump pattern requires a trusting and obedient horse. After completing a fence, the rider has to pull the horse up so he won't tire himself and so he can properly pace himself for the next fence. If the horse doesn't listen, they're both in trouble! Feeling the horse begin to shift his weight a few feet from the fence, the rider must know when to release the reins and give the horse his head so he'll be able to jump cleanly and clearly. The horse must trust his rider to do this. It's a two-way street; there must be real cooperation.

Augie and I had that kind of relationship. I knew his trust in me was absolute and complete. At my command he was eager to obey in an instant. It was the joy of Augie's great heart to do my will. It did not matter whether or not he understood the course of jumps before him. He showed no concern over how hard those four-foot rail jumps or five-foot triple spread jumps appeared. He simply loved to do my will.

For us humans, the path of life set before us often seems like a confusing maze of difficult, and sometimes painful, fences are expected to hurdle. The more perplexing the pattern grows and the more demanding the discipline becomes, the more we are tempted to doubt the wisdom of our Rider. We feel like disobeying by balking at the jumps and avoiding the course.

The apostle Peter knew about this when he wrote his first epistle. His readers lived during the reign of the madman Nero and knew what it was like to have the threat of a torturous death hanging daily over their heads. Of course, Peter assured them that a great reward awaited them in heaven. But what were they to do in the meantime? How were they to respond *now* to the overwhelming and perplexing course before them? Peter advised them this way: "So then, those who suffer according to God's will should commit themselves to their faithful Creator and continue to do good" (1 Peter 4:19).

Committing ourselves to our faithful Creator—that's *trusting* God. Continuing to do good—that's *obeying* Him. If you grew up attending church, you've probably sung that old hymn "Trust and Obey" many, many times. According to Peter, we couldn't find a better summary of what God expects of us when the hurdles are difficult and the pattern doesn't seem to make sense.

Trusting God

When you think about it, Augie's response to me didn't hinge on his approval of the course set before him. As a matter of fact, he didn't know or understand what was set before him. What counted was that he knew me. For years I had fed him, brushed him down, given him exercise, and led him to shelter away from the cold. We had built a relationship, and I had proven myself to him over and over again. By demonstrating myself trustworthy, I was able to so win Augie's confidence that he followed me in whatever I asked.

That same type of relationship built on trust was the key factor in saving our horses' lives several years ago. During the incident I mentioned earlier when someone set fire to my father's barn, our first thought was for the safety of the horses. Since fire can cause an otherwise calm horse to go wild with fear, we covered their eyes with blankets before leading them past the roaring flames and out to safety. Such an ordeal must be an unsettling thing for a horse. With so much noise and commotion surrounding him and the strange smell of smoke clogging his nostrils, one would imagine that then, of all times, a horse would desire the full use of his senses and faculties. But here these humans were covering his eyes with a blanket that ordinarily went on his back and asking him to follow them when he could not even see. To the horse, in the words of C. S. Lewis, "the whole proceeding would seem, if it were a theologian, to cast grave doubts on the 'goodness' of man."[6] But fortunately our horses weren't theologians; they were horses. In that confusing moment when they could not understand, they trusted us to care for them as we had always done. There was no rebelling, no challenging of our wisdom or authority, and as a result we were able to save their lives.

How unlike these simple animals we are! They put tremendous confidence in their masters, mere human beings, yet the great God who has chosen to save and redeem us at such a precious price does not have our trust. "An ox knows its owner, and a donkey its master's manger, but Israel does not know, My people do not understand," marveled the Lord in Isaiah 1:3.

What causes this senseless lack of faith? It is our failure to realize just how much God has already done to prove Himself to us. We really don't know who our God is and what He is like. The men and women of the Bible considered God's character and nature to be the rock foundation on which their faith rested. "This I recall to my mind, therefore, I have hope," Jeremiah reminded himself amid the horror and confusion of the Babylonian invasion of Israel. "The Lord's loving kindnesses indeed never cease, for His compassions never fail. They are new every morning; great is Thy faithfulness. . . . Therefore, I have hope in Him. The Lord is good to those who wait for Him" (Lam. 3:21-25). Jeremiah chose to depend on what He knew to be true about God from the Bible and from history instead of relying on his own assessment of things.

The apostle Paul's confidence during trials was not based on the assumption that he could say, "I know why this is happening to me." Rather, it rested on the fact that he was able to say, "I know whom I have believed" (2 Tim. 1:12). The God he trusted was the One why, by His own power, had set the sun, moon, and stars in motion. It was He who, in infinite wisdom, had ladled out the sea, dreamed up space and time, formed the mountains, carved out rivers, scattered rain and hail, and conceived in His mind our very existence. But for Paul, the supreme demonstration of the wonderful nature and character of this great God was when He laid aside His Divine splendor, took upon Himself the form of a servant, and died a martyr's death for us. "He who did not spare his own Son, but gave him up for us all—how will he not also, along with him, graciously give us all things?" (Rom. 8:32).

If God has done *that*, surely He has proved His intentions! When He covers our eyes with the blanket of a limited understanding, surely He deserves to be given "the benefit of the doubt," to put it mildly. He is worthy of our trust.

> The Hands that shaped the flaming spheres
> and set them spinning, vast light-years
>   away from Planet Earth,
> have laid aside the Robes of State,
> donned human likeness by the great
>   indignity of birth.
> The Hands, responsive to Love's Plan,
> that formed the God-reflector, Man,
>   of dust and destiny,
> outstretched—by Man's fierce hate impaled—
> wrought life anew, Love's Plan unveiled
>   upon Golgotha's Tree.
> The Hands that found it nothing strange
> to pucker up a mountain range.
>   or ladle out a sea,
> that balance Nature's systems still,
> and shape all History to His will,
>   hold, and are molding, *me!*
> —Marion Donaldson

What Is Trust?

When I speak of having faith in God during our times of suffering and crises, I am not talking about an emotion. Trusting God is not necessarily having trustful feelings. It is an act of the will. *Because essentially, trusting God is reasoning with yourself to act upon what you know in your head to be true, even though you do not feel like it is true.*

In those first months after my injury, the promises of God seemed anything but true. To my way of thinking, God was insane. How could this crazy paralysis possibly fit into a pattern of good for my life? I felt as though the despair of my soul was as bleak as the gray hospital walls which surrounded me. Even after I was able to return home, trusting the Lord seemed impossible. How could I be expected to believe when everything inside and outside of me screamed just the opposite?

The answer came on one of those long and pleasant evenings when Steve,

Diana, and I were sitting around my parents' living room fireplace discussing spiritual things. Steve had his Bible and was explaining a passage he had just studied that week. Opening to chapter twenty of John's Gospel, he began reading where it described the disciples several days after Jesus's burial, hiding from the Jews in fear behind locked doors. Suddenly, Jesus appeared in the middle of the room and assured the astonished men that He had indeed risen.

For some reason Thomas was out when it all took place, and upon returning to the room later, he failed to find the excited report of his fellow disciples convincing. "Unless I see the scars in His hands and side, I will not believe it," he protested.

One week later in the same house, again with the doors locked, Jesus appeared once more to the huddled group. Only this time Thomas was there. The Lord addressed him, "Come here, Thomas. See My hands for yourself; touch My side. Stop doubting and believe."

Faced with the visible evidence, the only response the amazed disciple could give was the confession of worship, "My Lord and my God!"

Steve leaned forward just a bit more to add intensity and then read slowly from verse twenty-nine, directing its content right at me. "Then Jesus told him, 'Because you have seen me, you have believed; *blessed are those who have not seen and yet have believed*'" (italics mine).

The verse hit me with the force of a truck. Jesus wanted me to believe what He said without having to have tangible or visible proof. Sure, He could appear visibly right in my room. That would make believing so easy. But He wanted me to take Him at His word. Didn't I like to be taken at my word? Hadn't it felt good when the local store clerk would let me off if I was a few nickels short, saying, "Pay me next time. I know you're good for the money"? Didn't Jesus want to be treated the same way?

It took some gut effort, but from that time on whenever I had doubts, I reasoned to myself from the things I knew in Scripture about God's trustworthy nature. And I still have to do that sometimes. Feelings or no feelings, I cling to Jesus' words that in heaven I will be rewarded, not because I have seen and believed, but because not seeing, not feeling, I have *still* believed. By taking God at His word, sight unseen, you and I have the privilege of honoring God and of being commended in a way the twelve disciples never could be.

Obeying God

When god allows us to suffer, sometimes our tendency is to use our very trials as an excuse for sinning. We feel that since we've given God a little extra recently by taking such abuse, He owes us "a day off" when we can do as we please. This is a continual inner battle for me. I'll be sitting out on our porch on a beautiful spring day when suddenly the reality of my confinement will hit me hard. A little lustful fantasizing is sure inviting then, or maybe a few minutes of bitterness and self-pity. And it is so easy to justify. *Don't I already have to give up more than a lot of Christians just by being crippled? I say to myself. Doesn't my wheelchair entitle me to a little slacking off now and then?*

When we feel like this, if we sit down and examine our lame protests in the light of the Bible, they will vanish one by one. I have discovered in the Bible at least three good reasons why suffering does not give me any excuse to sin.

First, *God has promised that He provides for me, and for every other Christian, the desire and power to do what's right—no matter what the circumstances!* I used to think my trials were an exception—that He couldn't expect from me what He did from others because it was "a different story" in my case. But 1 Corinthians 10:13 told me, "No temptation has seized you except what is common to man."

It always seemed to me as I lay in my hospital bed that God was putting me through more than I could take. But 1 Corinthians 10:13 told me, "God is faithful; he will not let you be tempted beyond what you can bear."

Sometimes when lust and bitterness would lure me, I reasoned within myself, "There is no way I can say 'No' to bitterness and break free of sin's clutches this time." But, again, 1 Corinthians 10:13 told me, "When you are tempted, he will also provide a way out so that you can stand up under it."

Now either I was right or He was right. Faced with a choice like that, I knew I just couldn't call God a liar. So when I sin during my sufferings, it's not because I have to. It's because I want to. God gives me grace to live in a wheelchair which He doesn't give you if you can walk; but He gives you grace to endure the death of a husband, the loss of your hearing, the plight of poverty, or whatever, which He doesn't give me. Each of us needs to use the grace of God gives and to bear up faithfully under our own unique burdens.

Now that I knew I *could* obey, the question to be answered was—*would* I? This brought up the whole issue of the lordship of Christ—the second reason why I have no excuse to sin. *Before any of us ever "sign up" to follow Christ, He makes it clear that He is to be the Master and that following Him will require some real hardships for us.* There is no fine print in the contract. What we are getting into is plainly spelled out in His Word from the beginning—"If anyone would come after me, he must deny himself and take up his cross and follow me," He tells us. "No one who puts his hand to the plow and looks back is fit for service in the kingdom of God" (Mark 8:34; Luke 9:62).

Besides all of this, it is absurd to use suffering as a reason for sinning, when *suffering's very purpose is to turn us from our sin and make us like Christ.* Peter said that the person "who has suffered in his body is done with sin. As a result, he does not live the rest of his earthly life for evil human desires, but rather for the will of God" (1 Peter 4:1-2). During my stay in the hospital I met many people who wouldn't have given God the time of day when they were healthy. But a good splash of ice-cold suffering sure woke them out of their spiritual slumber. How silly to use something that was meant to wake us up as an excuse to doze off spiritually.

But wiping out my excuses for disobeying God wasn't all that the Bible did for me. It also gave me some exciting positive incentives *to* obey. Like joy, for instance. What gives more heartfelt joy than having a clear conscience, knowing that you haven't brought on your own troubles? And even when those troubles are your fault, by starting to obey again, you know that you've taken the first step in getting out from under the rod of correction. To top it all off, we know that "Blessed is the man who perseveres under trial, because when he has stood the test, he will receive the victor's crown" (James 1:12).

One final thought. Obeying God's command to love others is one of the most difficult things we ever have to do while suffering. Our own needs, pains, and griefs scream for our undivided attention. Yet giving in would do nothing but hurt us, for often healing only comes when we get our minds off ourselves and show concern for others and their cares and interests.

Recently, at a wedding shower for my friend Sheryl, I was having anything but a good day. My back ached, my corset was too tight, and the two got together and made my head throb. I've got to admit that my conscience wasn't treating me all that nicely either. It kept reminding me of a few things I'd said to a member of my family that morning, even though I had confessed those things to God. And looking around at all those smiling faces didn't help things much. *I should be happy today. After all, Sheryl's one of my best friends, and this is her special day!* About all I could do was work up a polite smile and hope nobody would corner me in conversation.

Staring blankly ahead, I was looking at, but not really noticing Pop Bond—Sheryl's father-in-law-to-be, the only man at the shower. Oblivious to the girlish chatter, Mr. Bond was picking his way around boxes and presents, snapping photos from this angle and that. But when he began to zoom his lens in on me, he stopped being a blur in my vision and suddenly came into focus.

"Oh, no," I protested. "Please, not me."

"Why not?" he said with a smile, and began walking toward me. "You look very pretty today."

My gaze dropped. "Well, Pop, I don't feel very pretty."

"That's no problem. This camera can make you look great even on a bad day," he joked, taking a seat on the folding chair beside me. "Here, let me show you this new lens I just bought."

With that, he opened his leather case and began displaying proudly, one by one, his host of camera attachments, explaining as he went.

"Now, just take a look at this new two-hundred-millimeter zoom lens. Why, you can focus and zoom with just one hand."

I have to admit, I wasn't very interested in hearing about his camera gismos. But I listened as this white-haired gentleman with the sparkling blue eyes continued. He told me how excited he was about his basement darkroom. Pride beamed in his eyes as he described the local awards some of his pictures had won.

"Um hum," I nodded casually, still not particularly impressed. But he did begin catching my ear when he started recounting a recent trip he had taken to Sagamore Horse Farm to photograph some of their breeding barns and spring-houses. He went on to explain how he had returned to the farm weeks later to give the manager some of the finished photos he had taken there.

Pop really does love his hobby, I thought. *I admire that.* His story continued.

"The manager liked those shots so much, he asked if I'd come back and take pictures of their stallions," he exclaimed.

"No kidding!" I lit up a bit. "How did you get high-spirited thoroughbreds to stand still for a snapshot?"

"Well, it wasn't easy," he laughed and lifted a finger. "But we all got together and. . . ."

Before long, I began to realize I was interested in what Pop was saying and was really listing to him.

"Well, Pop," I smiled, "you'll just have to come up to our farm soon. Bring your cameras, and we'll make a day of it."

By the time the shower was over, I had discovered how much I really did care about this dear old gentleman and his hobby. More than that, I had genuinely forgotten all about my aches and pains and guilty conscience. The concern I had shown for him was the very remedy that worked wonders for me!

When God tells us to obey Him in our trials by putting others first, He knows what He's doing. He knows we won't be sorry.

Give, and it will be given to you. A good measure, pressed down, shaken together and running over, will be poured into your lap. For with the measure you use, it will be measured to you (Luke 6:38).

Nine

Don't Compare
. . . Share!

A S MY BARE feet positioned themselves on the edge of the wooden raft on that hot July afternoon in 1967, it never occurred to me that the murky Chesapeake Bay into which I was about to plunge concealed a shallow bottom. I should have know better, should have checked the depth. But the innocent-looking waters lured me into a trap which broke my neck and cost me the use of my hands and legs for the rest of my life.

There is an innocent-looking trap awaiting each person who suffers. It isn't a body of water, but an attitude. I am talking about the temptation to compare ourselves with others who seem to have it easier than we do. Just a few indulging dives into this perilous frame of mind, and we will find ourselves caught in a net of self-pity that robs our joy and dishonors God.

I was ensnared in this net during the early years of my paralysis. It's confining power particularly showed itself whenever I went shopping for clothes with my close friend Sheryl. Sheryl's clothes always fit her so well. In comparison, it seemed to me that mine hung on me like a sack. Watching her model an outfit for size made my face flush with envy, although I never told her.

"What do you think, Joni?" she would ask about a pants suit we were considering, turning first this way, then that, to see in the mirror from every angle.

"Looks great, Sheryl," I would answer, trying to sound excited in order to hide my jealousy. But inside I was burning. As she wheeled me up to the mirrors so I could model the same outfit, all I could think of was, *God, how come I can't look like her! I can't even compare myself to a mannequin and come out winning—clothes fit them great because they can stand up!*

At that time in my life I was just beginning to grow as a Christian, and my hunger for spiritual food spurred me to spend a good deal of time in the Bible. A bite of that food went down pretty hard one day—some spiritual spinach which tasted bad at first, but which I learned to appreciate later as I grew up in the Lord. My meal was served from John's Gospel, chapter twenty-one, where it seems Peter had the same problem I did. One of his friends appeared to be getting a better deal in life than he was! Jesus had just announced to Peter that years in the future he would be led to a martyr's death, but not a word had been spoken about John.

Perhaps jealousy stirred in Peter's heart. Wasn't John the one who'd gotten to sit next to Jesus at the Last Supper, the one who seemed to be especially intimate with the Master? Was Christ going to let John off with an easy death in his old age and an exciting ministry while he lived? It was too much for Peter to keep inside. "What about him?" Peter asked Jesus, pointing to John. "What's his future going to be like?"

The answer Jesus gave shocked me. I certainly would have expected a response like: "Don't worry, Peter. I'll be with you through whatever. Everything's going to be all right." But what He actually replied was more in this vein: "Look, if it's My will that John lives until I come again, what is that to you? What I have planned for John is not your business—your business is to make sure your own heart and life are right. So stop grumbling and follow Me!"

Now this sounds harsh at first. But when I thought about it, I began to see that Jesus was right in being so stern. In the first place, self-pity never helps anyone. It only magnifies a person's own misery. And it certainly doesn't help God. Can you imagine how ineffective Peter would have been as a preacher if every time he was scheduled to speak he was backstage sobbing for himself, wondering if this would be the sermon that would anger people to the point of killing him? In the second place, by comparing his situation with John's and demanding that God give them "equal rights," Peter was doubting that God's plan for him was good. And that is sin, for "without faith it is impossible to please God, because anyone who comes to him must believe that . . . he rewards those who earnestly seek him" (Heb. 11:6). To doubt God's good intentions is to sing: "Jesus hates me this I know, for my unbelief tells me so."

Besides, although it may seem God is being grossly unfair and is giving us a heavier cross to bear, we really don't know what the person next door has to live with. I may be grieved with a broken neck envying my healthy neighbor, never knowing that my neighbor is grieving with a broken heart. Peter probably had no idea that John, in his old age, would spend years languishing in an island prison, receiving the visions of the Book of Revelation. There John would gaze with longing upon the waiting glories of heaven, upon the special honors given to the martyrs (including Peter himself!) around God's throne, and would wish that his life, too, had been mercifully cut short.[7]

Because we don't have all the facts about how much each person has suffered, or what sins they need chastening for, or what qualities they do or don't need built into their lives, we just can't say what trials each person should be getting—or how many! But though *we* don't have all the facts, God does, and "Shall not the Judge of all the earth deal justly?" (Gen. 18:25). God is doing in each one of our lives something expressly different than He is doing in another's. He will give us the unique grace to bear our unique cross.

I'm excited to say that today Sheryl is still a part of an intimate circle of friends with whom I have real and deep fellowship—only minus the envy, thanks to Christ's words to Peter. When you think about it, wouldn't it be awful if, whenever we had deep trials, God allowed all our friends to be going through exactly the same problems? Who would be there to lift us up? Doesn't it make far more sense, instead of envying our friends who have lighter loads, to benefit from their supportive fellowship?

Fellowship

We should never be alone when we suffer. I don't mean never for a minute, or that we must not live in an apartment by ourselves. But we should never build a self-imposed wall around us that allows absolutely no one inside to see what we're going through and to hurt with our hurts. God never intended that we shoulder the load of suffering by ourselves. "Two are better than one. . . . For if either of them falls, one will lift up his companion. But woe to the one who falls where there is not another to lift him up" (Eccl. 4:9–10).

If you are single or widowed, you may feel as though such an intimate sharing of sorrows is impossible. But you do have a family—other Christians, the body of Christ. This family of believers is meant to be one of the warmest and most intimate circles of friendship in the world. I believe, and am told by my married friends, that even for a married person it is a mistake to try and rely on one's partner as one's total source of fellowship. God deliberately designed the church to consist of young and old, male and female, all types of people, and we need to rub shoulders with them all if our innermost needs are to be met. I absolutely could not make it without the sharing and caring of the Christian friends I have made in my church and community—friends of all ages.

Perhaps the saddest thing is to see Christian leaders who feel they cannot share any of their trials with those in the church who are under their spiritual care. Granted, none of us can reveal *all* our most private concerns to *everyone*. But we do need to share them with *someone*. And perhaps some should be shared with the congregation at large, or certainly more than are usually shared. The idea that

Christian leaders should be towers of strength who never admit to their own pains and sorrows doesn't come from the Bible. Paul boasted freely of his pains and weaknesses and frequently asked for prayer. A Christian leader who never shares his problems with those under his care teaches them by example to do the same thing!

But what if your relationships with friends and church members aren't as open as you'd like them to be? Then it's up to you to do something about it. *Fellowship is usually created, not found!* My friend Diana taught me so much about this when I was in high school. Diana was the type of person who felt like clawing the walls if a conversation never moved beyond the trivial. Not that she couldn't let her hair down and have fun. Far from it! But she had a way of getting people to share honestly their thoughts and feelings. I think her secret was that she really listened to people when they talked and asked them questions about *them*. Her facial expression showed that she really was interested—no wandering eyes or anything.

But Diana did more than listen. She shared. Now sharing your deep thoughts, fears, and concerns with another person is a scary thing. It's making yourself vulnerable. But isn't that much of what love is all about? Vulnerability. Diana tactfully and lovingly "invaded" the world of the people she met and knew and taught us something about what fellowship is all about. She would say things like, "Why don't we pray together for just a minute before you leave?" People who are suffering are in desperate need of deep and meaningful conversations with other believers. They shouldn't have to endure a constant diet of trite dialogue when they are around other Christians. They get enough of that out in the world.

When you suffer, there's something else you can do to foster close sharing and contact with other Christians. You can pray for it.

Not long ago the choir of a Christian college was touring some eastern states during spring vacation and gave a concert one evening at a church in our area. After the concert, the singers were assigned in groups of two or three to various families in the church who would house them for the night. Two girls were assigned to Mr. and Mrs. Estes, parents of my friend Steve.

As the four of them sat around the living room chatting and enjoying refreshments, Mr. Estes and his wife began bringing Christ into the conversation in their warm and tactful manner, asking the girls how they had met the Lord and what He was doing in their lives. To their hosts' surprise the two students looked at each other, smiled, and then let out a squeal of delight.

"Mr. and Mrs. Estes," the younger one exclaimed, "you don't know how glad I am you asked these questions." With that, she began sharing with them something of her background. She had become a Christian less than a year before. After that, naturally her thoughts and concern turned toward her parents. She wanted them to have the same personal relationship with Christ that she had, but

Diana Mood (partner in JONI PTL) and Betsy Sandbower (right) help Joni plan her schedule.

Joni's sister Kathy enjoys a typical Eareckson pastime—horseback riding.

Niece Kay (right) with friend and neighbor, Kathy Mettee.

Joni's parents, John and Lindy Eareckson.

A special headset enables Joni to use the phone.

On speaking tour in 1977
with Sheryl Bond and sister
Jay (right).

Joni at the desk in her studio where she works, draws, and reads.

Steve and Verna Estes and Joni work on *A Step Further*.

At work on one of her latest drawings.

Wisdom is a tree of life
to them that lay hold
upon her.

Proverbs 3:18

Charlotte Sherman (left) and Betsy work on mail at the
JONI PTL office.

Frank and Diana Mood discuss the new book with Steve and Joni.

Jay.

Joni and friend Dick Filbert.

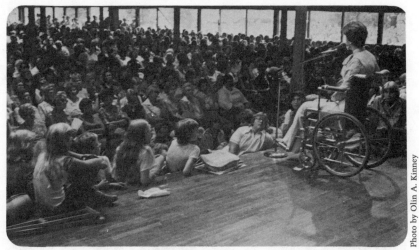

Addressing World Vision Conference, 1977.

Photo by Olin A. Kinney

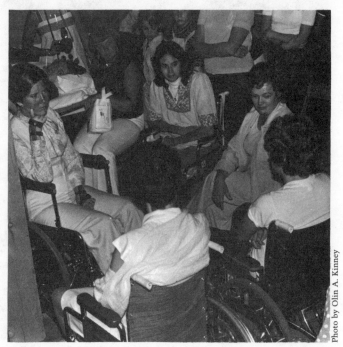

Talking with handicapped friends.

Photo by Olin A. Kinney

Billy Graham and Joni at Billy Graham Crusade, 1977.

Photo by Russ Busby

Photo by Russ Busby

Joni, Kathy, and Jay.

225

He that believed on me,
out of him shall flow
rivers of living water.

John 7:38

they didn't seem interested. For weeks she unsuccessfully tried to persuade her dad to go to church with her until one Sunday morning he finally agreed.

The service that day seemed to touch his heart. The people were friendly, the sermon appropriate—everything was perfect. In the vestibule afterward her father said, "I must say that the service today really moved me. Maybe I'll come around to seeing things your way in time. Just don't rush me." Inside the girl beamed with joy, said a prayer of thanks to God, and promised herself she would never force things on her father.

The family was just getting into the car when a gentleman approached them from the other side of the parking lot and hollered a greeting to her dad. The man turned out to be one of the church elders, someone her father had casually met a few times at his place of business.

"Say, how are you doing?" the elder asked as he smiled and extended a hand to her father. "Good to have you here. I see you've brought your wife and family," he said, bending down and nodding to them through the car window. Then he said something to her father which made the girl cringe.

"Hey, why not give me a call sometime and we'll get together and have a few drinks, okay? Well, gotta go. Take care," he waved, and off he went.

As her father got into the car and shut the door, the look on his face made the atmosphere so tense you could almost see it.

"You know," he said to his daughter as they pulled out of the lot, "I thought this place and these people were for real. But they're no different from me." With that he shut his heart to the gospel and never returned to church or discussed spiritual things with her again. In fact, her family had become so hostile to her new-found faith in Christ that when she and a friend arrived at her family's summer home that Easter for vacation, they politely requested that she leave.

"And that's why I'm here on this tour, Mr. and Mrs. Estes, instead of at home with my family this Easter," she concluded. "I've been really aching to talk to someone about all these things. The people whose homes I have stayed at this week have been very nice, but all we ever talked about was the weather. So my friend and I prayed this afternoon that we'd get assigned to a home tonight where I could really unburden my heart and where we could share and pray together! So when you moved the conversation in the direction you did, well . . . I just sort of exploded with joy!"

You see what happens when we ask God to send us fellowship and when someone reaches out to make that fellowship happen? Sharing with other Christians—it's one of the best responses to suffering I know!

Ten

While
We Wait

It's All Right to Cry

WHEN MY FIRST book *Joni*, came out in 1976, I had no idea God would use it in as many lives as He did. As a result I've been deluged with interesting mail, ranging from simple order forms for my artwork to friendly personal letters to distressed pleas for help. Some of those pleas sound like this:

> Dear Joni,
>   I have a nephew who recently broke his neck and is now paralyzed. He's so depressed and keeps asking "Why?!" I thought maybe you might autograph him a copy of your book. Do you think you could also write him a little note with a few tips on how to cope?
>
> Thank you.

My heart goes out to such people. It is frustrating to stand beside the bed of a suffering loved one and not be able to do anything. How good it would feel to be able to give a helpful book, or to share just the right encouraging word. But although I sympathize with those who are in this situation, I'm not sure that a book or a letter from me, or anyone, is the right prescription.

In the first place, a person usually isn't ready for advice and insights just after something drastic has happened to him. Thinking back on the time when I was seventeen, lying in a Stryker Frame those first few weeks after the accident, I'm not sure I would have been ready for a book written by someone who had successfully dealt with their handicap. In fact, the *last* thing in the world I wanted to see was someone in a wheelchair, smiling and full of answers.

At first it may seem that a person who has just lost a leg, discovered he has terminal cancer, or broken his neck is desperately looking for answers. "Why did this happen to me?!" he cries, and so we jump right in and give him sixteen biblical reasons why it happened. But more often than not, when he first asks "Why?" he doesn't really mean it as a question. He means it as an emotional release—sometimes even as an accusation. It's not the genuine "Why?" of a searching heart, but the bitter "Why?!" of a clenched fist.

It takes *time* for a person to realize that he never will walk again, or that he really does have terminal cancer, or whatever. After he has had time to cry, to agonize, and to sort out his feelings, *then* he gets into an "asking mood," and then our advice and counsel is helpful.

I think one of the reasons Steve was able to help me so much in dealing with my paralysis was that we met two full years after my accident—long enough for me to begin asking questions and begin listening to the answers. Others tried to give me the same help earlier, but I just wasn't ready for it.

There's another reason I wouldn't send books and Bible verses the instant a person has some terrible accident or illness. I wouldn't want him to think I was saying, "No, no! Stop your crying. Dry those tears and listen to all these Bible passages about suffering. Then you won't feel bad any more." I wouldn't want to give the impression that we are to learn what the Bible has to say about the value of suffering *instead of* feeling grief and sorrow. I have read books and heard speakers that implied that if we were really giving thanks for all things and seeing our sufferings in the light of God's Word, they wouldn't even seem like sufferings. But that sort of unrealistic, happy-go-lucky approach to trials can't be found in the Bible. "Giving thanks in all things" is not the same as "feeling like a million dollars in all things." We have the freedom to feel sorrow and grief.

Let me illustrate. This past year a friend of mine, Jeanette, and her husband lost their three-year-old son to cancer. Cute little Bradley, blond and blue-eyed—for a year and a half his parents had known death was coming. And, of course, when he died their grief was very deep. But throughout the whole ordeal they were never bitter toward God. They continued to love and serve Him, trusting completely that He cared for them and knew what He was doing.

About two weeks after Bradley's funeral Jeanette attended a women's Bible study at her church. Afterwards, as she walked down the hall with some other ladies, she spotted a little boy standing tiptoe atop some small steps, straining to sip from the water fountain. The sight immediately recalled memories of her own little Bradley who had always made a big production of climbing the little stairs to drink from that very fountain. She began to sob.

Walking beside her was one of her closest friends who sensed what had happened. This friend didn't say a word, just put her arms around Jeanette and silently held and comforted her. It was what she needed.

Then another woman, who didn't know Jeanette, saw her crying and obviously wanted to help. Coming up, she patted Jeanette and said, "I'm praying for you, honey. Praise the Lord."

The words stung like fire.

Later, Jeanette expressed how she felt at that moment. "I really had to ask God to help me with my feelings about that woman. I know she only wanted to help. But the way she said 'Praise the Lord' made me feel like I didn't have any right to cry if I was trusting the Lord." Pausing for a moment, she thoughtfully added, "Maybe she just didn't know that trusting the Lord doesn't rule out crying. Maybe she forgot that God told us to weep with those who weep."[8]

Jeanette was right. After all, Jesus wept at the reality of death when He stood at the grave of His friend Lazarus. Even though we will one day be raised to life, death is a horrible thing. All the sufferings of this earth are horrible things. It's foolish to think Christians can benefit from their trials without *feeling* them. And when Jesus shed those tears at His friend's tomb, He showed us that it's all right to grieve.

God doesn't ask us to stifle our tears. Let's not ask it from each other. For there is "a time to weep . . . a time to mourn" (Eccl. 3:4).

Songs in the Night

But mourning isn't enough. When your body is racked with pain, your heart is breaking with sorrow, your mind is a mass of confusion, and your soul is weighted with guilt, you have a need to know there is someone, anyone, who understands what you're going through. Well, one of the best places you can find this understanding is the Book of Psalms. This is no ordinary book, for many of the psalms were written out of the depths of despair, and they are meant to be read during the depths of despair.

David, the poet behind many of the psalms, knew what it was to suffer. In his early years, his life hung on a thread as the armies of Saul pursued him like a common criminal. He lost his best friend, Jonathan, in battle. After becoming king he was gnawed by the guilt of having committed adultery and murder. One of his sons died in infancy. For the rest of his life, his family and kingdom were plagued with incest, rebellion, murder, and war. Here's a man who really had problems!

Most of David's psalms don't supply any answers to our problems. Many of them are merely detailed and desperate pleas to God for help. But when I sit down and read the prayers of this man (and of the other psalmists, too), I know I am not alone. Here is someone who understands the way I feel—someone who felt the way I feel.

It's as if David and I are sitting together on a rock in the field beside his sheep. I listen as he, with all his poetic skill, pours out to God the aching of his heart. In doing so, he pours out my aching as well. *Yes,* I think, *those words capture what I am thinking. That's what I want to pray.* And it lets me know God has heard and understood my thoughts.

Listen as David groans before God in Psalm 6:

> I am weary with my sighing;
> Every night I make my bed swim,
> I dissolve my couch with my tears.
> (Ps. 6:6)

Doesn't that perfectly describe some sorrowful nights when your own pillow has been drenched with tears? Can't you feel with him as he cries out to God in anxiety and guilt in Psalm 38?

> For I am ready to fall,
> And my sorrow is continually before me.
> For I confess my iniquity;
> I am full of anxiety because of my sin. . . .
> Do not forsake me, O Lord;
> O my God, do not be far from me!
> (Ps. 38:17-18, 21)

As we spend more and more time with David, we trust our feelings to him because we see a man who has gone through what we're going through. So when his hopelessness turns into assurance that God has heard his prayers, his confidence becomes ours. Then we can say with him:

> Lord, all my desire is before Thee;
> And my sighing is not hidden from Thee.
> (Ps. 38:9)

The pain is still there. Yet the flicker of light refuses to die regardless of how much rain and sorrow is poured on it:

> For I hope in Thee, O Lord;
> Thou wilt answer, O Lord my God.
> (Ps. 38:15)

If David could hope like that, can't I? If the man who was an adulterer and murderer was able to face God with confidence despite his sins, can't I? That's worth shouting about! And sometimes David does just that. Like a refreshing summer shower in the middle of a heat wave, his sorrow turns to joy and he utters:

> I waited patiently for the Lord;
> And He inclined to me, and heard my cry.
> He brought me up out of the pit of destruction,
>   out of the miry clay;
> And He set my feet upon a rock making my footsteps firm.
> And He put a new song in my mouth,
>   a song of praise to our God.
> (Ps. 40:1-3)

Seeing the change in David's life makes us feel that we, too, can have strength to wait patiently for the Lord, that He will hear *our* cry, set *our* feet upon a rock, and give *us* a song. When we have heard this once-discouraged shepherd say:

> Thou hast turned for me my mourning into dancing;
> Thou hast loosed my sackcloth and girded me with gladness
> (Ps. 30:11)

we are able to believe that we, too, will one day laugh again. When he writes:

> Weeping may last for the night,
> But a shout of joy comes in the morning,
> (Ps. 30.5)

we begin to believe what before we could never believe—that our own crises, too, will eventually pass. And when we have heard this poet who so graphically expressed the dreadfulness of a sleepless night write:

> I lay down and slept;
> I awoke, for the Lord sustains me,
> (Ps. 3:5)

we, too, feel able to fall asleep at last. Somehow, God uses those soothing psalms to turn our tears of agony into tears of release. Like a person who feels better after he has cried and "gotten it all out," so the Psalms help us get things out— expressing to God our deep anguish and assuring our troubled souls that He is still worth trusting.

Six years ago my family and I boarded a chair-lift that cabled us to the top of a huge, glacier-scarred mountain overlooking the wilderness reserve of Jasper Provincial Park in Alberta, Canada. There our eyes met the spectacle of majestic pine forests, wild rugged terrain, and turquoise lakes. Shivering beneath our down jackets, half from the icy cold and half from the awesome view, we yelled our delight to one another over the violent roaring of the wind.

I marveled at the sight of a soaring eagle moving far across the wooded valley, a tiny speck against the distant mountain range. I watched as he circled and dove, admiring his grace and ease.

Eagles seem to have to do with big things—mountains, canyons, great depths, immense heights. It's always at the most stupendous and alluring spectacles of nature that we find them.

God talks about eagles. In one of the most well-loved passages of the Old Testament, He uses their flight to describe the adventure that will unfold to the suffering Christian who waits for Him.

> Though youths grow weary and tired,
> And vigorous young men stumble badly,
> Yet those who wait for the Lord
> Will gain new strength;
> They will mount up with wings like eagles,
> They will run and not get tired,
> They will walk and not become weary.
> (Isa. 40:30-31)

What does it mean to "wait for the Lord"? Well, some people think of the kind of waiting you do because you're forced to. (Like when there are ten people ahead of you in the waiting room at the doctor's office, and so you kill time flipping through magazines.) But when the Bible talks about waiting, it means *confidently trusting* that God knows how much suffering I need and can take. It means *looking expectantly* toward the time when He will free me from my burdens.

But not get weary? Not tire or stumble? How can that be when these are the very trademarks of those who suffer? Yet God's promise is clear that those who wait for Him in their sufferings will receive strength and endurance which others know nothing of.

Due to my condition, you'd think I would grow weary, weak, and tired of life. But because I know God and confidently look forward to the day when He will give me a new body, I am able to "mount up with wings like an eagle" even now. My expectancy gives me endurance and strength, like that of an eagle who with powerful wings is able to venture out in the mighty wind currents that whip through the canyons.

Oh, yes. There's one more way that waiting on God makes me like an eagle. My body is held by the limits of this chair. But the waiting hope I have in God's future for me gives me the freedom to soar to heights of joy and explore the canyon depths of God's tender mercies.

A year after I was released from the hospital I read the inspiring story of a French noblewoman named Madame Guyon. This saintly woman was arrested in

1688 and falsely accused of heresy, sorcery, and adultery by jealous church officials. She was convicted, and as a result spent the next ten years in prison. During those long and lonely years of her confinement, she penned the following poem. It is an eloquent expression of the strength God will give to the suffering heart that waits on Him.

> A little bird I am,
> Shut from the fields of air;
> And in my cage I sit and sing
> To Him who placed me there;
> Well pleased a prisoner to be
> Because, my God, it pleases Thee.
>
> Naught have I else to do;
> I sing the whole day long;
> And He whom most I love to please,
> Doth listen to my song:
> He caught and bound my wandering wing,
> But still He bends to hear me sing.
>
> My cage confines me round;
> Abroad I cannot fly;
> But though my wing is closely bound,
> My heart's at liberty;
> My prison walls cannot control
> The flight, the freedom of the soul.
>
> Oh! it is good to soar
> These bolts and bars above,
> To Him whose purpose I adore,
> Whose providence I love;
> And in Thy mighty will to find
> The joy, the freedom, of the mind.

HEALING:
A PIECE OF
THE PUZZLE?

Eleven

I Wish
I Were Healed

IT'S A RATHER quiet afternoon around our house today. The yellow school bus full of chattering students won't drop off my niece, Kay, for at least another hour. Through the bay window of my drawing studio I can see my green-thumbed sister, Jay, out in the garden mothering her radishes and zucchini squash. No friends or visitors have dropped by today—a rare thing at our house—so I have the place all to myself. It's a perfect time to catch up on some reading.

On the far corner of the desk at which I am seated lies a book I've been wanting to get into recently. It looks just within nudging reach. I use the word "nudging" because I don't have the use of my hands or fingers. What I can do is position my arm beside the book and with weak, awkward, jerky motions manipulate it toward me. It took me a long time after my accident to learn to do this, so I'm grateful for the ability to nudge. I can even turn the pages and keep them open by myself if the binding of the book is broken in.

But today, as my brace-supported arm inches past the pencil holder toward the book, I can see a potential problem—the small paperback is just on the borderline of being out of reach. *Uh-oh. This is going to take some stretching.* I can get my wrist beside it but not quite behind it to pull it my way. I need some strategy. *Hey, maybe I can zigzag it.* My cousin Eddie once taught me about sailing. "When you want to head a sailboat into the wind," he said, "you can't just head straight on. You need to weave your boat right, then left, back and forth, and inch your way forward." He called it tacking.

I'm going to tack. I'll push the book left to the edge of the desk. Then I'll push it right. I'll move it slightly back each time until it gets close enough to open. Handicapped people have to get used to little tasks becoming big chores.

But I'm not sure I'll ever get used to failing at tasks that even a handicapped person can usually accomplish. Today that little book is just an inch and a half farther away than I'm used to reaching. I can move it, but not towards me. *Come on, book, cooperate.* Every nudge seems to push it farther away. My only hope is to try to press the weight of my arm downward on top of the cover and attempt a quick jerk back towards me. With studied effort I place my wrist on the book, strain with weak muscles to push down as hard as I can, and pull back fast!

But all I succeed in doing is knocking the book off the table. *Oh, no! Book, there you are within eight inches of my dangling left arm, and I can't touch you.* I glance out the window. Jay's still outside. *She'd never hear me yell from in here.* Nobody's there to pick it up. No other book is within reach. So I will spend the next sixty minutes sitting exasperated at the desk, staring at the bookshelf, spending an anticipated hour of reading with nothing to do.

It's at times like this I wish I were healed. Please realize that I don't always feel this way—not even often. But on days like today it sure would help! I call them "I-wish-I-had-my-hands-back" days. Though I have learned to be content with my condition, and even to rejoice in it, the prospect of being restored to a normal life would be very exciting. I think in all honestly that any handicapped person, Christian or otherwise, would rather be well. So naturally, once my relationship with God began to get straightened out, and once I learned that regaining the use of my hands and legs was beyond medical hope, I became vitally interested in what the Bible might have to say about miraculous healing.

I began investigating in every way I could—studying the Scriptures, reading books, and gleaning counsel and advice from friends and various Christian leaders. What everyone agreed upon was the fact that God certainly *can* heal any person, no matter how serious the problem.

But what they could not agree on was whether or not God *wills* to heal all those who truly come to Him in faith. I found two extreme opposite positions. On one end of the spectrum were those who stated that the age of miracles is absolutely past and gone and that we should never seek and expect them today. At the other end were those who felt that miracles can be a part of the everyday life of each Christian and that healing from disease is an important portion of the believer's heritage. Between those two opposite poles, I found Christians at all points. This controversy continues in Christian circles right up to today. And I want to emphasize that there are believers on both sides of the fence who are totally dedicated to Jesus Christ as Lord and to the Bible as God's Word. This is not a discussion between people who love God and people who don't, between "the good guys" and "the bad guys." It is a kind of intramural debate.

With all these opinions facing me, I began narrowing down the possibilities. To start with, I just couldn't go along with those who were positive that God never heals anyone miraculously today. In the first place, who is in a position to say this? Just because I may not know of anyone whom God has healed in an extraordinary way, does that prove that He has never done so during my lifetime? God deals with His children as He wills. To one He gives a life of relative ease and comfort; to another He gives the privilege of suffering for Him in a concentration camp. For some, He rewards their faith in this life; for others, He waits until after they die (Heb. 11:32-39). I cannot take my own experience from the hand of God and set it up as the absolute norm for His dealing with others. For me to say with certainty that God has not supernaturally healed anyone during my lifetime would mean that I'd have to be at every single place to check out every alleged healing.

Besides, what about all the testimonies from Christians who claim they have been divinely healed? One such person is a personal friend of mine, a mature Christian lady who suffered from a severe bone marrow disease. Every known medical procedure having failed, the doctors gave her a short time to live. But she and others prayed, and when she returned to the doctor for examination he dropped his jaw in amazement. This man was not a believer in Christ, but after taking repeated blood tests over a period of time he told my friend, "There is no natural or medical explanation I can give. Your situation was beyond hope. All I can say is that this is a miracle." That was fifteen years ago, and she is still healthy today. I know this woman well enough to feel confident she is not lying to me nor was she deceived into believing something that never really happened.

Of course, it's possible that some of these testimonies of healing come from people who just *think* they have been healed—over-emotional people, perhaps. Some may have even lied in order to receive attention. And several biblical passages (e.g., Matt. 7:22-23; Matt. 24:24; 2 Thess. 2:9) imply that some of these miracles may even come from Satan. But to place everybody into such categories is something I not prepared to do.

Earlier I said there is only one way a person could be sure that no miracles of healing ever occurred during his lifetime—he would have to have been present with all persons at all times. Actually there is another way. Suppose there was a promise in God's Word that He would not miraculously heal anyone after a given point in time. Then we could be absolutely certain that any so-called divine healing after that was either a hoax or from Satan. There are a number of Christians who feel this is, in fact, what the Scriptures teach. And as a result, they write off each and every healing testimony no matter how convincing.

I've got to say here that I really agree with people who insist on judging experiences by the light of Scripture and not vice versa. Modern Christians tend to put too much weight on their experiences anyway. Then they set their conclusions up as some kind of absolute truth by which everything else is to be interpreted, putting those experiences on an equal level with Scripture.

But this *doesn't* mean we should totally *ignore* our experiences. There are far too many who have claimed to have experienced miraculous healing for us to just write them off. Lots of these testimonies come from people who are mature in the faith—and many are from the field of medicine. All this should flash a yellow light in our minds if we're among those who feel the Bible totally rules out miracles for our day. It should make us go back and be sure we have understood God's Word correctly.

So at least for the present, I myself have had to rule out that pole of the spectrum which says God never heals miraculously today. In my opinion the Bible doesn't teach it, and experience doesn't support it.

But what about the other position—the view which says not only is healing for today, but it is for everyone? What about the claim that none will be turned away who truly have faith in Jesus to heal their body?

Not long after I broke my neck, some of my friends and others who knew of my condition began sharing with me that they felt just this way. To this day I receive scores of letters from Christians who share the same conviction. Some have sent books. Many have taken the time to compile Scripture references in support of the idea that I not only could, but should be healed. Here are a few quotes:

> ". . . To get right to the point, I believe you could be healed, Joni. I'm not sure what you've been taught, or where you stand on the subject, but there are many scriptures saying that healing is for today and that it is for everyone, whatever their condition. . . ."

> "I have heard that you believe God wants you in the shape you're in, but I can't believe that. Here's why . . . [at this point, numerous scriptural supports are given]. Joni, you might say you are glorifying God in your paralysis, but how much more in your healing! When Jesus healed people, the Bible says they glorified God after they were healed. You are known all over the world, and if you were healed, you can imagine how fantastic a thing it would be? Can you imagine how much more God would be glorified?

> ". . . John 10:10 says we are to have an abundant life. Being paralyzed, can you honestly say you are having an abundant life? Jesus came to set people free. You're bound to your wheelchair. Your body is the temple of the Holy Spirit. Do you think He wants His temple to be broken and helpless? . . ."

> ". . . I'd like to see one more chapter written in your book. I'd like the heading to be, 'How God Healed Me.' "

It would be impractical to list here all of the reasons I have been given why any Christian can expect healing from God if he truly believes. But from the number of letters I've received, books I've read, and discussions I've had, here is a summary of the more common points posed to me:

1) Sickness and death are the work of Satan and his forces (Luke 13:16; Acts

10:38). Since the whole purpose of Jesus' coming was to destroy the works of the devil (1 John 3:8), those who believe in Jesus can expect freedom from disease.

2) Jesus healed people during His lifetime. Verses like Hebrews 13:8 tell us that God never changes, that Jesus Christ is "the same yesterday, today, and forever." Therefore, He must still be in the business of healing people today as He did centuries ago.

3) We have promises in Scripture that whatever we ask in Jesus' name will be done for us (John 14:12-14; Mark 11:22-24; 1 John 3:22 and many others). These promises would seem to include prayers for healing.

4) There are a number of Scripture passages which specifically guarantee the health and healing of believers. The most well-known is Isaiah 53:5, "By His scourging we are healed." Others are Psalm 103:1-3 ("Bless the Lord, O my soul. . . . Who heals all your diseases"), 1 Peter 2:24, and James 5:15.

These points which others had shared seemed to make sense. *Guess that answers my question about where I should go from here,* I thought to myself. Having considered the issue, I became convinced healing was for me.

୫ର

Twelve

Why Wasn't
I Healed?

O N A R A I N Y afternoon in the early summer of 1972 about fifteen people gathered together in a tiny oak church not far from my home. The group consisted of close friends, family, and church leaders—several elders and a few ordained ministers—whom I had called together to pray for my healing. It was a simple format. We began by reading aloud in turn from various Scriptures. Some read from the New Testament . . .

"We have this assurance in approaching God, that if we ask anything according to his will, he hears us. And if we know that he hears us—whatever we ask—we know that we have what we ask of him" (1 John 5:14-15).

some from the Old Testament . . .

"But those who look to the Lord will renew their strength. They will soar on wings like eagles; they will run and not grow weary, they will walk and not faint." (Isa. 40:31, NIV).

several read promises about healing . . .

"Is any one of you sick? He should call the elders of the church to pray over him and anoint him with oil in the name of the Lord. And the prayer offered in faith will make the sick person well; the Lord will raise him up . . ." (James 5:14-15).

others read the stories of those who were healed . . .

" . . .He said to the paralytic, 'I tell you, get up, take your mat and go home.' He got up, took his mat and walked out in full view of them all. This amazed everyone and they praised God, saying, 'We have never seen anything like this!' " (Mark 2:1-12).

After the readings, they anointed my head with olive oil. Then followed a time of direct, fervent, believing prayer for my healing. We asked God to glorify Himself by allowing me to walk again, and we trusted Him to do so.

By the time our brief service was over, the rain had stopped. Exiting through the front doors of the church, we were greeted by a beautiful rainbow in the misty distance, sparkling from a bath in golden sunlight. I cannot say it was an extremely emotional moment for any of us, but it gave me just one more reassurance that God was looking down on us right there and had heard our prayers.

I left the church parking lot in exactly the same frame of mind that I had entered it—fully expecting God to heal me. "Thank You, Lord," I prayed silently as the car pulled out, praising God for what I was convinced He had already begun to do.

A week went by . . . then another . . . then another. My body still hadn't gotten the message that I was healed. Fingers and toes still didn't respond to the mental command, "Move!" *Perhaps it's going to be a gradual thing,* I reasoned, *a slow process of steady recovery.* I continued to wait. But three weeks became a month, and one month became two.

You can imagine the questions that began popping into my mind. *Is there some sin in my life?* Well, of course, there is still sin in every Christian's life. No one is without it. But there was no area of conscious rebellion against God on my part. I was living in close fellowship with Him, keeping short accounts, confessing my sins and failures to Him daily and receiving assurances of forgiveness.

Had we done things right? My friend Betsy assured me on that point when I asked her.

"Of course we did, Joni," she defended. "That wasn't some off-beat group of immature Christians trying to do something apart from the authority of church leaders. Ordained men and elders led the meeting."

"I guess you're right," I nodded in agreement. "We did things just like it says to do in James 5 and other places."

But then came to my mind the ten-thousand-dollar question, the question that is in the minds of so many I've met over the years who have not been healed in response to their prayers—*Did I have enough faith?*

What a flood of guilt that question brings. It constantly leaves the door open for the despairing thought: *God didn't heal me because there is something wrong with me. I must not have believed hard enough.* You can easily see how this can produce a vicious cycle:

A Christian who is afflicted with some sort of physical problem asks a friend, "Do you think God would heal me if I asked Him?"

"Of course He will," the friend assures him. "But you mustn't doubt. The slightest trace of doubt may prevent your being healed."

So knowing that "faith comes by hearing, and hearing by the Word of God," the ill person spends hours in the Bible, reading about God's mighty power and wonderful promises, in order to strengthen his faith. Finally, he feels ready to pray. He prays by himself, with the elders of his church, at a healing service, or whatever, but he doesn't get healed.

"What happened? What went wrong?" he asks. Often he is told, "The problem isn't with God. He's always ready and waiting. The blame must be yours. You probably didn't really let your faith go and trust God all the way." Yet the poor guy *knows* he believed God in that prayer for healing more than he's ever believed God in his life.

What is the result going to be? Since he didn't get healed, naturally he begins to wonder if God really intends it. His faith has weakened. Yet he's been told that more faith is just what He needs to get healed. Each unanswered prayer makes him doubt more and more, which in turn makes his chances for healing less and less! It becomes a losing battle.

But thinking about it, I knew I had entered the prayer service in that little church with total faith that God would heal me. I had even surprised various friends by calling the week before and warning, "Watch for me standing on your doorstep soon; I'm going to be healed."

No, insufficient faith was not the missing ingredient. The answer must lie elsewhere.

Since that time I have had years in a wheelchair to ponder the question, "Why wasn't I healed?—time to read many books, talk with many people, and do much prayerful considering and studying of Scripture. I still don't have all the answers about healing. But I do have some of them—answers that come from the Bible and that have been of great personal help to me. In a moment I'll share with you the conclusions I've reached after my six-year search for answers, and what led to those conclusions.

But first, let me give a warning. Often we have questions about issues like this which require more than just simple answers, but we don't have the patience to hear those answers out. Sometimes in the past, my own attitude has been, "Don't give me any detailed theological stuff. Just answer my question." Then, because I refused to take the time or mental energy to hear and consider the answer, I would go away assuming no answer existed.

It's so easy to take a casual, surface approach to the Bible when searching for answers. We meander through its pages with a lazy mental attitude, taking things out of context and failing to understand figures of speech. But Paul tells us to correctly handle the word of truth (2 Tim. 2:15). Apparently, it's possible to *incorrectly* handle it. In 2 Peter 3:15-16, the apostle Peter warns us not to distort the Scriptures, reminding us that some things in the Bible are just plain hard to understand. We need to treat God's Word with respect, digging hard to find the intended meaning. This is especially true when studying something as controversial and charged with emotion as the miraculous healing issue.

With this in mind, here is the conclusion I've come to regarding miraculously healing: God certainly can, and sometimes does, heal people in a miraculous way today. But the Bible does *not* teach that He will *always* heal those who come to Him in faith. He sovereignly reserves the right to heal or not to heal as He sees fit.

To understand how I reached that conclusion, ask yourself this question: "Just what is disease?"* I don't mean "What is it medically?" nor "What is its physical cause?" I mean "What is it biblically? Why is it here? What is its purpose?" The answers to these questions will shed a lot of light on the subject of healing. And to find the answers, we need to go all the way back to our first parents and the Garden of Eden.

In the beginning God created the universe and gave the earth to man, appointing him as His "assistant ruler" over earth (Gen. 1:26). Adam and Eve ruled the earth under God's authority. There was no sin and, therefore, none of sin's awful results. Pollution was nonexistent. Nature was helpful, not hostile, to man. No hurricanes, floods, tidal waves, or volcanic eruptions threatened man's survival. Death and disease were unknown. There was no fear that one of Eden's luscious-looking fruits might secretly contain some fatal poison. For both humans and the world of nature it was truly Paradise.

But earth did not remain a paradise for long. Satan, who had rebelled against God in a prideful struggle, followed by his army of demons, had set up a rival kingdom against God. Planet earth became his headquarters. Mankind was enticed to sin, to eat the forbidden fruit, and as a result a curse fell upon the earth. Romans 8:20-23 makes it clear that not only man but the earth itself—the world of nature—became subject to futility and frustration, to the endless cycle of change and decay. It seems quite possible that before this time all animals may have been vegetarians. Now they fed upon one another, and violence brought about the law of the jungle.

Nature not only became hostile to itself but to man as well. Once they had worked together; now they were in conflict. Once the earth had yielded its fruit without much effort from man; now it became a world of weeds! Wild animals sought man's life, and floods and droughts threatened to wipe him out.

Man himself began to experience problems in both soul and body as a result of sin. Immediately after disobeying God, Adam and Eve began feeling guilty,

---

*I am using the word "disease" throughout these next few chapters to include all physical problems and disorders: sickness, deformities, handicaps, loss of limbs, pain, etc.

because they *were* guilty. This caused the world's first marital argument—Adam blamed Eve for his sin. Loneliness, frustration, sorrow, and all the internal problems people face began right there. Jealousy and murder were not long in coming. All humans forever after were born with a sinful nature, separated from God and spiritually dead.

Just as thorns and thistles attacked the earth, sickness and weakness attacked man's body. As we read through the Book of Genesis, the human life span becomes shorter and shorter. No longer did people live hundreds of years as the early generations did. Illness and disease infested the world. Deformed babies and retarded children became a fact of life. And worst of all—the whole process ended in death. Plants died. Animals died. People died.

Yes, sin brought its own special consequences and results. Satan became the king of planet earth, the "god of this age" (2 Cor. 4:4), the "ruler of the kingdom of the air" (Eph. 2:2), the "prince of this world" (John 12:31).

By this time we have answered our question: "What is disease as the Bible sees it?" *Disease is just one of the many results of man's sin, along with death, sorrow, guilt, and disasters of nature.*[9] It is part of the general curse from God that the human race must suffer collectively because of its sin.

So what about this curse with its death and disease? Did God merely abandon the world and leave it hopeless? No! Way back in the Book of Genesis He promised that one day a Redeemer would come who would deal both with sin and with sin's results. The whole Old Testament foreshadows this coming One, and as its pages unfold, pictures of this coming Messiah become increasingly clear.

In the first place, the Old Testament makes plain that *the Messiah will deal with sin.* He will do this by forgiving the sins of God's people and by destroying pagan sinners who refuse to obey God.

Secondly, the Old Testament makes plain that *the Messiah will deal with sin's results.* Take the Book of Isaiah for instance. Listen to what it says about how the world of nature will be restored. "For waters shall break forth in the wilderness . . . and the burning sands will become a pool, and the thirsty ground springs of water . . ." (Isa. 35:6-7 RSV). Both the physical earth and the animals will be affected. "The wolf and the lamb shall feed together, the lion shall eat straw like the ox; and dust shall be the serpent's food. They shall not hurt or destroy . . ." (Isa. 65:25 RSV). The ancient prophet foresaw that the sorrow and frustration of mankind would change, and "the ransomed of the Lord . . . shall obtain joy and gladness, and sorrow and sighing shall flee away" (Isa. 35:10 RSV). And as for disease—"Then the eyes of the blind will be opened, and the ears of the deaf will be unstopped. Then the lame will leap like a deer, and the tongue of the dumb will shout for joy" (Isa. 35:5-6).

With promises like these and others, the air of expectation for the Messiah's coming was at fever pitch by Jesus' day.

But there were two misunderstandings held by many who read the Old Testament prophecies. First, many didn't realize that all these good things were to be for the whole world—not just the nation Israel. Secondly, many people—perhaps most—thought that everything the Messiah was to do would be accomplished in a single coming. They didn't understand that their King would come first in humility as a servant, and only later in all His regal splendor. They were right about the fact that the kingdom of God was coming. Their mistake was that they thought it was going to arrive all at once.

In the early portions of the Gospels, a rugged preacher named John the Baptist emerged from the Judean wilderness. From the banks of the Jordan River he called upon the crowds to repent, saying that the kingdom of God was "at hand"—that is, very near (Matt. 3:2).[10] But when Jesus appeared, He announced that the kingdom of God had come.[11] Once, after freeing a demon-possessed man, Jesus said, "If I drive out demons by the Spirit of God, then the kingdom of God *has come* upon you" (Matt. 12:28; Luke 11:20, italics mine). Another time, when some Pharisees asked Jesus, "When will the kingdom of God come?" Jesus gave a surprising reply. "The kingdom of God does not come visibly, nor will people say, 'Here it is,' or 'There it is,' because the kingdom of God is among you."[12] (Luke 17:20-21 NIV—marginal reading).

You see, these Pharisees were expecting the kingdom of God to be an all-at-once affair (Luke 19:11), when God would destroy His enemies and set up His rule in Jerusalem with a spectacular display of divine "fireworks." But what they did not realize was that the King Himself was standing right there in their midst, and because of that, the kingdom of God had in one sense already begun. Though its fullness was still to be in the future,[13] it had already been launched with the coming of Christ. That is why Matthew 4:23 calls the message that Jesus preached "the good news of the kingdom." Jesus had come to challenge Satan's claim as ruler of the earth and to establish His own kinship, claiming back what was rightfully His. He had come to begin to reverse the curse which had followed man's fall into sin. He had come to deal with sin and with sin's results.

How did Jesus deal with sin? He dealt with it by paying its penalty on the cross and by confronting sinful actions and attitudes in people He met.

How did He deal with sin's results? He reversed their effects. Confronted by guilt, Jesus forgave men's sins. Finding disease, He healed the sick. Faced with demon possession, He cast out the spirits by His forceful command. Threatened by the hostilities of nature, He rebuked the storm. "Quiet! Be still!" His amazed disciples breathed a sigh of relief when their boat and their lives were saved, astonished that "even the wind and the waves obeyed Him." Jesus wasn't just proving He can help us through the "storms of life." He was demonstrating His power to reverse the effects of sin upon nature, showing that He was retaking the rule of earth for Himself. It was as if He were saying, "Don't you waves know that I am king here? Satan has ruled this planet long enough, causing you waves to be hostile to man. But I have come to put an end to all of that."

Yes, in dealing with sin and sin's results, Jesus began His kingdom. But underline the word *began* here, for it is so important to the whole question of healing. Jesus put the process in motion, but He didn't finish it then and there. Acts 1:1 refers to the record about Jesus given in the Book of Luke as "all that Jesus *began* to do and to teach" (italics mine).

Sure Jesus cast demons out of people. But He didn't totally wipe out demon possession. Demoniacs still existed after Jesus returned to heaven.

And, yes, Jesus healed the sick. But consider all the people, even in His own country, whom Jesus never met and never healed, let alone those in other parts of the world. And those He did heal grew old and died later on.

Jesus stopped the storm, showing His power over sin's results in the realm of nature. But does that mean all catastrophes of nature were forever erased? Absolutely not.

He raised the dead, and that was wonderful. But there were many godly people whom Jesus did not raise. And even those He raised had to face death again later.

Jesus forgave men's sins—made them righteous in God's eyes. But did He, in their lifetime, free them from the very presence of sin? from having a sinful nature? No. *His purpose wasn't to cement the final brick in His kingdom right then. If He had done that, most of the world would never have had time to hear the Gospel. His plan was to begin the kingdom, to lay the foundation. He wanted to give a foreshadowing of what things would be like at the end of time when the kingdom of God would be a completed building.*

The men who wrote the Epistles stress that we who are Christians are living in two ages at once. We experience the trials, temptations, and problems of this present age, even though we have tasted the powers of the coming age. God is king right now, but He doesn't always "flex His kingly muscles." Rather than totally wiping out sin and its results, He gives Christians a mere taste or "down payment" of what the kingdom in its fullness will be like.

For example, when we get to heaven we will become perfectly righteous and holy. But in the meantime, though we are still sinners, God has given us "the promised Holy Spirit, who is a deposit [or down payment] guaranteeing our inheritance . . ." (Eph. 1:13-14). The way in which the Holy Spirit helps us love God and want to do right in this life is a foretaste of the future when He will make us totally holy and pleasing to God. As a mother gives her children a taste of stew before dinner, so Jesus by His miracles, and the Holy Spirit by His working within us, show us what heaven will be like. But in the meantime, "though inwardly we are being renewed day by day," "outwardly we are wasting away" (2 Cor. 4:16). Though we will one day get the whole package, "meanwhile . . . while we are in this tent [i.e., our bodies], we groan and are burdened" (2 Cor. 5:2-4).

Do you see now why I have sawed through so much theological lumber on this whole subject of sin, sin's results, and the kingdom of God? *Disease is just one of the many results of sin that Jesus began, but didn't finish, dealing with when He started His kingdom while on earth.* Jesus' miracles, including healing, didn't guarantee the end of any of sin's results for those who follow Him.

From time to time God, in His mercy, may grant us healing from disease as a gracious glimpse, a "sneak preview," of what is to come. It is my opinion that He sometimes does. But, in view of the fact that the kingdom has not yet come in its fullness, we are not to automatically expect it. Why should we arbitrarily single out disease—which is just one of sin's many results—and treat it in a special way as something that Christians today shouldn't have to put up with? We are living in "this present age," and the emphasis on earthly trials in the New Testament gives the impression that we're going to have to put up with plenty!

Does Jesus want the best for His children? Sure He does. But that doesn't mean a life of ease and comfort cushioned on a velvet pillow. So when bedsores afflict me as boils did Job, I must say with him, "Shall we indeed accept good from God and not accept adversity?" (Job 2:10). And when I feel bound to my chair as Paul was to his chains, I will say with him, "For it has been granted to you on behalf of Christ not only to believe on him, but also to suffer for him" (Phil. 1:29). I will remember his words:

> "Not only so, but we ourselves, who have the firstfruits of the Spirit, groan inwardly as we wait eagerly for . . . the redemption of our bodies. For in this hope we are saved. But hope that is seen is no hope at all. Who hopes for what he already has? But if we hope for what we do not yet have, we wait for it patiently" (Rom. 8:23-25).

✿

Thirteen

Satan Schemes
. . . God Redeems

WHEW! THAT LAST chapter covered quite a bit of ground, didn't it? I'll bet some of you are thinking by now, "But what about those four points mentioned back in chapter eleven?"

I haven't forgotten them. But I did want to approach the matter of healing in a general way first. Having sketched a broad background, let's now chalk out answers to the specific points people have written to me about healing as summarized on page 121.

First, what about the idea that since Satan causes disease, and since Jesus came to destroy Satan's work, then Jesus will always heal disease if we ask in faith?

I think this sort of reasoning shows a failure to understand the Bible's teaching on an important subject: the relationship between God and Satan in causing disease (and in causing all calamities, for that matter). The first principle we need to grasp is that *though Satan often causes disease, he can only do what God permits.*

Deep inside, in our less consistent moments, I think we almost unconsciously see the conflict between God and Satan as an arm wrestling match. Their wrists go first this way, then that; God's arm is on top one moment, Satan's the next. God will win in the end (we remind ourselves) because He's slightly stronger and can hold out longer. But it's going to take much time, effort, and a few close calls. It's almost as if we think Satan's schemes throw a monkey wrench into God's plans, catch Him off guard, and present Him with problems He wishes wouldn't happen.

But how silly. The truth is that God is infinitely more powerful than Satan.

First John 4:4 tells us, "the one [God] who is in you is greater than the one [Satan] who is in the world." Why, Satan owes his very existence to God. He had to receive God's permission before afflicting Job, and even then was under definite restrictions. His demonic hordes feared Jesus and obeyed Jesus' commands. And the Bible is clear that when our Lord is ready He will crush the Evil One forever.[14]

No, Satan doesn't sneak out and cause pneumonia and cancer while God happens to be looking the other way listening to the prayers of His saints. He can only do what our all-powerful and all-knowing God allows him to do. And we have God's promise that nothing will be allowed which is not for our good or which is too hard for us to bear (Rom. 8:28; 1 Cor. 10:13).

But when we say that God "allows" Satan to do the things he does, I think we sometimes get the wrong idea. It isn't as if Satan twists God's arm and God hesitantly grants, "Well, I guess it'll be okay for you to do such and such . . . but just this once and not too much!" Nor are we to imagine that once God grants permission, He then nervously runs behind Satan with a repair kit, patching up what the devil has ruined, mumbling to Himself, "Now how am I going to work *this* one out for good?" Worse yet is it to suppose that when a Christian becomes ill he has missed "God's best" for him—that the Lord is now forced to go with some divine "Plan B."

No, not only is God not frustrated and hindered by Satan's schemes, but *God actually uses Satan's deeds to serve His own ends and accomplish His own purposes.*

For instance, take the crucifixion of Jesus. Satan clearly played the leading role in instigating the whole thing. He entered the heart of Judas Iscariot, the betrayer of Jesus (John 13:2, 26-27). Satan-sponsored evil was working in the hearts of the Jewish mob as they clamored in Jerusalem's streets for the execution of Jesus. Satan-sponsored pride and fear were behind the mock justice handed down by Pilate as he condemned an innocent man in order to gain political popularity. Satan-sponsored sin provoked the cruel soldiers to increase the anguish of the harmless prisoner by torture and ridicule in His last hours of life.

But how did the early Christians, who had God's perspective, view it all? They praised God that the men responsible for Christ's death had only done "what your [God's] power and will had decided beforehand should happen" (Acts 4:28). In his most daring attempt to frustrate the plan of God, Satan cut his own throat and performed the deed which was God's final provision for man's redemption. The world's worst murder became the world's only salvation and dealt the death blow to sin and Satan.

Now suppose God the Father had taken the view many modern Christians take—the view which says: Anything Satan wants must be bad for God's people—the view which implies: If Satan wants one thing to happen, God must want the exact opposite to happen. What would have been the result? Well, God would have stopped Judas from betraying Jesus and stopped the Romans from crucifying Him. In short, He would have canceled the Crucifixion! And if God had canceled the Crucifixion what would have been the result? None of us would be saved!

The truth of the matter is, Satan and God may want the exact same event to take place—but for different reasons. Satan's motive in Jesus' crucifixion was rebellion; God's motive was love and mercy. Satan was a secondary cause behind the Crucifixion, but it was God who ultimately wanted it, willed it, and allowed Satan to carry it out. And the same holds true for disease.

I can imagine someone responding, "But, Joni, how can we possibly say that God is behind disease—that it exists because He wants it to? The Bible tells us that Jesus *healed* disease. Surely that proves God doesn't want it to exist."

Well, let God's own words to Moses speak for themselves—"Then the Lord said to him, 'Who has made man's mouth? Or who makes him dumb or deaf, or seeing or blind? Is it not I, the Lord?'" (Exod. 4:11 NASB). And hear the words of Jeremiah the prophet—"Is it not from the mouth of the Most High that both good and ill go forth?" (Lam. 3:38 NASB). And through Isaiah God says, "I form the light and create darkness, I bring prosperity and create disaster; I, the Lord, do all these things" (Isa. 45:7 NIV).

Does this say God wants disease? I think the key here is how we use the word "want." God doesn't want disease to exist in the sense that He *enjoys* it. He hates it just as He hates all the other results of sin—death, guilt, sorrow, etc. But God must want disease to exist in the sense that He *wills* or *chooses* for it to exist, for if He didn't He would wipe it out immediately.

It's like this. Suppose you were a judge, and a teen-age boy who was caught robbing a store was brought before you. Suppose, too, that the boy's father was your best friend. Would you *enjoy* giving the boy the sentence he served? No. Emotionally it would grieve you. But still you would *choose* to sentence him, for that would be the moral and just thing to do.

So God chooses to allow sickness—for many reasons. One of them is in order to mold Christian character. In this way God uses one form of evil (sickness) to help remove another form of evil (personal sin). And there are other reasons, too. The benefits mentioned earlier in this book applying to other trials apply to disease as well. But perhaps the most comforting reason was mentioned in the last chapter. God is delaying closing the curtain on sin and its results until more of the world can have the chance to hear the gospel. For if God erased all disease today, He would also have to erase sin, the cause of disease, and that would mean the destruction of all sinners. It is God's *mercy* which delays His judgment on disease and sin.

But I can imagine another objection some may raise to the way I have viewed God's relationship to disease in this chapter. It has to do with Satan. Is it true that God grants permission for Satan to spread disease? "Since everything Satan does stems from sinful rebellion," some reason, "then to say God allows Satan to act sinful and cause disease makes God a sinner."

That's a tough objection to handle, and I certainly don't understand everything about God's relationship to Satan. But the Bible does make two things absolutely clear: On the one hand, God sovereignly controls even Satan's actions. On the other hand, God is in no way a sinner nor the author of sin![15]

When the Bible presents us with two truths like these which seem opposed to one another, how are we to handle them? How can we fit them together? The easy way out is to deny one side or the other. (In this case that usually means denying God's sovereignty.) But that's wrong. What we should do is first be sure that both truths are really what the Bible is teaching. Once we're sure of that, we must humbly bow our reason to the authority of God's Word, accepting both truths in faith. When God tells us something we're to believe Him, even if what He says seems paradoxical to our finite minds.

The best illustration of this I can think of is the doctrine of the Trinity. Scripture plainly says there is but one God. Yet it also plainly teaches that the Father, Son, and Holy Spirit are each God although they are three distinct persons. No true Christian denies any of these truths even though human reason can't fit them together. Why should we treat the biblical truths about God's sinless nature and yet His sovereign control over Satan any differently?

Satan, as king of this world, has been granted the power to wreak havoc and disaster. He does so because he is going to hell, and misery loves company. He sends disease and trouble because he hates mankind and he hates God. But God exploits Satan's evil intentions and uses them in His own service—just one more example of His ability to work "out everything in conformity with the purpose of his will" (Eph. 1:11).

Satan intends the rain which ruins a church picnic to cause the people to curse their Lord; but God uses the rain to develop their patience. Satan plans to hinder the work of an effective missionary by arranging for him to trip and break a leg; God allows the accident so that the missionary's patient response to the pain and discomfort will bring glory to Himself. Satan brews a hurricane to kill thousands in a small Indian village so he can enjoy the misery and destruction; God uses the storm to display His awesome power, to show people the awful consequences that sin has brought to the world, to drive some to search for Him, to harden others in their sin, and to remind us that He is free to do as He pleases—that we will never figure Him out. Satan schemed that a seventeen-year-old girl named Joni would break her neck, hoping to ruin her life; God sent the broken neck in answer to her prayer for a closer walk with Him and uses her wheelchair as a platform to display His sustaining grace.

As a friend once said, "God sends things, but Satan often brings them." Praise God that when Satan causes us illness—or any calamity—we can answer him with the words Joseph answered his brothers who sold him into slavery, "As for you, you meant evil against me, but God meant it for good" (Gen. 50:20).

So much for the relationship between Satan and sickness. Let's move on to the second point people have written to me regarding miraculous healing (remember? back on page 121). The point was: because Jesus Christ is "the same yesterday, today, and forever" and because in the Gospels He healed all who came to Him in faith, mustn't He do the same today? This subject came up some time after the healing service in the little oak church.

It was one of those cold winter evenings when Steve and I were sitting by the fireplace. Some of my family were in the kitchen dressing warmly to go out in the falling snow. Steve caught that longing look on my face as I stared at my sisters while they bundled up in their scarves and coats.

"You'd really like to go out there with them, wouldn't you?" he said.

Startled, I answered, "Oh, no, I don't . . ." But I paused, then continued, "Well, yeah, I guess it *would* be nice to be on my feet. You know, Steve, it's been more than a year since that healing service at the church."

Steve, sensing I wanted to get into something heavy, pulled his chair closer.

"Look," I questioned, "do you know of any place in the Bible where it says that Jesus turned down someone who wanted to be healed?"

He thought a moment with a contemplative wrinkling of his forehead. "No, I can't think of any," and shook his head.

"Then you believe the Bible when it says in the Gospels that Jesus healed those who were brought to Him, right?"

"Oh, certainly," he replied and reached for his Bible on the table.

"And God's Word says that Jesus Christ is 'the same yesterday, today, and forever,' doesn't it?"

"It sure does."

"It also says that God never changes, right?"

"Right."

"Then if Jesus healed all those who came to Him in faith, and if He never changes, won't He surely heal all those who come to Him in faith today?"

Steve stood up and started slowly walking around the table. He took a deep breath, paused to collect his thoughts, and then responded, weighing his words. "Joni, your logic sounds inescapable. Jesus did heal those who asked Him back then. And He doesn't ever change. But to conclude that He has to act in the same way today—I've got to answer 'no.'"

Seeing the "why?" written on my face, he began to explain himself. "I think the basic mistake in that line of reasoning comes from failing to distinguish between *who God is* and *what He does*. Who He is never changes, but what He does often will."

He went on to explain that God's character and attributes are the things about

Him that cannot change. For instance, He could never become more holy than He is now, or more loving, or more faithful. Neither could He become less of any of these. That's because God is already perfect in all His traits, and for Him to change in any way would mean a move toward imperfection.

Allowing time for that to sink in, he walked over to the hearth to place a log on the fire. "Here, let me make it clear. It's like a person standing at the North Pole," he suggested, talking with his hands in typical Steve fashion. "When you're there, you're as far north as you can go. Move one step in any direction, and you've moved south."

I asked, "You mean if God were to change, He wouldn't be God any more?"

"Exactly," he confirmed, slapping his hand to his side. "When you're at the top, if you're going to move, there's no place to go but down. And because God's character and traits are 'at the top,' they're never going to change—or as the Bible puts it, 'He's the same yesterday, today, and forever.'"

Steve continued, "But that's not to put God into a box and say that He can't act. It's wrong to picture God as a meditating mystic who sits motionless for hours and doesn't even budge to swat a fly from his nose. The Bible is full of God's acts, and any act involves change."

"Not change in His character," I echoed, "but a change in what He does." Things were beginning to fit together, and my face brightened as Steve agreed.

He elaborated on the fact that God has a plan for the human race and that history is constantly moving toward a climactic goal. At one time God acted through a nation; now He acts through His church. Once Jesus submitted to those who mocked Him; someday He will take vengeance on His enemies. What is fitting at one time in His plan is not fitting at another. The God whose character is never-changing is directing a grand play where the props and lines are constantly changing, ever moving toward the final scene and the closing of the curtain.

Glancing out the window at my sisters returning with their sleds, I mused, "Then in answer to my question, are you saying that miracles of healing aren't fitting for today?"

"Joni, we just can't generalize about that. It may be good for God to heal one person and not another, or even to heal a person at one time in his life and not at another time. I believe that God sometimes still heals miraculously today when people pray. But I do think that miracles had a *special* place for the days of Christ and His apostles." He wheeled me away from the window and pushed me to the table.

Sitting down beside me, he opened up his Bible and went on to explain. I learned how miracles had a special place *for the time of Christ* because they proved He was who He claimed to be—Israel's Messiah. They showed that His kingdom had the power to reverse the awful effects of sin, such as death and disease.

Miracles had a special place *for the time of the apostles* because they proved that the apostles, too, were who they claimed to be—Christ's specially chosen men to get the wobbly-kneed, newborn church on its feet. The Book of Acts (where we read about the apostles and all they did) is the record of a unique time in the history of God's people—a unique time with unique problems. Thus, they needed special leaders such as the apostles.

In the first place, there had never been any Christian missionaries before. Yet Christ had told His followers to spread the gospel to the whole earth. What a task! And so God assisted the early church's first splash into an icy cold world by giving them leaders who could do miraculous deeds. Acts 2:43 tells us that "Everyone was filled with awe, and many wonders and miracles were done by the apostles."

Another unique problem the early church had was the confusion that so many new Christians felt who had been raised in Judaism. Steve asked me to imagine myself as the father of a Jewish family recently turned Christian, living in Palestine early in the first century.

"Picture this, Joni," he grinned. "For centuries your people have faithfully followed Jewish law regarding offering sacrifices, circumcising all males, not eating certain meats, and not associating with Gentiles. Naturally, the old way of life lingers on. After all, you *are* still a Jew. One day your best friend, also a Christian Jew (but acting a bit strange lately), springs some news on you.

> "Hey, old buddy, did you hear?"
>
> "Hear what?"
>
> "About the big change. Since God's Son has died on the cross as the final sacrifice for sin, we don't have to offer animals at the temple any more."
>
> Flinging your arms up, you exclaim in amazement, "Are you out of your mind?! Not offer sacrifices? I mean, I believe in Jesus, but we've *always* offered sacrifices."
>
> "And that's not all," he continues excitedly. "We don't have to circumcise our sons any more."
>
> "Not circumcise our boys! Why . . . (cough!) . . . that's . . . (sputter!) . . . how can you . . ."
>
> "And there's more—we can eat any meats we want to. And we're supposed to love all Gentiles as if they were our brothers! In fact, I'm inviting you and old Flavius Marcus over for pork dinner tonight."
>
> "*Me* eat pork?!" Holding your hands to your head, you run out screaming, "With Flavius, the pig herder?!!"

I laughed as Steve finished his story. "Well," he concluded, "you can imagine the difficulties that arose between Jewish and Gentile Christians. There needed to be some respected and capable leaders, such as the apostles, who could take charge and settle disputes."

He went on to tell how there was something else that made the apostolic age a special time. There was no New Testament as such yet, and the teachings of Jesus might easily be forgotten or distorted. Though the Holy Spirit was giving some Christians prophecies and revelations to fill in as stop-gaps until the full New Testament message could be written down and made permanent, there were many impostors. False teachers, hungry to feed their own egos, lurked behind every tree, waiting like wolves to pounce on God's flock and lead them into error. Since there was no New Testament to appeal to as an absolute standard by which to measure truth, the apostles were God's men to "ride herd" over the situation and authoritatively guard the church from error.

Yet with all the phony apostles running around, how were the real apostles of Christ to prove themselves genuine? Paul answers that question in his letters to the Corinthian church. He claims they can know he is for real because of his consistent life and the success of his ministry with them.[16] But his final defense is found in 2 Corinthians 12:12. "The things that mark an apostle—signs, wonders and miracles—were done among you with great perseverance." *Miracles had the definite purpose of spotlighting those men whom God had appointed to begin and lead His church.* God also added weight to the apostles' authority by the fact that, in addition to doing miracles themselves, others received miraculous gifts under their ministry. Apparently this did not happen under the ministry of non-apostles.[17]

"Special men for a special time," Steve summarized. "That's what the apostles were. In fact, they were so special that Ephesians 2:20 tells us the whole church was built upon the foundation of the apostles and New Testament prophets, with Jesus Himself as the chief cornerstone. Now that's quite a rank and honor, a position not given to the rest of us.

"Look at all those books about healing up on your shelf," Steve pointed up above my desk. Taking one down, he said, "I've read this one myself. Let me show you something in here." He flipped through the pages.

"See, here the author quotes Jesus' words to the Twelve in Matthew 10:8—'Heal the sick, raise the dead, cleanse those who have leprosy, drive out demons. Freely you have received, freely give.'" His finger moved down the page to the next paragraph.

"Down here he uses that verse to say we should be out doing the same. Joni, if Jesus' words there apply directly to us, it means we should all be out raising the dead!

"One more thing," he concluded. "No matter what we believe as to how important miracles were for then as opposed to now, one thing is certain: we can't point to what God did yesterday as proof that He's got to do the same thing today. If that were true, He'd have to keep our shoes and clothes from wearing out today because He did it for the Israelites as they wandered in the wilderness!"[18]

It began making sense to me. Although we can learn much from reading about the apostles, that doesn't necessarily mean we can do everything they did. God sent them to help the church at a time when they were desperately needed. Instead of getting frustrated and jealous because we can't do everything the apostles did, we should be praising God's wisdom in giving them special gifts appropriate to their situation and in giving us special grace appropriate to ours.

Neither Steve nor I had kept track of the hours as they had slipped by. The snow had stopped, the fire had died, and it was long past the time when I should have been in bed. Steve yawned, stretched, and got up to leave.

Picking up our empty Coke bottles, he hesitated a minute and then said, "Jon, this talk hasn't been easy for me. I've really had to wrestle with these things watching you these years in that wheelchair. If there's anyone anywhere who'd love to see you walk, it's me."

"I know that," I assured him.

"I don't want you to just blindly accept everything I've told you tonight. I'm just asking you to give it some prayerful thought with an open mind."

And that's all I'm asking you, the reader, to do.

❧

Fourteen

Prayers And Promises

BUT THE VERSES we read in that little oak church seemed so clear! I'm talking about all those Bible promises which seem to guarantee Christians that *all* their prayers will be answered, including prayers for healing. Remember?

> "I will do whatever you ask in my name, so that the Son may bring glory to the Father. You may ask me for anything in my name, and I will do it" (John 14:13-14).
>
> —Jesus
>
> "I tell you the truth, if anyone says to this mountain, 'Go, throw yourself into the sea,' and does not doubt in his heart but believes that what he says will happen, it will be done for him. Therefore I tell you, whatever you ask in prayer, believe that you will receive it, and it will be yours" (Mark 11:23-24).
>
> —Jesus
>
> "I can do everything through him who gives me strength" (Phil. 4:13).
>
> —Paul

And this brings us to the third and fourth points in chapter eleven: We have promises in Scripture that whatever we ask in Jesus' name will be done for us—including health and healing.

These are staggering promises, but they pose a problem. I mean, when's the last time you actually saw a mountain throw itself into the sea? Godly Christians pray in faith and in Jesus' name for a lot of things that never happen. So when Christians don't get their prayers answered (that is, when God's answer is "no"), what are we to do with verses like these? We can't just avoid them or attempt to make them mean something we'd feel comfortable with. Yet to put these verses by themselves on a plaque over our fireplace and then view them as God's word-for-word promise that all our prayers will be answered our way can really bring frustration. I'll be the first to admit that I've sometimes felt as though my prayers just bounced off the ceiling and never got through. Haven't you felt the same way?

Now I don't know all the reasons why God says yes to some prayers and not others. And I don't know the complete meaning of all these verses. but I've found it a real help to compare different sections of Scripture and let one throw light upon another. And you know that? God sure does guarantee answers to prayer. When Jesus gave His disciples these promises, He was saying, "Look, I'm giving you a job to do, and I promise you'll have everything you need to get it done. If there's a mountain in your way, ask Me and I'll mow it down." And those apostles did see mountains move as they changed the course of history!

But I also found that God gave two conditions which must be met if our prayers are to be guaranteed answers: we must be living in close fellowship with Him, and our requests must be in line with His will.

Fellowship With God

When I was a high school student, I, like many Christians, tended to think of myself as the center of life rather than God. Oh, I was trusting Christ as my Savior from sin, and I more or less tried to do what was right. But the basic thing on my mind when I thought about God was, "What can He do for *me?* How can serving Christ give *me* joy? How do *I* feel at the end of a worship service?" Naturally, this "God-exists-to-make-me-happy" mentality carried over into my prayer life. Forgetting that God expects and demands holiness from His children, I reasoned, "If God wants only the best for me, then surely He will answer my prayers, even if I don't exactly live like an angel."

But I was in for a rude awakening. Leafing through the Psalms during devotions one day, I stumbled upon this verse: "If I regard wickedness in my heart, the Lord will not hear" (Ps. 66:18). *Gulp! How can that be? I thought God listened to everybody.* But over the years I found other verses which said the same thing. James 5:16 says that the prayer of a righteous man is powerful and effective. *Oh, I don't need to worry about that,* I consoled myself. *Since I'm a Christian, I'm righteous in God's eyes no matter how I live.* But someone pointed out to me that all through his book James isn't talking about the *legal* righteousness God gives us, but the *obedient* righteousness we give Him. In other words, if I wanted God to hear me, I'd better start listening to Him.

Peter adds his voice to James' by cautioning husbands to treat their wives with respect. He goes on to tell them why—"so that nothing will hinder your prayers" (1 Peter 3:7). Remember that Peter was standing right there when Jesus gave all those astounding promises in the Gospels. Yet he didn't take Jesus to mean, "Prayer is like a blank check. Just fill in the amount whenever you like, no matter what your spiritual condition, and I'll cash it for you." No, God only guarantees that faithful Christians who "telephone" Him get through immediately. Backslidden believers might expect a busy signal unless they're calling to say, "Forgive me. I'm sorry."

Jesus Himself, who gave these promises, qualified what He meant in John 15:7. *"If you remain in me and my words remain in you*, ask whatever you wish, and it will be given you" (italics mine). When he says "remain in me," He's talking about a consistent life style of closeness to Him, not a sporadic spirituality.

When I was in high school, we ran several weeks of cross-country in gym class every fall. When the whistle blew, most of us started out at a relaxed pace, and soon the majority of girls found the pace they knew they could keep up for the whole distance. But there were always a few who shot off sprinting like a kid who had just hit a baseball through the neighbor's window. Before most of us had made the bend, they were half-way around the field. Pretty soon we would pass them as they slowed down to catch their breath. Then they'd zoom by us again, only to fall behind the second time. At the end of the race the steady, consistent runners always did the best.

In the same way, when we dash off with a sudden surge of spiritual zeal, that doesn't necessarily mean we are "remaining in Christ." Sudden zeal isn't bad, but it may be deceptive. As I know from personal experience, we can be "super-Christian" one week and a discouraged quitter the next. Now, God promises to answer the prayers of those who maintain a steady walk with Him, and that involves some maturity. Of course, all Christians will have their ups and downs, so I'm not talking about perfection. The very best Christian falls infinitely short of that. And because God is so gracious, at times He may hear us even when we are out of fellowship with Him. But the more consistent our life with Christ becomes, the more we can expect our prayers to be answered.

Jesus wasn't speaking in general terms when He told us to remain in Him. He got specific by adding the phrase, "and [if] my words remain in you." This refers to more than just the actual words He said while on earth, the words printed in red in some Bibles. He meant the Bible in general, for Christ's Spirit inspired all the Scriptures. To have Christ's words remain in you does not mean you have to get a seminary degree or Bible school diploma. Nor does it require memorizing "grocery lists" of biblical names and places so you can win a game of Bible Trivia when someone tries to stump you with "Who was Zechariah's mother-in-law?" You can know tons of Bible and theology without ever letting it grip your soul. I think Jesus was referring to running Scripture through your mind over and over again in order to find new ways to please God and bring Him praise. Like David's attitude when he wrote, "Thy word I have treasured in my heart, that I may not sin against Thee" (Ps. 119:11).

So there we have it. To get our prayers answered we need to walk with God and be in His Word. But I fear that too many of us want the power of Paul's prayers without the discipline of Paul's life. At one time or another we've all been guilty of approaching God as though He's some great spiritual Vending Machine in the sky—drop in a prayer and out comes the answer. But God isn't a machine; He's a person.

My sister Kathy can feel free to ask my sister Jay, "May I borrow your car tonight?" because Kathy is close to Jay, loves her, treats her well, and has cultivated a relationship with her. But if you're a supposed "friend" of Jay who hasn't even called for two years, don't expect to casually drop by one day, turn on the old charm, and con her into loaning you her car.

Human relationships don't work that way. Neither do relationships with God. We can't expect Him to hear our prayers if we only come running to Him when we want something or get into trouble. And even when we're living close to Him, we have no license to expect "healing upon demand" or anything else upon demand. Because we exist to serve God, not vice versa, we're to humbly request things from Him, remembering who He is. Then, as the apostle John says, we will "receive from him anything we ask," not because we demand it, but "because we obey his commands and do what pleases him" (1 John 3:22).

God's Will

But what if you're a Christian who is really trying to remain in Christ and yet you're sick? Perhaps it's a head cold. Perhaps it's leukemia. But after four healing services and countless prayers and tears, you're still sick. What's wrong? Maybe you could relate when I shared my own experience of not getting healed because you, too, feel guilty that nothing's happened. Perhaps you've searched your heart for any hidden sins until you'd almost invent some so you could confess them and be healed. It could be that certain pages in your Bible are over-worn from where you've underlined different promises in ink and have read those promises aloud to God. But though you've rung heaven's phones off the hook and have promised God you'll do anything if only He heals you, all you get is silence.

If this is your situation, you are not alone; thousands of other Christians are just like you. And my heart goes out to you because I know exactly what it feels like to have well-meaning Christians give subtle hints that my condition is self-imposed.

But after looking everywhere else for the reason why my prayers for healing weren't answered, I was forced to return to God's Word and take a closer look. It was there I found something which shed light not only on my questions about divine healing, but on the whole issue of why Christians suffer. It's such a simple thing. If you have tried everything to be healed but nothing has changed, then *has it ever really hit you that the reason you are in your present condition is that God, in His wisdom, wills it to be so?*

You see, the same apostle John who recorded God's promise that whatever we ask in Jesus' name will come true (John 14:13) also said that God puts a condition on that promise. In 1 John 5:14 he tells us, "We have this assurance in approaching God, that if we ask anything *according to his will,* He hears us" (italics mine). Now that's quite an "if." Not . . . if we ask anything we think we might like . . . or anything that would make life easier . . . or even anything that we imagine God would want . . . but anything that's actually "according to His will." For God to answer our prayers, they must be in line with His will.

But why in the world would it possibly be God's will to deny a Christian's request for healing? In some ways, this whole book is about that very thing. The pages of Scripture teem with good things that can come from suffering. Pain and discomfort get our minds off the temporary things of this world and force us to think about God. They drive us to pull His Word off the shelf far more than usual and to pay more attention when we do. Trials knock us off our proud pedestals and get us relying on God (2 Cor. 1:9). Then we learn to know God better, for when we have to depend on someone to get us through each hour, we really get to know them. Problems give us the chance to praise God even when it's hard. This pleases Him and proves to the spirit world how great He is to inspire such loyalty. And it proves something to us—it gives us a gauge to measure the depth or shallowness of our own commitment to Him.

Sometimes sickness serves as God's chastiser to wake us from our sin (1 Cor. 11:29-30; 1 Peter 4:1). This proves to us that He loves us, for every good father disciplines his children (Heb. 12:5-6). Sometimes God uses suffering to help us relate to others who are suffering (2 Cor. 1:3-4). And the list could go on. If nothing else, the fact that while Jesus was on earth God matured Him through suffering should tell us something (Heb. 2:10). It should make us ask ourselves the question, "Should I expect anything less?"

I sometimes shudder to think where I would be today if I had not broken my neck. I couldn't see at first why God would possibly allow it, but I sure do now. He has gotten so much more glory through my paralysis than through my health! And believe me, you'll never know how rich that makes me feel. If God chooses to heal you in answer to your prayers, that's great. Thank Him for it. But if He chooses not to, thank Him anyway. You can be sure He has His reasons.

I can hear someone saying, "Joni, if we think that way, if we don't expect God to heal us, He won't! Ending a prayer for healing with the words 'If it be Thy will' actually shows a lack of faith. Shouldn't we strive to reach the place where we're so in touch with God that we can just sort of sense what He wills in every case and then prayer with full faith and assurance?" But what a contrast this view is to the biblical picture of our God! He is so above us that we will never figure Him out: "O the depth of the riches, the wisdom and the knowledge of God! How unsearchable his judgments and his paths beyond tracing out! Who has known the mind of the Lord? Or who has been his adviser?" (Rom. 11:33-34).

The authors of the New Testament didn't claim to always know God's mind. James tells us we shouldn't say, "Tomorrow I'm going to go to such and such a place and do so and so." Rather, our attitude should be, "If it is the Lord's will, we will live and do this or that" (James 4:15). Once when Paul was asked by some Christians to stay in Ephesus to help teach them, he didn't pretend to be able to read God's mind, but merely said, "I will come back if it is God's will" (Acts 18:21).

One of the main reasons we need to pray with an "if-it-be-Thy-will" attitude is that it's so easy for us to make mistakes and misread God's will. Countless times I have fooled myself into believing the prayers I prayed were for God's glory when actually they were for myself. "God, don't let me make a fool of myself when I give my talk in speech class. If I do, the kids will think that all Christians are weirdos, and that'll hurt Your reputation." Now if that's what I had actually meant, my prayer would have been okay. But deep inside, I think what was really on my mind was, "God, don't let me flop this talk because I don't want to have my bubble burst." Maybe God knew that what was *really* hurting His reputation was my self-centered attitude at school and that a lousy speech would serve His purpose better than answering my prayer.

But out motives don't need to be selfish or sinful in order for us to misread God's plan. We can make honest mistakes.[19] Let me give you an example.

One afternoon about a year ago a nice-looking, dark-haired young man in his mid-twenties, whom I had never met before, appeared at our door asking to see me. My sister Jay invited him in and left the two of us to talk in the den. During the awkward conversation which followed, I learned he had driven all the way from his home in the Southwest just to meet me. Obviously nervous, he said God had revealed to him that I was to become his wife and that he should propose to me. In his mind, it was clearly God's will that we be married. He became very unsettled when I told him that, strangely enough, he was about the tenth such person in the past two years whom "God had told" to propose to me. Had God misled him? Had He misled the other nine?

No, we concluded after discussing it for a while. God is not a God of confusion. He doesn't mis*lead* us; we mis*read* Him. Then we went on to talk about some "safer" ways to discover God's will—like applying principles from His Word, getting the advice of mature Christians, and waiting to see which doors God opens and closes. By the time the young man left, he was much more at ease. Convinced God hadn't played a joke on him, he drove away feeling that the things he had learned had made his trip worthwhile.

It takes real humility and self-denial to put our pleas for healing before God and then willingly leave the answer with Him. Jesus so beautifully illustrated this in His prayer of anguish in Gethsemane. In His personal desire He desperately wished to avoid the horrors of the cross, saying, "Father, if you are willing, take this cup from me"; but His last clause made possible the salvation of mankind— "yet not my will, but yours be done" (Luke 22:42). Surely, at least part of what it means to pray "in Jesus' name" is to pray in the same spirit in which He prayed in His darkest hour—giving God our requests but leaving the results with Him.

Look How Far We've Come—A Summary

Jesus gave wonderful promises to His disciples; whatever they needed to get God's work done on earth, He would give. But Jesus' own words and the rest of Scripture make it clear that there were at least two conditions to any prayer they made—they must be remaining in Him, and their request must be in line with God's will. Since God hasn't chosen to reveal all of His will to Christians, then we must leave our requests in His hands and wait to see what He decides to do. And if He chooses to refuse our request? Well, there is more than one way to "move a mountain." The New Testament stresses that God loves to use weak vessels (people) to do His work so that He, and not they, gets the glory. And in light of all the spiritual benefits resulting from sickness and suffering, God may choose that our very sickness be His way of moving the mountains before us.

As we grow in our faith, our way of looking at things changes. Once it seemed as if the only way God could glorify Himself would be to *remove* our sufferings. Now it becomes clear that He can glorify Himself *through* our sufferings.

As for healings and other miracles of God—just because they had a *special* place for the days of Christ and His apostles doesn't mean they have *no* place for today. In reacting to the "God wants to heal everybody" extreme, many of us have over-reacted and joined the "God never wants to heal anybody" extreme. In this case, what we mistakenly call "unemotionalism" in reality is probably plain unbelief. We do not have because we do not ask.

But that's not to say that any time we ask in faith for healing God is obligated to give it to us. Even in apostolic times godly Christians sometimes had to endure illness. During his travels, the apostle Paul, whom God used to heal many, had to leave his friend Trophimus sick in Miletus (2 Tim. 4:20). In 1 Timothy 5:23 Paul urged his friend Timothy to "use a little wine because of your stomach and frequent illnesses." He didn't say, "Pray more about it," or "Come and see me about it." He said, "Take something for it." Christians are to pray for healing, but they are not necessarily to think something is wrong if God refuses the request.

Finally, we should not deceive ourselves into believing that miracles are the ultimate weapon to convince a sinful world. At the end of Jesus' own life, though He had done all kinds of miracles, some men jeered, "If you're really the Messiah, come down off that cross and then we'll believe." Before going to the cross, Jesus confided to His disciples that their generation was especially guilty because they had seen so many wonders and still, on the whole, didn't believe (John 15:24). No, we can be certain that if a man's heart is hardened in sin against God, even the most spectacular divine sign won't change his mind, unless the Holy Spirit opens his eyes.

Do you remember the book that fell off my desk several chapters ago? Well, I still can't pick it up. It sure would be nice to have the use of my hands again so I could reach it. But the wish is fading. For my paralysis has drawn me close to God and given a spiritual healing which I wouldn't trade for a hundred active years on my feet.

WHEN
THE PIECES
DON'T SEEM
TO FIT

❦

Fifteen

Let God
Be God

DURING MY FIRST year in the hospital I would sometimes leaf through my Bible using a mouthstick. I suppose I learned some things, but reading was mainly a pastime—on par with watching soap operas and listening to the radio. Not until I got home did I give God's Word any kind of serious study. When I did, it made the difference between night and day. Seeing things through God's eyes instead of my own helped me to begin fitting together the puzzle pieces of my suffering. I was getting a taste of genuine wisdom. *Maybe if I keep at it,* I reasoned, *one day I'll be fully wise—able to understand ALL of God's purposes in EVERYTHING that happens.*

But as my Christian life progressed, thing didn't work out that way. Often I could see how some specific trial was working out for my good. But sometimes I couldn't. For instance, I knew that trials are sent to build us up. But there were days when the problems were piled on so high they only seemed to wear me down—even when I took them as from God. *The Lord promises that days like this will turn out for my good,* I thought, *but HOW! I just can't see it!*

And that wasn't all. In addition to my own unsettling experiences, I began learning about others who endured trials for which I had no answers. People began writing me with problems I just couldn't understand, even with an open Bible. Oh, sure, in one sense I could understand. I knew the various explanation in Scripture for why God lets us suffer. But matching up which explanation fits each particular trial was another story. What would you have said to the young girl who wrote this letter?

Dear Joni,

  . . . My father died when I was two years old and my mother has been very ill with cancer for a year now. . . . I am trying to understand why God allowed this to happen. Sometimes I spend a lot of time just wondering what it will be like when Mom dies and I am alone. I have been trying to get closer to God so I will not be bitter when this happens. I have already received Jesus as my Lord and Savior, but the depression I have from watching Mom suffer causes me to have a hard time concentrating long enough to read and study His Word. Just sitting around watching TV and sleeping seems to all I can handle.

I could give this girl some helpful advice as to how to respond to her problems in a God-honoring way. But give her the specific "Why" behind her troubles? That was a different story. Was God's purpose in her trials to make her more like Christ or to get her thoughts on spiritual thing? To make her an example to the angelic world or to give her the ability to comfort others? I might guess, but I didn't know. Whatever God's reason, at least on the surface it didn't seem to be working.

In fact, some of the trials people wrote to me about actually seemed to *hurt* God's cause.

Dear Joni,

  Please understand as I write this that I am not feeling sorry for myself and I am not an atheist. I thought that after I read your story I would be finally able to see things differently. But though I admire you if you honestly believe the way you do, I still have just not been able to understand the cruel things in your life and in the life of my brother.

  My brother is 26 years old and has been a Quad [i.e., paralyzed in four limbs] since 1965 due to an auto accident. . . . Like you he had quite a bit going for him at the time of his accident. Being a Quad yourself you know what he went through.

  He finally made up his mind to do something with the only thing he had left—his mind. He studied Psychology at home, went to work as an aide for the Governor of Indiana and was going to go to college in Ohio for more Psychology. He lost his job after only two weeks because Medicaid could not pay his medical bills if he was working. He *wanted* to work, he didn't want to be dependent on other people, and like you he *didn't* want pity.

  I talk in the past tense because my brother is now in a nursing home in a comatose state as of October 1976 due to a freak accident. He lived like a normal person the way he *wanted* to, and he kept his mind alert at all times. Now, Someone has decided to take his mind away. If you feel that's fair or that there's a reason for that, please help me understand it.

Any explanation I might have sent to this young man would probably come off sounding like hollow little formulas—trite clichés. And to be honest, they probably wouldn't have satisfied me deep down inside either. Sometimes the magnitude of a person's problems seems to outweigh any potential benefit which might come as a result. I felt that way when I read this woman's letter.

Dear Joni,

I am a 22-year-old triplegia (paralyzed in three limbs). This happened to me in 1968 after my mother hit me on the head. It took six surgeries to save me. I was at Cook County Hospital for one year. Then I was sent to the Rehabilitation Institute of Chicago for a year and a half. Then I went to Grant Hospital for surgery on my arms and legs.

I have been back to the Rehabilitation Institute eight times. So far I have had 22 surgeries. I am still the same. I am in a chair. I have no family and I take care of myself. I have read your book and would like to know how to cope with depression. I don't have a lot of faith in God. I feel I cannot overcome this. Please tell me how you feel about this.

I began to wonder, "Will I ever become truly wise and be able to understand God's mind in all of this?" My friend Steve didn't help matters any when he told me about the experiences of his cousin, a young woman who until recently lived not far from me. She shares those experiences here:

When My mom was only sixteen, a local alcoholic a few years older than she said he'd kill her parents if she wouldn't marry him, so she did. He was like a maniac and used to beat her black and blue when he was drunk. We grew up extremely poor on a farm in Tennessee, and mom had to work hard in the fields to keep food on the table. . . . I remember once mom gathering us kids and running to the hills behind out house. I thought the reason dad was chasing us with the gun was that he was only playing cowboys and Indians (I was so little). But when I saw the fear in mom's face, I knew it was for real. Later that night we sneaked back to the house when dad fell asleep drunk and it was safe. . . . One time when he was drunk he lined us up against the wall, pointed a loaded gun, and said he was going to kill us one by one and then kill himself. If a neighbor hadn't happened to drop by and then help us, I guess we'd be dead. Dad drowned when I was seven.

Even after mom remarried and we moved north, trouble seemed to follow us. Mom had a gun pulled on her up here. And two years ago when she worked in a store three robbers tied and gagged her, locked her in the ladies' room, and put a knife to her throat. They said they'd kill her if she screamed. . . .

She's spent the last nine weeks in the hospital with raynauds disease. It turns your hands and toes dark black and hurts like frostbite wearing off. She hasn't had a good night's sleep the entire time from the pain—pain so bad she can't even stand to have the sheet touch her fingers. When her left foot got gangrene, they thought they might have to amputate, but they were able to save it. . . . Three fingers of her left hand had to go, though, down to the first joint. We all keep trusting the Lord, but it sure gets hard sometimes.

Could even the most mature Christian fully explain God's reasoning in all of this? But that wasn't all! Steven's cousin went on to tell of her stepfather's serious health problems and surgeries, the crushed shoulder her brother received in a car accident that left his left arm immobilized, and her own operations for cancer. But the last episode she shared was the most unbelievable. It took place on her farm early one morning in August of 1975:

I had seen my husband, Buddy, and the kids off for the day. After getting dressed for work, I came downstairs to go out through the kitchen door to my car. When I got to the kitchen I was startled to see a man there, leaning over the washer. But when he turned my way I recognized him as the teen-age boy from the farm a quarter mile up the road. "What are you doing here?" I asked, thinking it strange that he hadn't knocked. Usually the dogs bark at a stranger, but they hadn't today. But he didn't say a word, just sort of stared with a kind of dazed look. Then he showed a knife in his hand and began walking towards me.

I backed up and started to scream, but he kept coming. Finally he stopped right in front of me and then stabbed his knife into my right side. When I felt the hot liquid pouring out, I put my hand over the wound to keep from losing too much blood. But it didn't do any good, because he started stabbing me all over. All the while I kept screaming, "Why?! Why?!" When I went for a kitchen knife to defend myself, the drawer just came out and fell to the floor. I think the scariest thing was when I saw my own blood all over the floor. I slumped to the floor, and after what seemed like ages he finally left.

After he had gone I got hold of myself and then began faltering over to the phone to call for help. It wasn't until I heard the kitchen door open behind me that I realized he had never really left, but had waited outside to see what I'd do. My heart sank, and I knew I'd never make it to the phone. "I'm going to kill you this time," he said very matter-of-factly. Then he raised his knife and started stabbing me all over again. After slashing my wrist and behind my knee he pricked his knife in my stomach over and over. It was more awful than I can describe.

He asked me if my husband was home, and I said, "Yes, and he's coming downstairs!" But when nobody came he knew I had lied and came at me again. I managed to yell, "You've already killed me. Why don't you just leave me alone!" Then just as calm as anything he wiped his mouth with his sleeve and turned and left.

I was getting weaker and weaker as I lost more blood, but I knew I'd have to wait until he left for good before trying anything this time. When I was almost ready to black out, I know it was God who gave me the strength to get to my feet and stumble to the phone. I pushed the "0" button and had just enough time to tell the operator the bare essentials before a black curtain fell and I was out.

They tell me that it was two days before they knew if I'd live or not. It took somewhere around fifty stitches all over my body. I had to have my spleen removed, and they had to repair my liver, pancreas, and collapsed lung.

Steve tells me that after serving only one month in a minimum security detention home the attacker was transferred to a mental institution and was allowed home on weekends. Fourteen months later he was freed. Although God has given Steven's cousin remarkable ability to forgive her assailant and not be bitter, after three years she still feels the effects. In order to go to the bathroom she must first wake her husband because she fears walking down the dark hall alone.

When I heard the story of this young woman, I just sat in stunned silence. How could anyone make sense out of that? She'll feel the effects of it for the rest of her life. Steve's cousin did say that the incident drew her family closer together. It also brought her somewhat closer to God.

But though technically one could point to these things as reasons why God allowed all of this to happen, surely they couldn't be the whole story. She had already been close to God, and they already had a better-than-average family life. Surely God's whole purpose couldn't have been just to move their good family life and Christian life up a few notches. A much milder trial could have done that. What was God thinking? The burden of the questions seemed to outweigh the answers.

If I was to be involved in a ministry to people who suffer, it seemed to me that I should know the solutions to questions like these. But how could I help others understand what I didn't even understand myself?

I will always be grateful for a book which God sent into my life about that time, one which I say without hesitation is among the best I have ever read. In his book *Knowing God*, J. I. Packer included a small chapter called "God's Wisdom and Ours." There he tackles this very problem of our inability to understand the purposes of God behind every event.

Now the mistake that is commonly made is to . . . suppose . . . that the gift of wisdom consists in an ability to see why God has done what He has done in a particular case, and what He is going to do next.

What do you mean that's a mistake? Isn't wisdom the ability to always figure out the mind of God?

People feel that if they were really walking closer to God, so that He could impart wisdom to them freely, then . . . they would discern the real purpose of everything that happened to them, and it would be clear to them every moment how God was making all things work together for good. . . . If they end up baffled, they put it down to their own lack of spirituality.

He's sure got my number. Has this guy been reading my mind?

Such people spend much time . . . wondering why God should have allowed this or that to take place . . . or what they should deduce from it . . . Christians . . . may drive themselves almost crazy with this kind of inquiry.

Amen to that! I'm about to go bananas myself. Then you mean that we can't always understand what God is thinking? Wow, I thought. *Then if that isn't wisdom, what is?* The next few pages held some answers that were real life-changes for me, and that got me searching in the Bible for some answers of my own.

I came across the story of Job, the classic example of suffering. If anyone ever needed to understand the "why" behind his condition, it was Job, His family had been killed, his property ruined and stolen, and his body inflicted with boils. Not until the last five chapters of the book does God finally walk onstage to answer the questions and challenges of Job and his friends. And when He does, do you know what reason God gives Job for all the suffering he had experienced? None. Not a word! He doesn't sit Job down and say, "Listen carefully while I give you the inside story on why I've let you go through all of this. You see, My plan is. . . ." In fact, so far is God from answering Job's questions that He says, stand up, Job. I've got a few questions to ask *you!*"

For the next four chapters God does nothing but describe in detail the awesome majesty of His own works in nature, and then asks Job if he can match them. The Lord paints vivid word pictures of the creation of the world, the vastness of the stars and space, the might of the ox, the majesty of the horse, the miracle of animal instincts and the way earth provides food for every living thing. "But of course you know all this!" God mocks Job, "For you were born before it was all created, and you are so very experienced!" (Job. 38:21 LB).

I could almost feel Job cringing as God spoke to him. (I was cringing myself.) *Why put Job on the spot?* I thought. All those descriptions of God's wisdom and power in nature were certainly interesting. But what did they have to do with Job's trials? Job never claimed he had created the world. He never said he could explain the habits of wild animals. Why was God talking about that? Job hadn't pretended to know all the mysteries of weather cycles and birth and life. All he wanted was for God to help him understand the death of his family, the loss of his property, and the boils all over his body.

I continued reading. More nature scenes. More descriptions of God's greatness. More taunts from God like, "Do you know how mountain goats give birth? . . . Can you shout to the clouds and make it rain? . . . Do you realize the extent of the earth? . . . Tell Me about it if you know!"

It still seemed so confusing. But as I came to chapter forty, some light began to dawn. God finally asked Job a question that seemed to focus in on what He had been driving at all along. "Do you still want to argue with the Almighty! Or will you yield? Do you—God's critic—have the answers? . . . Stand up like a man and brace yourself for battle. Let me ask you a question, and give me the answer. Are you going to discredit my justice and condemn me, so that you can say you are right?" (Job. 40:1, 7-8 LB).

So that was it! God understood that when Job demanded "Why?" he was really asking God to be accountable to him. It seems so innocent, but in a sense, to insist on such answers from God is to set oneself over God. How absurd! We, like Job, often think God is not treating us fairly. We act as if there were some imaginary court in the sky where God must answer to something called "fairness." But what we forget is that God Himself *is* the court; and He invented fairness. What could we possibly measure His fairness against? What He does is as fair as you can get.[20]

Look at God's awesome wisdom and power demonstrated by His marvelous works of creation. How could such a God be answerable to a puny mortal like Job, who couldn't begin to fathom God's infinite greatness? As God said in Jeremiah 49:19, "Who is like Me, and who will summon Me into court?" It was as if God were saying, "Job, if you can't even understand the way I do things in the natural world, what gives you a right to question Me in the spiritual realm, which is even harder to understand?"

When Job realized this, all he could say was, "I am nothing—how could I ever find the answers? I lay my hand upon my mouth in silence. I have said too much already"(Job 40:4-5 LB).

What made Job feel this way? He got his first glimpse of who God really is. All his life he had worshipped God, but for the first time he saw God as He really is, not just his own limited concept of Him, Job put it like this: "I had heard about you before, but now I have seen you, and I loathe myself and repent in dust and ashes" (Job 42:5 LB).

My thoughts turned away from Job's situation and back to my own. I was grateful for the things I had been able to see from God's point of view. But, like Job, I still had unanswered questions. What about the things God hadn't revealed? How had I handled them?

Immediately I was convinced. The Bible tells us our God is so trustworthy that we are to throw our confidence on Him, not leaning on our own limited understanding (Prov. 3:5). God has already proved how much His love can be trusted by sending Christ to die for us. Wasn't that enough? Not for me. I always wanted to be on the inside looking out—sitting with the Lord up in the control tower instead of down on the confusing ground level. He couldn't be trusted unless I was there to oversee things!

What a low view of my Master and Creator I had held all these years! How could I have dared to assume that almighty God owed me explanations! Did I think that because I had done God the "favor" of becoming a Christian, He must now check things out with me? Was the Lord of the universe under obligation to show me how the trials of every human being fit into the tapestry of life? Had I never read Deuteronomy 29:29: "There are secrets the Lord your God has not revealed to us" (LB)?

What made me think that even if He explained all His ways to me I would be able to understand them? It would be like pouring million-gallon truths into my one-ounce brain. Why, even the great apostle Paul admitted that, though never in despair, he was often perplexed (2 Cor. 4:8). Hadn't God said, "For as the heavens are higher than the earth, so are . . . my thoughts [higher] than your thoughts" (Isa. 55:9)? Didn't one Old Testament author write, "As you do not know the path of the wind, or how the body formed in a mother's womb, so you cannot understand the work of God, the Maker of all things" (Eccl. 11:5 NIV)? In fact, the whole book of Ecclesiastes was written to convince people like me that only God hold the keys to unlocking the mysteries of life and that He's not loaning them all out! "He has also set eternity in the hearts of men; yet they cannot fathom what God has done from beginning to end" (Eccl. 3:11 NIV).

If God's mind was small enough for me to understand, He wouldn't be God! How wrong I had been.

I thought back to those early days of studying God's Word when the puzzle pieces of my suffering began fitting together. How sweet that first taste of wisdom was. There's nothing like seeing our difficulties from God's perspective. But what a mistake to think that I would ever be able to complete the *whole* puzzle of suffering. For wisdom is more than just seeing our problems through God's eyes—it's also trusting Him even when the pieces don't seem to fit.

WHEN IT ALL
FITS TOGETHER

Sixteen

Heaven

"CLOUDS," I MUMBLED to myself, staring out the window of the plane.

"Hmm?" Sheryl glanced up from her book.

"Those clouds out there," I answered. "Look at them."

Sheryl leaned over my shoulder and stared out at the beautiful expanse of puffy billows. It was close to dusk, and the cloudscape was one of the most gorgeous we had ever seen—deep purples, light pinks, hazy blues, bright oranges: a celestial mountain range arrayed in panorama against the setting sun.

"What do they remind you of?" I asked.

"Mountains," I said. "Spongy mountains in a million colors."

"I know," I answered, eyes still fixed on the view. "You'd almost believe they'd hold you up if you jumped out onto them."

But they wouldn't. Beautiful as they were, solid as they seemed, they were just fading mists of vapor—wisps of smoke. Here today, gone tomorrow.

I thought about our life here on earth and what the Bible says about it. "What is your life? You are a mist that appears for a little while and then vanishes" (James 4:14). I glanced about the cabin of the plane. Stewardesses serving refreshments. Businessmen with their *Wall Street Journals*. Mothers and babies. Tourists with tennis rackets. Some dozing. Some staring out the window. Flying to sales meetings, vacations, grandchildren.

It doesn't seem like a mist that quickly vanishes, I thought to myself. We really don't believe it's all going to end, do we? If God hadn't told us differently, we'd all think this parade of life would go on forever.

But it will end. This life is not forever.

Nor is it the best life that will ever be. The good things here are merely images of the better things we will know in heaven. It's like the artwork I produce. I draw scenes from nature around me, but those drawings are only a feeble, sketchy attempt to mirror what I see. I imitate with a gray pencil what God has painted with an infinite array of colors. My drawings, bounded by the edges of a sketch pad, can never fully portray God's boundless nature above, beneath, and around us. And just as my arkwork pleasantly but imperfectly reflects the nature I see, so this earth that we know is only a preliminary sketch of the glory that will one day be revealed. Reality—the final painting—lies in heaven.

Our problem is—we get too caught up in the "reality" of life.

"A month from now I'll be sipping lemonade on the sands of Florida," dreams the overworked secretary.

"Three more weeks till we're out of here!" thinks the high school senior looking forward to graduation.

"Isn't he the most wonderful person on earth," sighs the engaged young woman.

"If only I get this promotion," plans the rising executive.

But getting what we want is seldom as wonderful as our imagination told us it would be. The long-awaited vacation ends up being too short and too expensive. College assignments make high school homework seem like child's play. The maiden's knight turns out to be an average husband with chinks in his armor. And that promotion at the office brings with it added pressure and headaches. The good things in life rarely turn out to be as satisfying as we expect. And even when they do, they never last long enough.

That's why God tells us in the Bible that we are to set our hearts on heaven (Col. 3:2; 1 Peter 1:13). Life's pleasures were never meant to fill us. They are merely to whet our appetite for what is to come—and to cheer and inspire us as we trek through this earth toward heaven. "Our Father refreshes us on the journey with some pleasant inns, but He will not encourage us to mistake them for home."[21]

The trouble is, we do mistake them for home. It's hard to think about heaven when it seems so far away. Besides, we've got to die in order to get there. Who wants to think about that! And so God gives us a little help in getting our minds on the hereafter. He does it in a way we usually don't appreciate at first, but later we're grateful for it. Samuel Rutherford described this help in an essay he wrote back in the seventeenth century:

> If God had told me some time ago that he was about to make me as happy as I could be in this world, and then had told me that he should begin by crippling me in arm or limb, and removing me from all my usual sources of enjoyment, I should have thought it a very strange mode of accomplishing his purpose. And yet, how is his

wisdom manifest even in this! For if you should see a man shut up in a closed room, idolizing a set of lamps and rejoicing in their light, and you wished to make him truly happy, you would begin by blowing out all his lamps; and then throw open the shutters to let in the light of heaven.[22]

That's what God did for me when He sent a broken neck my way. He blew out the lamps in my life which lit up the here and now and made it so exciting. The dark despair which followed wasn't much fun. But it sure did make what the Bible says about heaven come alive. One day, when Jesus comes back, God is going to throw open heaven's shutters. And there's not a doubt in my mind that I'll be fantastically more excited and ready for it than if I were on my feet. You see, *suffering gets us ready for heaven.*

How does it get us ready? *It makes us want to go there.* Broken necks, broken arms, broken homes, broken hearts—these things crush our illusions that earth can "keep its promises." When we come to *know* that the hopes we cherished will never come true, that our dead loved one is gone from this life forever, that we will never be as pretty, popular, successful, or famous as we had once imagined, it lifts our sights. It moves our eyes from this world, which God knows could never satisfy us anyway, and sets them on the life to come. Heaven becomes our passion.

When I think of longing for heaven, I think of Rick Spaulding, a 23-year-old paralytic who wrote me shortly after reading my first book. His letters were so full of joy and love for the Lord that they encouraged all of us who read them. I thought I would enjoy meeting him someday; perhaps I could find out more about his injury, and we could share spiritual insights or talk shop about wheelchairs.

On July 4, 1976, I had opportunity to visit Rick. Some friends had taken me to Philadelphia for a few days where I had several speaking engagements. On that bicentennial afternoon we had nothing scheduled. So remembering from Rick's letters that he and his family lived in Valley Forge, not far away, we called and asked if we could come see them. Within minutes we were on our way.

When we arrived at the house, Mrs. Spaulding drew us aside to explain a bit about Rick's condition and prepare us for meeting him.

"Rick was in a fist fight at school when he was fifteen," she described. "He fell and hit his head on the gym floor, which put him in a coma. When he woke up, he was paralyzed."

Well, I thought, *so he's paralyzed. I'm paralyzed.*

But she went on to tell us just *how* paralyzed he was. You see, I can move my shoulders. I can move a little bit of my biceps muscles. I can smile and talk. But Rick couldn't do any of these things. The most he could do was turn his head and blink his eyes—and it had taken him months to learn even that.

"You're going to have to learn to read eyelids," she warned, and in we went.

From the moment we met Rick, we liked him. There he lay in a reclining chair, unable to chew his food and unable to speak a word. But could those eyes ever talk! As we communicated (for we could not actually converse), I learned to ask the type of question he could most easily answer—questions to which he could blink a "yes" or a "no."

Rick's parents shared with us a method they had discovered which allowed Rick to make full sentences. It was an alphabet chart. Whenever he wanted to spell a word, his mom would watch as he pointed his eyes to either the right or left side of the chart. Then he'd look up, straight ahead, or down to indicate which line he wanted. Finally his mom would read aloud each letter on that line until he blinked. She'd write the appropriate one down, and he'd go on to another.

By using the chart to write term papers and by listening to his textbooks on tape, Rick had gone on to finish high school and two years of college. In his college work he received one A, one C, and the rest Bs! (His only C was his first semester of Russian language. He later pulled it up to a B.)

We "talked" about a lot of things that afternoon, but the most exciting time was when we began talking about our mutual faith in the Lord and about heaven.

"Rick," I said, hoping to express for him what he could not, "can you believe how neat it's going to be when we get our new bodies in heaven!"

His eyes lit up.

"I don't know about you," I continued, "but when I was on my feet I never thought much about heaven. I pictured it as a boring place where everyone wore angel costumes, propped their feet up on clouds, and polished gold all day long."

Rich laughed although he couldn't smile (if you can imagine that).

"But since I lost the use of my body, I've learned that one day I'm going to trade it in for a new one.[23] No angel wings! Just hands that work and feet that walk. Think of it. We'll be on our feet—running, walking, working, talking with Jesus—all kinds of things! Maybe we'll even play tennis!"

As I spoke Rick began fluttering his eyelids up and down, up and down, as fast as he could. It was his way of expressing excitement, his way of smiling. He was telling us in the only way he could just how anxious he was to go to heaven. His eyes blinked a shining testimony of his faith in God and his desire to go to be with Him and receive a new body.

Sitting and sharing in that room that afternoon made all of us—myself, my friends, Rick, and his family—long for heaven. But since Rick had the most to gain by going there, I think he longed for it most. One month later he got his wish. In August of that same year, Rick went to be with the Lord.

What suffering did for Rick, it can do for all of us—get our hearts on things above, where they belong. But suffering does more than make us want to go to heaven. *It prepares us to meet God when we get there.*

Just think for a moment. Suppose you had never in your life known any physical pain. How could you at all appreciate the scarred hands with which Christ will greet you? What if no one had ever hurt you deeply? How could you adequately express your gratefulness when you approach the throne of the Man of Sorrows who was acquainted with grief (Isa. 53:3)? If you had never been embarrassed, if you had never felt ashamed, you could never begin to know just how much He loved you when He took your shameful sins and made them His.

Don't you see—when we meet Him face to face, our suffering will have given us at least a *tiny* taste of what He went through to purchase our redemption? We will appreciate Him so much more. And our loyalty in those sufferings will give us something to offer Him in return. For what proof could we bring of our love and faithfulness if this life had left us totally unscarred? What shame would we feel if our Christianity had cost us nothing? Suffering prepares us to meet God.

And suffering does one more thing. If in our trials we are faithful, *they win for us rich rewards in heaven.* "For our light and momentary troubles are achieving for us an eternal glory that far outweighs them all" (2 Cor. 4:17). It's not merely that heaven will be a wonderful place *in spite of* all our sufferings while on earth. Actually, it will be that way *because* of them. My wheelchair, unpleasant as it may be, is what God uses to change my attitudes and make me more faithful to Him. The more faithful I am to Him, the more rewards will be stored up for me in heaven. And so our earthly sufferings don't just aid us today; they will serve us in eternity.

Now I don't know exactly what these rewards and treasures will be, but they'll be worth it. Remember back in second grade when one of the kids was the class hero because he had an especially neat yo-yo? To all the other kids, what mattered most in the world was to own the same kind of yo-yo. But when you were in high school, you no longer cared about yo-yos. Then what mattered most was being on the varsity team, or owning a sporty car, or being popular with a certain crowd.

In the same way, when God gives us our perfect hearts, the things that matter so much to us now won't seem important any more. The passion of our hearts will be to honor Him who alone is worthy of praise. In one sense, those who have been faithless in this life, to whom God does not give many rewards, will probably not want them. I believe their purified hearts will gladly admit that they don't deserve them. And those to whom God gives rewards? It seems that all they will want will be to serve God more fully and completely. And He will grant them their wish. They will be privileged to serve Him in special ways—as rulers over His affairs and pillars in His temple (Matt. 25:23; Rev. 3:12).

I said that one day God will give us perfect hearts. To me, that seems the single greatest marvel about heaven. If God were to take us to heaven today without changing us inside, heaven wouldn't be heaven. The purity and holiness there would only repel us and make us feel guilty. And we'd become terribly bored after awhile, just as we do with even the most exciting activities on earth.

The thing that will make heaven heavenly will be the change God will make inside us. Can you imagine what it will be like to never again have the desire to sin? to never again feel guilty? or depressed? or upset? We will know the wonderful harmony of not only being in paradise, but also of having hearts that are able to enjoy it.

When I think of heaven, I think of a time when I will be welcomed home. I remember when I was on my feet what a cozy, wonderful feeling it was to come home after hockey practice. How pleasant to hear the familiar clanging of bells against our back door as I swung it open. Inside awaited the sights, sounds, and smells of warmth and love. Mom would greet me with a wide smile as she dished out food into big bowls ready to be set on the table. I'd thrown down my sweat suit and hockey stick, bound into the den, and greet daddy. He'd turn from his desk, taking off his glasses, then he'd give me a big "hi" and ask me how practice was.

For Christians, heaven will be like that. We will see old friends and family who have gone on before us. Our kind heavenly Father will greet us with open, loving arms. Jesus, our older brother, will be there to welcome us, too. We won't feel strange or insecure. We will feel like we're home . . . for we *will* be home. Jesus said it was a place prepared for us.

We'll have new bodies and new minds! I myself will be able to run to friends and embrace them for the first time. I will lift my new hands before the hierarchy of heaven—shouting to everyone within earshot, "Worthy is the Lamb who was slain to receive blessing and honor. For He freed my soul from the clutches of sin and death, and now He has freed my body as well!"

The wrongs and injustices of earth will be righted. God will measure out our tears which He has kept in His bottle, and not a single one will go unnoticed. He who holds all reasons in His hand will give us the key that makes sense out of our most senseless sufferings. And that's only the beginning.

> He will wipe every tear from their eyes. There will be no more death or mourning or crying or pain, for the old order of things has passed away.

Can't wait?

> He who testifies to these things says, "Yes, I am coming soon."
>
> Amen. Come, Lord Jesus.
> (Revelation 21:4; 22:20-21)

A Concluding Word

I JUST REREAD the last chapter with you, a chapter that Steve and I penned many years ago. In it, I found sentences like, "I myself will be able to run to friends and embrace them for the first time." My eyes scanned the next page, and I paused to read: "The wrongs and injustices of earth will be righted. God will measure out our tears which He has kept in His bottle, and not a single one will go unnoticed."

It is as thrilling now as it was then to voice these words from my heart. I've covered a lot of miles in my wheelchair since my accident in 1967, and yet timeless, changeless truths such as these will ignite my spirit, still bring tears of joy to my eyes.

I also think of hurting, handicapped people I know whose lives exhibit the same joy because of the Lord Jesus. People like Donna from Texas who is a ventilator-dependent quadriplegic, bedridden for more than three years and holding confidently on to hope. People like Diane from California who, despite the painful and crippling encroachment of MS, still manages to spend hours a day in prayer. People like Patti, a recovering alcoholic from New Jersey, who goes to God daily for grace. These believers, and many more, put life and breath around the truths described in the previous chapters.

A Step Further has been more than just a further step in the sharing of my life with you, the struggle and lessons, downfalls and victories. In a way, it is a defense, a proof if you will, for the goodness of God. It is a personal and definitive statement on why you, too, can trust and obey God, not *in spite* of your hardships, but even *because* of your hardships. Believe me, I'm not boasting—it is not my personal story that has impact, but the Word of God that has power to change your life.

A father who lost his son in a brutal murder once wrote me, "Joni, I used to have a million questions for God . . . and no answers. I still don't have all the answers down pat, but you know what? I don't have any more questions. Knowing Him is enough."

I pray you will be able to say the same.

Joni Eareckson Tada
Woodland Hills, California
Summer 1990

NOTES

Notes

Putting Together the Puzzle of Suffering

1. Philippians 1:29.

2. The next page is taken from Paul's argument in 2 Corinthians 10-13. Many of the ideas have come from: Frederick D. Bruner, *A Theology of the Holy Spirit* (Grand Rapids: Eerdmans Publishing Co., 1970), pp. 303-315; Walter J. Chantry, *Signs of the Apostles*, rev. (Edinburgh, Scotland: Banner of Truth Trust, 1973), pp. 71-81.

3. C. S. Lewis, *The Problem of Pain* (New York: Macmillan Publishing Co., Inc., 1962), p. 93.

4. Ibid.

5. John W. Wenham, *The Goodness of God* (Downers Grove: Inter-varsity Press, 1974), p. 56.

While We're Working on the Puzzle

6. Lewis, *Pain*, pp. 43-44.

7. Source for this idea was Edith Schaeffer, *A Way of Seeing* (Old Tappan, N. J.: Fleming H . Revell Co., 1975), p. 64.

8. Romans 12:15.

Healing: A Piece of the Puzzle?

9. Please don't misunderstand and think that when we call disease a result of sin we mean that every time someone is sick or deformed it is because of some specific sin or sins in his or her life. Jesus' disciples made this mistake once. Upon seeing a man who was blind from birth, they asked Jesus, "'Rabbi, who sinned, this man or his parents, that he was born blind?'" But Jesus corrected their misconception. "'Neither this man nor his parents sinned,' said Jesus, 'but this happened so that the work of God might be displayed in his life'" (John 9:1-3). Then He healed the man. Now Jesus wasn't saying that the man and
his parents were totally sinless. He merely meant that the man's blindness was not the result of some direct sin. It was part of the general curse from God that the human race must suffer collectively because of its sin.

10. While the other Gospels use the phrase "the kingdom of God," Matthew alone uses the phrase "the kingdom of heaven." Although many Christians take these to be two different things, it is our belief that the two phrases are interchangeable and refer to the same thing. A quick comparison to parallel passages in Matthew and the other Gospels will bear this out. Compare Matthew 4:17 with Mark 1:15, and Matthew 13:11 with Mark 4:11 and Luke 8:10.
Matthew's Gospel is directed at Jewish readers who hesitated to verbalize the name of God for fear of misusing it and, therefore, often substituted "heaven" or some other word for "God." See, for example, Luke 15:21: "Father, I have sinned against heaven and against you'" (also Matthew 21:25, and Mark 14:61 where "the Blessed" is used to refer to God). Thus, "the kingdom of heaven" is merely the Jewish form of the phrase, "the kingdom of God," the Greek form.

11. Several other references to the kingdom as partially present now, or as present in some senses now, are: Colossians 1:13; Romans 14:17; 1 Corinthians 4:20; Matthew 13:44-46; Mark 12:34; Matthew 12:28; and Luke 17:20-21.
If this view of the kingdom was interesting or helpful to you and you would like to investigate it further, see: George Ladd, *The Presence of the Future* (Grand Rapids: Eerdmans Publishing Co., 1974), pp. 45-119; *Crucial Questions About the Kingdom of God* (Grand Rapids: Eerdmans Publishing Co., 1974); *The Gospel of the Kingdom* (Grand Rapids: Eerdmans Publishing Co., 1959); Herman Ridderbos, *The Coming of the Kingdom* (Nutley, N. J.: Presbyterian and Reformed Publishing Co., 1975).
Our primary purpose here is not to enter any sort of debate over eschatology (i.e., the doctrine of the end times). In our presentation of the kingdom of God as partially present and partially future, we are merely trying to say that God has not totally finished everything He is going to do in removing sin and sin's results. (Christians of all echatological persuasions will agree with this.) Using the concept of the kingdom of God merely seemed to us to be the simplest yet clearest way of doing this.

12. This verse could also be translated "the kingdom of God is within you," but since Jesus was talking to men who didn't believe in Him, some versions prefer the equally acceptable reading "the kingdom of God is among you" or "is in your midst" (NASV).

13. See Matthew 6:10; 25:31-34; Mark 14:25; Galatians 5:21; 2 Thessalonians 1:5; Revelation 11:15.

14. John 14:30; 12:31; Matthew 28:18; Colossians 2:15; Hebrews 2:14; 1 John 4:4; Daniel 4:35; Isaiah 40:25; John 1:3; Job 1:12; 2:6; Mark 1:24; 5:7; 1:27; Romans 16:20; Revelation 20:1-3, 10.

15. "Thine eyes are too pure to approve evil and thou canst not look on wickedness with favor" (Hab. 1:13); "For God cannot be tempted by evil, nor does he tempt anyone" (James 1:13). "God is the author of the author of evil, but he cannot be the author of sin itself for sin is the result of a rebellion against God. How can God rebel against himself?" (E. J. Carnell, *An Introduction to Christian Apologetics* [Grand Rapids: Eerdmans Publishing Co., 1948], p. 302).

"All evil is either sin or the punishment for sin" (Carnell, p. 2). God can be said to be the author of the punishment for sin (calamity, hell, etc.), but the Bible will not allow us to call Him the author of sin itself, even though His plan allowed it to come about. Though we can't understand this, still we cannot "draw a straight line" between God and sin.

16. 1 Corinthians 9:1-3; 2 Corinthians 2:17; 11:23ff.

17. In the first five chapters of Acts, only the apostles are mentioned as performing miracles (Acts 2:43; 3:6; 4:33; 5:12; 5:15-16). In Acts 6:6 the apostles laid hands on seven godly men (all non-apostles) and prayed for them. Among these men were Stephen and Philip. Immediately the text records the fact that Stephen did miracles among the people (6:8). After the account of Stephen (6:8-7:60), the text records the fact that Philip worked miracles in Samaria. The clear implication is that they got this ability when the apostles laid hands on them.

It seems also that non-apostles were not able to transfer their miraculous gifts to others without the aid of an apostle. When the apostles heard that the Samaritans had "accepted the Word of God" (8:14), they sent Peter and John to Samaria because "the Holy Spirit had not yet come upon any of them; they had simply been baptized into the name of the Lord Jesus" (8:16). When the apostles laid hands on the Samaritans, they "received the Holy Spirit" (8:17).

Some students feel that the Samaritans were not truly saved until Peter and John came, for how could a person be saved without having the Holy Spirit? It seems more likely to us, however, that "they received the Holy Spirit" means "they received the miraculous gifts of the Spirit." For one thing, 8:14 says that the Samaritans "accepted the Word." For another, in 8:18 Simon the Sorcerer, "*saw* that the Spirit was given at the laying on of the apostles' hands." This implies that the Samaritans received outward, visible signs, not an inward work of grace. It seems, therefore, that as a non-apostle (in the technical sense of the word "apostle"), Philip received miraculous gifts from under the supervision of the apostles. It seems also that those receiving such gifts were not able to confer the power to others without the aid of the apostles *themselves*.

18. Deuteronomy 29:5. This idea came from *Miraculous Healing* by Henry Frost (soon available from Zondervan).

19. Even the apostle Paul did once! See Acts 16:6-7.

When The Pieces Don't Seem to Fit

20. It seems to me personally that our failure to have as complete and perfect an understanding of "fairness" as God does stems from two things. First, we just don't have all the facts. Trying to decide if what He does in a given situation is fair or not is like coming into a room halfway through an argument. Not having all the background information, we are in no real position to cast a verdict. And we won't have all the information until Judgment Day, when we'll be able to see things in light of an eternal perspective.

The second reason we don't always view what God does as fair is our own failure to appreciate the seriousness and hideousness of sin. I know that it seldom really strikes me that God owes this utterly rebellious and ungrateful planet absolutely *nothing*. In fact, that is an understatement. Actually, He does owe us something—hell. My father once commented how strange it is that we Christians say we deserve hell, but then complain when we get the slightest taste of it here on earth. If we just for once could have a clear picture of the extent of our own sin, I'm sure we could agree with C. S. Lewis when he says that "the real problem is not why some humble, pious, believing people suffer, but why some do *not*" (Lewis, *Pain*, p. 104).

One objection that is often raised against attributing fairness to God goes as follows: "There are some things God allows in the world that seem so unfair to us (e.g., children dying in war, etc.) that if God were to call them 'fair' we must be using a totally different dictionary than He. If our 'black' is His 'white,' the discussion becomes meaningless." C. S. Lewis answers this objection convincingly (*Pain*, pp. 37-39). If you are wrestling with the whole issue of God's goodness, by all means read this excellent book.

When It All Fits Together

21. Lewis, *Pain*, p. 115.

22. Samuel Rutherford, *Letters of Samuel Rutherford.*

23.1. Corinthians 15:42-44; 2 Corinthians 5:1-2.

CHOICES
CHANGES

To Ken

Contents

Acknowledgments

SPECIAL THANKS TO World Wide Pictures for taking a bold step with the movie *Joni*. Their film gave shape to my conviction of how the power of Christ can slice through the anger or indifference of someone with a severe disability. And much gratitude to the Billy Graham Evangelistic Association for their encouragment and support in the launching of Joni and Friends, our ministry that brings together Christians and disabled people throughout the world.

Dr. John MacArthur and the Special Ministries Department of Grace Community Church have lent time and staff in helping Joni and Friends design and implement its materials and workshops.

Dr. Sam Britten and the Center of Achievement for the Physically Disabled have also provided their expertise and advice on understanding and meeting the needs of those with disabilities.

I am grateful for the understanding Joni and Friends staff and volunteers who quietly passed by my closed office door as I shut myself away to write this book. Also my appreciation to Judy Butler for telling me, "You can do it!" She along with Bev Singleton, Francie Lorey, and Joe Davis were my sounding boards as well as my hands in pulling together the manuscript.

Thank you, Judith Markham, my editor, for teaching me more about the craft of writing.

And thank you, Steve Estes, for helping me find "my style."

In my third episode, several ideas were borrowed from Mike Mason's *The*

Mystery of Marriage. He put into remarkable words what my husband and I are experiencing each day.

Also, Ken and I have enjoyed using Chuck Swindoll's devotional *Seasons of Life,* and I have echoed his essay on "Risking Liberty" at the close of my first episode.

Liv Ullman's autobiography, *Changing,* touched me deeply, and I often read her chapters for stylistic inspiration.

But God's Word and its constant admonition to "speak the truth in love" remained the plumb line of my content.

He changes times and seasons.
—Daniel 2:21

All of us, then, reflect the glory of the Lord with
uncovered faces; and that same glory, coming
from the Lord . . . transforms us into His
likeness in an ever greater degree of glory.
—2 Corinthians 3:18 (GOOD NEWS BIBLE)

Introduction

HERE I SIT in the middle of eternity, asking God to transform me into His shining likeness. That, to me, is an exhilarating prospect, even if a bit frightening. But that's not all. He expects me to uncover my face—a thought more frightening than exhilarating.

There is danger in doing that. A risk. My books *Joni* and *A Step Further* were a risky uncovering of my life. But there have been so many choices and changes since then. Sometimes I have cowered behind a carefully constucted façade. Other times I have been too much the bold spiritual exhibitionist, wearing my faith on my sleeve.

But mostly I have lived life between the two extremes.

So I've prayed—really prayed—about opening my life in this book. It's not *Joni*. Twenty years have passed since I broke my neck in that diving accident. Nor is it a walk through theology like *A Step Further*.

Instead, you hold in your hands my journal in which I write about sin and its subtlety to deceive and manipulate my heart. About a choice to grow, changing from a young girl into a mature woman. And about the risk of opening my life to one man, the man I believe in with all my heart.

Why do I put these things in a book? Obviously, I hope to play a small part in building up your faith in Christ. And for those who remain skeptical about God and the Bible, I believe I offer some reasons why life in Christ makes real sense.

But there's more. And it has a lot to do with "sitting in the middle of eternity." This wheelchair has helped me sit still. I've observed with curiosity the way we Christians grasp for the future, as if the present didn't quite satisfy. How we, in spiritual fits and starts, scrape and scratch our way along, often missing the best of life while looking the other way, preoccupied with shaping our future.

In my least consistent moments I too try to wrestle the future out of His hands. Or worse, I sink back into the past and rest on long-ago laurels. But God is most concerned with the choices I make now. I know—truly know—what God expects of me. An uncovering. An unmasking. He expects me to change.

And what sort of change, may I ask so gently, does God expect in you? Are you impatient about sitting in the middle? Do you feel you must grab ground for your future, a future in which you hope God won't mind going along with your plans and dreams?

God, standing silently and invisibly and presently with us in the middle of eternity, is interested in a certain kind of change. And as Oswald Chambers has mused, "If we have a further end in view, we do not pay sufficient attention to the immediate present: if we realize that obedience is the end, then each moment as it comes is precious."

For this reason I write *Choices . . . Changes* in the first person present. Because it is happening now—right now. I do not know how the Spirit of Christ performs it, but He brings us choices through which we never-endingly change, fresh and new, into His likeness.

Uncover your face with me. It's a risk. But the journey is full of surprises.

THE MOVIE

Surely you desire truth in the inner parts.
—Psalm 51:6

TANNED HANDS GRASP the edge of the raft, and in one graceful motion she lifts her body out of the water. She reaches us and smooths her blond hair back, wringing it in a tiny knot at the base of her neck. She tugs at the elastic of her royal blue bathing suit and shakes the water from each leg. In another fluid movement, knees bend, arms swing, and she pitches forward in a dive. Her body slices the surface of the water. She is under.

"Cut! That's a print!" the director, Jim Collier, yells from a rubber raft floating nearby.

I am jarred back to the present. The actress, tall and brown with a blond wig, could easily be mistaken for me. Except that I sit at the water's edge. In my wheelchair.

They will film me next. Taking over where the actress left off, I am to float face down in the water. Another actress, playing the part of my sister Kathy, will rescue me.

I wait while the crew members position lights and reflectors, anchor the movie camera to the crane, and float the sound equipment out by the raft. Sound men and cameramen bustle about quietly.

They eye me politely, and I sense a tension in them. Either they are apprehensive because this scene is being shot without rehearsals or because they think I'm nervous. I'm not. The past is far behind me. I can't be touched by memories of my accident so many years ago. God is in control of my life now. I have His grace. I am content.

I eye the crew politely in return, feeling my own form of hesitancy. I wonder what they think of my faith. I'd like to help these men and women know Jesus. Maybe they'll see Him in my life or hear about Him in the script. The producer has given them each a copy of my book *Joni*. I hope they read it.

A sound man carries a boom mike on his shoulder and smiles as he passes. I return his smile and imagine his thoughts: "Handicapped people need religion."

The girl in the blue bathing suit is back on shore now. She flings a terry towel over her shoulders and presses a corner of it to her face, smiling and chatting with another crew member.

My mind replays her short scene. The velvet way she slipped out of the water, hands slicking the wetness from her hair and suit. The hot sun glazing the natural tawny glow of her skin. She waves at me. Embarrassed to be caught staring at her, I quickly acknowledge her greeting and then look down.

I sit slouched. I watch a breeze lift the towel off my lap, exposing my legbag and catheter. My bulky corset is buckled on the outside of my suit so I can breathe while I sit and wait. The strap of my bathing suit—my blue bathing suit—has slipped off my shoulder.

"Okay, we're ready for Joni. Let's get her out here!"

Two paramedics lay me on a rubber raft, take off my corset, and float me out into the shallow bay.

"Way to go, kid." The assistant cameraman waves from the crane above.

"Not to worry. You'll do fine," the property master calls from the shore.

Miss Blue Bathing Suit wades knee deep into the water, watching intently. I'm touched that she cares. I should have told her—should have told all of them— that I float in pools all the time. I'm not afraid of the water. Really.

Shivering a bit, I float on my back and wait for the cast and crew to get in position. Everyone is quiet. I take a deep breath, and Jim Collier signals the paramedics to flip me over, face down, in the water.

Above water, the camera begins rolling. In the curious underwater acoustics I hear Jim yell, "Action!" I strain to hear "Kathy" splash through the water and call my name. I hear her voice, muffled. Seconds tick by. The bay is cold and dark. My lungs are hungry for air.

I am going to shake my head—a prearranged signal to warn the paramedics that I need help. Suddenly, hands grab my shoulders. As "Kathy" lifts me from the water, I sputter and gasp for breath.

It's real. But . . . oh, yes, I am supposed to act. "Kathy. Butch. I can't move. I . . . I can't feel," I manage to splutter as they carry me to the shore. A crane follows. Cameras whir. People take notes. Gaffers tilt reflectors.

"Cut! It's a print!"

I breathe deeply with relief. A pat on the back and smiles break the tension. The scene has come and gone so quickly. The reality we just filmed is now at a distance, recorded neatly on a strip of celluloid encased in a can. The cooks from the catering truck set out snacks and everyone gravitates toward donuts and coffee.

The pretty girl in the blue bathing suit has taken off her wet wig and donned a fresh white sweat shirt. She approaches and we greet one another warmly. I feel the camaraderie. We are a team.

Yet something is troubling me. I glance at the raft still anchored off shore. It looks bleak and lonely, no longer surrounded by the crew and their trappings. I look toward the catering truck where everyone is chatting and laughing. I glance again at the raft, rocking slowly on gentle swells.

The gnawing stops. I know what it is. It has been a long time since I've listened to its whispers, felt its icy fingers around my heart. Pity, an old enemy, is trying to move in on old territory.

"Me? . . . Pity?

How can that be? I've learned not to compare myself with others. I've written chapters in books about it. I speak about it to audiences all the time. God knows, I wouldn't be doing this movie if all those old matters weren't settled.

But what is happening? Have so many years passed since that July day in 1967 that I've become too comfortable? Has the camera lens focused too sharply today on those old details? This July day in 1978? I marshal fragments of faith. Something about contentment. Something about grace. A simple Scripture verse floats to the surface of my mind and turns to face me: "Therefore let him who thinks he stands take heed lest he fall."[1]

"Lest he fall . . ." That's fair warning. Especially since I've never done anything like this before. Playing the lead in a movie about my life. Re-creating my own experiences before the cameras. What do I know about acting? Oh, sure, I sold toothpaste to my bathroom mirror when I was a kid, but that's about the extent of my dramatic experience.

But I'm up to it. I talked it over thoroughly with my family and friends, with Bill Brown, executive producer at World Wide Pictures, and with Billy Graham. With absolutely no pressure from anyone, I was the one who decided to play my own part. I figured if the real person could say the real thing to a lot of people with problems, then the film would have an even greater impact. And wouldn't it be wonderful to create something lasting, something permanent? It couldn't be that much different from writing a book or painting a picture.

"Let him who thinks he stands take heed . . ." *Lest he fall*, I ponder again. If anyone were to fall, I suppose it could easily happen in Los Angeles, the City of the Angels. Fallen angels. And Hollywood, the film capital of the world, is a long way from my desk at the farm in Maryland or from the art easel in my study.

But World Wide Pictures wants the movie *Joni* to be a top-notch production that can hold its own against other movies shown in local theaters. Here in Hollywood they can assemble some of the most talented sound engineers, set designers, gaffers, and grips in the industry.

Being fresh off the Maryland farm, what do I know about these people and their cosmopolitan ways? Yet here, for six months, I'll be living and working with them, rubbing shoulders with their world every day. I tingle at the thought, at what kind of witness this could be.

No. I won't fall. And I should, at least, be a match for the glittery, empty trappings of Hollywood.

Hollywood. It brings to mind a dark and foreboding verse out of Ephesians: "So I tell you this, and insist on it in the Lord, that you must no longer live as the Gentiles do, in the futility of their thinking. They are darkened in their understanding and separated from the life of God because of the ignorance that is in them due to the hardening of their hearts. Having lost all sensitivity, they have given themselves over to sensuality."[2]

Hmm. Heavy words. In these surroundings—by this bay, on this beautiful beach—they seem stuffy, strait-laced, even out of place. The crew, the cast, even the girl in the bathing suit—they're genuinely nice people. No, this world won't touch me. I'll touch it for Christ!

So why all the fuss? Everything is under control. Dr. Graham himself has cautioned me that this filming will be difficult. I understand about reliving hospital experiences, complaining before a camera that I long to be healed, rehashing old relationships—some successful, some splintered.

World Wide Pictures has bent over backwards, rallying people to pray daily for me and the crew. They've made arrangements for my sister Jay to stay with me, along with a nice English lady named Judy Butler from the Billy Graham office. They've even rented a little house nearby for us on a quiet tree-lined street.

But as urgent as everyone is to calm me, I am equally insistent on calming them. Hollywood may be "way out," but it's still on planet earth. And my diving accident was many years ago. Those painful memories of my early days of paralysis are all but clouded over. I proved that today in the water. I wasn't nearly as unnerved as everyone else.

No, it wasn't the scene in the water that bothered me.

It was what went on behind the scene.

I AM DISCOVERING that people in movies wear masks. They substitute one kind of reality for another. It seems all the more confusing since my lines aren't, in fact, voiced from my heart as they were years ago. They are read from a script. The mask of a hospitalized seventeen-year-old girl doesn't quite fit me any more. They have to re-create "me" with palsy, pale foundation, dark make-up under my eyes, a matted blond wig, and a wrinkled hospital gown.

Today I lay face down on a Stryker frame—a narrow canvas bed. With my chin and forehead resting on cushioned strips of cloth, I can follow everyone's steps. I memorize the shoes of the cast and crew. The sound man with the boom mike stands over my head. A strip of adhesive tape on one of his shoes reads, "Hi," and on the other, "Joni."

Minutes tick by. Camera rehearsals take time. I wish they would hurry, though. My chin and forehead are beginning to ache from the pressure. This mask is real.

I must concentrate. The director and the cameraman are almost ready. Footsteps across the sound-stage floor become attendants and nurses. The director flips through a script much like a doctor making notes on my chart. Cameras and lights become giant X-ray machines positioned around my body.

"Let's make a movie, children." Jim Collier claps his hands for positions. "Remember, Joni, you're dazed. Disoriented."

"Yes," I say obediently. I am, in fact, dazed and a little disoriented.

Filming begins as Cooper, the actor who wears the mask of my boyfriend, smuggles a puppy up nine flights of hospital steps, makes his way past a nurses' station on hands and knees, and into my room. He pulls the panting puppy from under his jacket and lifts him to my cheek. "Here, pup. Lick Jon's face."

"Oh, he's so cute," I mumble. Under the heat of the stage lights the puppy droops and whines to be let loose.

"Cut! Change the slate for another take!" The crew takes a break, stretching and talking idly as the camera is repositioned.

We begin again, but the pup ignores his lines.

We try a third take. A fourth. They bring in a second puppy.

Offstage, the dog wrangler tries to tease his pups into a playful mood. Onstage, my mood sours. My chin and forehead are hot and sore. Yet I apologize to the director. Perhaps my frightful wig and pallid features put the puppies off?

We try the scene again. I strain to reach the pup with my cheek. *Oh, please lick my cheek!* By now, the crew members chuckle every time a new puppy goes into his "I'm not interested" routine. I realize I'm not smiling and weakly join the laughter.

Four puppies and fifteen takes later, I lamely give permission for the wrangler to smear liver-flavored baby food on the side of my cheek away from the camera. I apologize again. It must be my fault.

"Action!"

The puppy wriggles and squirms in Cooper's hands. He catches a whiff of the liver and furiously licks my cheek. The camera catches this precious bit of action, everyone cheers, and Jim finally calls a wrap.

It takes just minutes to pack the camera, clear the set, dim the lights, and say good night. It takes longer to flip me face up on the Stryker. Oh, the relief!

Jay and Judy lift me in their familiar and friendly embrace into my wheelchair. They push me to the dressing room. It will take even longer to remove the pasty make-up, wig, and gown. Before they begin, the girls walk back to the sound stage to gather up our sweaters and other belongings.

Alone in the front of the brightly lit make-up mirror I look into a pale, drawn face. The hair is askew. The hospital gown is oversized and obliterates the body underneath. The girl is alive only from her shoulders up, just like in the hospital. Even the dry, crusty food on her cheek is a reminder of those first sorry attempts at feeding herself. She is exhausted and humiliated. Cowing before dogs and directors, she has allowed herself to be intimidated. Just like in the hospital.

Tired and hurting, I feel so sorry for the girl in the mirror. The past overpowers me. It eats away like acid. I look at my paralyzed legs and a feeling of claustrophobia envelopes me—I can't move. Hot tears well in my eyes. Who am I crying for? The girl in the mirror or the woman in the chair? Is it the past I grieve for . . . or the present?

Ashamed and embarrassed by these thoughts darting beneath the surface, I lean my head back and let the tears drain behind my eyes. I press my nose against the sleeve of the white gown, dabbing at the wetness as though painstakingly retouching the flaws on a mask. The smile I hastily assume as Jay and Judy return from the sound stage is just that—a mask.

I stare straight ahead as they wipe away the thick make-up with cotton balls and astringent. A steaming-hot washcloth brings quick color to my cheeks. The make-up man inches the wig from my scalp. The wrinkled gown is folded away. My hair is brushed, my sweater buttoned, and refreshing drops are put in my eyes. I like what I see in the mirror now.

But I don't like who I am. My self-image has been slammed back into the wheelchair. How clever I've been at learning the art of masking the "handicap" part of my disability, whether with an attractive hairstyle, a fashionable outfit, or a streamlined wheelchair with color-coordinated leather. But strip away all those props and stick me in a hospital gown with messy hair and a lifeless complexion, and my grip on life—even paralyzed life—seems lost.

Perhaps I am not so content after all.

"TIME FOR RUSHES!"

"Time for what?" I power my wheelchair toward Rob Tregenza, the assistant to the director, who is flipping through sheets of dialogue.

"Rushes. Dailies. Every afternoon the lab sends back footage shot the day before." He tucks the sheets under his arm and helps maneuver my bulky chair through the narrow door to the screening room.

Only a handful of people are gathered in the dimly lit room. The cameraman is here to check his angles, while his assistant examines the focus and the gaffer makes notes about the lighting.

The director, who is here to oversee the general look of the film, waves his arm as the lights dim. "Okay, roll it."

It is like watching home movies as the unedited footage of the day before begins. Still it's a little fantastic to think of me on such a big screen. Huge out-of-focus hands holding a slate suddenly appear. Loud beeps begin the sound track. The image on the screen sharpens into focus and the slate claps, marking the first print of puppy number one who whines to be let loose. As the film continues to roll, Rob huddles close to my chair to give me information. He explains that the clapping of the slate helps the lab synchronize the sound track with the screen images.

The next slate marker claps and a second print begins. Another puppy fails. I glance at Jim Collier who is shaking his head and penciling notes. The screen goes dark. More beeps tell us another print is coming on the roll.

"Get ready." Jim leans forward in his chair. "This is the one."

The slate appears on the screen. A voice off-camera drones, "Sound."

"Speed," says another voice.

"Camera?"

"Rolling," comes the reply.

"Mark it. Scene 29, take 14." The slate claps, and I hear the director's voice whisper for action.

DICK: "Hi, gorgeous."

Seconds pass.

JONI: "People die here, Dickie."

The camera dollies smoothly, following Cooper as he crawls underneath the Stryker frame. The focus remains sharp as he lifts the puppy from his jacket. There is plenty of underlighting. The audience will be able to see the actors' expressions. The microphones pick up the nuzzly sounds of the pup licking the girl's face.

Rob is still kneeling by my side, making comments about the acting. I am not listening. My attention is not on the finer points of film making—the lighting, directing, sound, or focus. My attention is riveted on the pale, lifeless expression of that seventeen-year-old girl on the screen. She is paralyzed. She is helpless. She is . . . me.

In the darkened screening room before an image that looms larger than life, I neglect the grace which God offers me.

"So WHAT IS it like—starring at yourself in your own film?" The interviewer, his glasses propped on his balding head, leans back on the couch and taps the point of his pencil on his steno pad. His khaki safari jacket, properly crumpled and oversized, gives the impression that he has been published in the *New Yorker* or the *Atlantic Monthly*. We are alone in the small press room. I wish Jay or Judy were here, but they have gone to get our lunch while I do the interview.

"I . . . I don't feel very comfortable with that word. I mean it's not like I'm a star or anything," I reply. In an effort to make my role more comfortable, I suggest that it is more like "playing my own part" or "re-creating my life story."

The man writes for a daily paper. We don't speak the same language. I sense he is looking for a dirty angle to tarnish the Christian purpose behind our movie. "The Billy Graham people are just great . . . the movie crew is helpful and very nice . . . World Wide is even providing an art instructor to give me painting lessons," I ramble, hoping he'll pick up on the good points.

I willingly tell him my own weaknesses, ladle out how really ordinary I am, hoping all the while I will charm the socks off him.

I relate a funny story about a policeman pulling me over as I wheeled across the street near NBC studios.

"Were you going too fast?" the reporter asks with a hint of a smile.

"Oh, no. I was jaywalking . . . er, jaywheeling, I guess you could say." My story falls a little flat.

Hiking his collar, he settles again into a serious vein. He sips black coffee and occasionally jots certain of my comments on his pad in shorthand. When I want him to record a point, I speak more slowly, giving him plenty of time to quote me accurately. It's a game, and we both know it.

"How do you think starring . . . er, portraying yourself will change your plans for the future?"

"Do you mean if I want to act in more movies or something?" I ask.

He shrugs his shoulders and waves his hand. "Whatever."

"No. No, I have no designs on doing *Joni: Part Two*, or, ah, *Son of Joni*," I laugh. He loosens a bit. "Seriously. After it's over, I think I will just go back to the farm in Maryland and continue to paint and maybe write some more. Whatever," I say, mirroring his gesture. "I love the farm, my sisters, our horses. It's pretty this time of year. . . ." My voice trails off. I have not thought much lately about the barns or horses or the fact that the folks at home must be cutting and baling hay right now. Admit it or not, this movie is beginning to consume my thoughts.

I am relieved when the grilling is over. But I have a cramped uneasiness that I have been far too aware of my own actions, as though I were auditioning for the approval of the reporter. A mask, it seems, can be worn even behind the scenes.

I am glad when Jay, Judy, and I break out through the swinging glass doors at the end of the day. The sun has dropped behind the Hollywood Hills, flattening them to a one-dimensional shade of maroon. The bottoms of the clouds are underlit in pink and mauve, an effect the gaffer would love.

"Cut. That's a print!" Jay points to the sunset.

"Put it in the can," adds Judy. Laughing at the lingo which has become a part of us, we head for the car.

We resolve to leave work behind and visit a nearby shopping center. Light relief from the heavy pressure of the shooting schedule. Something ordinary and everyday to get us back in the real world. Yet as we wheel and walk through the mall, we jabber about the film. People we like on the crew, amateur criticism of wardrobe and set design, reviews of the latest rushes. We find it difficult to leave the movie world behind. And who could blame us? We are a secretary and two farm girls come to town.

"Let's choose a salad place for dinner," I suggest. Jim Collier has asked that I lose a few pounds for the remaining hospital scenes. "No dessert for me."

"Hey! I've got an idea," Jay says. "We just passed a T-shirt place. You know, where they paint anything you want on the front?" She waves for us to follow and then disappears into the store.

I stop at the front window to look at the shirt styles, colors, and slogans. In a short while Jay comes out and announces, "You now have the perfect answer for those guys on the crew who keep stuffing donuts in your mouth." She holds up a T-shirt that reads DON'T FEED ME!

"And you're not the only one who needs to lose weight," she adds, whipping another T-shirt out of the bag. It reads OR ME. Judy stands behind her displaying a big grin and one more shirt that says NOR ME.

We giggle our way through supper on leftover movie adrenaline, guessing the crew's reaction to our silly shirts.

Behind the smile, however, I calculate calories: a salad, no dressing; no cream in real coffee. No breakfast tomorrow. No donuts at the studio. Maybe a light lunch and no dinner tomorrow evening.

I am not hungry anyway. I live on energy.

I am becoming obsessed with myself.

I LISTEN EAGERLY to every direction Jim Collier gives for each scene. He wrote the screenplay and directed the movie *The Hiding Place*, and I know I can learn a lot from him.

"You're angry at this point. Angry at God. Angry at your friends." His voice is quiet but intense as he strokes the page of script with his fingers. I appreciate his suggestions, but I wish he'd give me more technical cues.

He leans back and adjusts his glasses. "It's important that you come across as natural as possible," he says, as if guessing my thoughts. "We've talked about it. Just relax and let it happen."

He rises and walks with Rob toward the cameraman, I suppose to discuss important technical things. Jim folds his arms, rubs his chin, and listens to the cameraman. With outstretched arms they peer through their hands to frame the shot. Jim examines the set through the eyepiece of the camera. They motion the gaffer over and point to several stage lights above.

I watch and wonder about Jim's work on *The Hiding Place*, the movie about the life of Corrie ten Boom. I read her book several years ago and was impressed with the film version of her years with her family in Holland, hiding Jews in their attic during the war, her ironclad faith during her internment in the Nazi concentration camps. The movie was stirring. Jim did a good job.

But it was Corrie's life. I wonder how she felt about watching her experiences come back to life on screen. How did she react to seeing others play the parts of family or friends? What did she feel when they portrayed those awful scenes in the death camps? Were the memories too painful? Here on the edge of the sound stage I have a hard time imagining her, like me, watching Jim Collier and his crew translate pain, horror, and even faith through actors and a script.

Jim has told me that Corrie ten Boom is now praying for this movie. She's praying for me too. I picture her in a wheelchair by the fireplace in her home, sipping tea, gently turning the thin pages of an opened Bible on her lap. She is in her eighties, limited in her traveling and speaking. But now she ministers through her powerful and effective prayers.

I smile, remembering a recent convention where she was honored and presented with a large bouquet of yellow roses. As the crowd stood to applaud her, she lifted the bouquet heavenward, and I knew she was saying, "Lord Jesus, this is Yours."

And picturing her by the fireplace in my thoughts, I decide, *No, Corrie would not have gotten caught up in any movie. Certainly not to the point of worrying.*

But here I am—upright, stomach in knots, biting my nails as I wait on the edge of the sound stage.

$\mathscr{S}$

I FORCE MY eyes to make contact with the young boy sitting rigid and upright in a body cast. A metal halo bolts into his skull, keeping his neck stabilized as it heals. The fluorescent light of the occupational-therapy department washes any color from his skin. I angle my chair closer to his side. Still, with his head fixed forward, he must strain to see me from the corners of his eyes. He smiles and weakly lifts his thin arm in a greeting.

"They tell me you're filming here today." His voice cracks.

"Yes, I am. I mean, we are. They're making a movie about my diving accident and rehabilitation and stuff." I try to sound casual, to include him, to make myself "one of the guys."

I notice his arms and hands are supported by an overhead sling attached to the back of his wheelchair. He must feel so bulky, I think to myself, like some sort of mechanical contraption. I back up my chair so he can see me better.

"You're moving your arms. That's a good sign," I offer.

"Yeah, they've got me in O.T. to do some work." He points to a painted ashtray with the brush a therapist has taped to his armsplint. The table beside us is strewn with newspapers splattered with red and yellow. A Mason jar holds colored pencils and brushes. Several other chalky ashtrays and candy dishes are organized neatly, waiting for the kiln.

I look around the table and smile at the other young guys working on projects. Some look up and grin. A few study me suspiciously. Others seem not to notice me, their lifeless eyes and tired expressions fixed on weaving a potholder or painting a dish.

"You were here at Rancho, huh?" one paraplegic asks as he wheels away from the table to get another jar of paint.

"Yes. About ten years ago, though." I try to spot a familiar face among the therapists. "Lots of things have changed."

I am uncomfortable. All our movie paraphernalia and personnel seem an intrusion into the private lives and pains of these patients at Rancho Los Amigos Hospital. The fellows know they are about to be filmed. Some are interested, while others shrug their weak shoulders indifferently. I want to put everyone— them and me—at ease. I explain that this film will help others understand the everyday difficulties people like us face.

By now the sound technicians, the grips, and their helpers are pulling in large electric cables, carts with tape recorders, and lighting stands. The occupational-therapy department is beginning to look like the sound stage of a movie studio. Nurses and therapists are grouped in the corner, watching. I hope the production people will be careful.

The gaffer begins to anchor lights on tall stands above an art easel. I am to be filmed against the backdrop of the fellows at the table. Along with them, I am to "learn" how to do as much as I can with what little I have left. An actress playing the part of a therapist is to teach me how to write with a pen between my teeth.

I'm glad that they do my make-up and wardrobe in the dressing-room trailer in the hospital parking lot. I don't want to be made-up in front of the young boy in the halo cast.

A knock on the trailer door tells us that filming is about to begin. I power my wheelchair back over the cables into the O.T. room and take my place at the easel. The young black actress who plays the part of my therapist resembles the real woman from my past. But then every prop and person in this film is reminding me of too much already.

Slab of clay is thrown down to table by Joni's easel.

JONI: "You gonna throw that at me?"

THERAPIST: "I want you to draw something on it."

JONI: "You gotta be kidding."

Therapist has two sticks in her hand.

THERAPIST: "Draw something you like. Use these."

JONI: "It won't work. I used to do a lot of sketching in charcoal. My father's sort of an artist. But that was when I had my hands."

THERAPIST: "The skill, the talent, comes from up here." (*Points to her head.*) "With a little practice you can do as well with your mouth as your hands."

The lens focuses tightly on me as I take the stick in my mouth and press it into the soft clay. I carve a line that wiggles and worms its way across the surface, and

I try hard to control the shaking. The frightening part is I'm not acting. Every tense muscle in my neck, every raw nerve communicates directly through the stick onto the clay. I want to relax. I'm afraid that others will know I am not pretending to be a novice with the mouthstick. Thankfully, I hear someone say, "Cut."

"Is that real enough?" I ask the director.

I shake my head to clear the scene from my mind, then slowly turn my neck, tilting it back and forth to relax the tightness. This is another bit of filming I am relieved to see finished. Too many real things caught up in movie things.

During break I wheel outside to the therapy courtyard. Some brawny fellows in wheelchairs are playing a fast game of basketball. I watch them for a few moments and then wheel over to a group of girls in wheelchairs. They are smiling and chatting under the shade of some palms. The group looks friendly and inviting. I want to get over these stupid feelings of uneasiness and awkwardness. I battle to come up with a conversation opener.

"You're Debbie Stone, aren't you?" I say to a smiling girl whose wheelchair is stickered with a plastic "Because He is God, Jesus Lives Yesterday, Today and Forever."

"Yes, and you're Joni," she says, reminding me that we met earlier. World Wide has asked Debbie to round up people in wheelchairs for several movie scenes. I had forgotten that her permanent place of work is here at Rancho, collecting information and preparing patients for the outside world.

Debbie's disability is obvious—polio at a young age. She sits upright with her brown hair cascading down her small bent body. She smiles her way through an incredible story of abandonment, adoption, rejection, hospitals, and rules and regulations. Debbie is the first disabled person I've ever met with such an upfront testimony in the midst of an irreligious environment. I can tell that she tries to spread good news around this cold and impersonal institution. She is an oddity in this place, but everyone likes her.

"You met the guys in O.T.?" she asks, turning the conversation away from herself.

"Yes." I nod and then add, "Things in occupational therapy haven't changed much . . . potholders and paints and stuff. But those guys seem to have a good attitude about it."

Debbie's smile fades. "Well, not all of them. Did you meet the boy with the halo cast?"

I nod again.

"His parents don't want anything to do with him. He broke his neck in a motorcycle accident, driving when he was drunk. They figure he got himself into this mess, so he can get himself out." She sighs and shakes her head.

I wince and look toward the window of the therapy room. I wish I had said more to him.

"And the good-looking paraplegic? His wife just filed for divorce. I've tried talking to him about God, but he just won't listen. He's losing himself . . . in pity. In drugs."

I stare at the therapy room windows. The stories she relates are strikingly similar to many I heard when I was at Rancho as a patient years ago. But they didn't touch me then as they do now.

Debbie picks up on my mood. "Joni, you wouldn't believe the problems most handicapped people face. Spiritual struggles, yes. But down-to-earth, practical problems too."

Debbie is doing what I would like to do. In a real world, in a real way, she is helping people see Christ. No masks here.

"HEY, GET A LOAD of this!" Jay is reclining on the couch, crunching an apple while flipping through my script for the following week. "They've got a kissing scene in here, and guess whose name is on the call sheet." She rises to show me the page, her Cheshire-cat grin shining.

The script describes the scene in less than half a page. I have a line or two. Cooper, the actor playing my boyfriend, has even less to say. The rest is action.

Only a half page for all those memories. The real scene held all the drama. When my boyfriend Dick came to the hospital, there was no place he could wheel me so we could be alone. The solarium was filled with visitors, and the auditorium was off-limits. The only place we could hide and escape my six-bed ward was the elevator. We'd catch an empty one, press the third-floor button, and then flip the "stop" switch between floors. There we had plenty of privacy . . . until a nursing supervisor tracked us down one evening.

"I'm glad they've included that in the script. It'll add a fun moment to all those other drab hospital scenes," I reason.

"Yeah, and you'll have all the fun." Jay tousles my hair on her way back to the couch.

But will it really be fun to do a kissing scene in front of a movie crew with an actor I hardly even know? Cooper is very nice and very handsome, but what I know about him goes no further than his 8 x 10 glossy tacked to my dressing-room wall along with other cast members. Taking no chances, I decide to prepare. That night when I'm alone I practice the best kisses I can remember—on my wrist.

In the following days Cooper and I are thrown together frequently as we act our way through other scenes. Always, I wonder what he is thinking. Has he read ahead in the script? Does he have the same silly thoughts about the elevator scene as I do? Probably not. He's a Hollywood actor. He probably kisses leading ladies all the time.

The day arrives, and we go on location at a local hospital. An elevator is rigged with stage lights, microphones, and electric cables. The large camera is anchored on a tripod in the corner.

Cooper walks up behind me. "Think we'll fit in there?" He grins, popping a breath mint in his mouth. I envy his nonchalance.

When all is ready, I'm pushed into one corner of the elevator, and Jim pulls Cooper next to me, briefing us on our few lines. "The rest," he says, smiling, "will come naturally."

Then Jim shoulders up to the cameraman to discuss the mood he wants to capture. Cooper carefully sits on my lap, taking cues on how close to me he appears through the lens. The script lady, armed with her clipboard, pulls up a stool and sits within feet of us. She is ready to record every word and movement for the editors who will piece the film into one smooth scene.

"You'll do fine," Cooper whispers as he pats my shoulder. I admire his confidence.

"Action!"

Cooper turns toward me, brushes my cheek with his hand, and tilts my chin. His lips touch mine. Electricity. The foreign feel of lips on mine melts in an instant. I forget the lights and camera.

The director asks for a cut. Cooper breaks off his embrace, leaving me in mid-emotion. The lady on the stool fans us with her script. It is getting warm under the lights.

"Boy, you kiss good," Cooper laughs, patting my hand.

"Okay, let's do another," Jim scribbles a few notes and motions to begin.

Again Cooper leans toward me, only this time I am quicker to respond. I am surprised how easily I relax into his kiss. We linger a big longer past the "Cut."

"We don't need another take, you two," Jim breaks in. Everyone laughs. I glance at the cameraman and the script lady and laugh nervously. Do they know it wasn't all acting?

I purse my lips. They feel hot. My heart rushes with passion—another foreign feeling. I'm hit with guilt and the rush instantly vaporizes. I smile, still a little shaky. After all, God knows I haven't kissed anyone in a decade. The thought of never kissing anyone for another decade registers and my smile quickly fades.

A new day of filming other scenes with other actors helps me put—or try to put—that silly kiss out of my mind. Late in the afternoon they call for rushes, and we head for the screening room. I smother—or try to smother—my excitement about reviewing the footage of yesterday's kissing scene.

As the rough prints roll by, I gaze like some heart-struck moviegoer. The screen sizzles. But the scene is short, and as quickly as the footage begins, it is completed. Jim Collier and the rest of his crew scrawl a few notes and comment on the color intensity, then leave.

"Wow, that sure looked real," Jay says as we wheel into the blast of air conditioning in the hallway.

I feel humiliated. Silly, foolish, and even a little angry. That kiss was nothing but celluloid, to be clipped, cut, and edited.

THIS MOVIE THING mustn't take control of my life. Why do the script, the cast, the crew, and even the way I look on film mean so much to me? Why can't I just go back to our little rented house at the end of a day and put it all out of my mind?

I take deep breaths and try to relax in front of the large art easel. I have many paintings to complete for scenes in the movie, and time is slipping by. James Sewell, the art director, coaches me on the various brushes and paints I should use, but the harder I try to pay attention and concentrate, the further my mind wanders away.

"Joni . . . are you listening?" James asks. "Which shade of pink do you believe would work against this cool color?" He fans several tubes of paint in his hands for my inspection.

"Wh-what?" I say, startled. "I'm sorry, James. I guess my mind is elsewhere. I have such a difficult time concentrating these days."

James lays the paints on the table, folds his hands and leans on the corner of the canvas. He takes the brush out of my mouth, wipes it with a damp cloth, and sets it next to the other brushes.

Between scenes, this kind and fatherly, yet exacting professional has worked hard to instruct me about my artwork. I hate to disappoint him. After a long moment, he leans down and gives me a warm hug. "It's near lunch. Why don't we break early?" he says as he straightens.

I nod sheepishly.

"I'll push you out to the courtyard. You look like you need some fresh air." He smiles and tweaks my cheek.

The cement courtyard on the third floor of the studio is a nice place to escape movie commitments for the moment. Today a breeze has swept away the heavy smog, and the California sun shines bright and hot. Here, there is time to think.

Jim Collier warned that once this movie began we'd be on a greased slide—movie lingo for "no stopping." He was right. These first weeks of filming have been a wild initiation. There's hardly been time to think about the unexpected: the girl in the blue bathing suit, that ridiculous dog, the unnerving visit to Rancho Hospital—and that kiss.

It is all so perplexing. Like déjà vu. I've been here before. I look at the script on my lap, opened to a new page of dialogue. I didn't write these lines, but they are mine. And somehow, I'm acting . . . but I'm not. Feeling inferior, even ugly next to an attractive girl in a blue bathing suit. Feeling the pain of rejection from a mere dog. Fighting off intimidation. And that kiss. Old desires bubbling to the surface of my heart.

I catch my reflection in the large glass panel that separates the courtyard from the studio. The wheelchair takes up three-quarters of the space that makes up "me." I look like a bulky movie prop.

This movie image is too real. The script is about my life ten years ago, but the scenes are much too close for comfort. I am actually reliving the same old problems—from self-image to singleness!

Suddenly the sun is to hot. My skin prickles with anxiety. The shade of a small potted tree in the middle of the courtyard and a light breeze offer little relief from the heat of my thoughts.

I retrace my steps one by one. *How did I get myself into this predicament?* Prayer should have prevented this from happening.

Prayer. I have been praying, concentrating on the crew, the actors, the believers who will be inspired by the film, the unbelievers who will be brought into the Kingdom, the folks who are supporting the movie. But prayer for myself? No, I have assumed that my past, neatly shelved, is so far behind that it cannot touch me. Now I'm not so sure. Must I learn the same old lessons? In a new way? I don't think I can . . . I'm so tired.

And my Bible. For the past two weeks I've barely opened it. Oh, I've rehearsed a few familiar verses on my way to work each morning, verses memorized some time back. But nothing new. Nothing fresh. Just cruising on the top of a wave of God's grace.

One of those verses comes to mind now: "Do not think of yourself more highly than you ought, but rather think of yourself with sober judgment."[3]

Lots of things are beginning to slip on the greased slide. I've gotten my back against the wall spiritually. I'm growing tired. I'm failing. I feel like I'm letting people down. What if they knew?

I throw my head back and open my mouth in a silent scream. *How can I act out my love for God in a film when I can't get my act together for real?*

"Joni, got a minute?" Rob Tregenza jolts me out of my thoughts.

I erase the panic from my face and switch gears too easily from meditation to movie making.

Rob motions me into the screening room and spreads sheets of music on the carpeted floor. A girl sits at the piano and begins toying with a melody while Rob sings the words.

> Father, set my soul sailing like a cloud upon the wind,
> Free and strong to carry on until the journey's end.
> Each mile I put between the past and the future in your
>   hand
> I learn more of your providence and find out who I am.

"What do you think of it as a song for the close?" Rob holds the second page of music for me.

"I like it . . . keep singing." I close my eyes.

> I want to thank you for the gift of your Son
> and for the mystery of prayer
> And for the faith to doubt, and yet believe,
> that you're really there.[4]

Rob gathers the music sheets and taps them together on the piano lid. "Jim wanted me to run this song by you. Get your input."

"Well, the words are great. Especially the part about putting miles between the past and the future. You know, seeing it all as in His hand," I say. "But I don't get that line having faith to doubt and yet believe."

He smiles knowingly, nodding his head as he closes the lid on the piano. "We all have doubts, Jon," he says. "Don't you think the faith God gives us is large enough to handle even them?" He speaks with a hint of challenge in his voice, as though his own faith has been stretched at some point.

I want to mouth a stock answer to his rhetorical question, like a recording on replay. But I don't. This conversation seems isolated for a special reason, as though I am the one who had something to learn. I can't counter with a quick reply.

I know I have the faith to doubt and yet believe. The miles between my past and future are in His hand. But I'm beginning to wonder—do I know who I am?

Ⓢ

MY CHAIR JOSTLES up the gravel driveway, and I wheel into the shade of a spreading coast oak. The dusty, sweet aroma of a barn with hay. A green pasture bordered with rusting barbed wire. A corral with horses. It's not the farm in Maryland, but the movie people have found a convincing counterpart here behind the hills of Santa Barbara.

We have traded the smog of Los Angeles for the dust of a country road near Solvang. The cast and crew have swapped their Porsches for pickups and cowboy hats. There's an air of freedom and fun. No more hospital scenes for me.

It's easy to act these outdoor scenes. Being in Solvang is as exciting as my first real break from the hospital. It's easy to relax with the cast and crew. This morning one of the guys presented me with a cowboy hat of my own. The cameraman gave me a ride on his crane. During a break, I talked horses and saddles with several grips down by the corral. These people are so friendly. They have so much to say. Nobody here sounds like that verse from Ephesians— having a darkened or hardened heart.

I sit in the shade of this oak, reveling in the new freedom. It's not only a change in scenery and scenes; it is my brand-new power wheelchair. My arm straightens against the joystick and the chair inches forward. No more being pushed everywhere. Pride combines with independence as I choose to move or not move. I can turn my chair to chime in on a conversation. Or I can turn away.

Jim Collier introduces me to the young actor who will play the part of Steve Estes, the dear friend who was instrumental in getting my feet on the ground spiritually.

"I'm Richard," the boy says with a broad smile and seats himself on the stump of a log beside me. He resembles Steve at sixteen—tall, lanky, a little shy at first. "I've read all about Steve," he begins as he gestures with a *Joni* book. "He had a big impact on your life, didn't he?"

The make-up artist approaches and sets his bag on the gravel. "Mind if I start on you two?" He wets his brush and begins to line Richard's eyes for the camera.

"Yeah . . . uh, yes," I say absently as I return my attention from the actor's eyes to his question. "I mean . . . yes, Steve had a big impact on me."

Richard cracks open the book to show paragraphs he has highlighted in yellow. "I was hoping I could learn more about him from you."

The make-up artist wipes his brush and begins on my eyes.

"Well, I was barely out of the hospital when I met Steve . . . he was a teenager like me . . . but he was so enthusiastic about the Bible. He taught me how God had control over my accident and—"

"Okay," Richard interrupts, "but I guess I need to know more about his mannerisms. You know, how he would gesture and stuff."

"Oh. I see." I quickly switch gears and push away enthusiasm for Steve and those wonderful old truths. I concentrate instead on the importance of the moment—the art, the drama. The mask this actor needs to wear.

The assistant director calls the crew together over his megaphone. We are ready to start the next segment of filming. "Steve" and I are to exchange a few lines down by the barn.

While they fasten the camera to the huge crane, I practice wheeling my chair up and down the dirt path that parallels the barn. I'll have to drive straight while I deliver lines and look up at "Steve" sitting on the barn roof. After practice runs and rehearsals with the crane, we are ready.

"Action!"

As instructed, I drive slowly up the path, watching for the crane to rise above the backside of the barn roof. I look up at "Steve" as the camera slowly swings into position behind him.

"Whatcha reading?" I say my first line.

He looks up from the open book on his knee. "The Bible. 'They that wait upon the Lord shall renew their strength; they shall mount up with wings as eagles; they shall run, and not be weary; and they shall walk, and not faint.' "[5]

The words seem distant. From the past. Rather than inspired Scripture, I am hearing just lines from a script.

I shake my head on cue and say dryly, "That's very poetic." The dryness comes too easily. Too naturally.

Upon direction, I continue to power my brand-new wheelchair, leaving "Steve" behind on the roof.

THE SUMMER SUN above the Solvang farm is already high and hot, but the script calls for the cool days of fall. Autumn scenes need to be shot around the barn. I sit at a distance and watch the crew spray-paint the green summer leaves of an oak tree with tints of gold and red. The movie company goes to incredible lengths to re-create reality.

While I wait, I occasionally glance down at the open book on my lap. I'm attempting to catch up on my reading with a book by an English pastor about Jesus' sermon on the mount.[6] Each sentence is a stumbling block, the language weighty with old and stiffened words. But I ought to work through at least several pages.

The author is speaking about the verse, "Blessed are they that mourn."

"Let us, then, try to define his man who mourns. What sort of man is he? He is a sorrowful man . . . he is a serious man . . . he is a sober-minded man . . . he is a grave man."

I only scan these words from the book. My attention is easily diverted to the spray-painting of the leaves. I observe with an artist's eye how they choose the colors for different branches. I return to the page.

"The true Christian is never a man who has to put on an appearance of either sadness or joviality. No, no; he is a man who looks at life seriously; he contemplates it spiritually, and he sees in it sin and its effects."

Something about this paragraph nettles me. Perhaps I should read more closely.

"That is the man who mourns; that is the Christian. That is the type of Christian seen in the Church in ages past, when the doctrine of sin was preached and emphasized . . . a deep doctrine of sin, a high doctrine of joy, and the two together produced this blessed, happy man who mourns, and who at the same time is comforted."

The words sour as I reread the paragraph. I check the cover. Is this the same book I started reading months ago? Back then it was a favorite. Now the pastor seems to be writing for stuffy English saints from years ago. His words don't apply. Especially now.

I forget the book and wheel over to the director and "Steve" to rehearse my lines for the day.

Much later I drop into bed, exhausted after another emotionally charged day of filming and of too much caffeine on an empty stomach. My body is weary, but my mind does instant replays of the afternoon. The laughter. The chatter with the cameramen. The pats on the back.

In the middle of my thoughts, other words stick out like a sore thumb. *"The Christian is a man who looks at life seriously . . . contemplates it spiritually . . . sees in it sin and its effects."*

I lie alert for a moment, letting the two worlds play against each other. Like pieces of a puzzle. I make a half-hearted attempt at fitting them together. But oddly, they don't.

I sigh, turning my head and nestling into the pillow. I can't ponder such weighty matters at this hour. Tomorrow is another busy day.

THE MORNING SUN rises and crests the mountains, exploding like a diadem into the sky. Jay and I are being driven from our Solvang hotel to the movie farm. In high spirits, we sing Linda Ronstadt style. I look at my sister. Hair, long and blond, just as she wore it in her twenties. Granny glasses. Faded blue jeans. I am glad she is here. She brings a touch of stability and reality to this movie mania.

But even Jay is not above change. Rob Tregenza, who has researched so many details for the film, has spent a good bit of time researching my sister. I noticed him admiring the way she handled the horses for one of the scenes. I've watched them sit and talk much during breaks.

Our driver turns onto the dirt road leading to "our farm." The shaded lawn and tranquil house are overrun with cables and light stands, movie trucks and cranes. Everywhere there are people putting up props, hammering, and sawing. The excitement draws us in.

I wheel into the house over power cables and through a maze of trunks and boxes. The interior is to resemble the living room back at our Maryland farm. The old farm is difficult to picture with all this film-making paraphernalia. But in the middle of the set stands my art easel. A familiar touch. My heart warms, and I smile, remembering those first sketchy attempts to paint with a brush between my teeth—an experience I must soon re-create on film.

Jim Collier rallies the crew. Jay finds my place in the script. I am to be filmed painting a beautiful butterfly making its journey from caterpillar to cocoon to winged flight.

I watched the kind elderly prop man ready his jar of caterpillars. Through the network of this crazy industry, he has located a supply house for bugs and insects. He has ten or fifteen, in case any die, crawl away, or fail their screen test. (Memories of the puppy linger.) We tease him about being a caterpillar wrangler. He responds with mock dignity. Why, he has trained these caterpillars to crawl, on cue, across the window sill of the set. I laugh. All this for the movie to suggest that I am the one coming out of the cocoon.

For the camera to film my painting and then switch focus to capture the tiny creature on the window sill, the gaffer is asked to brighten the set with extra lights. I sit on the sidelines watching him converse with Jim and the cameraman. Their comments become as heated as the room from the glare of lights.

"It's too much light," says the gaffer. "We've got to think of Joni under all this heat." My ears catch his defensive tone. It's nice to be the object of such consideration.

"But we need the depth of field to have the foreground and the background in focus. Look at those shadows by the window!"

As a compromise, they decide to cut the glare with flags and nets. But as I move into position under my easel, I still feel the intense heat of the stage lights above me. My advocate approaches with a solid flag, a rectangular frame covered with black cloth. He stands and shields me from the dazzling lights as the camera readies.

"Please, I'll be okay."

"Not to worry." The gaffer smiles.

I hardly know this man. He is merely a name on my prayer list for the movie crew. But I've observed his friendly manner with everybody. He's even-tempered and flexible. He's also strong, I register, thinking back on his discussion with the cameraman and Jim.

"This is helping," I add, groping for something to say. "I don't handle heat very well. It's my, uh . . . handicap."

Our exchange is cut short as Jim calls for action. Despite the heat, the caterpillar and I perform on cue. We applaud the prop man for his excellent coaching, and we break for coffee.

As I wheel off the set, I glance toward the gaffer and his helpers dismantling the heavy lights. Jay has difficulty clearing cables from my path. The gaffer quickly comes to help, as though assisting me is far more important than juggling thousand-dollar stage lights.

"Sometimes . . . this wheelchair . . . ," I half apologize for interrupting him.

"You don't seem handicapped at all to me." He smiles and returns to his work.

"Wrap" comes early. A small group clusters to make dinner plans. The camera assistant and the gaffer want to join us.

Our movie making is finished for the day, yet I freshen my face to prepare for my next "scene." The location will be a little Scandinavian restaurant that has received rave reviews. I plan the dialogue carefully—the sorts of questions I want to ask, the direction I want the conversation to take. The meal is incidental. Plates are props. I will make the gaffer center stage.

Our dinner conversation is spirited. I am delighted that my new friend is sitting next to me. As on the set, he doesn't seem to mind helping—cutting my meat or lifting a glass of water to my mouth. Without prompting, he dabs my mouth with a napkin at the end of the meal.

Our little group chatters idly as we meander up the street outside the restaurant, stopping now and then to peer through shop windows. Rob reaches for Jay's hand as they walk.

It's a warm Southern California night and a clear, starry dome twinkles above us. Crickets court in the woods beyond the little town and the air is sweet with gardenia. Under the street lamps, I discover my own sense of backlighting.

I'm not above change either, I decide.

I push the joy stick of my new wheelchair, powering ahead. With sly pleasure I choose to leave my sister and the rest behind and wheel beside the gaffer.

W E ARE BACK in Los Angeles, away from the camera. The gaffer—handsome, wealthy, kind—has asked me to dinner. I wonder what to wear. A simple blouse with matching bow? No. An elegant V-neck sweater? Perhaps. Yes.

"You don't seem handicapped at all to me." I recall his words and his smile. I picture the hills of Santa Barbara. The quiet California night. The blanket of stars above us. Back there I didn't feel handicapped—for a change.

Waiting by the window, I watch the shiny red Porsche pull up outside our house. It is familiar on the studio lot, but parked in our driveway it moves out of the professional world and into the personal. I am ready.

"Are you sure it'll fit?" I cringe. I don't want my clunky push wheelchair to damage the leather of the tiny back seat.

"Not to worry." My gaffer friend struggles to angle the chair behind his seat. "There!" The chair is lodged into place. Thank God. Who would have guessed a wheelchair would fit into a Porsche?

I am surprised at how much we have to talk about. There is no awkwardness. Our working together every day for many weeks now has not drained ideas for conversation. I don't feel uncomfortable trying to bridge the gap between our worlds.

"So this movie's a lot like your real life?" he says soon after we're on our way.

"Yes." I lean back into the cushiony headrest and sigh. "It's pretty much the way it happened."

"You know, what I said the other day is true," he interjects. "None of us on the crew even notice your wheelchair."

I am flattered by his attempt to put me at ease, but I am also uneasy with this talk about me. Surely he is tired of hearing about "Joni" stuff. I am.

"I bet you've filmed other things a lot more exciting," I say in an effort to turn the conversation back on him.

He shakes his head. "I wouldn't exactly call Pepsi commercials exciting."

"That's because you own stock in Hawaiian Punch. I've seen you drinking cans of that stuff on the set. Come on, where's your Pepsi spirit?"

"In my garage. They gave us cartons of the stuff after the shoot." His eyes and smile meet mine for an instant, warmed in the glow from his dash lights. I snap a mental photo.

We speed up the on-ramp of the Ventura Freeway, the lights of the Hollywood Hills twinkling like stars. He is right. Tonight this handicap is not going to get in the way.

I plan not to drink any water so my legbag will not need to be emptied. I have lost a great deal of weight during this movie, so I know I'll be easy to lift. I think about what I'll order for dinner—something easy to eat so that no food will fall off my special spoon. I glance at my feet. It's early in the evening, and thankfully, my ankles aren't swollen and unsightly.

I listen to the click of the turn signal as we shift into the fast lane and watch the people in the cars we speed past. An elegant blonde with her hair in a sophisticated chignon drives a black Mercedes—it's night, but she wears dark glasses, hiding any trace of an expression. A rowdy group of teenagers out for a good time—the windows of their Pontiac Firebird are shut, but I can see them lip-syncing to a rock beat on their radio. A man in a station wagon, eyes straight ahead and hands clutching the wheel in driver's ed. form—he ignores his wife who leans into the back seat to slap their child's knees.

The freeway is a drama with its own players and plot, a teeming world rushing this way and that. I feel a part of its pulse, its beat. With my wheelchair tucked out of sight behind the seat, the people in the cars we zoom by would never think I am handicapped.

We pull up sharply in front of an exotic oriental restaurant. The Porsche idles while my friend walks toward the valet, slips him a folded bill, and explains our need for special parking. The boy smiles and runs ahead to escort us.

Within minutes my wheelchair is unfolded and ready for me. I hope my shoes don't fall off while he's lifting me. And I hope I don't hurt his back!

There are steps, but my friend handles my chair with confidence. He has obviously studied my sister's technique. I breathe a sigh of relief. My legs fit underneath the table. I order a dish I can handle easily with my special spoon in my armsplint.

"Okay, so how would you light your glass if you were doing a wine commercial?" I ask, wanting to show my interest in his work.

He thinks for a moment, lifting his glass to the light, letting the wine swirl. He sets it down and runs his fingers around the rim. "I'd place the wine here." He gestures toward the glass, leaning back. He pulls an empty chair closer to him. "Then I'd sit a beautiful woman here." He pats the arm of the chair. "A dark brunette. Full mouth. High cheekbones. Long neck. Lots of skin."

My smile stiffens.

"Then I'd put a nine light or an H.M.I. here and a couple of twinnes for back light and a lee filter to soften things up." He uses the language of his profession. "In other words I'd light the wine to outshine the girl. Who needs the beautiful woman?" He smiles as he sips his drink.

I laugh. I'm still in the fast lane. I fantasize that my hands can gesture . . . long graceful fingers, polished nails, stirring coffee as I talk.

During the drive home, the Cinderella magic begins to wear off. My legbag needs emptying. (Is that a faint whiff of urine?) My sweater has pulled out of my slacks from all the lifting. My corset has ridden up, digging into my skin and making it harder to breathe. I'm getting "sweats," which tells me something is wrong somewhere. My reflection in the mirrored visor tells me my make-up needs repairing, but there is nothing I can do about it. I look closer. My face has that same pale, lifeless expression I once saw in the movie mirror.

I'm glad Jay is home when we arrive. I feel heavier as they lift me into my wheelchair. My friend senses I am uncomfortable so our good-bys are quick. I am happy to get out of the sweater, unstrap the corset, take off the legbag, and be in bed where I don't feel quite as paralyzed.

I think back on the evening—the light, the sound, the action. I have edged closer to a world I've known little of in the last decade. I wonder how close I can get without it weakening me.

Tomorrow is another day of filming. More scenes about adjusting to a wheelchair. More about being handicapped. More about coping. I am getting tired of hearing about "those days." I am getting tired of hearing about "Joni" and how she has it all together.

But I almost had it all together tonight. The thin mask very nearly, but not completely, stayed intact.

꧁

"JAY! JUDY!" MY voice is urgent. I have been awakened in the middle of the night my a pounding headache. My heart is racing. It is not with fear. Something is desperately wrong with my body.

"Jay!" I wait for an answer or for someone to flick on a light in the adjoining room.

Jay stumbles into the room. "What is it?" She reads the panic in my eyes. "Oh, Joni, you're sweating buckets!"

"I think it's my catheter. It must be blocked or kinked or something." I breathe deeply, trying to control my heart rate. "Do something, please, quick."

Jay goes into high gear and throws back my covers. She turns me on my side and discovers that I've been leaking around the catheter. "The bed is soaked. Your bladder must be bursting!"

I think of the two quarts of water I drank before bed, a necessary part of my nighttime routine. I haven't gotten rid of any of that fluid. I'm in dysreflexia—a dangerous reaction in spinal cord injured people that can result in a cerebral hemorrhage.

"I'm going to change it. We don't have time to fool around." Jay scrambles urgently through the dresser for a new catheter, syringe, sterile solution, and scissors.

My head is hammering. I know my blood pressure is shooting up rapidly uncontrollably. I try not to think about a brain hemorrhage.

Within minutes, a new catheter is inserted. "Come on . . . drain bladder, drain," Jay whispers nervously as she looks for a flush of fluid in the clear urological tubing.

I cannot tolerate the pain. "What's happening? Why isn't it working?" I cry.

"I don't know. I don't know! I've checked everything. It must be a faulty catheter."

I read panic in my sister's face. She knows as well as I how dangerous this is. Doctors have warned us. We've read about it in books. But this is the first time it has happened.

A tight band squeezes my head. "Oh, God, forgive me. Forgive me for knowing what to do one minute, then forgetting the next," I mumble. "Please . . . if this happens . . ."

Jay fumbles for the phone and calls the transportation captain of the movie. "Get the paramedics for Joni. Quick!"

"Praise the Lord . . . praise the Lord," I say as deliberately as my breathing and the pain allow. I wait—either for the paramedics to arrive or for the rising pressure to stop or for my brain to snap. I wait and fight off the panic with praise.

As I am rushed to the hospital some of the pain in my head subsides. My bladder must be draining. I breathe deeply with relief. I know I am soaking the sheets and stretcher. But who cares? I'm alive!

In the emergency room I am fitted with a new catheter. They monitor my blood pressure and pulse for an hour, waiting to make sure everything is stabilized. It is 2:30 in the morning by the time we head back to the hotel. I joke about looking bright-eyed and bushy-tailed in just a few hours for the morning's film schedule.

"You can't be serious." Jay looks stunned. "Don't you think you ought to take the day off? The production can wait. Nobody will mind."

I consider her concern. Yet I know I will feel better if I don't lie around worrying and wondering about what could have happened. "Okay, let's compromise. We'll sleep in and ask Jim if we can start filming at noon."

Back in bed, where just hours ago I panicked, I remember my praises to God. I'm relieved I had enough sense to rush to Him when I needed Him. But now I only rush a quick prayer of thanks to heaven. After all, I need to get to sleep for tomorrow's schedule. I fight off guilt. God will understand.

Later that day when we arrive on the set, the crew is unusually quiet. No "How ya doin' there, kid!" Obviously, they have heard about my middle-of-the-night emergency. I suppose I look tired. Judy floods my eyes with Visine to cover the redness.

Since it is after noon and time is short, we quickly enter the first thing on the schedule: Scene 648.

JONI: "I'm okay. I can still feel."

Cut to Jay.

JONI: *(continuing)* "And I guess I'm alive. I just wanna be alone for a while."

After the scene is shot, I curtly dismiss Judy's suggestion that I take a nap or an early break. She and Jay just don't understand. I've got a job to do. I can't let Jim and the cast and crew down. I must make sacrifices. I can handle the pressure. And I really do just want to be alone.

THE VARIOUS MOVIE scenes are slowly linking together, forming a strong message about the hope that can be found in Christ. But I'm growing weaker—physically, emotionally, and spiritually.

I sit on the sidelines of the sound stage and watch. But I don't want to just watch; I should be doing something,. *Like praying.* I sense the faint suggestion from God's Spirit. I remember the clogged catheter and the answered pleas, so I push myself into an obligatory prayer.

The camera assistant looks tired. *Lord, help him find rest in You.* I wonder if the prop man understands the message behind this film yet. *Lord, may he find You to be the answer to his deepest longings.* That actor I kissed . . . *Lord, he's not needed in the filming schedule any more. Whatever he's into now, bring Yourself often to his memory.*

I watch the gaffer. He wears a red plaid flannel shirt. His jeans, though faded, are nicely creased. He raises a can of Hawaiian Punch in my direction, smiling his broad, easy grin. I cannot, will not, pull my eyes away.

Prayers for him? Yes, I pray. Although I wonder about my motives. I seem to be more concerned about my heart than his soul. And he has no idea.

But I have ideas. Some of the cast and crew will be flying back East to Maryland to capture the fall colors. We will shoot beautiful scenes among real trees this time—fiery red maples and tall yellow oaks. Everyone will see the real farm, meet my real family and friends. I'll show the crew—including the gaffer, of course—other horse farms in Maryland, parks up in the mountains, and maybe even Washington, D.C. Maryland in the fall. They'll love it.

In the scenes to be shot there even the script is beautiful . . .

Shot of wheel of Joni's chair moving through leaves.

STEVE: " 'And just as there are different kinds of seeds and plants . . .' "

Steve and Joni moving through woods.

STEVE: *(continuing)* " 'so also there are different kinds of flesh. . . . The angels in heaven have bodies far different from ours, and the beauty and glory of their bodies is different from the beauty and glory of ours. . . . But all who become Christ's will have the same kind of body as His.' "

Pan from leaves to Joni and Steve moving away down path. Music starts. Steve reading out in front of Joni as they move up hill.

STEVE: " 'I tell you this, my brothers—' "

Joni gets stuck and Steve goes back and pushes her up hill.

STEVE: *(continuing)* " 'an earthly body made of flesh and blood cannot get into God's Kingdom. These perishable bodies of ours are not the right kind to live forever.' "[7]

All who become Christ's . . . Oh, how I wish these words would get through to all the crew—the prop man, the script lady, both cameramen, and, yes, the gaffer. I sit on the sidelines, this time on the edge of a field in Maryland, and watch them film footage of the trees.

The Californians look like foreigners in their down jackets next to Marylanders who need no coats against the nippy air. Betsy and Diana, close companions of mine since high school, seem comfortable with only sweaters. They have come on location near the Sykesville farm to watch. I am glad my Maryland friends show an interest in the movie making.

"So what's this thing do?" Diana points to a large white sheet of styrofoam.

"It's a fill card," my gaffer friend begins. "Like when a face is too dark on one side? You'd bounce light onto the cheek with a tilt of this white card." He angles the reflector to focus the sun's rays toward Diana.

"So *that's* what I'm missing." Diana poofs her hair in Marilyn Monroe fashion. "I just need to walk around with a fan in front of me for the windblown look, and a fill card to get the sunken cheeks." She flattens her hands against her face. "Then a spot behind me for backlighting. Au naturel."

"That's right." The gaffer laughs and points. "That's right. We do that to Joni every day. But you know . . ." He grows serious. "No matter what light I use, it's hard to make her look bad."

I should be studying the script on my lap, but all I can do is stare at this man. His compliment is sincere and innocent. And my heart is probably making far more of it than he intends. But I don't care. Diana sees the silly moon-struck look on my face and shoots a glance to Betsy.

After the break my friends join me behind the set to watch more filming. The big camera silently records the sight and sound of wind in trees. For several minutes we look on with no words between us.

"It's neat watching them, isn't it?" I whisper and motion toward the crew and equipment. A gust of wind tousles the crisp skirts of the trees. We gather closer for warmth.

Betsy leans over from behind my chair and wraps her arms around me. "Just so you're okay, Jon." She pats my arms and straightens up.

Her comment annoys me. "What's your problem?" I snap. "There's nothing wrong."

Betsy backs away slightly. "Oh. I was just thinking how thin you've gotten. You know, and tired." She looks puzzled. "I love you. The pressures of this movie and all . . . I'm just worried about you."

Her soothing words are convicting. "Look, I'm okay, you guys." I paste on a smile. "There's nothing to worry about." My rehearsed line is a trowel, smoothing out their concerns like bumps and unsightly pebbles until the surface appears glossy and flat.

I must not let them know that I truthfully don't prefer their company . . . that I hardly read my Bible now . . . that I'm nearly anorexic—I cannot eat . . . that my prayers are lifeless, even self-centered . . . that I want to date anybody . . . and that I don't like this wheelchair.

All who become Christ's . . . I think of the crew. Yet I stubbornly push away any meaning the thought may hold for me. People in movies wear masks, substituting one kind of reality for another.

THE CHANGE OF Maryland seasons sweeps in with the north wind which blows across the farm fields and roars through the trees. The colorful leaves are drying to a dull brown and falling off the branches. The few remaining scenes must be shot quickly.

In a shaven cornfield across the river from the farm, "Steve" and I fly a kite for the camera. The fickle fall wind lifts and drops the kite far out of the frame of the camera. We have to do many retakes.

Steve, flying a kite high, looks at Joni.

JONI: "My life is like that, full of ups and downs."

I say the phrase almost shamelessly and am pricked that nearly every line in this movie reads too close for comfort. But so what, I rationalize. Everybody has ups and downs, and I'm no exception. So I've had a few struggles lately.

Ups and downs. Jay seems to be the only one whose life is on an even keel these days. Although she and Rob have known one another only a short time, those weeks have been filled with hours of long, heart-to-heart talks—more conversation than Jay has ever shared with anyone before.

Frankly, I haven't paid much attention until recently. I did notice them during coffee breaks between scenes when they would sit in directors' chairs by the edge of the sound stage, discussing the lifelikeness in the set design. And in Solvang I did think it curious that they spent so much time together after each day's shoot. But now I see the change coming. And it is not simply the season.

In fact, being home in Maryland—surrounded by family and friends—has pushed something new to the surface. Marriage. It doesn't surprise me. I've often wondered why some white knight hasn't galloped up sooner. When Jay sits in her rocking chair, her Scandinavian blond hair shining and swaying, no one could be more beautiful. She tends her garden with the care of a mother for her children. Her home on the farm exudes warmth and welcome. She has shown total commitment in all the years I've lived with her and her daughter Kay.

Though Jay and Rob will marry, they assure me that life as we've known it on the farm will continue. But now I must look at Jay's life and mine from a clinical distance. An incredible change—not a movie scene but a real one—is about to upheave my life and hers. What do I feel?

I don't feel anxious or even envious. I don't even consider myself adrift because of this great new direction in my sister's life. Oddly, I don't feel anything. It occurs to me that I'm simply numb. My sister is about to be married, yet I am pleasantly numb, as if in a silly stupor.

For the first time I am scared to death. It has little to do with Jay's marriage on the horizon. But it has everything to do with the realization that I am at a surprising distance from the real me. Somehow I have become surgically separated from familiar and reasonable emotions that should be a part of who I am. I am also frightened and a little disgusted that, once again, I am consumed with thoughts about myself.

It all happens so quickly. Jay and Rob celebrate their wedding on Friday afternoon after the last Maryland scene is shot. The sky is gray with heavy clouds, diffusing what fall colors remain. Nothing is diffused about the ceremony, however, as our pastor reads from the Book of Common Prayer. Amid lilting strains of classical music, the exchange vows before family and a few friends in the farmhouse living room. The warmth of the wedding matches the simplicity of their love for one another.

My life is full of ups and downs. The phrase rolls over and over. I am happy for Jay, of course. But what does such a change free *me* to be? To do? Just who *am* I, and where, in God's name, am I going?

STREAMERS OF WATER flatten against the window beside me as our plane slices through the fog and rain on the flight back to Los Angeles. Once on the ground, we find the freeways slippery and slow; our rented house is damp and dark. It is the first time I have seen bad weather in L.A.

As Judy and Jay unpack and settle in, I glance over the script and call sheets for next week's filming. Names of actors are missing. They are no longer needed in the story line. There are several crew changes. We have more short pick-up shots than usual, and the schedule looks slower-paced. The production on *Joni* is definitely winding down.

Monday morning is still gray and chilly, but I am warmed by the friendly greetings from the crew and cast at the studio. The heavy lights on the make-up mirror drive the chill further away. Jim Collier pulls up a chair. "You look rested." Our eyes meet in the mirror and he waits for a smile. We both understand that I have been through a lot of changes lately. "I know many people have been praying for you. I've heard you got a pressure sore." He takes off his glasses and wipes them with a corner of his shirt.

I lower my head. "Yes, just a small one. I suppose I've gotten a little too thin."

"A little?" Jim replaces his glasses and rubs my shoulder. "Those hospital scenes were months ago."

"Well, I'll try and gain some." I tell a lie. "And Jim, I need the prayers." I tell a truth. Strength is what I need—physical stamina—to give my fullest energies to these last weeks of filming. But I know that emotionally, even spiritually, I am still backed against a wall.

"Listen, I know the rest of the crew has missed you. How about speaking to them as a group before we start in this morning?" Jim suggests as he leaves, tucking his clipboard under his arm.

I wheel downstairs to the sound stage where the producer has gathered everyone. "Good to see you, kid." The camera assistant gives me a hug. "She's back!" The prop man spreads his arms in welcome. The wardrobe and sound people greet me with hugs and kisses. James, the art director, waves his brush as he paints a backdrop. The gaffer, who is looping a cable on his elbow, waves and smiles from the other end of the set. My emotions are just below the surface as I mentally collect a few ideas to share. I do love these people. I have prayed for them, talked to Jesus about them, and talked to them about Him. But to avoid tears, I avoid the heavy, heartfelt speech on the tip of my tongue.

"I just want to tell you how much I've . . . I've enjoyed being with you these months. This film . . . uh, work of art, is . . . has meant so much to me. It has stretched us all creatively. It has put us all through many changes. And because of our teamwork," I say as I gesture toward the sound stage, "very many people will learn about the Lord . . . as I hope you have too."

The crew applauds. Their appreciation is warm, sincere. I want to say something more, something specific about the gospel, something more direct. to challenge these people about where they are with God. But some inkling of a double standard keeps me from going further. Tears spill over. I cry, not only because I love these people, but because I have let them down. I've let God down.

"Joni, we have a little surprise for you and the crew," interrupts Bill Brown, the executive producer, as hand-clapping subsides. "Billy Graham is at the other end of the building for a World Wide board meeting. He has asked if he can come over and talk with us for a few minutes." There are oohs and aahs and another smattering of applause.

Mr. Graham and several board members walk onto the sound stage. The tall, striking evangelist takes time to greet everyone personally, shakes hands, chats in a relaxed way as if he's known us all for years. Although I have met him several times before, I am nervous as he approaches. Stammering a bit, I keep my greeting brief. I want to direct his eyes off me and onto the crew.

"This film will speak to millions," he says as he turns to the group. "Millions who are paralyzed spiritually. People without Christ are crippled far more than Joni here." He motions toward my wheelchair. "But this movie you fine people are working on will tell of Joni's victory in Christ. What a great encouragement to so many who are suffering in so many different ways."

The group is quiet. Some lean on stage props; a few stand behind lighting tripods or sit in directors' chairs. Billy Graham is saying what I am too weak to utter.

"World Wide Pictures thanks you for the hard work you are doing," he continues as he turns to me. "And we thank you, Joni, for selflessly giving so much . . . reliving so many difficult memories for the spiritual benefit of thousands."

The image of thousands of nameless, faceless people crowds my mind. The powerful message of this true story—a young teenager's struggle to believe in God from a wheelchair—will, as he says, benefit thousands.

But what about the "me" behind the scenes? I'm afraid that people will think I'm a superhuman saint. Because of this movie, they may assume I am far more than I really am. I don't know what to say, how to respond. I manage a weak "thank you" and muster the courage to look Mr. Graham straight in the eye.

I have the sinking feeling he can look right through me.

ONE OF THE last scenes we shoot is an important one. We are re-creating a conversation I had with a man who attended my first art show. I have a lot of dialogue, and I've been memorizing it for more than a week now.

The wardrobe people have planned a nice outfit for me. I'm allowed to wear my current hairstyle and even my own make-up. Jim hasn't guided me much either. He knows I've said these lines scores of times before. It should come naturally.

On location at the small restaurant reminiscent of the little downtown café back in Baltimore, I sit across the table from an actor dressed in a marine uniform. He has an eyepatch and wears a metal hook on his right arm.

"Lights . . . camera . . . action" cues us to begin our off-the-cuff conversation.

MARINE: "Hey, when did you get outta high school?"

JONI: "Oh, sixty-seven."

MARINE: "Yeah, me too. They never told us about this in Senior Problems." (*He gestures with his hook.*)

JONI: "No they sure didn't. I think in our school they called it Contemporary Issues in Social Sciences."

MARINE: "Exactly."

JONI: "There are a million questions, and only a couple decent answers in life."

MARINE: "Half the guys in my class went to college, the other half went to Vietnam.

Some lived, some died, some of us got caught in the cracks." (*Long pause.*) "No one ever told us the world's an outhouse! Did they?"

JONI: "I am sure of only one thing. I know who put me back together.

MARINE: "How can you know?"

JONI: "I sleep nights and I laugh a lot. . . . Look, if there really is such a place as heaven and if . . . if Jesus really died on that cross because He wanted to bridge the gap between God and us, then getting to know Him and all that that means . . . well, it should be worth looking into, even for you. You see, I'd rather be in this chair, knowing Him, than on my feet without Him. And I never really knew that for sure until this moment."

I'd rather be in this chair, knowing Him, than on my feet without Him. That piece of script replays itself long after the director calls a wrap, long after I've gone back to our little house.

How can you know? I hear the actor say tauntingly.

"I sleep nights," I whisper into the darkness as I lay in bed, wide awake.

℘

I AM GOING home. This time for good. I lean back against the headrest of the TWA jet and think about what lies ahead. For me, right now, the movie seems to be the only thing heading forward in a charted direction, and even it is not in my life any more. Other people have the film now. Color processors. Editors. Musicians. And eventually promoters and distributors. People will pray. The movie's message, just as Mr. Graham predicted, will change lives.

The mask of that seventeen-year-old girl and her long-ago experiences must be torn off. Somehow I must pick up where I left off a year ago. The cast and crew have gone their separate ways. Judy Butler has returned to her work with the Billy Graham Association to set up a crusade in Nashville. I glance at Jay and Rob, asleep in their seats beside me. Perhaps now my life can get back to normal.

The plane drops within sight of the patchwork of snow-covered fields, farmhouses, and pastures. Our farm will be a picture postcard of drifts shouldering up to the stone house with its candlelit windows. Horses in their winter coats will be stamping their feet in the corrals, and pine trees dressed in heavy white will frame the scene. Leaving palm trees and freeways, I wonder how quickly I'll ease back into life at home.

Rob and Jay and I drive from the airport through the snowplowed slush on the highway till we reach the country lane of the farm. Inside the house a few things have changed since Jay married—a new rug, a different chair, the living-room furniture rearranged.

I glanced around the corner into my study. My desk and books are as I left them, along with a new stack of folders and letters that need attention. The Mason jars holding my brushes and paints await my return. My sketch pad lies opened on the art easel. The page is blank.

The setting is the same. I'm the one who has changed.

I don't fit any more.

And I'm not sure why, I think to myself in my own not-so-familiar bed that night. The blankets suddenly seem as heavy as the darkness, and I'm tempted to call Jay to pull down my covers. *It's probably just a little anxiety, the strain of adjustment to the months away from the farm. I'll try thinking about some Scripture verses . . . or praying.*

"They are darkened in their understanding . . . separated from the life of God . . . hardened in their hearts, having lost all sensitivity." The words, as clear as black ink on a white page, come back to haunt me. This time, the verse from Ephesians seems neither stuffy nor out of place.

God, are those words for me? The conviction, like darkness, presses in. *Darkened . . . hardened . . . could that be me? Not so much people in Hollywood, but me?* Where are the thoughts coming from? I am too dull to discern. God? The Devil? Is the Holy Spirit doing the talking, or am I shadow-boxing imaginary problems? I'm tired and I'm weak and I've been through a lot. Maybe I just need sleep.

LATE DECEMBER COMES blustering across the fields, whistling through every crack in the farmhouse. Rob, between researching and scripting his new film project, dons a heavy coat and scarf to split more wood for the fireplaces. Jay sets up a little space heater in my study as I go back to work at my art easel.

It is winter 1978. I try desperately to keep my attention on the present, on my sketch pad. But every time I look away from the paper, my eyes focus on the movie. The people. The places. Photos of the gaffer and me framed in brass on my desk.

I look at Rob, still a new face in the farm setting. His smile and voice are linked so closely to those memories I battle. I stare at him and think of the dinner we all enjoyed in the little town of Solvang behind the mountains of Santa Barbara. Candlelight dinners around the farm table somehow seem empty by comparison.

I watch a program on television, oblivious to the story line and dialogue. Instead, I scrutinize the lighting. Are the shadows too harsh? Why aren't they using a fill card? My gaffer friend would have put in more backlighting.

A late-night movie comes on, with Burt Lancaster playing the Bird Man of Alcatraz. Don't they realize he has two shadows behind him in his cell? What sort of a professional did that? How would "our" crew have lighted it?

The bars on the cell window . . . the prison . . . the Birdman won't be released. He's in there until he dies. . . . Oh help me, God—I'm in this wheelchair till I die. A cell. A prison . . . I can't breathe.

"I can't breathe," I call out. "I can't breathe!"

Jay rushes in, knotting her bathrobe. She quickly sits me up in bed. "What happened?" She presses her hand against my abdomen, helping me get my breath. My gasps quiet when I feel her arms around me.

I forced myself to take long controlled breaths. "I don't know." On the television screen, the prison movie has broken for a commercial. I inhale slowly. "For a minute I felt like that man behind bars."

Jay lowers me back into bed. "Shh. It's only a movie." She smooths my hair back and waits by my bed in silence.

Only a movie, I think to myself as she flicks off the set. "Only a movie," I mumble in exhaustion.

The next day I am back at my easel. It has been months since I've drawn anything. I am rusty, out of practice, and everything I sketch looks wrong. Maybe I've lost my talent, my creativity. Perhaps I'm so dry I will never be able to draw again. Evil, ugly panic raises its head once more. With eyes wide, I glare at my feeble attempts on the art pad. I can't even draw a straight line.

Pushed to the brink, I spit the pencil from my mouth. Lodging my shoulder against the easel, I sweep my arm across the desk. The pad, the pencils, the books—everything goes flying, crashing against the wall and hitting the floor. The noise attracts Jay who is vacuuming in the next room. She comes running.

"I can't draw! I can't do anything!" I scream hysterically.

Jay stands dumbfounded, looking at the mess on the floor, her hands open in question. Incredulous, she raises her eyes to me.

I shake my head and sob, "I don't know who I am . . . I don't know who I am." My voice cracks. Tears blur my vision. My nose runs and I lick my lips. Helplessly, I look at my sister.

I don't know who I am.

GOD IS PUTTING pressure on.

I debate with Him, having enough faith no doubt and still believe that He is there and listening.

"God, this movie was all Your idea. I didn't knock on anybody's door, anxious to bare my soul and share the struggle of those early years in my chair. I didn't want to be anybody's idea of a star. . . . I just wanted to do something for You, for Your Kingdom.

"What You have here is not sin, God. Give me a break. Look at all the sacrifices I've made. I'm drained. Tired. I've lost weight. I've been slapped with hospital memories. I've been tempted, sure, but You must know I'm in a wheel-chair. . . . It's only understandable that my heart would get out in front of my head. And isn't it about time? Look, I've been content with my singleness for years. So what's the big deal in going out with somebody, even if they don't know You? What's wrong with an occasional date?

"And look at all those other changes. Living in 'Hollyweird' is bound to make anybody a little batso. Besides, there was so little time to read or fellowship with lots of Christians. . . . It was up at dawn, run to work, scarf down dinner, cram a script, and into bed early.

"And Jay's married now. Shouldn't that give me every reason in the world to wonder about my own future?

"And look what else those months away from home did. I sacrificed weeks away from my art easel. It's going to take me forever to feel comfortable with that pencil in my mouth again. Little wonder my creativity has shriveled up.

"This isn't sin! This is life. I'm expected to be exhausted. I am *not* darkened in my understanding or hardened or insensitive. I've made big sacrifices, and I deserve a little time off and a bit of understanding on Your part. On everybody's part."

But the pressure doesn't let up.

Another morning dawns after another fitful night. My first thought is that the sunlight pouring through the gauze curtains will, I hope, stick to my senses. Will somehow brighten me from the outside in. But I am antsy and bored, still tired, and anything but peaceful.

Doors click shut and faucets run. Somebody flicks on "Good Morning America" in the other room. I smell sausage frying and coffee brewing.

"Morning," Jay says as she enters my bedroom carrying two mugs. She wedges my coffee next to my pillow, placing one end of a flexible plastic tube into the mug and the other end in my mouth.

"You're in here early," I comment, sipping coffee.

"Well, there's somebody at the door to see you," she explains.

I give her a puzzled look.

"It's Bill Mock, Dad's old wrestling buddy." She sounds equally puzzled. Bill is not a regular visitor to the farm. He comes only for special get-togethers that my parents occasionally have with Daddy's wrestling crowd.

"Bill says he has a message for you," Jay explains. "Do you want him to come in or shall I tell him to wait until you get up?"

I know Bill has come some distance at such an early hour. How peculiar that he didn't call last night. "It's okay. Let him come in now."

Jay smooths my blanket, straightens my pillow, and leaves to get my unexpected guest.

It's odd to see Bill walk through my bedroom door. His face and hands are still red from the cold. That makes him look even more out of place in my warm, cozy room. I can sense that he feels the strangeness too as he takes off his cap and approaches the foot of my bed.

"Joni, I know this is unusual," he begins. "When I woke up this morning, God gave me a clear message. And He told me to give it to you right away."

I am stunned by Bill's directness about something that obviously has nothing to do with my father or wrestling. I am numbed by his seriousness. But I nod with a smile and watch him turn to a marked place in his Bible.

"First Samuel 15:22," he announces, his voice steady. "'To obey is better than sacrifice.'" He closes his Bible, and for an awkward moment we are both quiet.

"I don't know what to add," he offers meekly. "Do you know what this is about, Joni?"

"Obedience . . . is better . . . than sacrifice," I repeat quietly. "Yes, I know . . . I mean, I think I understand the message."

As quickly and oddly as he came, Bill leaves.

BILL MOCK'S VISIT haunts me, though I do my best to rationalize it away. It couldn't have been a message from God. Come on now, really. It just appears that way because of the timing. It was just a coincidence. . . . Yes, that's it. Just a coincidence, a strange twist of timing. . . . Besides, I can't get all hung up in figuring out that kind of thing right now. Old Testament messages will have to wait. I've got more urgent concerns.

The Billy Graham Crusade in Tampa, Florida, is coming up soon, and World Wide needs one last bit of filming for the movie. The ending. I am to speak from the crusade platform to conclude the movie *Joni*, and I've got a script to memorize.

Jay spreads the three pages neatly on my desk. I read words that are—were—mine:

When I think of Jesus paralyzed on the cross simply because He loved me, even when I couldn't have cared less about Him, I know I've discovered something priceless. And that healing is His gift of love to you and me. You know, trusting Christ is not necessarily having trustful feelings. It is an act of the will. We need to *believe* it; lay our sins and brokenness at His feet and receive spiritual healing that will start us on a great eternal journey.

I became a Christian when I was a high-school sophomore. I believed my grades would go up, homework would be less boring. I'd be more popular. It didn't exactly work out that way, though. To follow Christ may cost something—you may be asked to fellowship in His suffering. But I can promise on my own experience that over and over again you will see, feel, and touch His sustaining power.

I look up after reading the first page. A wet glaze blurs my eyes. I am sincerely moved by my own words. Honest words. Ever since my accident I have clenched and clawed my way by God's grace to say those things from the heart.

My tears are nostalgic, telling me I have now, somehow, lost the heart for these words.

JUDY BUTLER LEAVES her office in Nashville to fly with me to Tampa. It is the day before I am to speak.

Florida is a refreshing change from the last weeks of panic and pain. The sun, the fragrant breeze, the coconut palms with their silvery tips clicking in the wind. I sit beside the motel pool absorbing it all, rehearsing my lines silently.

I'm glad this life is *not* forever. That's a dark subject, right? We all get so caught up in *now*. It's hard to think about heaven when it seems so far away. Besides, you have to *die* in order to get there.

But if God were to take us to heaven today without changing us inside, the purity and holiness there would only repel us. And we'd become terribly bored after a while just as we do with even the most exciting things on earth.

Can you imagine what it will be like to never again have the desire to sin? To never again feel guilty, alone, or depressed? Heaven will be heavenly because God will give us new bodies and new minds, and the Bible promises that we will *enjoy* Him forever.

I find myself in that crazy, unreal world again, listening to this *Joni* character tell me things I should already know. But I do wonder as I lean my head back and gaze up the skirts of a coconut palm . . . I wonder . . . at never having the desire to sin . . . at never feeling guilty or depressed.

An hour before the Saturday night crusade begins, I sit in front of a large mirror ringed with bright lights. The make-up man—nobody I know from the old crew—sponges thick pancake color on my face and neck. He works quietly while I nervously scan my lines one last time.

So many words. Important words Jim Collier has carefully selected to wrap up the message of the movie. And they've just told me that 30,000 people are seated out there in the stadium. I swallow, trying to clear my dry throat. I stare distractedly at the crinkled sheets of script on the counter.

> And I can't wait! I intend to stand before the Lord with legs that walk and arms and hands that work, and I will lift them high and shout out to the whole universe that Jesus Christ is who He claims to be as the very Son of God, the King of Kings and Lord of Lords, and *that's* only the beginning!
> If I hadn't decided to go swimming in Chesapeake Bay on that hot July day in 1967, I wouldn't be sitting here, speaking to you about the glory of God. But *I am!*

The make-up man has finished with me. I'm now sitting in a draped and carpeted corner of the stadium locker room. Couches and chairs disguise the ugly concrete. This is where the platform party, including Mr. Graham, Cliff Barrows, and Bev Shea, will meet and pray. I'm glad, privileged, to be included.

After we pray, Mr. Graham greets me. He is flanked by several men in dark suits holding walkie-talkies. He reminds me how happy he is about the progress on the movie. He'd been told that the editors have nearly finished; all that's needed is the last minutes of footage to be shot tonight. Then he turns and walks out the stadium tunnel. The rest of us follow.

Our small group steps onto the field and moves past the television crew and press tables to the platform. The glaring stadium lights are blinding, and I have to squint to see the thousands filling the stands.

In the moments before I'm introduced, I fidget. My eyes dart to the script folded open on Judy's lap. A knot grips my jittery stomach. I am afraid. I try to smother the butterflies, to breathe calm to my pounding heart. It is not like me to be this unnerved.

"Joni, move. That's your cue!" Judy elbows me.

Startled, I realize that I somehow missed my introduction. I power my wheelchair up the makeshift ramp to the microphone. I smile and acknowledge Cliff Barrows who welcomes me with applause. After a quick, silent *God, help me,* I launch into the beginning of the script.

> "Someone once asked how I had managed it—getting my life together. At the time I couldn't say much more than that Jesus had done it. I only knew a handful of Bible verses then, but I did feel that God had taken the broken pieces of my life—physical, emotional, spiritual—and made something beautiful!"

Each word, each phrase that booms and echoes across the huge stadium flashes in black ink on the white page of my mind. This isn't so bad. I relax.

"This was at least eight years ago. Today I know that the Lord is creating something in me that I could never create for myself. That is not to say that I now understand all the 'whys.' But I know *who* holds the answers, and I can wait!"

This is a breeze. And what powerful things are being said. I can't see expressions on the faces of people seated so far away in the stadium, so I say my lines to the cameramen. Oh . . . oh! It is . . . one of the cameramen from the movie. And the gaffer. He is another one of the crew people they've flown in from Hollywood. For a split second I lose my place, then quickly rivet my focus back on the script.

"And anyway, the exciting thing is that you don't have to break your neck to find God!"

The audience laughs, as the script suggested they would. I nervously join them, welcoming the break to gather my thoughts. When the rumble of laughter subsides, I zero in on the next line of black-inked words imprinted on my memory.

"I wanted to put you at ease about that. Suffering can help the search along. Your priorities get rearranged. But I imagine most of you would catch on faster than I did.
"Still, handicaps come in all shapes and sizes . . . broken homes, broken hearts, anxiety feelings that threaten to take over. Burdens of doubt. A deep loneliness. The confines of your soul may seem as limiting as—a wheelchair. I *know* that feeling. But I also know that . . .
"I also know that . . ."

Oh, god! What is my next line? Seconds tick by. Nothing. It's not coming. Here I sit in front of 30,000 people . . . *God, what is my line?*
I drop my head. Tears well in my eyes. Several more seconds tick by. I don't dare look at Mr. Graham or Mr. Barrows or Judy, who has my script. I raise my head and start pulling something, *anything*, out of the air.

"I know that . . . that God's Word is real. And . . . and Romans 8:28 has meant . . . so much. And all things really do fit together for our good . . . and, and His glory."

I ramble, repeating bits and pieces of things I have said so many times before. All the while, through tears, I try desperately to pick up the script. I can't. Several minutes later, I finish.
The crowd stands and applauds. Mr. Graham does the same, leading the rest of

the platform party in an ovation. It is only then that I realize my tears have moved these people. I'm so ashamed—my words didn't make sense—not to me anyway. I'm certain the film shot cannot be used to adequately conclude the movie. But, incredibly, God has made use of my ramblings.

"I blew it!" I whisper to Judy as she wipes my tear-streaked face. "In front of all these people . . . I blew it!" I begin to cry again.

I leave Florida, humiliated and defeated.

My SOUL SEEMS as dull and dim as the gray sky outside my study window. Snow is threatening. How I wish it would come. Late winter is never pretty on the farm. A fresh coat of white would at least cover the mud and manure around the barn and blanket the stark leafless trees and barren fields.

My Bible reading is just as muddy and barren. Try as I will, nothing gets through. God's Word is supposed to be sharper than a sword to my soul. But I don't feel the cutting edge.

Yet I refuse to think of myself as hardened. Insensitive. Darkened in my understanding. I understand plenty—I'm tired. Just taking a little longer than usual to get my spiritual bearings.

The movie editors call. They want me to return to California to do some voice-dubbing sessions for the film where the sound is a bit garbled. They also want me to repair those lines I flubbed in Tampa.

The idea of escape appeals to me. A getaway to palm trees and sun and warmer weather. More than two months have passed since I left California, and it will be odd to work with new people. All of the original crew will be busy on other projects by now.

While in Los Angeles, I visit Grace Community Church for a Sunday service, a church I had occasionally attended during the many months of shooting. I sit in the back and watch people file in, their faces clean and fresh. They all look alike. They have notebooks and Bibles in their well-manicured hands. Their pencils are sharpened, their skirt hems are at the proper length. Their hair is cut neatly over the ears. I wonder if they ever get their hands dirty with the world's problems.

I'm being a snob.

The choir enthusiastically sings a triumphant hymn. But only after the last note do I realize that my spirit was not lifted by the tune nor did my heart respond to the words. The service is for the other people sitting in the pews, not for me.

The pastor, John MacArthur, begins to preach his sermon. His topic, the obedience that marks the Christian. He quotes the Bible. His voice is urgent. He talks about narrow gates and straight paths, He punctuates his words with a pointed finger aimed at his congregation. Everyone around me listens attentively, nods in agreement, scribbles notes in notebooks and Bible margins. The deeper he gets into his sermon, the more distant I am. Above it all. On the outside looking in.

Listen to him. MacArthur has really changed . . . gotten legalistic lately. I don't remember him being so uptight and hardlined. He's become so narrow since I heard him last. I watch with amazement as people around me take it all in without a questioning look.

We've been freed from living out a bunch of rules and regulations, I argue with him. *A whole book in the New Testament was written about that. Life can't be that black and white when we're led by the Spirit. And what about God's grace? Doesn't it cover a multitude of mistakes? Life's too short to sweat the small stuff. We're not under law.*

The microphone picks up his words and booms them out over the sanctuary. "'What then? Shall we sin because we are not under law but under grace? By no means!'"

I am stunned at the uncanny timing of that verse. Why, I was just thinking about the law and grace. I quickly try to explain away the painful truth of the text, while keeping up in the race with MacArthur.

He cites another verse from Romans. "'Shall we go on sinning so that grace may increase? By no means! We died to sin; how can we live in it any longer?'"

Now the congregation has faded into the background and I am the only person in the entire church. MacArthur is speaking to me.

"'If they have escaped the corruption of the world by knowing our Lord and Savior Jesus Christ and are again entangled in it and overcome,'" he reads about apostates from 2 Peter 2:20, "'they are worse off at the end than they were at the beginning.'"

Apostasy? Ugh! What an awful word! That's not me, I am relieved to think. *But corruption?* I linger o that word while MacArthur passes me. *I know Christ, and He's pulled me from the corruption of the world—there's nothing even appealing about a walk down Sunset Boulevard. The sordid materialism and dog-eat-dog decadence.* To my dismay, I'm being arrogant again. It is the corruption of little things—snobbery, pride, toying with temptation or rebellion—that makes a fool of me.

It is not John MacArthur who has changed! This sudden realization is a shock. It is I! And it isn't his words that are needling me. It is God's words!

I pick up his roll of verses as he quickly flips back to Matthew 23. " 'In the same way, on the outside you appear to people as righteous but on the inside you are full of hypocrisy and wickedness.' " I listen wide-eyed. The verse is about religious leaders who fool themselves into thinking they are right with God when actually they don't know Him at all. Again, I'm relieved to think I'm not a false prophet. But hypocrisy? My heart sinks. I've edged awfully close to seeing black as white. Bad as good.

MacArthur expounds a bit further and then goes to 2 Peter to close. " 'Therefore, dear friends, since you already know this, be on your guard so that you may not be carried away . . . and fall from your secure position.' " Another sigh of relief—my position in Christ is secure. But my experience with Him? Oh, I grieve. I know I've let down my guard. Gotten carried away.

My heart is racing and I am short of breath. I've been grabbed and jerked up short, as though I were dizzily peering over the edge of a dark and murky pit, thankful that someone has caught me.

" 'The word of God . . . judges the thoughts and attitudes of the heart. Nothing in all creation is hidden from God's sight. Everything is uncovered and laid bare before the eyes of Him to whom we must give account.' " That verse from Hebrews seems fresh, brand new, as though I have never heard it before. It isn't so much that MacArthur is right or that my father's friend Bill is right. It is God's Word that's right—alive and active. It has sliced into me sharper than any double-edged sword. Dividing my soul and spirit.

I leave church deeply humiliated, my soul wounded and cowering. But in the deepest part of my spirit I know that truth has gotten through.

I'M BACK AT my desk on the farm, feeling shaky and a little sick. And I gingerly take Scripture now as though it were a healing prescription, reading portions as if I were swallowing medicine.

I lean my head back and stare at the ceiling, remembering what it was like to be sick when I was a child and have my mother or father take care of me. They would hold a spoon of medicine to my lips. Touch my fevered brow. Walk quietly in and out of my room. I was always comforted by the sound of their voices downstairs. It was also a comfort to know that soon I would get better. I wouldn't always be sick.

Judy sends me a postcard with a get-well message. She simply pens Philippians 1:9: "And this is my prayer: that your love may abound more and more in knowledge and depth of insight, so that you may be able to discern what is best and may be pure and blameless until the day of Christ." She knows. She knew all along, just as Betsy, Diana, Steve, Jay, and the others did.

Could it be? . . . Yes, it could. The movie, the very piece of creativity I was most proud to be a part of, was God's way of pressing me up against myself. And I don't like what I see: hidden resentment, discontent in almost every situation, envy, the pull of temptation, a lazy attitude toward His Word, self-centered prayers.

The list looms and my stomach gets queasy again.

For months I have been wrestling with my problems, not even certain what is at the bottom of those struggles. *Could all that "struggling," it slowly dawns, be nothing but a polite word for postponed obedience?*

Even though I still feel the burnt edges of exhaustion, the taint of humiliation, I very much want to be well. I know the answer, somehow, is in the Lord Jesus. The compassionate, sensitive way He dealt with sick people is always comforting. Sweet and gentle Jesus.

But now as I read the stories of His dealing with sin, I notice that He overthrows tables and flails a whip at people who pollute His Father's temple. He confronts those who try to mask their sinful attitudes. He exposes uncleanness in the lives of His disciples. He even sharply rebukes His closest friends.

I don't like reading these things, but they are there. He does not let selfishness or pride slip by His notice. He squares off against sin.

And He squares off against the sin in me. My sin—the word itself stings—has gone from a tiny trickle to a raging torrent that cannot be ignored. And now it's as if Jesus Himself is holding it up before my face and saying lovingly but firmly, "See! This is what you've become. What are you going to do about it, Joni?"

Do I hate sin in my life as much as He must? My heart breaks. The answer is no. I'm nowhere near as close to Christ as I had assumed.

I read from the book of James: "Wash your hands, you sinners, and purify your hearts, you double-minded. Grieve, mourn and wail. Change your laughter to mourning and your joy to gloom. Humble yourselves before the Lord, and he will lift you up."[8]

Tears stream down my cheeks and splatter on my desk. This verse, I'm ashamed—no, pleased—to say, was written for me.

I read a page from an old Puritan book. It becomes my prayer:

O God,
I know that I often do thy work without thy power,
   and sin by my dead, heartless, blind service,
      my lack of inward light, love, delight,
      my mind, heart, tongue moving without thy help.

Help me to rejoice in my infirmities and give thee praise,
   to acknowledge my deficiencies before others
   and not be discouraged by them,
   that they may see thy glory more clearly,

Teach me that I must act by a power supernatural,
   whereby I can attempt things above my strength,
   and bear evils beyond my strength,
   acting for Christ in all, and
   having his superior power to help me.[9]

Oh, how I want to do His work in His power. Not mine. And I want very much to serve. But not heartlessly. I want to admit my weaknesses and not be discouraged by them. *And Lord, if I attempt things beyond my strength, may I always find help in You.*

The healing is happening.

I reread my book *A Step Further* with great interest, swallowing the advice Steve and I wrote for others to read. I notice in the introduction the words, "Oh, I'm still paralyzed. . . . But I'm no longer depressed." I smile at the confidence with which I penned that phrase. Little did I realize then that depression would one day hit me so hard. And I cannot presume that it will never return. I call my editor and ask her to delete that line in the next printing.

My mind, much clearer now, wanders back to that sermon on obedience I heard in church just weeks ago. What about my argument against law and for grace?

I realize that I can hardly abuse a religion where I am slavishly chained to obey a bunch of rules and regulations. But I have abused the freedom Christ has given me. The hazard in any system of choice is that I take the risk of misusing it.

I'm a prisoner of Christ. Me, this humbled and sorely disciplined child of His. But I am also free in Christ, and I pray with wrenching and heaving pleas that God will take a risk with me—that is, let me keep making my choices.

Yes, I admit to God, there will always be the danger of choosing the wrong thing, the sinful thing. But instinctively I know that if I am to change into a responsible, mature, and godly woman, I must still make choices even if, occasionally, they are wrong.

And Father, I want to yield to your Holy Spirit who can make those choices the ones that best honor You. And I believe You will sovereignly perfect me no matter what I choose.

THE MINISTRY

Serve wholeheartedly, as if you were serving the Lord, not men.
—*Ephesians 6:7*

IT IS 1979 and a chilly, early spring day in Maryland. The yellow forsythia along the pasture fence promises that the barren farmland will soon be green with life. A gust of wind stings my cheeks, and I'm grateful when Jay takes off her sweater and wraps it around my shoulders. Standing behind my wheelchair, she leans forward and folds her arms around me. I can tell a question is coming.

"Are you sure you know what you're doing?" she asks as we watch my other sisters, Kathy and Linda, carry boxes, packages, and suitcases out to the waiting pickup truck. *Am I doing the right thing? Is this move to Southern California really in God's will?* My carefully packed books, clothes, medical supplies, and keepsakes seem to know where they're going. Do I?

Thinking back, I marvel over the circumstances that have brought me to this decision. A book and the recent movie have detailed the long journey toward accepting my paralysis. But I have learned, all too painfully, that you can't live in a world of books and movies. They can only reflect, in part, who you really are. Their glitter fades quicker than a spotlight.

Now I must get on with living.

I am thirty years old. And I sense a conviction, a certainty that things must change—just as surely as Jay and Rob, the farm and I are changing. The circumstances are right for it.

I cannot continue to be the girl whose faith wavers and weakens at every new juncture. I must grow. That faith must stretch further. And I cannot just be a "hearer" of God's Word. I must be a "doer" and practice these new lessons I've learned.

It simply is time. Time for me to launch out on my own.

Another cold gust of wind whistles through the pines in the pasture. "Brr . . . I'm freezing. Jay, pull this sweater tighter around me, would you?"

Jay knots the woolen sleeves, tugging their warmth snugly around my neck. Without prompting, she reaches up and pulls my stocking hat down around my ears. I feel instant relief and watch appreciatively as she holds my hands in her warm grip. She knows just what to do. In fact, she knows my routine needs better than I do.

Oh, I love her. I will miss her.

As I watch her adjust my feet on the wheelchair footpedals, I push a frightening thought out of my mind: life without Jay will mean the loss of a great deal of security. Our lives have been intricately entwined for years. We have lived together on the farm, traveled everywhere, done everything together. Jay is more than my sister. She is my confidante, my nurse, my roommate. Above all, she is my friend. Though she has her own life—her daughter Kay and now Rob—I know she will miss me too. That hurts.

The pickup truck is packed tightly now, engine idling and ready to go. The driver, a friend who is heading to the West Coast on other business, pulls off his gloves and climbs into the truck. Gunning the motor, he calls good-by and heads down our driveway. Within a week he and my things will arrive in sunny Southern California.

"Well, Joni, you're next!" My sister Linda smiles as she walks toward me, rubbing her hands together.

"You know, it's still not too late to change your mind." Jay reminds me that I have not answered her earlier question. She scoops Charlie, our farm cat, into her arms and rubs his chin.

"I know, Jay. I know all of you . . ." I swallow and glance at each one. "You want what's best for me. But I believe this is the right choice. . . . Besides, spring days in California have got to be warmer than this!" Our laughter breaks the poignancy of the moment, and we head into the house for some hot coffee around the log fire.

Sitting alone by that fire later in the afternoon, I think more about my decision to move so many miles away.

Decisions. Choices. I'm forever bumping up against those words. The decision to write a book about my life. Should I make the movie? Just what is God doing in my life, and where am I going? Who am I? Is a move away from the farm wise or not? And choices bring change.

My track record with God hasn't been the greatest this past year, but I've confessed inward rebellion, and I believe He is faithful in cleaning and clearing the slate. I sense the presence of His Spirit as I read the Bible. More than ever, I want to delight myself in Him. And if my life is truly lined up with God's will in these areas, then I know I can follow my heart's desire.

Mentally, I list those things making up my "heart's desire." I feel it is time to step out on my own. To step into a new dream. To be a "doer" of God's Word, I must help others—*disabled people with dreams of their own.*

I keep remembering my brief conversation with Debbie Stone that day at Rancho Los Amigos Hospital. Her words have haunted me as I have pondered my decision to begin such a ministry: "Joni, you wouldn't believe the problems most handicapped people face. Spiritual struggles, yes, but down-to-earth practical problems too."

I am a handicapped person who has experienced the overwhelming love and grace of God. I have the added advantage of loving family and friends who have cared for me faithfully, whether by lifting my spirits or lifting me into a wheelchair. Out there beyond the pasture and the walls of my cozy home are thousands of men and women, young people and children, who have none of that. They need not only comfort from God's Word, but practical caring from His people. I know I have been called to give it . . . somehow.

As incredible as it seems, the call includes Los Angeles. There, I can put together such a dream. I already know a few rehabilitation professionals from my own stay at Rancho years ago. I'll be returning to Grace Community Church. I have friendships with people connected with World Wide Pictures. And I do love the climate. I will have to face some painful memories—and the smog. But even after weighing these things, Los Angeles is still ideal.

As the afternoon fades into the early dusk of a spring evening, I sit alone in the shadowed living room; my only light, the glowing fire. Peace settles in my heart. No doubt. No panic. Just peace.

I don't know what lies ahead. But I do know who I am. I have a dream, and I know where I am going.

"**H**AVE YOU GOT the tickets?" I call to Kerbe as she unloads her bags at the airport curb.

"Uh . . . no, I don't think Jay gave them to me." She rummages through her purse, searching for the airline envelope. "Maybe Rob has them!"

Rob pats his jacket pockets. "Nope, not here," he says.

What a way to begin my new life out on my own! I can't even find the tickets to where I'm going! I scan the travel bags and carry-on luggage stacked around me on the sidewalk. Something tells me to look on my lap. "Here they are," I call out. Someone has wedged the ticket folder between my leg and the side of the wheelchair.

Kerbe grabs the tickets and shoves them into the hands of the impatient skycap who has already tagged most of our luggage and loaded it onto a cart. Making one final check, my eyes catch sight of the purple check-through tags. *Purple . . . that's not Los Angeles. Those tags will send our luggage to San Francisco!*

"Rob, stop that cart!"

Jay unlocks my wheels and hustles me through the automatic doors. "Don't forget to find a good doctor and a medical supply store," she reminds me as we rush through the security gate. "And don't forget to order new catheters and legbags. You're almost out."

Frantic moments later the tags are changed, the tickets stamped, good-by tears shed too quickly, and Kerbe and I are settling in our seats on the plane.

As the engines whine to full power, I strain to look out the window, hoping to catch a final glimpse of Jay and Rob, Mom and Dad, Kathy, and the others who came with us to say good-by. It was such a maddening rush at the gate. There wasn't time to say all that I wanted to say. Not that we won't see each other again. It just feels that way right now.

I picture Daddy standing at the curb, leaning on his crutches, wanting to help but unable to. He didn't know I was studying him. I could tell he was hiding concern for his youngest daughter about to leave the nest—in a wheelchair no less. He worries about where I'll live and who will help me, though I've told him at least ten times that John MacArthur, the pastor at Grace Community Church, has arranged for me to stay in a little house next to the church. And Kerbe, my cousin, will be living with me, along with Judy Butler, on loan for a year from the Billy Graham Association to help set up my new ministry. "Everything's okay, Daddy," I have told him loudly and repeatedly, pushing past his hearing impairment.

"Anything you say, hon." His blue eyes twinkle but his lip quivers.

Mother, on the other hand, was a pillar of strength this morning. Giving directions to everyone. Helping unload luggage from the station wagon. Like the calm in the eye of the storm. I hope I'll carry some of that family trait in the unknown months ahead.

Our jet takes off and banks left, heading west, and I let my head sink comfortably into the cushion. Fields and towns below us become obscured by clouds as we sweep higher into the sky. The edges of the morning's memories grow fuzzy, blurred by time and distance. Just as my eyes close on the edge of sleep, I feel the presence of someone standing by my seat.

"Aren't you the girl who just did that movie?" I look up into the smiling face of a woman in a high-fashion suit heavily accented with jewelry. "I'm sure I saw your photograph in a magazine recently."

"Well, I guess it could have been me. I just finished playing my own part in a movie about my life."

We chat about the movie. She explains that she and her husband prayed for me during the filming. They had difficulty imagining how anyone could relieve such painful memories, and I assure her it was only possible because of the prayers of people like herself.

Kerbe puts down her magazine and listens in. After the woman returns to her seat, Kerbe turns toward me, tucking one leg underneath her. "What *was* it like, Joni? I mean, you know, doing a movie?"

I look into my cousin's clear blue eyes. She is a pretty girl—young, excited, and happy to be starting this new adventure with me. Just entering her twenties, she is anxious to follow the Lord's leading in her life. But her question reminds me that few people really know what I have been through emotionally and spiritually in the past year.

"You've got to understand that it wasn't very glamorous," I sigh.

Choosing my words carefully, I describe the pretty actress in the blue bathing suit—her grace and elegance, her striking figure—and the contrast of my embarrassment over my own appearance that day. The awkwardness. The ugliness. I rein in any temptation to enlarge the facts and become a spiritual exhibitionist.

As I wind out the story like the string from a ball of yarn, I wonder to myself what God saw that day. How He viewed me that afternoon on the beach. I was so concerned about the way I looked, but that was nothing compared with what God must have seen on the inside. If a mere bathing suit exposed useless, puffy legs, how could I have ever have thought I could hide a resentful spirit from the Lord?

As I tell Kerbe about the rest of the movie months, the remaining hours of our flight pass quickly. The jet shifts altitude, and we begin our descent into Los Angeles.

We can see the gleaming white HOLLYWOOD sign propped like a billboard on the hillside overlooking the city. It reminds me that I must never again say I can't be touched by resentment. Never again take God's grace for granted. I am free in Christ. But I am a prisoner of Christ.

We land smoothly and taxi to the gate. Kerbe and I wait as the other passengers grab carry-on luggage from the overhead compartments and shuffle up the aisle to the front exit.

I feel a hand touch my shoulder and look up into the smile of the fashionably dressed lady. As she is pushed along by the flow of people, she turns and says, "Well be looking for the movie . . . you're a really great person."

I want to say thanks but I can't. She has no idea of what went on in my heart behind the scenes of that film. But I know. And God knows.

"You're kind, but," I call after her, "don't we have a great God!"

"CALIFORNIA, HERE I come, right back where I started from," I hum as we speed along the Hollywood freeway past borders of dusty oleanders that hide endless subdivisions.

Traffic thickens and we close our windows against the heat and fumes. Air conditioning brings cool and quiet. Images of the Maryland countryside flash before my eyes: spreading maples rustling in a fresh breeze, the spring house beside the pasture creek on our farm, and the sweeping valley down to the nearby river. What a different life I will have in Southern California. The only valley I've seen here is the San Fernando Valley, and it is overflowing with spreading housing tracts and sweeping freeways. Will I find a real home here?

We exit at the turnoff that takes us to Grace Community Church and arrive at the little stucco house that will be our temporary home. We see that someone from the church has hammered a sturdy ramp in place at the front door and widened the doorways. Others have provided a couch, a dinette set, lamps and cushions, pictures and plants, all arranged by someone with decorating skill. It is a welcoming, friendly place to begin.

Church people detour from their car-pool routes and grocery shopping to drop by and introduce themselves, casseroles in hand. Housewarming cards nest themselves in our mailbox. Freshly baked chocolate-chip cookies appear on our doorstep.

In all these ways and more, Grace Community goes out of its way to show kindness. Even John MacArthur takes time from study and appointments to visit.

He comes as a brother, informal in slacks and a pale blue golfing sweater. I thank him for arranging all this, nodding toward the little house.

"We're just glad you're here," he says and taps the armrest of my wheelchair. I'm pleased he feels comfortable enough to touch. "How are plans for your ministry coming along?"

We discuss the budget Judy and I have laid out and the small office we plan to rent nearby. We are wasting no time in putting my dream into motion.

"You're welcome to look at what we've got going here." He gestures toward the church buildings. "But . . ." He hesitates. "You should spend more time with Dr. Sam Britten, one of our elders. He started our handicap outreach. He's also the director of quite a big center at the university."

I have already met Dr. Britten at our first board meeting. He was very personable, asking to be called Dr. Sam, putting his hand on my shoulder, and pulling up a chair to talk. I suppose that sort of warmth comes from his twenty years of working with disabled students.

The day after John MacArthur's visit, Kerbe makes an appointment for me to visit Dr. Sam at California State University.

The campus is not far from the church. Kerbe drives me there, and we search out the Center of Achievement for the Physically Disabled, which Dr. Sam directs. Kerbe parks her Camaro in the student lot and hails a passing student to help me out of the car.

I immediately feel comfortable on this campus. A row of parking places for the handicapped lines the front of the physical-education building, our destination. A girl in a power wheelchair, like the one I use at the house, is lowering herself from a van on a mechanical lift. A muscular young paraplegic in a tank top wheels by me in his sporty racing chair, books on his lap and bag draped over his wheelchair handle. I follow the dusty tracks of his wheels to the entrance. This, I figure, must be Dr. Britten's center.

Inside, the shiny linoleum of the long corridor reflects the sunlight streaming through the glass door at the far end, and we follow the echoes of laughter and voices to a door on the left, which opens into a large room. We stand in the doorway and watch.

Young men like the student we passed on the sidewalk are out of their wheelchairs, doing sit-ups on red gym mats. A girl who looks like a staff person braces the elbow of an elderly man as he takes shaky steps with stiff legs and the aid of a cane. Leg braces hang on the walls like pots on a kitchen rack, each in its orderly group. Canes, crutches, and walkers are neatly lined by the parallel bars at the far end of the room. Pulleys with weights fill one wall next to a floor-to-ceiling mirror. The place has all the trappings of Rancho Los Amigos but is somehow different.

Weights slam, straps buckle, people chatter and laugh.

Laughter. That is the difference.

I spot Dr. Britten. Tall, with a clean-cut athletic build, he stands by a young quadriplegic whose gloved hands are strapped to the pedals of an exercise cycle bolted to a table. He gives the boy encouragement while adjusting knobs on the machine. The boy leans forward in his chair, straining to throw his weight into each turn of the cycle. Dr. Britten smiles and squeezes the boy's arm. When he turns away, he spots us in the doorway.

"Come on in," he calls above the clamor. "I've been expecting you."

Kerbe wheels me into the room, and I feel as though I belong here. I can tell this is a place where things get done.

"Nice to see you again," I say as I balance myself forward and extend my arm in an awkward greeting. Dr. Sam takes my hand in his and smiles, clasping my elbow. His brown eyes are warm, sincere.

"Have you thought more about my suggestion that you can drive?" he asks as he glances at his clipboard. I am surprised, having entirely forgotten about our discussion at the board meeting a few nights ago. At that time he said he thought I could drive a van, but I politely dismissed it as impossible. "The best universities in the country have tested me. Everybody knows I don't have the muscles to turn a steering wheel," I told him.

"If you're open to it, I've got you scheduled for an evaluation," he says. "Now."

"Well, yes . . . but do you really think someone like me ought to be on the freeways. I mean, honestly?" We slowly make our way through the maze of people and machinery. Before he answers, he takes time to introduce us to various staff and students. We end up at an exercise table neatly piled with evaluation forms and medical consent slips.

"Did you see those vans parked out front?" He scoots a stool next to me and extends my arm, feeling my bicep muscles with his fingers. I nod absent-mindedly, absorbed by his work. He bends, twists, and stretches my arms, asking me to offer resistance now and then. As he jots notes on several of the forms, he motions with his pencil toward a handicapped girl wheeling by. "She drives one of those vans."

I stare at the back of the girl as she wheels away. She looks far more disabled than I. I return my attention to Dr. Sam, who begins to test my coordination and reflexes.

Later in the day, after I've talked with several disabled people who drive, Dr. Sam pushes me up to one of the exercises cycles—the same one I saw the quadriplegic boy cycling with his arms. He takes a pair of leather gloves off the wall and rips open the velcro straps.

"Your evaluation looked great." Dr. Sam smiles. "I see no reason why you can't begin some simple strengthening exercises right now."

"Driving, huh?" I challenge him with an unbelieving smile.

"You can do it." He looks directly into my eyes as he straps my hands to the cycling machine. "I know you can. We'll worry about the steering wheel later."

What in the world does he mean? I begin pedaling. Maybe answers come later. Then again, I did come here to ask questions. Sam Britten's obviously an expert, and I do need direction on starting a ministry to disabled people. I just didn't realize I'd be the first one on the receiving end.

Heaving my shoulders to push the cycling pedals, I begin to feel a part of the pulse of the place. My heart rate quickens within minutes, and I breathe deeply, remembering athletic advice from days when I was on my feet. It feels good. For the time being I forget my questions. I think about how my father could benefit from a place like this.

Everyone is busy with routines except one young woman, who sits in the corner like a statue, her arms propped on the wheelchair armrests. Her lovely Latin looks and her mass of curly dark hair overshadow her wheelchair. An attendant speaks to her in Spanish, and I wonder whether it is her striking appearance or the distant way she observes the rest of us that sets her apart so distinctly. I wonder about her and her almost tangible isolation. Perhaps she is some movie star from South America.

Puffing and panting, I take a breather as Sam Britten approaches.

"That's enough for one day," he commends as he loosens the velcro straps on my gloves. "After I design an exercise program for you, you'll be on those freeways in no time."

We laugh—he with sincerity, I with skepticism. I do like this man, though. And I like the positive atmosphere of this place. I'm looking forward to coming back to his center on a regular basis.

"If I gather a group together," he says, "would you mind saying a few words to my students before you leave? They all know you . . . your book is required reading in my class."

I say yes, of course. Talking to these people about the struggles I've faced—dealing with pity and stares, learning how to live on my own and yet depend on others, and seeing God's part in it all—is what my dream of a ministry is all about.

Dr. Britten introduces me to the cluster of people in wheelchairs and walkers, and then joins the small group of staff members standing at the back. I can tell he is pleased to have me talk about my faith and my acceptance of my wheelchair. I sense that my having worked alongside these people today has helped. We're on common ground.

All except the beautiful lady with large green eyes that rarely blink. She sits in the back, as statuelike as before.

꧁ꕥ꧂

THE FULL MOON hangs pale and mysterious over the orange tree behind the little stucco house. It evokes memories of summer evenings on the back porch of the farmhouse when Jay and I would sit around the redwood table and sing old country songs. Tonight I sit in the backyard and sing a favorite hymn to the moon and hear Jay's harmony in my head. I wonder what my family is doing tonight.

It was good to talk to Jay on the phone earlier. I imagined her sitting on the kitchen steps, leaning her shoulder against the doorsill, twining the phone cord with her fingers. I had lots to tell her.

Our ministry, now christened "Joni and Friends," is a month old. Volunteers who type and take shorthand are helping me answer hundreds of letters that have come as a result of the movie and the two books. An office with job descriptions and procedures is unfamiliar territory to me, but Judy, having helped set up Billy Graham Crusades across the country, is right at home. Kerbe and I soon fit in with the typewriters and telephones.

I wish Jay were here.

I ward off creeping homesickness by keeping busy—working at the office and my art easel, looking through real-estate ads for a permanent home, and visiting Dr. Britten's center.

Sam is teaching me more than muscle-strengthening exercises. I watch how he deals with people who have no hope—people who have been shifted from one hospital to the next, people who feel they are a burden to families or friends. But not to Sam. Like Jesus, he seems to be moved with compassion, not pity, when he sees the crowds. I marvel at how he keeps up with his overloaded schedule. He takes time, so much time, with the young girl, alone, without a ride home, or the boy with cerebral palsy who confesses his shame over uncontrolled drooling. I watch him kneel on the floor next to a student stretched out on his lab table. Sam seems to be talking to him, but he is probably praying.

I am making headway on the cycling machine. I pedal it faster, easier. I still am not convinced I will drive, but all this exercise isn't going to waste. I haven't felt this well, this strong, in a long time. I am gaining some weight and sleeping better.

"That's not bad," an attractive woman in blue warm-ups observes as she eyes the counter clicking off my number of cycles on the machine. I have often seen her here working with people and assume she is Sam's assistant. She introduces herself as Rana Leavell.

"How much longer on this thing?" I get dramatic with my huffing and puffing.

"I'm the wrong one to ask." She looks around for Sam.

"You don't work here?" I slow my pace. "I've seen you helping out."

"Well, I'm just here to earn a credential to teach phys. ed. to handicapped high-school kids. I'm near burnout with my junior high schoolers." She laughs. "In fact, see that girl in the wheelchair over there?" She points in the direction of the attractive Latin woman with abundant coffee-brown hair. "She just told me she had me for junior-high phys. ed. years ago. Talk about feeling old."

I stop pedaling. Rana knows the mystery lady. "Who is she?" I try to make it sound like a casual question.

"Her name's Vicky Olivas. She's only been paralyzed a few years. She's had a tough time." Rana speaks quietly. "She can't move much."

"Yes, I . . . guessed that." Sam is stretching Vicky's arms, both of them preoccupied, so I feel free to watch her as we talk. Suddenly I'm conscious of staring and in embarrassment say to Rana, "I've been praying for her."

"Praying?" Rana looks at me with a strange smile. "Yeah, well . . ." She slaps the cycle machine. "Let me get somebody to take you off this thing." She walks away.

So the mystery lady has a name. As Sam unstraps my hands and we talk about my progress, I watch from the corner of my eye as Vicky Olivas is pushed outside by her attendant. I wish I could catch her before she leaves, but I don't want to hurry Sam. Time and talk are an important part of his work. So by the time Kerbe pushes me outside, the lady in the wheelchair is gone.

"You need help?" Rana walks out the door behind us.

"Yes, if you would. You can help Kerbe get me into the car." I nod toward my cousin who is crossing the parking lot. Late afternoon shadows stretch across the campus toward a group of students kicking a soccer ball. The shade and the trees remind me of the cool earth smells of home. I wonder if I am making any progress. Not the sort Sam is after, but progress in making this area my home. A home with a ministry and a house and friends.

Friends.

Rana, standing next to me, rummages through her purse and pulls out a pack of Virginia Slims.

"Would you like to get together sometime?" I ask.

"Yes, I'd like that. Your cousin," she says, pausing to strike a match, "has already said something. I told her she could exercise my daughter's horse while she's visiting friends in Europe." She shakes the match and pulls deeply on her lighted cigarette.

"You have a family?"

"You could say that," she says as though she's given this information many times before. "I'm divorced." She sighs, then adds, "My daughter—she's twelve—and I are very close. I really miss her." She fumbles with the cigarette pack. The shadows shift and the sun reflects on her hair. It's much more blond than it appeared inside.

"Well, I couldn't help Kerbe with the horse," I laugh, "but the offer is sincere. It'd be fun to get together."

Kerbe steers her Camaro close to the curb, and Rana pushes me to the passenger side and takes off the armrest of my chair. My cousin reaches through my arms and grabs my waist while Rana positions herself in front and locks her hands under my knees. Together they lift me onto the car seat. While Kerbe heaves my folded wheelchair into the trunk, Rana buckles my seatbelt.

"Speaking of getting together," I comment as Rana adjusts the belt, "I'd like to get to know Vicky Olivas."

"So would everyone," Rana says without looking up. She slams the car door and leans down to look through the open window. "This setup is not the greatest in the world." She slaps the door. "A van would do better."

"That's what Sam keeps telling me," I say as Kerbe backs the car slowly from the curb. "But me? Drive fifty-five on the freeway?" I call as we pull away.

We go home to the little house by the church. Home. I call it that, but the three of us are still camping out of suitcases, our bedroom floor cluttered with open luggage, hair dryers, and boxes of books. So many things are borrowed. Even our pots and pans are on loan. But as we wheel up the wooden ramp to the back door and smell the dinner Judy is preparing, it feels like more than just a house.

That night I lay in bed by the open window and watch the waning moon cross the curtains. I think about the sounds of a summer night on the farm—crickets clicking, frogs croaking, and the distant bark of the dog over the next hill. Nothing like the noise of speeding cars on the boulevard that rattle the warm night air here. But the homey sounds of Judy in the kitchen and Kerbe murmuring to one of her new friends on the phone drift in to me.

Perhaps home is not that far away after all.

I WHEEL ALONGSIDE the wrought-iron fence of the hilltop house which is for sale. The manicured lawn is bordered by a wall of pink bougainvillaea on one side and Indian paintbrush on the other. I stop beneath three silk oak trees. I decide they are the tallest of any as I scan the neighborhood from the edge of the backyard. It's not the farm—the house and the lot are small, and it's nowhere near as private. But it's beautiful. I take a deep breath and smile at the realtor.

I will have to draw up papers, get a loan, buy a washer and dryer, contact the telephone company and post office. And just a month ago I was biting my nails over opening a new checking account.

But my confidence comes and goes.

The same day Judy pushes my chair down the aisle of the supermarket. My lap is a catchall for a can of soup, a package of hamburger, mustard, and Comet cleanser. I block the aisle when she leaves me to backtrack for a forgotten item.

A woman with a loaded cart inches closer to me as she examines the shelves. I am sure she is wondering how she will maneuver her way around my chair. I decide not to speak until our eyes meet. She will have to follow my instructions and parallel park my wheelchair closer to the pancake mix in order to pass. I wonder if she's nervous, as I choose carefully what I will say. As I'm about to speak, Judy returns with the tea bags.

The woman smiles—with relief, I imagine—as Judy pushes my chair past her loaded cart. I suppress the urge to apologize for almost being in her way. The rest of the trip down the aisle, past boxes of cake mix and sugar, I argue with the urge.

I'm welcomed here just as much as any cart pusher in the place, wheelchair or no.

These mental gymnastics are silly, I decide after Judy enlists the help of a bag boy to load the groceries and me into her car. But how do others handle life out on their own? I picture the faces of the people I've met at Sam's center. How do they feel in situations like this? What does Vicky Olivas do? Or does she manage at all?

It is another day at the center. As my cousin and I approach the entrance, I spot Vicky sitting in the shade at the corner of the building with her attendant. She comes out here to smoke and, presumably, to escape the others. I gather courage. This is the day we will meet.

"We've both been so busy we haven't had a chance to talk," I begin as I'm pushed up to her, disguising the fact that we really haven't even met.

"Yes, I've noticed you too." She speaks perfect English with a heavy Spanish accent. Close up, she is lovelier than I imagined. Sophia Loren, I think to myself, as I grope for a comparison. She sits straight, almost too rigid, her hands propped on a flowered pillow, spread fingers displaying perfectly polished nails. Her jeans, ironed and starched to a sharp crease, come to a precise point over high-heeled sandals. Even her toes are painted. Her attendant holds her cigarette and coffee.

"What's your reason for coming to the center?" I ask the safest question I can come up with to try to begin to dispel the mysteries that surround her.

She looks at me incredulously with the expression of an aristocrat. "To get healed," she says. After an awkward pause, she adds, "Isn't that why you're here?"

I'm not prepared for this. I'll be late for my appointment if I get started. But this opportunity is answered prayer, and I do want to get to know her. "I'm just trying to strengthen whatever muscles I've got," I say truthfully. "If I get more in return, that would be great." I shrug my shoulders. "Whatever God wants."

"God?" She pauses. "My psychologist says it's all in my head."

"Your paralysis? In your head?"

Vicky Olivas looks down at her lovely lifeless hands. I realize I've said too much too soon. I start to say that perhaps, yes, such things happen . . . rarely, but . . .

"My psychologist says I may snap out of it if I keep coming here." She talks slowly, as though speaking is difficult. "I went to a hypnotist . . . that didn't work. The spiritist didn't work either." My heart twists at her last statement.

The mysteries surrounding this woman are not unfolding. If anything, she is more of an enigma than before. "Healing is really important to you," I conclude, filling the space while her attendant lifts the styrofoam cup of black coffee to Vicky's lips.

"Yes." Another pause. "I was in Russia not long ago. I read about research going on at this institute in Leningrad. My relatives in South America are involved in international politics, so the arrangements for my trip were easy."

"And?"

"And so you see," she says, pointing to her hands with her chin, "the Russian doctors couldn't do much. But" she adds hastily, "I had pneumonia and I got a bed sore. I was too sick to work that hard." She goes on to describe the battery of people who gave her deep muscle massage, braced her legs to help her stand, and told her to concentrate on moving her fingers.

"But I can do this." She leans ever so slightly forward in her wheelchair and shrugs her shoulders. She is proud of the small bit of movement, convinced the trip to Russia helped. "And I'll do more. I know I will." She tilts her head toward her attendant, a signal for another puff of cigarette and sip of coffee.

I wonder if she sees the strange contradiction she presents as she sits in the shade and talks about what she will do, while the real work of pushing and pulling toward such dreams goes on even now inside the walls behind her. Although Vicky Olivas is convinced she will begin moving at any time, she is doing nothing more than waiting. Waiting as she sits in a corner of Dr. Britten's lab, watching the rest. Waiting as she avoids the group and takes a cigarette break outside the center. Waiting while conferring with a psychologist, a hypnotist, even a spiritist.

It also occurs to me that Vicky Olivas probably does not go to supermarkets. Instead, others do her living for her while she waits to be healed.

"There you are!" Rana rounds the corner of the phys. ed. building. "Sam's been looking for you. You're late for your appointment, you know." She lifts her arm and points to her watch. "Hi, Vicky," she adds as she joins our circle. "Are you coming in, too?"

"No. I think I'll catch the early van home."

"Suit yourself," Rana replies in her matter-of-fact tone. I sense she's trying to make a not-so-subtle point.

Rana pushes my chair through the open glass door and down the long corridor to the lab. "What did you find out?"

I listen to the rhythmic squeak of my rubber wheels on the shiny linoleum, measuring my words. "She's got a lot to learn." I try not to sound condescending.

"Haven't we all." Rana sees people like Vicky all day long. Her commend adds a healthy perspective.

I do have a lot to learn. How can my dream of helping other people with disabilities become a reality unless I know how to put God's love into practice with someone like Vicky Olivas. Isn't that what sharing Christ in a real way with a real world is all about?

"By the way," Rana adds, "wasn't that some story of how she landed in that wheelchair?"

"I'm afraid I didn't get that far," I confess. I can't believe I didn't even ask Vicky the obvious question.

"You didn't?"

I shake my head.

"Well, I'd like to know where God was when all that awful stuff happened to her!"

ﾟﾂ

A NEIGHBOR'S SWIMMING pool provides a good place for Rana to stretch and exercise my arms and legs. But now we take a break and float lazily as the currents from the wind and the pool filter send our rubber rafts in slow circles. Her hands drape in the water, her fingers splashing an occasional ripple.

It's a quiet Saturday afternoon and I'm not anxious to get back to my exercises. Instead, my mind drifts back to my conversation with Vicky Olivas. So many unanswered questions. I seize this moment as a chance to hear more about her.

"Rana, what can you tell me about Vicky?" I tilt my head and squint against the sun to see her.

I relax into the damp cool towel folded under my neck and listen to what she tells me. . . .

March 26, 1976, is a beautiful Friday morning in Los Angeles. But for Vicky Olivas it is a grim reminder of happier, brighter mornings. Her husband has turned his back on their young family, broken his marriage vows, and left Vicky alone to care for two-year-old Arturo. Saddened and shaken, facing an uncertain future, Vicky must get a job to support herself and her young son.

A woman at the employment agency has just called, and although it is Friday, with the weekend fast approaching, she insists that this one job interview could be an opportunity Vicky won't want to miss. "Probably by Monday the job will be taken by someone else," she has warned.

It means taking Arturo to her parents' house, a long drive back to Hollywood to change clothes—she will have to borrow gas money from a neighbor—and another trip back to the Valley. Vicky sighs and shrugs. Why not?

Driving her sporty car makes the distance a pleasure—something she hasn't felt since her husband packed his bags and left. A rush of air through the open window revives her hopes. Maybe with a job and a new apartment her life could begin again.

Vicky has difficulty finding the address she has been given. There seem to be only factories in the general neighborhood. She debates about forgetting it and just going home. But after showing the address on the slip of paper to a receptionist in one of the buildings she passes, she is directed up the block. She parks her car at the curb, then hesitates again when she walks to the corner and looks down a long dirty alley. The address, the receptionist said, is at the last door on the right.

I've got to start somewhere, Vicky thinks as she listens to the click of her high heels on the cement take her closer to the warehouse at the end of the alley.

The door is unlocked and she steps into a dim front office. There is dust on the typewriter, the floor is strewn with papers, and a damp closed-in smell fills the place. *I hope I don't get this job,* Vicky thinks. Peeking around a corner, she cautiously makes her way down a hallway. "Hello . . . is someone there? Hello?"

She walks through the warehouse and comes to another office where she finds two men, one sitting behind a scarred formica desk and the other slouched in a molded plastic chair with his arms folded.

"My name is Vicky Olivas. The employment agency sent me over."

The man behind the desk, obviously the boss, leans back and looks her up and down. Suddenly, Vicky is aware of her peach pantsuit. She feels the weight of her waist-long hair. She blinks her eyes, her lashes false and feathered and heavy. Everything seems weighted under his stare.

"Yes. I've been expecting you. Do you have a resume?" he demands.

Tell him you left it in the car and get out of here, something warns her.

"Well, do you?"

"No . . . no," she stammers. "I don't have one with me."

"Here." He slides an application across the desk. "Go into the front office and fill it out while I finish."

Vicky, shaking slightly but resigned to seeing the interview through, obediently begins to fill in her address and social-security number. She checks the box which indicates that at her former job she was an accountant's secretary. She glances up once and notices the two men loading television sets and stereos into a van parked at the open doors of the warehouse. By the time the other man pulls away in the van she has completed the form.

At that point the owner enters the room, closes the door behind him, and clicks the lock. Another chill of apprehension goes down her spine, but she dismisses it as nerves.

"Are you finished?"

"Yes. I just have to sign my name," she says and pens her signature at the bottom of the document.

"Let's go into my office." He motions her through a door. Vicky walks in front of him as he points the way. They are in another warehouse.

Then the nightmare begins.

Suddenly the man grabs her from behind, wraps his arms tightly around her chest, and throws her against the wall. She hits a tool chest and stumbles, her back against the bricks. The man stands several feet away from her, hands at his side, and says, "Do you realize this is all planned . . . all planned."

"Wh-what are you talking about?"

"I asked them to send somebody just like you," he says as his eyes hungrily scan her again. "I've sent everyone home," he hisses through clenched teeth and steps toward her.

He grabs her blouse, and Vicky twists and squirms violently to break free. Out of the corner of her eye she spots the glint of something metal. A gun! She wrestles even harder to free herself. Suddenly, a loud bang. The room and the man spiral round and round as Vicky slumps to the floor.

Her thoughts spin out of control as her body slides across the floor. She is being dragged. But to where? And what? She feels the cold tiles of a bathroom against her face and smells urine and dirt. Something wet and warm trickles down her neck. That is the only sensation. No pain. She strains to see where her legs are. She can't feel them. She struggles to brush her hair from her face but cannot lift her arms.

The man leaves the room, then returns after a few moments. He wipes his brow with his hand, nervously shakes his head, leaves again, and returns. He repeats this pattern several times. "I didn't mean to shoot you. . . . I didn't mean it."

The odor of the filthy bathroom and his sweaty body make her dizzy. She tries to think of something to save herself. "Would you be kind enough to call my brother," she says. As she makes this calm suggestion, she tries to keep her tone polite, cooperative, tries to control her panic and fear. "He'll come and get me. We won't say a thing. Everything will be all right." She gauges each sentence with a breath. She recites the phone number.

Amazingly, the man dials. He listens, then slams down the receiver—a busy signal. *Oh, Arturo, stop playing with the phone.* The man dials again. No answer.

He paces in and out of the bathroom rubbing sweating hands on his pant legs. "Please take my keys out of my pocketbook," she says. "If you would get my car . . . a Camaro, light blue . . . just up the street. You can't miss it." The man nervously struggles to decide what to do. Finally he leaves. In a few minutes he is back.

"Okay, I've got the car," he says as he reaches under Vicky's armpits to help her up. Her legs refuse to support her weight. They seem numb. Useless. He becomes angry and lets her go. She falls back to the tile, hitting her head and shoulder.

"Why aren't you helping me?" he yells. He storms out of the room, switching off the lights as he goes, and slams the door. In the dark stillness the odors of sweat, urine, and filth are suffocating. The silence is eerie. Has he left her to die in this awful place?

The room begins to spiral again. In her dizziness, Vicky thinks she hears a woman's voice, urgent and angry. She takes a deep breath. "Help! He-e-e-e-elp!"

A girl in her late teens rushes in. "What have you done?" *She must know the man*, Vicky reasons through her faintness. "What are we going to do?" Vicky can feel the girl's panic as she stuffs a dirty towel under her bleeding head. *Are they going to kill me?*

The glaring light and the girl's presence revive Vicky's senses. "How about if we say that the two of you were walking down the street and saw my car pulled off to the side with me slumped over the wheel." Hope is in her voice. She doesn't know whether she is making sense, whether they are even listening, but she has to try. "And you pushed me over to the passenger side and drove me to the hospital. You could say that you didn't know what happened to me or anything." Vicky's eyes dart to the man, to the girl, and back to the man. "I won't say a word. You won't be dragged into this. I promise!"

The two deliberate over the story, with Vicky coaxing to make it sound better and better. Finally, the perspiring man threatens, "We'll do it. But you'd better not say anything. We have your application. Your address. If you say any-thing . . . I know you have a son. I'll kill him."

"So THEN WHAT happened?" I press Rana. Behind her sunglasses, her skin shining with Bain de Soleil, Rana, the no-nonsense lady with sharp wit and ready words, seems sincerely moved by the story she has related.

"Well, those jerks threw her into the front seat of her car. The girl drove and Vicky gave her directions." Rana lifts her sunglasses and looks at me. "Isn't that incredible?"

I shake my head and awkwardly splash my hand in the water to keep my raft facing her.

"So . . . they pull up in front of this hospital, and the girl runs into the emergency room and says, 'I found this woman. I don't know if she was shot or stabbed.' Amazingly, there were several police there on another matter, and Vicky was taken in on a stretcher. Feeling safe at last, she told the whole story to a policewoman while the doctors worked on her. Anyway," Rana says, taking another deep breath, "nobody believed her until they went back to the warehouse and found her purse and sunglasses, blood, and a gun in a trash pail. The guy was arrested."

This story sounds like a murder mystery or a television movie-of-the-week— unbelievable, improbable—but it is not fiction. And the ending has an even sadder twist.

"He was released after three years in jail. And Vicky spends the rest of her life completely paralyzed in a wheelchair."

"How does she live?"

"Although the employment agency wasn't connected, they should have known the guy's record—three other convictions of attempted rape. Because of a small settlement, Vicky is able to live alone with her attendant and son. It's the only security she's got."

For the moment all is quiet except for the pool pump at the far edge of the backyard.

"It'll be a real miracle if that woman ever smiles again," Rana concludes, after sensing I have no comment. The fact is, I am thinking that Vicky's story must not end here. Not if my dream to help other people has anything to do with it. But where do I begin?

"I don't see how you handicapped people do it," Rana says in mild disgust. "And I don't know how you can believe in a God who would allow all that stuff."

I am still silent, but my thoughts have shifted from Vicky to Rana. I sense a pressing need much closer to home. I recall my conversation with Rob exactly a year ago on the movie set. Something about having the faith to doubt and yet believe. As then, but for a different reason, I am not quick to mouth a stock answer. Rana is asking about one of the great mysteries of my faith. It can't be handled in a trite or prepackaged way. That's something else I learned from the movie.

I also can't ignore her comment. Yet movie memories bring other concerns to the surface. *Who am I to tell anybody about the gospel?* Barely months have passed since my own time of rebellion against God. I'm still slightly shaken from the trauma of those months even though I know God has forgiven me. My head knows He has wiped the slate clean. My heart is still having a hard time catching up. So who am I to tell anybody anything?

Besides, I hear whispers from an even more distant past, *Vicky's story would test the faith of the most steadfast of saints. Who could explain it?*

"Well?" Rana is waiting, lazily splashing her hand, making little eddies in the water.

Well, I asked for the chance to talk to real people in a real world. Here it is.

"What we need here is wisdom," I begin, leaning my head forward to shade my eyes so I can look directly at her. "And wisdom is not the ability to figure out why God has done what He's done and what He'll do next."

"Then what is it?" she says flatly.

I plop my head back on the raft. "It's trusting Him even when nothing seems fair." I add what is fresh on my mind. "You know, we can have faith to doubt and still believe."

Rana has come out from behind the dark lenses. She props her sunglasses on top of her head. I sense that in expressing her doubts she is truly asking for understanding. "So what's the big deal about God that He's worth that kind of trust?"

I grin, liking her honesty. "Look, Vicky's case is bad—no getting away from it. But far worse is *why* people pick up guns and shoot and rape and . . . whatever.

In other words, sin. And not only the sin in crazy jerks like that man in the warehouse," I add quickly. "I'm talking about you and me. We're sinners too."

"Sin. There's something I know about," Rana says in mock pride. In the next breath she begins to tell her story. How she has come out of a divorce and gone looking for good times with reckless abandon. Why should it matter what she does as long as she doesn't harm anyone? As she exposes more seamy details about herself, I nod thoughtfully. The flow of words stops. She waits. For what, I'm not sure. Shock? Disgust? Astonishment?

My expression doesn't change. My ears are no longer tender, having been toughened by the movie experience. And my own sin is a glaring reminder of the sorts of things I am actually capable of doing, of being.

"Sin should never surprise us," I finally answer her unspoken question. "I am really . . . really . . . no different . . . no better than you." I squint through the glare of the sun. "The surprise is that God forgives any of us," I say, convinced that Rana knows her past of deeds and pleasures is wrong.

"And that," I say, turning my face back toward the sun, "is the big deal about God."

"I don't believe I understand," Rana concludes. She cools her skin with handfuls of pool water.

"Well, don't worry. I think it'll all come clear," I say, feeling my raft drift away from hers.

Several days later Rana and I find ourselves sitting at the edge of the same pool. I'm not surprised when she brings the subject up again.

As we talk she becomes even more real, opening the inside of her heart, describing her pain and disappointments. I describe for her the Savior who entered this real world and died on an agonizingly real cross for our terribly real sins. He was buried in a real tomb of cold hard stone. He rose in a real body.

"I'm sure God's Word would do a better job of explaining things to you than I can." I show her several verses in the New Testament and several in the Old, including Isaiah 53. She thinks the descriptions of Christ in the Old Testament are rather amazing. So detailed. So accurate.

She goes home that afternoon with a Bible in her hands. She promises, without prompting on my part, to read more. The next afternoon she comes for another visit. An unexpected one. "I have something to tell you," she says.

My new friend has prayed to acknowledge Christ as her Lord.

The thrill in Rana's voice, the new light in her smile, are like a fresh wind that blows new strength and excitement into my own soul.

CLUNK! MY HEAD hits the edge of the car door frame. "Drat it!" I exclaim, squeezing my eyes against the pain. Kerbe's car is easy enough to be lifted out of, but grabbing a novice off the street to help has its disadvantages.

"I'm so sorry," Kerbe apologizes as she lightly rubs my throbbing head. "Uh-oh. A bump."

"Oh, it's nobody's fault," I groan. "Rana's right. Getting lifted in and out of a car all the time is a real pain—no pun intended."

Kerbe begins to smile. Rather cheeky, I think, still wincing from the mishap. My head smarts, and I want to ask her what's so funny.

As we wheel to the center, I spot Dr. Britten beside a new cream-colored van. He is wiping the shiny fender with a cloth. Kerbe stops my chair beside him as Sam straightens and spreads his arms.

"Well, how do you like it?" he says.

"Nice." I wonder why he wants my opinion on a van.

"Our church wanted to help your ministry. The elders put it before the people, we took an offering, and it's yours to drive." Sam beams as he opens the sliding door to show me the interior.

I don't look at the van. My gaze is fixed on Sam as he chatters on. "Of course, it has to be adapted. The mechanical lift will go here." He motions with his arm. "We'll take out the driver's seat so your wheelchair will fit there."

"How can this . . . be?"

Sam stops his tour of the interior and leans against the passenger door. "Still don't think you can do it, huh?"

"No, it's not that. This van—," I say, sweeping my head in a scanning motion. "How . . . I mean, it's a gift . . . to me?"

"Joni, you've been asking me all kinds of questions about churches helping disabled people. Just think of this as an example of what a church can do." Sam gestures toward the van. "And you can get the word out better than I or anyone else in our congregation."

Sam's idea intrigues me, but I'm still not certain I can drive. I push myself even harder, lifting wrist weights, cycling at the machine, developing my balance in the chair.

Weeks fly by as my power chair and I are measured for width, height, and weight to fit the van. The mechanisms are fine-tuned to the strength in my arm. The new van is fully equipped. The moment of truth is here.

Sam and Rana climb into the van while I jab at the outside controls to open the automatic door and lower the mechanical lift. Once I am lifted into the back of the van, I power my wheelchair into the driver's alcove. My chair couples and locks into place. Sam fits my hand into a cuff on top of a metal joystick that rises from the floor where the "four on the floor" would ordinarily be. He explains that I should push forward to accelerate, pull back to brake, swing my arm to the right for right turns and vice versa for left.

"Very simple," he concludes.

I lean my head to reach for a mouthstick. With it, I jab at the ignition button on the control box bolted to the door. The engine turns over easily and roars when I lean my shoulder forward slightly, applying pressure with the joystick. I examine other buttons on the box—a red one for the emergency brake, white for air conditioning, blue for windshield wipers, and yellow for headlights. I press another button with my mouthstick and shift into drive.

"I can't believe I'm doing this!" The van inches out of the parking lot onto the street. "What if a policeman stops me?" I ask Rana, looking at her in the rear-view mirror.

"Got your learner's permit?"

I nod nervously.

"Well," she laughs, "you'll just have to pretend we're not here. He'll have to get it out of your wallet himself. Simple!"

I drive through back streets, a little disoriented to be sitting on the driver's side. Teeth clenched, I brace myself for an approaching stop sign. Trying to remember all that Sam has taught me, I cautiously flex my bicep, pulling back on the joystick. The van jerks to a halt several yards before the sign. "Stay calm. Every move is carefully planned," I say in my best Inspector Clouseau accent. As my muscles relax, the drive becomes smoother.

I breathe deeply and glance at the houses that flow by. I am driving. I am moving. Just like everybody else.

After a few more days on the road, I am convinced I can drive—even the freeways. The only people Sam and I need to convince now are those at the Department of Motor Vehicles.

Rana, who has learned to manage the sensitive controls of my van, drives me to the D.M.V. building the following week. She grills me on questions from the student-driver's handbook.

Although we are early, the lines are already long. We wait. Time and the people in front of us inch forward. *This is crazy.* I look around at the scores of people waiting at other windows. I grin, imagining their thoughts. *I can't even lift a glass of water to my mouth and here I am about to tell these people that they ought to let me on the road!*

Finally, it is our turn at the window. The official-looking woman sitting behind the desk stamps a few papers and gives a "next please" look to Rana.

I clear my throat. "Good morning. I'm here to take the written exam for drivers. I . . . uh . . . can't use my hands, but my friend here—"

"May I have your learner's permit please," she replies in a monotone, reaching for an application.

"As I was saying," I continue, "I can't write with my hands, but my friend here," I nod toward Rana, "can help me take the exam."

The government lady thumbs through more papers and without looking up says, "I'm sorry. You'll have to come back next Friday morning a little earlier. Handicapped people may only take the oral examination with one of our employees in the conference room." She glances at her watch. "The room is closed now."

Rana and I look at each other in disbelief. It took a mountain of effort for her and Judy to get me up and out of bed even *this* early. I whisper to Rana through the side of my mouth, "We're not leaving here until I take this exam."

I reassume a smile and clear my throat again. "Well, I think we can come up with a creative alternative here." I adopt a tone of official authority to match the woman behind the window, who continues to look at me without expression. "You seem, I'm a mouth artist, and I hold brushes and pencils between my teeth." The woman's eyes widen. "And if my friend will be allowed to hold the test on a clipboard, I can take it that way."

She sits rigidly now, ignoring her paperwork. She rises and walks from the window, advising us to wait while she finds her supervisor. In a few minutes she returns and motions Rana to the window. Leaning forward, she whispers, "I do think she'll be too much of a distraction to the other people taking the examination. Do you know what I mean?"

"Do you know what she means?" Rana turns to me.

Those old feelings of inadequacy begin to encroach. I will not be intimidated by this woman and her silly red tape. "Well," I say, my smile in plaster by now, a tinge of anger in my voice, "how about this. Let's tape a pen to my wrist. And if you don't mind my straying out of the little true and false boxes a bit, I can take the exam that way."

"I don't believe this," I say to Rana through clenched teeth as the woman leaves to confer with her supervisor again.

"Hmm. I felt like telling her that tall guys with big noses and glasses distract me." We smother our chuckles.

The license lady returns with a roll of masking tape and leads us to the examination area. We are pleased with ourselves—until I look up and see the desks. They are designed for people to stand and take the exam—too high for me to reach from my chair! But I am not about to back out now. We devise a scheme to place a waste basket on my lap and prop the exam paper on top within easy reach. "Although frankly," I say to the woman, "I believe I am far more of a distraction doing it this way."

Later I do prove to be a distraction, however—to the examiner riding with me as I take my road test. He is so fascinated that he keeps forgetting to tell me where to turn and when to park.

But I pass the exam, and move one step closer to independence.

Oh, if my Maryland friends could see me now. I can drive to meet someone for dinner. I can drive myself to work at Joni and Friends. I can drive to watch a sunset. I can drive alone. For the first time in fifteen years, I can actually go somewhere . . . anywhere . . . by myself. It's almost like getting healed!

My driving is an occasion that calls for my parents to make a special trip out to Los Angeles. They've heard I can drive, but they must see it for themselves. As they clutch their seats, I drive them to meet Sam. They are amazed at my accomplishment and immensely impressed with his work at the center. Meeting some of his disabled students gives them a better perspective of what I'd like to do through Joni and Friends.

Mother and Dad bite their nails as I sign the papers for my new hilltop home. They stay an extra week to help move things from the little stucco house to my new address. I am proud of my home and anxious to copy decorating details from the house on the farm—Indian rugs as wall hangings, a George Washington spread on my bed, and a stained-glass lamp over the kitchen table. Daddy has brought a handmade driftwood lamp, a wooden chest, and several oil paintings of cowboys and horses. I even buy a miniature schnauzer puppy who reminds me of one of our old dogs on the farm. My California home has an air of the Maryland farm, but it is distinct, unique, and mine.

I take more steps toward independence.

Mom and Dad help me pick out a washer and dryer, a dining room set, and a rug for the kitchen. They buy dog toys for Scruffy, my new pup. Pushing aside shrubbery with his cane, Dad examines the backyard fence to make sure Scruffy can't escape.

Mom enjoys a game of tennis with Rana. Vicky Olivas and I watch from the sidelines and keep score. My parents take great interest in my friends. They think Judy and Kerbe are absolutely wonderful for taking such excellent care of me. (Parents never change.)

Every time I see my mother smile or my father nod, I am further convinced that I did the right thing in moving to Southern California. They approve of and enjoy my independence.

"Joni, this decision you made to move was a good one," they say.

"Just imagine," my mother says, shaking her head in the back seat of the van, "Joni driving us down the Ventura freeway. I can't wait to get home and tell everyone about it."

I laugh as I savor the proud smile on her face. And I recall Sam Britten's comment: "Just get out there and tell other churches what they can do."

"OKAY, HOW ARE we going to pay the bill?"

I think for a minute. "I don't know. Maybe it could be my treat. But then again . . ." I hesitate. "I don't want to offend her."

"Maybe if I treat, it would look a little less patronizing," Rana replies. "Vicky has a lot of pride."

"Okay. So she's disabled and doesn't want a handout. Then she pays for her own dinner."

"Maybe she can't afford it. It's an expensive restaurant."

"We're making this into a big deal." I sound exasperated. "You treat. Judy and Kerbe and I will even up with you afterward."

"Then it's set. I'll pick her up, and we'll meet you all at Benihana's on Friday."

We smile good-naturedly. Perhaps we're both overly concerned for Vicky Olivas. But Rana has seen the emptiness in Vicky's life. And she has felt her own emptiness vanish with her new peace in God. I'm proud that she wants to make a difference in Vicky's life. I want to also.

Finally, it seems to be happening. Vicky has agreed to go out to dinner with us. If I can really spend time with her, perhaps I can get behind the enigma.

We will be friends, I plan. We will learn from each other, as friends should.

The evening of our dinner engagement arrives, and we gather at the well-known oriental restaurant. We sip fruit drinks while we wait to be seated. In the corner, a man plays background music on a piano. After a few tunes we are ushered to a large U-shaped table, the middle of which is a metal cooking surface.

Vicky and I have to have the footpedals on our wheelchairs dismantled so we can fit under the table.

Vicky sits across from me, and I glance at her over my menu. She sits straight and rigid, her hands on the flowered pillow, towering over the girls beside her. She wears a silky blouse, low cut and belted. I wonder if she does something special to her hair to make it so thick and full. Someone has pulled part of it back with a pearly comb and a flower.

A Japanese waitress in a kimono greets us politely with a slight bow as she places our plates and chopsticks before us. I look at the chopsticks, then at Vicky, shrug my shoulders, and laugh. A busboy carrying a tray of water glasses bumps into her wheelchair and mumbles a quick apology. It's an awkward beginning.

"We almost didn't get here," Rana says with a hint of exasperation as she shakes the folded napkin and places it on her lap. "I got a phone call today from Arturo wanting to know where his mother was." She smiles at Vicky as she places her napkin on her lap.

"A call . . . from Arturo? He's only five years old," Judy responds.

"I know. Don't ask me how he tracked down my phone number." Rana shakes her head and takes a sip of tea. "But he knew I was somebody from Sam's center. The thing was . . ." She pauses. "He was desperate. Not out of fear for himself, but for his mother. He told me that somebody should have had her home from the center hours ago."

Vicky looks at Rana, waiting for her to continue her story. I take that as permission to probe. "What'd you do?" I ask.

"Well, I told him not to worry. That I'd find his mom. But honestly . . ." She opens her menu as she speaks. "I didn't know where to begin looking. I figured she missed the van, so I tried the campus. There she was," Rana says, gesturing toward Vicky, "quietly, patiently, waiting."

"Wow, Vicky . . . that's some kid you have."

"Yes, he's that all right," Vicky replies. Rana lifts the small porcelain teacup to her mouth. After a sip, Vicky continues. "He takes good care of his Mamita." She blushes a bit, and I wonder if it is from pride in her son or embarrassment over the incident. Does she wish she could take better care of him?

There is a lull in the conversation as we examine the menus and order.

"'Mamita.' Is that his special name for you?" Judy asks.

"Yes." It seems she doesn't intend to say more. No one offers to change the subject, however, and Vicky finally continues, "Arturo and I depend on each other. We live alone." Her tone is matter of fact. "That is, except my attendants who never seem to stay very long. I'm always training someone new to help me out."

When I hear this, I squirm a bit in my chair. I never seem to lack for someone to help. I live in a brand-new house with new furniture. I can paint. I travel. My van—an expensive gift—sits out in the restaurant lot. And I think of Vicky and five-year-old Arturo clinging to each other.

"Just the other night, I was feeling so . . . so sad." Vicky glances at us as we sit listening intently. "I was in bed, thinking how nothing is really going very right. Dr. Britten's exercises aren't helping . . . that is, I'm not getting any better. I couldn't help crying." She laughs, trying to make light of it. "And there was Arturo, sleeping next to me in his bed on the floor. He does that when he gets sick," she explains. "Anyway, he had a cold . . . his breathing was stuffy. And that made me feel worse. I couldn't get up to check his temperature or give him an aspirin, wipe his nose, or cuddle and cover him." She shakes her head, emphasizing each phrase.

"My crying woke him up. Then, without saying anything, he got up and found a Kleenex, wiped my nose and my tears. He went and got this big blanket—he's only a little boy, you know—and climbed up onto my bed so he could pull up the covers." She smiles broadly. "Isn't that something? He's such a good boy," Vicky says as she leans toward Rana, a signal for more tea.

At this point the Japanese chef approaches the stove with a tray of raw shrimp, chicken, and steak. He smiles and, with a quick bow of his head in the tall white chef's hat, scrapes the meat and raw vegetables onto the sizzling stove with a sharp knife. Steam hisses and billows and rises to the copper ceiling vent. Rana, Judy, and Kerbe lightly applaud as he begins his fanfare of cutting and slicing.

I watch the flying steel, but my thoughts are absorbed by the beautiful woman sitting across from me. I can hardly believe she's revealed as much as she has. Yet I know it has not been to gain sympathy. Rather, she has told the story to boast about her young son who is so responsible for his age.

"So you don't live with your parents?" Judy asks, reaching for a fork rather than chopsticks.

"No. You see . . ." She hesitates. "Although they don't live far away, I really want . . . need to be my son's Mamita, to raise him by myself."

No one presses her further. She is obviously a private person. Perhaps she feels she has shared too much already. For the remainder of the evening we talk about the food, Judy spins some yarns about her days as a midwife in England, Kerbe chatters about the career group at church, and Rana describes her daughter's recent trip overseas. Like life, our conversation just rambles on.

Rana feeds Vicky. She holds a morsel of chicken poised in question over the dishes of hot mustard and soy sauce. With a nod, Vicky selects the mustard. Rana cups her hand underneath the chopsticks and lifts the chicken to Vicky's mouth. Vicky leans forward and daintily takes a bite. I'm suddenly aware of my own way of eating as I lift my shoulder and angle the bent spoon attached to my arm splint. In a practiced motion, not quite smooth, I bring the spoonful of food to my mouth. I chew and swallow, feeling a bit guilty because I can feed myself. I wonder if Vicky will be able to feed herself one day.

That strange feeling urges me to say, "Your level of injury is about the same as mine, Vicky. I'll bet you'll be using your arms like me one of these days." I remember her poor attitude about God and exercise, and add for encouragement, "I know, I'm convinced God has some wonderful plans for you. With prayer and hard work, I've seen it happen."

After our dessert of green tea ice cream, the waitress presents the bill on a porcelain dish. I shoot a glance at Rana; I've forgotten what we decided to do. After a second of hesitation I announce that dinner is my treat and ask Judy to reach for my wallet.

Before anyone can quibble about the bill, I grab for Vicky's attention again. "I can't say that I know what you've been through. But I do know that God is a big part of the answer. Maybe," I continue, with a questioning look, "we can talk about it sometime." I look for a response. "I'd love to meet Arturo," I add, hoping that will be an incentive.

Vicky doesn't reply. Instead, as Rana backs her wheelchair from the table, she tosses her thick hair in that aristocratic manner and turns her head in the direction she wants to go—the door. Rana repositions her hands on the pillow and pushes her toward the exit. I back my power wheelchair into the aisle and follow them. Whatever closeness we had gained has somehow been lost.

Judy and Rana lift Vicky into the car while I watch and wait to say good-by. A valet slams the door. Vicky sits slumped, the comb in her hair beginning to fall. I don't want her to feel self-conscious, and I wish I could reach in and fix it for her. She turns her head slightly and offers a stiff smile, mouthing the words, "Thank you," through the closed window.

I move to the back of the car where Rana is loading Vicky's folded chair into the trunk.

"Well?" I say.

Rana shoves the spare tire further into the luggage compartment before she speaks. "Well, everything went fine up till the end there." She straightens and dusts off her hands. "Look, I'm a novice at being a Christian, but . . . I don't know how to put this . . . but, you . . . we just can't waltz into her life with ready-made answers, no matter how much we want to help. For anybody to pattern their life after you is a big order. Things just don't happen for others the way they happened for you." She slams the trunk.

I am hurt. God has used this baby Christian to point an admonishing finger at me. I am humiliated. I want so to do the right thing, say the right thing, say the right words to help Vicky and her young son, but I am embarrassed as I realize that she has become less of a person and more of a project. My own thoughts, my plans, condemn me: *We will be friends.*

I think about formulas, plans, designs, programs, and organized efforts. Perhaps I am relying more on these than on demonstrating God's love to a real person.

I wonder, what would Jesus have done?

I'VE OBSERVED SAM Britten for months now. His hands communicate love as he gently lifts a boy from his wheelchair or stretches the sore and spastic muscles of an elderly woman stiff from years of inactivity. Even his voice is tender and gentle. I am learning a lot from Sam's love and compassion.

"How do you . . . where do you . . . begin?" I ask as he unstraps my hand from the cycle machine. "So many people need so much."

Several cerebral palsied boys bide their time by the classroom door, waiting to begin their treatment. There are not enough classroom aides. Not enough equipment. Not enough room. And there is always a long waiting list.

"Just one at a time, Joni," Sam replies, motioning for an aide to greet the boys at the door. He returns his attention to me and the velcro strap on my other hand. "All you can do is try your best to help one person at a time."

He neatly refastens the straps to the gloves, smoothing the leather over and over again. Exasperated with his own limitations, it's obvious he wants to say more, and I stretch my aching arms, waiting for him to continue.

"I visited Tante Corrie ten Boom this weekend," he says, plopping tiredly into an empty wheelchair.

I've talked with Sam about Corrie before. In her late eighties now, this old saint of God, who survived Nazi concentration camps and went on to a worldwide ministry, has recently suffered another stroke. Severely disabled, she can no longer travel and speak. Now she lives a quiet life in a sunny little house south of Los Angeles. Disability is the great leveler, and Tante Corrie, like millions of others, now must struggle through the confusing world of wheelchairs and pressure sores, tubes and catheters.

An edge of excitement creeps into Sam's tired voice. "Joni, it was . . . was indescribable. Walking into that woman's room was like entering a sanctuary. We talked, although she could only answer with lots of smiles and nods." He shrugs his shoulders and his eyes focus on something far away. "When I rubbed her feet, I kept thinking about the hundreds of thousands of miles that woman has traveled. I kept thinking about her bare feet on the hard, cruel dirt of that death camp."

I don't speak at all—just listen and learn.

He straightens his back, his hands on his knees. "I devised a pulley system so she can do some exercises and get more strength in those frail arms of hers. And I instructed her companions on how to properly lift her in and out of bed, positioning her in her wheelchair, things of that sort.

"It's amazing to think that at almost ninety years of age that devout woman should have to start all over again . . . a whole new and different ministry."

I look at him questioningly.

"A ministry of waiting . . . of silence. Of being still before the Lord. Oh, uh . . . prayer." Sam looks back at me with his own questioning expression. "She was such an active woman—"

I nod. "Now she is the one who needs help."

"But you know what's strange?" Sam smiles. "Doing those few things for her, meeting those few needs—*I* was the one who came away blessed. She ended up giving more to me than I could ever possibly give to her."

We are interrupted by a sudden call from one of the aides who needs Sam's help to lift a young girl back into her wheelchair. He gives my shoulder a friendly squeeze and hurries to the other end of the room.

I watch him switch gears as he gives the young girl on the mat his entire attention, his complete devotion. I bite my lip at the poignancy of the moment, recalling his words about helping people one at a time. He gives as much to this girl as he would to Tante Corrie. To anyone.

Each person is special.

I learn another lesson.

THE WEEKEND BRINGS a new month with a promise of cooler days. Welcome days. But how I wish the weather would act like it's supposed to in November. Instead, the California sun lingers lazily high in the sky, smiling warmth on palm trees and swimming pools. I long for the rustling of crisp leaves in the wind. The fragrance of burning cherry wood from a neighboring chimney. I miss the steam of frost on my breath and weather cold enough to wear a wool scarf. Fall of 1979 has been so busy that I have forgotten such things.

I call home on Saturday. I tell Mom and Dad about our progress with the ministry. I ask how Jay and Rob are doing. How's Charlie Cat? How's Kathy's new Appaloosa colt doing? Does everyone miss me?

"And how is your friend Vicky doing?" The three thousand miles of telephone lines cannot filter out the warmth in her words.

"Oh . . . we went to dinner last week. It was nice. I feel so bad for her though. Mom, you wouldn't believe what she's been through."

"Give her our love." I can hear the smile in my mother's voice.

"I'll do that," I say sincerely. I do want to give Vicky love.

After I hang up, I think about my closing words. Like Sam Britten, I want to love and help people as individuals. See each person as special and unique.

But somehow I got bogged down at Joni and Friends this week. Every day there were scores of letters to answer. Tuesday I met with Sam and Greg Barshaw, another elder at Grace Church who works with disabled people. On Wednesday I contacted Debbie Stone at Rancho Hospital and found that she's going to move into the little stucco house and work full-time at the church. We talked about new programs for the church. Thursday and Friday I studied independent-living manuals, attendant-care manuals, source books for the disabled, architectural codes, and anything else about "handicaps" I could get my hands on.

It's so hard to think of people as special and unique while absorbing overwhelming statistics and impersonal manuals.

On Sunday morning I drive to church alone. There are dozens of handicap parking places in the church lot, and almost all are taken. I poke along, mindful that many people are unloading from vans and cars, wheeling their way across the lot to church. Several wave.

First service is just letting out. I glide down the ramp and greet the people walking up the ramp who must squeeze against the wall to avoid my wheels. Church is crowded, and I'm glad I'm early enough to get a good seat. Or, I should say, an aisle.

People in wheelchairs line up like a row of parked cars alongside the end of each pew. I stop and greet a few who aren't preoccupied with friends or the church bulletin. Then I wheel into place beside Kerbe, who is already seated at the end of the sixth row.

The choir sings. We are led in prayer. The congregation stands and sits, appropriately, as Scripture is read or hymns are sung—all except those who sit at the ends of the pews next to the wheelchairs. They hold our hymnals and turn pages for those of us who cannot.

It is time for the morning message. People pull out their Bibles and look for pens and paper. John MacArthur walks up to the pulpit. I smile, remembering a time not too many months ago when I couldn't wait to pull his sermon apart. My attitude sure is different now.

Somewhere near the beginning, MacArthur flips to a verse in the Gospel of John.

His voice carries across the congregation of three thousand. "And the Lord cried out from the cross, 'I thirst.'"[1] He makes his point and moves on.

My attention, however, is still on that verse from the Gospel of John. I close my eyes and picture the cross. The scattered crowd. The dark clouds and the soldiers. I picture Jesus crying out in thirst.

I wonder what I would have done. I ponder as the minister's voice fills the background. I imagine myself huddled in that crowd. If I had heard Jesus say He was thirsty, what . . . just what would I have done?

Well, I wouldn't have stood there like a nincompoop, as my mother would say. I think—I hope I would have run, not walked, to the nearest well. Forget the sponge and vinegar. I would have brought Him the real thing—a cool cup of water.

Then it hits me. I inch my chair closer to the edge of the pew where Kerbe sits.

She is listening intently to the sermon, but I interrupt her briefly as I whisper, "Flip to Matthew 25 for just a second."

She thumbs back a few chapters and lays the Bible open on my knee. My eyes scan the page for a particular phrase. I glance at the second column where Jesus is having a conversation with His disciples. There it is.

"I was thirsty and you gave me something to drink. . . . I tell you the truth, whatever you did for one of the least of these brothers of mine, you did for me."[2]

I raise my head and straightened my shoulders, staring into the distance. I am struck with the obvious. This is what Jesus wants me to do. To do for others with the same sense of urgency and concern what I would do for Him. Not just talk. Not just give advice. Jesus wants me to *do* something. For others. For Him.

I imagine something else. I picture Jesus being moved with compassion when He encountered the blind or the hungry or the widow who had lost her son. He was not overwhelmed by needy crowds. It was just part of His nature to roll up His sleeves and help one person at a time. That's what Sam Britten is doing every day at his center. Seeing needs. Making a difference with love and compassion.

I try to place myself in that picture, and squirm, knowing that so often what I feel edges close to pity. *"I feel so bad for her."* My response to my mother's question yesterday about Vicky haunts me. Pity, I decide, sees a need at arm's length. Compassion reaches out to touch. Pity never becomes more than a feeling. Compassion compels us to act.

I look around at the people in their parked wheelchairs. A man with cerebral palsy wails his way through a hymn. A woman taps her cane in time with the organ music. Each one in this crowd, myself included, has needs.

Vicky Olivas has a need. I place her here in my imagination—sitting across the aisle, singing, smiling, surrounded by friends. She, like these people, is neither a statistic nor a sociological grouping in a manual.

And I can . . . I really can make a difference in her life. But not with pity.

Jesus wants me to do something about it in a loving and compassionate way.

$\mathcal{P}$

"AND THIS SCARLETT O'Hara contraption is my corset," I say as Judy pulls up on my blouse and down on the waistband of my jeans to reveal the stiff, white garment of stays and buckles around my middle. "It helps me breathe and sit up straight. Honestly," I add, as Judy tucks my blouse back into my jeans, "it's the only reason I can sing or even talk loudly."

"Hmm . . . interesting." Vicky inspects my posture.

"I've got an extra one here." I motion toward my dresser drawer. "Would you be willing to give it a try?" I don't want to sound pushy, so I add, "It's no big deal. You can take it home and try it on there if you want to."

"No, I'll try it on here. I'd like to see what a corset does for me." Judy and Rana lift Vicky onto my bed and shift and roll her body to position the corset under her middle. She grunts and puffs as they tug at the straps and fasten the buckles.

"I betcha feel like John Wayne's packhorse, don't you? I always do," I say laughingly.

Back in her wheelchair, Vicky fights to gain her equilibrium from her new center of balance. "This isn't easy," she comments. And then, "Oh, my! Oh, my goodness! What a difference this makes in my voice," she says, surprised at the depth and projection she can already hear. Rana tucks in her blouse while Judy reshapes her corduroy cuffs to a point. They stand back and we all take inventory.

I am so pleased that she has responded to our help, but I want to make sure she understands that the decision is hers. "Look, I'm not pushing corsets. And a lot of people don't wear them and do quite fine. But for some, it's a real plus."

Vicky looks at me directly with a broad grin for the first time since I've known her.

"Watch out for pressure sores, though. I'm still battling a leftover one from the movie days."

We spend the rest of the afternoon talking, crowding in practical ideas and suggestions. I show her more of the tried-and-true hints I've accumulated in my many years in a wheelchair: support hose for better circulation, attractive leather armsplints to stabilize wrists and hands, and a portable easel to begin learning how to write with a pen between her teeth. She asks about the kind of catheter I use. We talk about exercises and the importance of drinking lots of water. Transferring properly to and from bed. Vitamins. Nutrition.

And bed baths.

"Yes, I know about those," she says with a blush. "There are just some things I'll never get used to. Like showing a stranger how to give me a bath."

She hits a sensitive chord. "Yeah, I have those feelings too." I try to throw some light and laughter on the subject. "But, listen. Even the disciples protested when the Lord Himself washed their dirty feet. Maybe they too had a thing about being bathed by somebody else, even if it was God wielding the washcloth." After I say it, I realize I've just mentioned a story from the Bible in a totally real and natural way.

Again, Vicky smiles. "Legbags. Corsets. My, there's so much to learn." She glances over Rana's shoulder at all the notes and scribbles she has made on her yellow legal pad.

"I'd like you to have that corset . . . but," I caution, hoping I'm not saying too much, "you should see your doctor and get measured for your own. And the easel is yours too if you'd like it. I have an extra.

Vicky is an aristocrat. Proud. Untrusting. Skeptical. Mostly unsmiling. But she says yes to my gifts.

"We could get together with your attendant and explain how to put the corset on and—"

"I'd *like* to get together with my attendant," she sighs. "The last one just left. Thankfully."

"What do you mean?"

She hesitates, as though deciding whether to trust us with her personal problems. "We got into this argument. I don't even remember what it was about. She got so angry. She took a pillow and . . . and she put it on top of . . ." She looks up, her eyes iced with tears. "On top of my face. She was so mad she wanted to . . . to kill me," she says, as though she still can't believe it.

The room is silent. At the far end of the backyard, Scruffy barks. The spray from the law sprinklers patters on the concrete ramp outside the sliding glass door. This woman, like many others I am beginning to discover, lives in a world that is foreign to anything I have ever known.

"Luckily, my brother was upstairs. The woman didn't know that. We both thought the house was empty. He ran down the steps when he heard me scream. He grabbed her by her hair and threw her out the front door. Then he raced upstairs, dug her things out of her room, and threw them off the balcony to her, yelling, 'Don't ever come back!'"

I lean on my arm propped on the wheelchair armrest. Judy sits slumped on the edge of the bed holding a corset. Rana dog-ears the corner of her tablet over and over. Just like that night in the restaurant, it is clear that Vicky has not shared this story to tug at our emotions. She has simply told us the facts.

I finally break the silence. "Well, we'll just have to . . . to *do* something." I look toward Judy and Rana, shaking my head. "I don't know what." I look back at Vicky. "But something."

Vicky tosses back her thick hair and sniffs. "I need someone . . . anyone. Arturo and I can't go on alone this way."

"Let's start by praying," Rana says softly. Her suggestion is sudden and jarring. A trace of a smile crosses my lips as I look at her sitting calmly with hands folded on top of the tablet on her lap. A soft breeze gently rattles the blinds of the glass door, and we wait for someone to second the motion.

"Jesus can't help me." Startled, we look at Vicky who continues, almost questioningly. "It isn't Jesus who can put me to bed or get me up in the morning. He can't get me a drink of water. It's nice that you all believe in God, but I need somebody more . . . more real than God. I need people."

"I need them too," I say out of nowhere. "The difference is that I know Judy and Kerbe and others are like . . . like the hands of God for me. I guess you could say it *is* God who gets me up in the morning." I pause and then add, paraphrasing a Bible verse, "Things happen that we might not rely on ourselves, but on Him."[3]

"And has one of your people ever tried to murder you?"

I don't answer.

Vicky hangs her head, embarrassed at the sarcasm behind her words. Swallowing hard, I divert the conversation back to something positive. "As I said, we all want to help. Corsets and the easel are a beginning. I don't know what is next, but we're in this together."

I think of Jesus and a glass of water.

We have begun.

I AM PAINTING today in the quiet room adjacent to the office at Joni and Friends. The brick floor is cool. The brilliant color chart is a treat for my eyes. My art books and cloth samples are stacked on top of a metal art file in the corner. Mason jars filled with brushes and tubes of acrylics are lined, soldierlike, on wooden shelves. Even the clutter of papers and color swatches tacked to the cork board are a relief from the office efficiency of telephones and typewriters on the other side of the closed door.

When I paint, I am supposed to think of nothing else. Just the brushes and colors and canvas.

But that's impossible today.

I keep thinking of Vicky and her new easel, wondering how she is progressing with a pen between her teeth. I recall my first easel and my feeble first-time efforts. I glance around—

"Phone for you, Joni." Judy sticks her head in the door. "Want to take it or are you still painting?"

I wheel to my desk phone and tilt my head to the receiver clamped to a gooseneck. "Hello?"

"Yes . . . uh, my name is Bee. We met the other night at a concert. Remember? I was the guy in the striped shirt with my friend Jack Fischer?" He is speaking fast. "I'm calling with really bad news. Jack just broke his neck in a parallel bar accident—"

Details come into focus. One night last week I went to a concert. There, I met two young men, both national gymnasts. Yes, one was named Jack, a handsome and happy fellow. He just wanted to meet me since he had finished reading my book *Joni* a few days earlier. He said something about using gymnastics in some way to talk about his faith in God. And now . . .

"An accident. But . . . but . . . I just met him—," I interrupt.

"Yes, well, he wanted you to know that you and your book . . . you know, what you said to him that night . . . everything is really helping."

I get Jack's address and tell Bee that I will write to him. "And please," I urge, "please tell Jack we will be praying for him."

I hang up, wishing my parting words hadn't sounded so hollow. "We will be praying for him" doesn't ring true in a situation like this. It sounds like a convenient way to end a distressing conversation. I need no further prompting. I bow my head and pray for Jack Fischer.

Later, at dinner with Judy and Rana, I tell them about Jack. We talk about Vicky. These are not statistics in an attendant-care manual. They are people with very real needs.

"What program could be set up to help them?"

But out discussion lacks energy. Our ideas seem stale. We play idly with our cheesecake.

As we lean back and wait for the busboy to clear our table, I think about needs. *Suppose a brother or sister is without clothes and daily food. If one of you says to him, "Go, I wish you well. Keep warm and fed," but does nothing about his physical needs, what good is it?*[4]

"What was it that helped *you* most, Joni?"

Judy's question seems naïve. "My situation was so different," I say as I brush her off. "My family's unusually close, and I've got great friends."

She stares at me. "Well?"

"Well, what? Do I stick you two in a Xerox machine and pass out the copies?"

"Sort of. Why don't you train others to help like we do?"

"Who?" I ask.

Rana rolls her eyes. "Look at all those people in churches on Sundays. Some of them must have some free time."

"Hmm. You're thinking of a class or something? Teach folks how to push wheelchairs or whatever?"

"Yeah," Rana says. "And maybe they'll even learn how to empty a legbag. Why wait around for social-service groups to teach those things? I've always heard Christians should set the standards for caring. Right?"

Judy fumbles in her purse. "Rana, have you got a pen? . . . Thanks. Hand me that napkin. Let's see . . . how to greet someone whose hands are paralyzed . . . how to talk to somebody who is mentally retarded or who can't speak . . . how to lift people out of a car into a wheelchair."

Judy pulls out her calendar as the ideas gather momentum. She scribbles on another napkin.

"Maybe we can use Dr. Britten's center."

"Or a room at Grace Church."

"We need compassionate people—both to teach and to learn."

Judy interrupts, jabbing her pen at us to emphasize her words. "Gene Newman over at church writes great curriculum. And Greg Barshaw can lecture," she adds as she jots down more names.

"The office girls can help with registrations. We'll invite church people from all over the Valley."

The ideas go from paper napkins to planning sheets, from lesson plans to notebooks, from brochures to a professional workshop. But as registrations from scores of churches begin pouring in for our first "People Plus" in the spring of 1980, a conviction deepens in my heart: a program—even one well-planned and well-prayed for—is not the entire answer.

The night before the launch of our weekend workshop I read a story about Jesus in the Gospel of Mark. "Some men came, bringing to him a paralytic, carried by four of them. Since they could not get him to Jesus because of the crowd, they made an opening in the roof above Jesus and, after digging through it, lowered the mat the paralyzed man was lying on. When Jesus saw their faith, he said to the paralytic, 'Son, your sins are forgiven.' "[5]

It's people who must make the difference. Not a program. People who will go to the same kind of lengths as those four friends, I think to myself.

Somehow we need Christians who will push through crowds, scale walls, and rip up roofs with that same urgent yearning to meet an ordinary human need.

$\wp\eth$

OUR FIRST PEOPLE Plus workshop. Crutches and cycling machines have been pushed aside to make room in Sam's lab for the more than one hundred people present: college students, some nurses, teachers, mothers, several businessmen. I listen from the sidelines along with a smattering of others in wheelchairs. A tall man with curly blond hair rests his chin on the mouth control that operates his power wheelchair. The wheezing rhythm of someone's respirator drifts across the classroom, and I spot the woman who, I surmise, has had polio. Her attendant occasionally leans over to adjust knobs on the machine.

The speaker is Greg Barshaw, the elder at Grace Church who helps disabled people. He shuffles his pages into order, adjusts the level of the microphone, and grabs our attention with a story. In his Sunday school class for mentally handicapped teens, it seems there was a young girl who was catching on rapidly . . .

"The girl's mother called me on the phone the other day," Greg explains. "She said she couldn't understand how her retarded daughter was learning so much, grasping concepts far beyond her natural ability. Her daughter wasn't doing anywhere near that well in public school. This lady couldn't understand what was going on. 'What are you doing different?' she asked me."

At this point Greg puts his hands in his pockets and strolls out from behind the podium. "This mother was shocked. But she shouldn't be. We don't discern biblical things with the brawn of our brain, so neither do the mentally disabled." He reaches for his Bible on the lectern. "It says in 1 Corinthians 2:12 and 13, that 'we have . . . received . . . the Spirit who is from God, that we may understand what God has freely given us. This is what we speak, not in words taught us by human wisdom but in words taught by the Spirit, expressing spiritual truths in spiritual words.'" He looks up and smiles. "Time and time again I've seen the Holy Spirit bypass the mind and teach mentally handicapped people truths that are far beyond their comprehension."

I turn to Vicky Olivas and Rana beside me. We give each other the look that says, "Hey, I never knew that." Obviously, the students in this workshop aren't the only ones learning.

"Look at Peter's famous confession of Jesus as the Christ," Greg goes on. "Immediately the Lord pointed the finger and said, 'Flesh and blood has not revealed this to you, but my Father who is in heaven.' He wanted to remind Peter that no one needs a super IQ to interpret God's Word. Just the Spirit within us."[6]

He looks directly at the audience and asks, "So who's mentally handicapped?"

A young college student raises his hand and says quietly, "I guess we all are."

"That's right. Any one of us is mentally disabled when we try to think our way to God. He doesn't need the muscle of your mind to get His truths across. In fact, pride of intellect sometimes gets in the way."

We laugh.

"All we need is faith. And the mentally handicapped have plenty of that. Remember, 'God chose the foolish things of the world to shame the wise.'[7] . . . Bet you came into this workshop thinking folks like that couldn't teach you a thing." Greg grins and shakes his finger at the class.

Again I glance at Vicky and Rana. The notebook they share is marked in the margins, with points underlined. More than a few Bible verses are circled or marked with asterisks. Greg holds their attention.

When coffee break is announced, people close their notebooks and several walk to the front to ask Greg questions. I am curious to know what Vicky and Rana think.

"So . . . do you think we're getting through to these folks?" I ask as Arturo stands on tiptoe to give his mother a sip of coffee.

"Oh, yes. You can tell they're learning a lot." I watch Arturo stretch his little arms around his Mamita to pull her to him and give her a hug. Then, as if it were a perfectly natural way to end a hug, he pushes Vicky back to an upright position.

Vicky is relaxed, at ease, a far cry from the aloof woman I met a few months ago, the woman who viewed other disabled people from a distance.

Rana pats the cover of her notebook. "You know, I understand what Greg means about learning from handicapped people. I remember giving this guy—he was cerebral palsied—exercises when I was at Dr. Britten's lab. And all the while I kept stretching and bending his legs, he kept telling me how I ought to know God. I thought the guy was sweet," she says, using a syrupy tone. "I mean, I thought, 'Isn't that nice . . . he's religious and he wants me to be too.'" She scoots forward in her chair. "And you know what? In my own mind I was set—absolutely determined—that there was no way anybody was going to talk me into thinking about God. I could not have cared less. But here I was listening to this guy talk my ear off about his faith." She laughs. "I only put up with his preaching because he was handicapped." A softness enters her voice now. I hear the difference and wonder if she does. Rana too is far different from the tough, calloused woman I first met.

"It must have been the Spirit of God that got through to me. Honestly," she says with surprise, "I was more handicapped than that guy with cerebral palsy."

Vicky listens intently as Arturo leans on her shoulder. "Actually, I'm learning a lot too," she admits to us. "I used to have a million questions and no answers." She draws a deep breath. "I still don't have any answers. But I'm learning that the questions aren't . . . aren't—"

"—aren't as pressing as they once were?" I finish her thought for her.

She tilts her head, thinking. "I guess you could say that."

"I know what you mean," I say, feeling myself drawn to some other time of my own. "It's just like Greg was saying. Sometimes the intellect gets in the way when we try to think our way to God." I ponder a moment and then add, "That doesn't mean there are no answers. It just means they don't come all at once."

&

I WONDER IF Vicky has found an attendant yet, I think as I watch Kerbe. She and Judy take turns giving me a bath and exercises each morning, fluffing my pillows, straightening my sheets, and making breakfast.

They work compassionately, yet efficiently. They have to. My speaking and traveling, the driving, workshops, and painting have cost me. I've been sitting up too many hours each day, and now I am in bed with my old nemesis, a pressure sore. The old one from movie days is now a full-fledged wound, open and oozing.

A week has passed—it seems like two. My doctor says I've got two more months to go. Two months in bed. Somehow God provided the grace to handle years in a rehabilitation institution. But that was long ago. Now time ticks by with slow monotony.

I read the Bible. This is not easy, though. The book must be pillow-propped on its end as I lay on my side. Words are hard to read sideways. Gravity works against me. And it is impossible to turn pages.

I read about the "day of evil" in the book of Ephesians.[8] *This must be it*, I brood. In the few places I can feel, I ache from inactivity. My hair is greasy and matted in back where my head has pressed on the pillow. Which reminds me, I must get a flatter, harder pillow. This puffy feather thing poofs around each side of my face in a suffocating, claustrophobic way. Little things—fitted sheets snapping their elastic corners, crumbs under my neck, a stuffy nose—irritate me.

"Therefore put on the full armor of God, so that when the day of evil comes, you may be able to stand your ground . . . take up the shield of faith, with which you can extinguish all the flaming arrows of the evil one."[9] . . . I reflect on verses like this. But in the hours idling by, my imagination does silly things.

I picture darts with red-hot tips coming at me while I weakly hold up a shield. Ha! Missed! I act out the struggle against "rulers, authorities, and the powers of this dark world."[10]

The truth is, my prayers seem to ricochet off the ceiling. I picture myself heaving heavy petitions on my shoulders, pushing them past the roof to heaven, clawing at the prison wall of my backyard. My life doesn't go past the border of yew bushes outside. I conjure up weird designs and scary faces out of the shadowy textures in the ceiling. I turn my head on the pillow and pull the same meaningless patterns out of the wallpaper.

Why do I tempt myself with such nonsense?

Depression does this. I remember that from my early days in the hospital. So I ask Judy to come up from the office in the afternoon. She sits beside me on the bed and goes through the mail. She gets me "outside," takes my mind off myself in this room and out to other people's concerns. Yet it's strange to be writing advice to others when I'm having a difficult time swallowing my own prescriptions.

She relates all the latest happenings at the office. I feel left out. I wonder if anyone has missed me.

"Of course you're missed." Judy smooths my dirty hair from my forehead and smiles warmly. I have discovered over these years that Judy, so very British and easily perceived as uncaring or unthoughtful, is truly compassionate. She folds back the blanket and examines the pressure sore, dabbing it with a swab and ointment.

"We need to keep the circulation moving around this area," she comments absently, her attention focused on massaging the skin around the sore.

But even with all the care and kindness, depression continues to eat away at me in my weaker moments.

I watch a videotape of *Gone With the Wind*. Hey! There's the name of the prop man from my movie. *That's right*, I recall wistfully. *He said he worked on that film in his younger days.* Memories of the *Joni* movie—the crew, Solvang, the challenge of film making—make me more restless during these doleful days.

I play backgammon lying on my side with the board balanced on the uprighted end of a suitcase pressed next to my bed. Frustrated, I search for exact words to describe where on the board I want my chips moved. I listen to the radio. I watch television. *Why do game shows depress me?* At least I have enough sense to avoid dumb reruns of "The Twilight Zone."

I look forward to meals. I eat a lot. The rest of the time I just lie here.

FROM MY BED I hear Vicky's wheelchair coming up the short hallway. She and Rana have come for a visit. I want to see them. Then again, I don't.

Judy has smoothed down the greasy cowlick on the back of my head and tucked in my sheet with nurses' corners. I wish I could be propped up in bed with pillows, but it would be dangerous for my sore.

Vicky enters and Rana positions her chair beside my bed. Vicky's olive skin has tanned nicely in the summer sun. Her hair has been cut for the hot weather. It's short but stylish. Her make-up is perfect. She sits so straight—the corset is helping. Wearing armsplints now, she appears to have more movement in her arms. As always, her corduroy slacks are perfectly creased. She has a new pair of summer sandals.

"So, how's the sore?" Vicky asks as Rana leaves to fetch some Cokes.

"Oh, it's coming along," I say, gesturing with my head toward the side of my hip. "How have you been?"

"Fine. I got a new attendant."

"Really?" I say with hope in my voice.

"It's working out great." It's wonderful to see her smile. Not stiffly as before, but with a new confidence. I'm curious to know whether her smile reflects something as wonderful happening on the inside.

She talks about her new helper, about her discussions over the Bible with Rana, about Arturo and the new van she's getting. I talk about the boredom of bed, about how behind I am on paintings and correspondence, and about how many speaking engagements I've had to cancel.

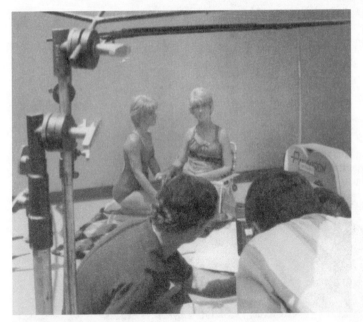

Doing a color test to make certain my double and I exactly match on film.

Face-to-face with "the girl in the blue bathing suit."

Make-up artist Bill Tuttle goes to work.

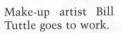

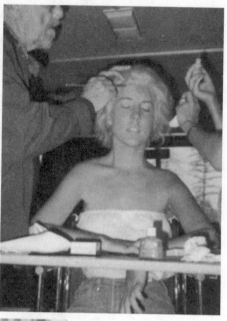

Bill and hair stylist Kaye Pow-
nall glue on the scalp line of
my wig.

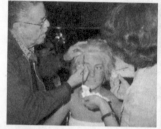

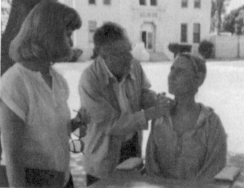

Friend Betsy Sandbower tries on my wig while Bill
pins my own hair tightly under a net.

Rob Tregenza, Assistant to
the Director, helps block
shots on the crane.

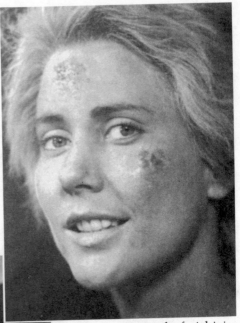

Make-up re-creates the facial injuries from my diving accident.

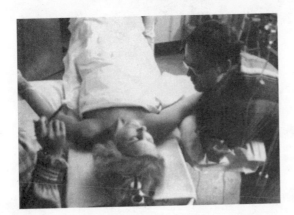

Jim Collier, Writer and Director, gives me direction for my scenes on the Stryker frame.

Dr. Sam Britten and Chris Ige.

Working at the cycling machine exercises my shoulders, biceps, and cardiovascular system.

Here Margie is helping develop my balance.

Margie Corbett, Dr. Britten's assistant, stretches my shoulder muscles to increase flexibility and reduce spasticity.

Dr. Sam Britten presents me with
the van, a gift from Grace Community Church. These snapshots capture my range of emotions at the
time!

On the left is my cousin Kerbe.

A mechanical lift enables me to enter and leave the van by myself.

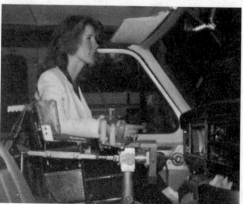

Behind "the wheel." My right arm is locked into the handcuff that controls the steering, accelerating, and braking.

Visiting a
rehabilitation
center.

In my office, dialing
a number with a
mouthstick.

Our radio ministry is a
vital part of Joni and
Friends.

Joni and Friends
staff and volunteers
gather for a picnic.

The first Joni and Friends workshop
in Southern California.

Steve Estes "talks" with a workshop participant who uses a wordboard.

A typical day's mail.

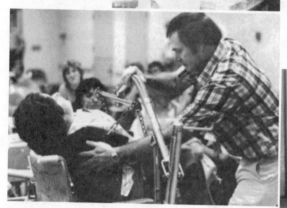

Some of the Joni and Friends staff and volunteers.

At a workshop Dr. Sam Britten and Debbie Stone demonstrate how some disabled people are transferred from bed to wheelchair.

Preparing a mailing.

Rana and I teach a People Plus class.

My armsplint and special spoon allow me to feed myself.

Having fun with my niece Earecka Tregenza and Ryan and Adrienne Estes (Steve and Verna's children).

Earecka feeds Aunt Joni an ice-cream cone.

I often borrow the hands of others. Here, Earecka, Ryan, and Adrienne help me shop, cook, and clean my wheelchair.

There are many important people in my life. Here are some who hold a special place in my life and in this book.

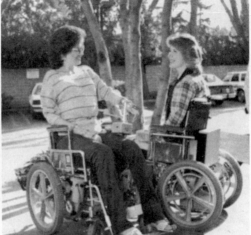

Vicky Olivas.

My sister Jay.

Scruffy's not a person, but he is special!

Vicky and her son Arturo.

Judy Butler, thinking and
planning as usual.

Rob and Jay.

Rana Leavell.

One of my favorite pictures of Ken, taken just as he was ready to leave for a game of racquetball.

My wedding gift to Ken was this fishing reel—big enough to catch a marlin!

Mother and I wait for the ceremony to begin.

Left to right: Ken's parents, Takeo and Kay Tada; Ken and I; Grandmother and Grandfather Minoru Hori, Ken's grandparents; and his sister Carol.

Left to right: my mother, Rob and Jay Tregenza, Ken and I, my sister Kathy Eareckson, my father, and my nieces Kay Trombero and Earecka Tregenza.

Our wedding party. Back row, left to right: Ed Hill, Larry Bonney, Ken, Dr. Sam Britten, Pete Lubisich, and Jan Janura. Front row: Betsy Sandbower, Carol Tada, Kay Trombero, Earecka Tregenza, Jay Tregenza, and Kathy Eareckson.

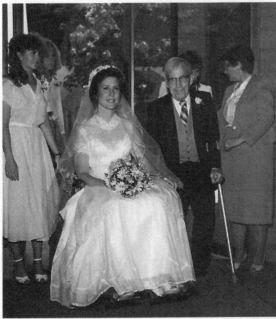

Daddy and I prepare to walk down the aisle.

My relaxed groom.

Mr. and Mrs. Ken Tada.

A few disabled friends gather to catch my bouquet.

435

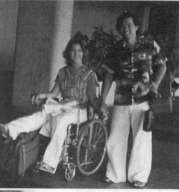

Arriving in Hawaii.

Some of our favorite moments are spent in the garden.

A farewell from Dad as we leave for our honeymoon in Hawaii.

Ken rigs a special easel for me to use during the long weeks in bed required for healing pressure sores.

Ken carves our first Thanksgiving turkey.

We visit a rehabilitation center in Poland.

Ken and I participate in a Wheel-a-Thon for the Center for Achievement for the Physically Disabled.

I stop short.

I'm whining. That makes me even more irritated with myself. Paranoia creeps in.

"Look, I guess you can tell I'm not in the best frame of mind at the moment," I apologize. "I'm not very . . . together." I laugh half-heartedly.

"That's okay. I guess the tables have turned."

I look at her in puzzlement.

"There was a time when I said the same to you." There's no spite in the tone of her voice.

"Go on," I urge her.

She seeks a kind of approval from Rana who is drinking a Coke. "Uh-huh," she says with her mouth full. It's up to you, she seems to say.

"Well, sometimes Rana would give me exercises, and I would snap at her with sarcasm, 'You want me to do these the way Joni does them, don't you!'" She searches for another example. "Or I'd look at you and sneer to myself, 'Joni can't be that happy, that together.'"

Vicky glances at my dresser, my walls. "And this house. And your van. So you wrote a book. And so what if you're a quad, I would taunt myself. Your problems are nothing compared with mine—or a lot of other people, for that matter. I used to think your life wasn't that big a deal."

She stops and shakes her head in a "tsk-tsk" manner. "I was so down on myself. I thought I could handle my problems better if I could cut you down to my size. I felt ashamed, though, when you wanted to be my friend. I couldn't even understand why you'd want me as a friend." She nods toward Rana. "Or why Rana was being my friend."

Openness. Honesty. The room—and me—are refreshed by the cross breeze of Vicky's candor.

"I guess it was just envy," Vicky says.

"I know what you're talking about," I break in. "I sometimes look at paraplegics even now and think they've got it made because they can use their hands and don't have to depend so much on others."

"Do you really do that?"

I nod sheepishly.

"I do too." Vicky laughs, delighted to discover a vice we have in common. I chuckle too.

"But it does help," she adds, her voice softened, "to see you . . . real. Struggling like the rest of us."

She whispers to Rana who leaves and comes back carrying a small potted prickly cactus tied with a bright bow. "Rana was showing me a verse out of her Bible that said something about looking out for another's interest as you would your own." She pauses as Rana places the cactus on my bedside table. "You've helped me. And although it's small, this cactus is my way of helping you along. You're tough . . . we can make it through these hard times. Together."

Her words glaze my eyes with tears. I recall something Sam once said of his visit with Tante Corrie: "*I* was the one who came away blessed. She ended up giving more to me than I could ever possibly give to her."

Vicky, in her unpretentious way of putting things, has given me much more than a surprise cactus. She has freely given me her friendship so that finally we can be real with one another. And that helps me see clearly through my depression.

Later that night as I fight off more demons in mad midnight moments, I grapple to hold on to the light of my friends' visit. *Being real hurts*. But this time it's easier to fight the battle. In the darkness the shadowy outline of a flower vase on my dresser could become a frightening form. Instead, I purposefully attach a brighter meaning to it. And in the dark and quiet, while crickets make peaceful, steady calming sounds outside, I am given something else. A new song inside.

> I have a piece of china,
>   a pretty porcelain vase.
> It holds such lovely flowers,
>   captures everybody's gaze.
> But fragile things do slip and fall
>   as everybody knows,
> and when that vase came crashing down,
>   those tears began to flow.
>
> My life was just like china,
>   a lovely thing to me.
> Full of porcelain promises
>   of all that I might be.
> But fragile things do slip and fall
>   as everybody knows,
> and when my life came crashing down,
>   those tears began to flow.
>
> But don't we all cry when pretty things get broken?
>   Don't we all sigh at such an awful loss?
> But Jesus will dry your dears as He has spoken,
>   'cause He was the one broken on the cross.
>
> Now Jesus is no porcelain prince,
>   His promises won't break.
> His holy Word holds fast and sure,
>   His love no one can shake.

So if your life is shattered
  by sorrow, pain, or sin,
His healing love will reach right down
  and make you whole again.[11]

＄

I FOLLOW THE snaking line of Interstate 15 on the map spread open on my lap. We pass the honor guard of eucalyptus trees that line the freeway, breaking the harsh hot winds for the new breed of stucco homes bordering the desert's edge.

It's exciting to leave Los Angeles behind. With pressure sores healed, I can finally take this long-awaited vacation. And I get to navigate while Rana is at the controls of the van. Judy and Vicky are with us too. Free from the confines of my bed, I am again an adventurer on the road of life.

We climb to the High Desert of sand and sagebrush, and speed past the offramps toward Barstow. Great red arrows and blinking neon lights warn us to stop at McDonalds or Burger King before crossing the hot plains to Nevada. We have our cooler filled with fruit and orange juice. We'll do fine, thank you.

On the dry and desolate outskirts of Las Vegas we find a Motel 6. Vicky and I wheel to the pool deck while Rana and Judy register. The desert sunset silhouettes date palms and hills in the distance. Winds whip ragged flags around the pool, and the halyards pinging against the metal poles sound like the sailboats on Chesapeake Bay. My mother would think this was an adventure too.

The next morning, dressed for the desert heat in a tube top, pigtails, sunglasses, and plenty of lip gloss, it's my turn at the wheel!

I drive slowly through truckstop burgs with names like Mesquite and Salina and Beaver, dusty little towns roadblocked with detours and busy corner cafés. Over a hundred or more miles of passing lanes I make friends with two trucks—a Peterbilt hauling timber and a Kenworth carrying steel beams.

We stop often at roadside rest areas or scenic points of interest. Vicky and I sit side by side under a shade tree while Rana spritzes our faces and arms with cold water from a spray bottle. Neither of us perspire—something else we share in common from our spinal-cord injuries—and our temperatures will equal the desert's if we aren't careful.

We pass wind-sculptured mesas and a few wind-beaten armadillos. Finally, hours past sunset, we pull into Green River, Utah. Weary and dirty, we sit in the darkened van while Judy checks in at the front desk. It's a large motel, but several tractor trailers are parked in the lot with their engines idling, keeping air conditioners going.

"Tomorrow we'll make Colorado by lunch and then have a late dinner in Estes Park, don't you think?" I speculate.

"I've never been to a Bible camp before," Vicky says.

Through the windshield we see Judy coming, stepping her way around huge muddy potholes in the gravel parking lot. We're ready to collapse into bed. But just as we click open the locks on our doors and heave our suitcases into our rooms, the phone rings. We look at each other questioningly. Who knows we're here?

"It's for you," Rana says, holding the receiver toward Vicky. "It's your mother." Judy drops a hanging garment bag on the bed and slumps down beside it. A bewildered Vicky leans her head to the receiver in Rana's hand.

"Halo . . . Mamie, que paso?"

Seconds pass. No change in her expression. Suddenly, her eyes widen. "Que? Estas segura?"

I don't need my high-school Spanish to tell me that something is desperately wrong.

"Quando paso?" She pressed her head harder against the receiver. "Todo?" Another stretch of silence. "No puedo es impossible. Mamie, yo te llamo mañana."

Rana replaces the receiver in the cradle, and we sit in silence, waiting. Whatever it is, Vicky can't take any more letdowns. Not now. Not when she finally seems to be getting a grip on her life.

"My mother says the peso in Mexico has fallen. All my savings are in those banks . . . everything is worthless." She finally is able to life her head and look at us. "The peso is almost worthless."

"Everything you have . . . in Mexico?" Judy says, stunned.

Vicky closes her eyes tightly. "The interest rates were so good . . . I needed the income just to make ends meet."

Rana flicks on the television to catch the late news. The commentator gives the headlines of the fast-breaking international story, accompanied by film coverage of banks in Mexico City where anxious people wait in long lines.

Vicky's income from her insurance settlement—everything she has to live on—will be cut to the core.

Rana lowers the volume after the report. "We can go back to L.A., you know."

Vicky sighs deeply. "No . . . no, we'll go on. There's nothing we can do. Let's just hope the value of the peso doesn't drop further," she laughs, "or I'll be flat broke. No house. Nothing." I can't believe she can laugh about it.

The news makes our time around the Bible that evening—a vacation ritual we promised each other—all the more meaningful. Amid open suitcases, heaped bedspreads, and scattered sweat shirts, we pray. Vicky listens. Before she and Rana go to their room, I ask Judy to flip to Psalm 50.

"This is . . . uh, . . ." I pause until Judy holds the Bible open in front of Vicky and points to the verse. "This is Psalm 50. The fifteenth verse says—"

"'Call upon me in the day of trouble,'" Vicky reads slowly in her heavily accented English, "'and I will deliver you.'"

"There's more," I prod.

"'I will deliver you, and you will honor me.'" She thinks for a moment. "Well, this is a day of trouble, no doubt about it," she says wearily.

I am convinced that in the night, alone in her bed, Vicky will call upon God.

T HE NEXT DAY we travel fast, make fewer stops, and arrive at our
destination at dusk. As we bounce up the rutted mountain road, our headlights
freeze a doe and her fawn in our path. The large chalet that is Ravenscrest Lodge
overlooks the twinkling lights of Estes Park, Colorado, a mountain resort
bordering the edge of Rocky Mountain National Park.

We don extra sweat shirts against the crisp alpine air and haul our luggage up
the small dirt path through the ponderosa pines to our cabin. Despite Vicky's
misfortune, we still sense adventure.

In the morning, I finally see the world we've entered as I sit outside our cabin
and wait for the others to get ready for breakfast. It is very quiet on the side of this
mountain, yet the air seems to roar. Does it breathe and sigh through the pines?
Or could it be a rushing stream? Pine needles sparkle in the sun, and occasionally
I hear the scratching of a rake on a dirt path.

The wooden screen door creaks open, and Rana wheels Vicky out beside me.

"Did you sleep okay?" I greet her.

"Considering," she replies with a smile, "yes." She throws her head back and
basks in the high-altitude sun. "That verse you gave me the other night about
calling on God helped," she says. "I guess I have nowhere else to turn."

"I understand. Even though things haven't hit me as hard as they have you," I
say, reflecting on her confession that day in my bedroom, "the fact is, I *have* had
it easier." Her eyes are open now, as she leans forward to listen.

I look deeply into her eyes. "But you've taught me to be so grateful for the
things I can do. Like something as simple as scratching my nose," I say as I lift

my arm to my face. "We both know what it means, though, not to be able to scratch our backs. So in some ways I . . . I think I can understand."

We are two paralyzed people, with injuries so similar and lives so different. Yet together we draw comfort from the sun and the things we share in common.

That afternoon, after lunch and a class on the book of Colossians, I power my wheelchair across the crunchy gravel toward our cabin. Judy is going to set up my easel so I can sketch the bark on the pine tree outside our cabin window. I am intrigued with the platelet-like shingles, the color and the texture. I pass Vicky and Mrs. Thomas, a kind gray-haired woman in a fresh cotton blouse and full skirt, the matriarch of sorts around here. She has wisdom, and she sits on a rock wall and talks over an open Bible to Vicky.

Later, Vicky tells me about it.

"Saying His name . . . the name of Christ . . . is so different." God's name, spoken in a gentle and accepting way, is foreign to her. "But that lady, Mrs. Thomas," she says, bobbing her head in the direction of the chalet, "says His name so warmly. Just like the rest of you. She talked about a personal relationship with the Lord Jesus . . . that's what she called Him. And that if I receive Him—" She spots Rana coming up the dirt path. "Rana, show Joni this verse. Right where my Bible's marked," she calls.

Rana places her half-eaten apple between her knees and reaches for the new study Bible on Vicky's lap. She opens it at the bookmark and smooths the stubborn page against the breeze.

" 'Just as you received Christ Jesus as Lord,' " Vicky reads, " 'continue to live in him, rooted and built up in him, strengthened in the faith as you were taught, and overflowing with thankfulness.' "[12]

Rana replaces the Bible on Vicky's lap, folds her arms, and continues to munch on her apple. Vicky gets to her point. "I'm already weak—in every sense of that word. I have nowhere else to go but up. And it makes sense that I'll only get stronger if I put my faith in Christ," she says with profound simplicity. "Don't you think?"

I glance at Rana who, more than any of us, has practically and consistently poured God's love into Vicky's life. She tosses the apple core and leans down to give Vicky a hug. "You know, you really *don't* have much else to be thankful for. Just purely and simply Jesus—and that's where He wants all of us to be."

We hear that night that the peso has weakened further. But our faith has been strengthened.

Ra

THE BIBLE STUDY we began during our vacation spills over into the following months. I watch in astonishing as the lovely, statuesque Latin woman in the wheelchair exchanges the mysteries behind her for the mysteries of God's Word. Less stiff, more trusting, Vicky accepts love without pride or question. Even more, she wants—needs—to give love in return.

One night, months later, we sit around the table after our Bible study, relaxing and nibbling on chocolates. No one is in a rush to leave. I talk about the farm and my family—a recent letter from my mother, the missions film Rob and Jay are doing in the Philippines, the few horses they've sold. A year ago it would have pained me to recount such homey details. I ponder aloud about this, reflecting on how in my wildest dreams I never imagined I would write a book or have a part in a move or leave the farm to start a ministry of workshops and radio programs, traveling, and speaking.

Judy leans on her elbow and says, "I never thought I would end up in California . . . full-time with Joni and Friends. It feels funny living in one place after moving from city to city with the Billy Graham Crusades."

"Yes," Vicky says, picking up the thread of our rambling conversation, "and a year ago I would never have seen myself in a situation like this." She scans the Bible, scattered commentaries, pencils, and notes cluttering the table. Her eyes take on a faraway gaze.

"I think it all started with me when my husband left," she begins. "And then God really grabbed my attention when I was attacked. And, yes, the gunshot . . . and paralysis . . . the divorce—Jesus really pulled me through that one. Let's see . . ." She mentally gropes for the list. "All those attendants who never worked out and that one who tried to murder me . . ." She laughs, shaking her head. "Oh, and I never told you about the one who refused to feed me, did I?"

We all look at each other, dumbfounded. She's really serious, recounting these matters in the same way we'd tabulate a day's minor irritations. "Uh . . . no . . . you never mentioned that one," I say.

Vicky checks off more of her list. "Raising Arturo on my own. The money crunch." She stops and asks Rana for a chocolate, takes a small bite, and continues. "But God has done it. And I never would have dreamed I could trust Him . . . after all those things. But I do." She smiles convincingly, even a little cockily.

Vicky has laid out the events like cards on the table, pleased to have been dealt such a good hand. "I don't need all the answers," she continues. "I just need the One who is holding those in trust for me."

What wisdom for one still so young in the faith. Yet it is wisdom I've heard before. *I said nearly the same thing in the movie, didn't I*, I muse with a smile, and an idea glimmers.

"You know, I got this letter the other day," I mention, "and I'm having a tough time answering it. Would you mind taking a look at it? Maybe even answering it?"

"Me? You're kidding! What do I have to say?"

"Listen. I'll send the letter to you. You tell me what you think."

Perhaps another part of my dream is beginning to take form: to see disabled people themselves reaching out to others in need. Before I send the Linda's letter to Vicky, I read it one more time.

I feel like I'm the only quadriplegic around. I so much dislike living in this nursing home. The only plus is its location—my mom lives only a block away and so I get to see my eight-year-old daughter. My divorce and custody battles are still not settled. It's so difficult at times to cope with first losing my husband, my daughter, my body, and my home because of some drunk driver. Many times I wonder if I'll make it.

I wonder if I'll make it. I've said those words too. Vicky has said those words. And somehow we must encourage this woman who has had her life jerked upside down and inside out by "some drunk driver"—let her know that she can make it. With the grace of God, she can and must.

After Vicky has had time to receive and read the letter, I press her, "What do you think?"

"I'm not sure I can help, but I'll give it a try," she replies.

Dear Linda,

My friend Joni shared your letter with me. Since our situations are so similar, she asked me to write to you.

Eight years ago I was shot in the neck. I needed the aid of a respirator but was lucky enough to be weaned off it in two months. During those months I had pneumonia most of the time, suffered from pressure sores, and was never really expected to live.

My son was eighteen months old at the time, plus I was in the process of a divorce. At that point my parents took custody of my son because they felt that even if I lived, I wouldn't be able to take care of him.

During that first year I felt I was in the middle of a bad dream, thinking any second I would wake up and everything would be okay. I went through all the motions of rehabilitation, but never allowed myself to learn. When I was released, reality hit me in the face. What to do?

Pity on me, poor Vicky! The pity lasted for two years—I refused to get out of bed or do anything for myself. I made everyone around me miserable.

Finally, it was like the Lord said, "Enough." Do I take the easy way and stay in bed in my parents' home while they make all my decisions, raising my son? Or do I move out on my own and start taking responsibility for my son and for my own life. How scary!

I got a house, and my attendant, my son, and myself moved in. I had to enroll my son in school—a giant step for me. Next, I had to go shopping to furnish my home. I was faced with mortgage payments, utility bills, food expenses, finding medical supplies, no transportation, and a need to be a meaningful part of my son's life. I didn't feel I could handle it. But it can be done.

Linda, I pray that you will have faith in the Lord that He will help you too. He was with me through all those rough times and the triumphant ones too. You will worry and wonder, but with God's grace, you'll make it.

I'm enclosing a book and a Bible with parts underlined. And Joni and Friends will send you a list of agencies and resources in your area. We will help you find a good church.

This is only the beginning, and I hope to talk to you soon on the phone. Please write. I'd love to know how things progress for you.

Yours in His care,
Vicky Olivas

My secretary folds the letter and sticks it in a Joni and Friends envelope. I look at the name of our ministry in the lefthand corner. The "and Friends" now includes Vicky.

The dream is coming true. Not here on my desk, but in the lives of people like Rana and Vicky and perhaps even Linda. People who, with God's help, are finding out who they are and where they are going.

∫∂

I READ IN a magazine this week that Corrie ten Boom has suffered another setback. It is simply a small paragraph at the bottom of a page, a few sentences highlighting her past ministry and a mention of this new stroke. *How old is she now? Eighty-eight? Eighty-nine?* I shake my head in amazement.

It's been far too long since I've seen her. And now, more than ever, we have much in common. My own battle with pressure sores is still fresh in my memory, and I recall the need to have visitors at my bedside, the comfort that people cared and prayed. I call Corrie's home and plan a visit.

Rana makes the long drive with me down to Orange County, to the single-story suburban house on the quiet tree-lined street that is now Corrie's sanctuary. We are greeted by Pam, Corrie's companion, a tall and strikingly graceful English woman. As we step into Corrie's home, it is like stepping into a different world. The air is fragrant with the rich aroma of good European coffee and Dutch chocolate. Old World clocks tick and a kettle steams.

Pam ushers us into the sitting room and asks us to wait while Tante Corrie is readied for our visit. Old photographs of the Ten Boom family crowd bookshelves and a buffet table. Photos in sepia of friends from Europe and from her travels. Each one is an individual treasure in a richly carved frame, proudly displayed on a lace doily. A reclining chair sits prominently in the room, and I wonder if it is a favorite of Corrie's, perhaps brought from the Netherlands.

A bunch of heavy, dewy pink roses crowd a vase on a small round table by the sliding glass door that opens into Corrie's backyard garden. A tree rustles and tulips sway. The breeze lightly wafts in the fragrance of orange blossoms. What a restful place.

Pam pushes Tante Corrie into the room in a wheelchair. She sits, slightly slumped, with her head resting in a forward position, but she greets us with a smile and a nod, waving her hand in a sing-song fashion with a finger raised. She mumbled a few garbled sounds.

It suddenly strikes me that this dear old saint who has ministered to thousands, even millions, with her speaking can now barely utter an intelligible word. I fight back tears of compassion and tell her how pleased we are to visit her. Her smile broadens. Her eyes sparkle.

Tante Corrie's silver-white hair, thin and wispy, is arranged in a soft roll. She wears a long white gown and a pink cotton robe. With her good hand she fiddles with the lace on the robe. Little round glasses perch on the end of her nose, and she peers over the rims at us.

I demonstrate my power wheelchair and recite some of the lessons we have both learned from long confinement. I do this not to exhibit my own spirituality, but to encourage her with what is really a litany from both of us to our loving God. "God's grace is enough for each day," I confirm, and she smiles and nods, pleased to agree.

I recall that Jim Collier, the director of *Joni*, had also endeared himself to Corrie in the making of *The Hiding Place*. She brightens when I mention his name, delighted to hear about his latest projects.

The mention of the movie triggers something else, and she gestures toward the shelf of video cassettes. Tante Corrie wants us to view one of her church films.

Pam puts on the video and leaves to prepare tea and cucumber sandwiches. I watch Corrie as she views her movie. She mumbles more sounds, accentuating her image on the film with a wave of her finger again. It seems she is not so much delighted with her appearance on the screen as she is with its message of hope from God's Word.

Corrie and I talk about heaven. It is a favorite topic for both of us. A new body. A new mind. A new heart. A new language. A new home. Even new ways to serve. Corrie underscores each of my words with a heavy Dutch "ja."

It seems appropriate to sing a song for her, one that has become particularly special to me because it captures all my thoughts and feelings about God and heaven and my disability. And as I begin, I realize how very fitting the words are for this dear friend of mine.

> Though I spend my mortal lifetime in this chair,
>   I refuse to waste it living in despair.
> And though others may receive
>   Gifts of healing, I believe
> That He has given me a gift beyond compare.

For heaven is nearer to me,
    And at times it is all I can see.
Sweet music I hear
    Coming down to my ear,
And I know that it's playing for me.
For I am Christ the Savior's own bride,
And redeemed I shall stand by His side.
He will say, "Shall we dance?"
And our endless romance
Will be worth all the tears I have cried.

   I raise my paralyzed hand and clumsily place it on the arm of Tante Corrie's wheelchair. She balances her good hand on top of mine and taps in rhythm while I sing the last verse.

I rejoice with him whose pain my Savior heals,
    And I weep with him who still his anguish feels.
But earthly joys and earthly tears
    Are confined to earthly years
And a greater good the Word of God reveals.
In this life we have a cross that we must bear,
A tiny part of Jesus' death that we can share.
And one day we'll lay it down
    And He has promised us a crown
To which our suffering can never be compared.

For heaven is nearer to me,
    And at times it is all I can see.
Sweet music I hear
    Coming down to my ear,
And I know that it's playing for me.
For I am Christ the Savior's own bride,
And redeemed I shall stand by His side.
He will say, "Shall we dance?"
And our endless romance
Will be worth all the tears I have cried.[13]

   Another breeze stirs the stillness, and it occurs to me that Pam, holding a tray of tea and sandwiches, has been standing for some time at the edge of the sitting room. None of us wants to disturb what has become, unintentionally, a holy moment.

Tante Corrie carries on the moment by grasping her paralyzed hand with the good one and then with great effort entwines her fingers. Pam, understanding this gesture, immediately puts down the tray, kneels by Corrie's wheelchair, and looks up into that determined face. "Tante Corrie, may we pray with you too?"

Pam rises and seats herself on the sofa beside Rana, and we bow our heads. After a moment, Corrie begins. Her words are indistinct, but her voice rises and falls as she prays earnestly in the Spirit. The Spirit is, in fact, the only one who understands her.

That night in bed, I relive each moment of my visit with Corrie ten Boom. I recall how our eyes met as we were fed our cucumber sandwiches. Helpless and for the most part dependent, I felt our mutual weakness. Yet I am certain neither of us had ever felt stronger. It makes me think of the Cross of Christ—a symbol of weakness and humiliation, yet at the same time, a symbol of victory and strength.

A stream of faces now flows through my mind—Vicky and Rana, Daddy and Jay, Debbie and Dr. Sam, Jack and Judy, Kerbe, Pam, and many more. Dependent or independent, being served or serving others, we are all trading our weaknesses each day for a far greater glory.

My thoughts focus on one of those faces—Vicky Olivas. I recall that day I first saw her at Sam's lab. The anger in her eyes and voice was iced over by her cool, calloused defense. She didn't seem then to hold the promise of one day being a child of God.

But through Vicky I have learned that, ironically, those who are icy cold—intensely belligerent—may be as close to the Kingdom as those who seem hotly interested in things of God. It is those who are lukewarm toward God who are in deepest trouble, Christ says. Suffering, in a mysterious way, pushes people to either extreme. And Vicky has now left the ice of anger and entered the warmth of heaven. I pray that our ministry may keep pushing thousands more of those who suffer out of their lukewarm complacency and into the vulnerability of either being hot or cold.

For a wheelchair may confine a body that is wasting away. But no wheelchair can confine the soul . . . the soul that is inwardly renewed day by day.

For paralyzed people can walk with the Lord.

Speechless people can talk with the Almighty.

Sightless people can see Jesus.

Deaf people can hear the Word of God.

And those like Tante Corrie, their minds shadowy and obscure, can have the very mind of Christ.

THE BUZZ OF Kerbe's hairdryer in the bathroom reminds me that it is Friday night. She must have a date. *We don't spend much time together*, I think as I look up from my book. I wheel out from under the kitchen table and down the hall to the bathroom. It'll be good to visit with her.

"Got a date?" I yell above the whine of the dryer. She turns, one arm held high above her head to stretch the strands of long brown hair twisted around a roller brush. She fans her hair with the heavy dryer and beams. The guy must be special.

"Yes." She raises her voice above the whine. "A potluck at church tonight."

We chat for a few minutes about her work at Joni and Friends, about the Bible study she's working on, a new milk-shake diet we're both trying, and the new colors Revlon is putting in their lipsticks.

I lean my head against the doorpost of the bathroom and watch her artfully handle her comb, teasing or pulling a curl here and there until her hair bounces like a thick mane.

"You look like a lioness," I laugh.

She turns to attack, threatening to paint a mustache on me with her blue eye pencil.

As I wheel back to my book, she heads for the door, shoulderbag and sweater draped on her arm. She's a gorgeous girl—so very popular at her church. Always a date. Always a party or a social or a Bible study to run off to. Yes, Kerbe fits right in to fast-paced California.

"Want some perfume?" She pauses by the open door and reaches into her purse for the spray atomizer.

"I'm not going anywhere," I say doubtfully.

"That's not the point." She sprays her neck and wrists as she walks toward me. "You don't have to be with anybody else to enjoy a little luxury." I tilt my head as she squirts the scent on my neck.

I like that attitude in Kerbe. On mornings when it's her turn to get me up and ready for work, I always arrive at the office looking like I've wheeled out of the pages of a fashion magazine. A contemporary hairstyle. A new blend of eyeshadow.

After she waves good-by and clicks the door behind her, I sit alone amid the lingering fragrance. My book doesn't hold quite the appeal it had earlier. My thoughts stray back to long-ago days when I was on my feet on a Friday night. Like my cousin, I'd spend an hour in front of the closet deciding what to wear and another hour at the magnifying mirror with a cover stick and make-up. I would leave the house polished and shined to a high gloss.

That was years ago. My only ventures into the dating scene now are when I catch a glimpse into Kerbe's world. I'm in my thirties—a bona fide single. I can't remember my last date. I sigh and shrug my shoulders.

That's not entirely true, I think abruptly. There was a dinner date with the movie gaffer. I shrink a bit, remembering those movie days when I abandoned my 20/20 vision and lived on blind feelings.

I push my attention back to the paragraph I have read and reread—several times. I glance around the kitchen. Judy and I may fix a snack later. We'll play a game of Scrabble. Maybe there's something good on television. I smile as I turn the page. *I could go out on dates like Kerbe. . . . But then again, no guy is exactly beating down my door*, I chuckle to myself.

Singleness. I have the gift whether I like it or not, whether I want it or not.

The evening slips by into a routine weekend. Grocery shopping, clothing sales at the mall, a few hours of painting, a phone call home to my family, an early night on Saturday. On Sunday, Judy and Kerbe get me ready for church.

John MacArthur is away, speaking at some conference, so we have a guest minister this morning. One of the elders leads the opening prayer and hymn. I peer over Judy's shoulder and scan the bulletin for the name of the guest speaker. Nobody I know. During the announcements people rustle in their seats, rummaging in purses and coat jackets for pens, checkbooks, and wallets. A few reach for visitor registration cards in the little pew boxes. I read the fine print in the bulletin, yawn, and look around. Sam Britten and his wife are sitting in a pew across the aisle. Our eyes meet, and we smile our greetings to each other.

After the offering, special music, and another hymn, the guest speaker climbs the steps to the pulpit. I settle down to listen. He introduces his sermon with a story. It gets a little long, and my mind begins to wonder. I slap my thoughts back in line. *Attention! Front and center! This is a worship service, Eareckson.*

My eyes settle on a dark head down front, four or five pews ahead. Thick black hair. My heart skips a beat. It's him. I can't see his face, but I know it's the gaffer. How is it that he's in church—this church? I strain to see, but . . . no, of course, it isn't. It's just someone who looks like him from the back. The tension and adrenaline drain away.

The power of those dormant feelings takes me by surprise, knocks me off balance. From nowhere I can taste the faint disappointment of old pipe dreams and false hopes.

The man tilts his head slightly, revealing a strong jaw and the smooth tanned curve of his neck. He leans to the left and in profile reaches for a Bible in the back of his pew. Other feelings force their way in—longings, wishful thinking, regret. Tiny darts of depression pinprick my resistance.

No. No. This must not happen. I will not sit here and squander this worship service on selfish notions! If I can't concentrate on the sermon, I will rivet these irksome thoughts into line—nail them down once and for all. *We take captive every thought to make it obedient to Christ.*[14] I remember the line from Scripture.

I find, though, that it takes a mountain of effort to pull my eyes away from the back of the man's head. In this instance, I cannot flee. That black hair—my heart knots. *Okay. Okay.* I challenge my feelings. *If that's the way you want to play, I can stand firm; if that's where the battle is, that's where I'll fight it.*

While the speaker drones in the background, I throw on my armor. I focus my eyes on the back of this stranger's head. *Oh, Father . . . You desire mercy rather than judgment. Now be merciful to me, a sinner. And bless You for not judging me according to these awful thoughts. Stupid, silly thoughts that distract me from worshiping You. Be merciful and help me win this battle—for Your honor and for the benefit of this man, whoever he is.*

I take a deep breath and gain more ground. *Father, if this man knows You, get him deeper into Your Word. Help him to obey. If he's dating somebody, convict him if he's messing around. If he's married, hold him to his vows. Don't let him get away with cheating, even if only in his thoughts. Strengthen him against the Devil and the world with all its temptations. Make prayer a big part of his life, and give him extra joy when he makes a stand for You.*

And if there are problems where he works, make his life shine as a real witness to his co-workers. If there is a lingering argument with his mother or father, resolve it, would You? Make his testimony at home consistent with what he believes here in this church. I stare at the man's head, his hair black and shining, and a wave of peace washes over me as I sense victory within grasp. *We're winning,* I smile to the Holy Spirit.

Save him if he's not in Your family. Strengthen him. Refine his faith . . . keep him from lies . . . clear up his bad habits . . . assist him in prayer . . . sustain his health . . . guard his mind . . . deepen his friendships . . . make him into the man You want him to be.

My heart is filled with honest-to-goodness joy. I know, through my prayer, that God is being exalted on this Lord's Day, even if in a most unorthodox manner. The speaker is winding up his message. It's too late for me to pick up his drift, so . . .

Almighty God, Father of all mercies—I begin a silent piece of liturgy I've known since I was a child—*we, Thine unworthy servants, do give Thee most humble and hearty thanks for all Thy goodness and loving kindness to us and to all men. We bless Thee for our creation, preservation, and all the blessings of this life. But above all, for Thine inestimable love in the redemption of the world by our Lord Jesus Christ, for the means of grace and for the hope of glory.*

As the speaker closes his sermon and asks the congregation to rise for the closing prayer, I continue my own petition. *And, we beseech Thee, give us that due sense of all Thy mercies that our hearts may be unfeignedly thankful, and that we may show forth Thy praise not only with our lips in our lives—by giving up ourselves to Thy service and by walking before. Thee in holiness and righteousness all our days through Jesus Christ our Lord. To whom with Thee and the Holy Ghost be all honor and glory, world without end. Amen.*

"Amen," the speaker says from the pulpit, and several in the congregation echo, "Amen." It is noon, and digital watches around me beep the hour in unison. The organist pulls out all the stops as the postlude permits everyone to gather sweaters, books, and purses. People begin shuffling out of the pews.

"I'm starved. Let's hurry home for lunch," Judy says as she steps out of the pew and over my footpedals.

"Let's!" I respond, but I am watching the man down front as he steps into the aisle and begins chatting with several people. I consider—only for a moment—approaching and introducing myself, perhaps mentioning my prayer for him. I instantly dismiss the notion. No. He'd think I was nuts! Or making advances or something. Besides, I don't want the morning's victory to be tarnished. I'll keep it between God and me.

A month or so passes. The memory of that morning battle with temptation has faded. I am at another worship service at Grace Church. Afterward, an acquaintance introduces me to a nice-looking oriental man. He looks familiar, and I study him with a puzzled air. Brightening, I ask him to turn around. He looks just as puzzled. "I want to see the back of your head," I explain. So he complies.

Sure enough, he is the man with the thick, black hair. We laugh when I tell him I prayed for the back of his head just a couple of months ago. I simplify my story, saying something about a boring sermon. We chat for a few moments.

As I start to power my wheelchair toward the exit, I realize I've already forgotten his name, and circle my chair around.

"Ken Tada." He smiles and waves good-by.

OUR MARRIAGE

As water reflects a face, so a man's heart reflects the man.
—Proverbs 27:19

ফ্ৰ

I T IS MAY 1980, and Jay and Rob's new baby, Earecka, is barely a month old. A strong sense of nostalgia overwhelms me every time I see snapshots of their family or imagine Earecka's crib in the corner of the farmhouse bedroom where my things once were.

I recall my visit East last year for Jay's baby shower. Still in faded jeans—with a sewn-in blue elastic band—she didn't let her swelling tummy dissuade her from farm chores around the vegetable garden and horse barn. Sitting in her rocker in the corner of the dining room, she looked resplendent, if not a little self-conscious, among pink and blue crepe-paper streamers and piles of presents. It seemed she would rather get her baby born so that the two of them might tackle farm chores together.

I examine a photo of Jay holding Earecka in her arms and imagine what it would be like—if I could feel, if I had the strength—to hold her. It makes me want to be home. I send a gift and several cards, and telephone the farm often.

I become philosophic. The choices and changes in Jay's life and mine are remarkable. She, in a ministry as a wife and a mother and a farmer—a rich blend of earthy, pragmatic sensibilities like breast-feeding and nurturing and gardening and giving. Me, in a ministry with handicapped people—seminars and churches and curriculum. So different. Do I have regrets? I wonder.

No. I see a parallel between our lives in the rich blend of art and music and speaking and creating, all of which fill my time along with the work of Joni and Friends. I have no doubts. The decisions I have made are choices with which I can rest. Like my older sister, I feel privileged to enjoy depth and soul and meaning in what I do.

I still know who I am—a happy single woman. And I know where I am going—forward with a singular dream.

S OMEBODY'S UP TO something. Why has Ken Tada been invited to my birthday party? I'm certain I see the fine hand of Carol and Twila, two friends from church who are giving the party at their townhouse. Plus, I keep running into this guy. At church. At a recent Young Life function where I spoke. But this birthday party seems a little too suspicious. After all, I don't really know him. Yes, I bet Carol and Twila are trying some matchmaking.

There's no doubt about it. This Ken Tada is an attractive man. He seems comfortable with himself and with other people as he sits on the sofa, gesturing with a can of soda as he speaks. He looks directly at people when he talks to them. He smiles a lot.

When I think no one is looking, I study his face. His thick black hair frames his high, wide cheekbones and dark brown almond eyes. He has a blockish build, square and stocky. As tall as he is and with those broad shoulders, I bet he's Hawaiian. And I bet he's an athlete, judging from his strong neck and arms. He seems reserved, neither brazen nor boisterous, even at this party among many friends. In fact, he seems somewhat shy.

For most of the evening I sit in a corner between the foyer and a living-room chair—the Emily Post thing for me to do in a small room crowded with this many people. I wonder if, at some point, he'll talk to me. But the evening passes, the party dwindles, and the guests begin to drift away. Some help pick up empty punch glasses and dirty paper plates. Most of them stop to say good-by as they funnel toward the door. Ken does too but lingers longer than the others. He leans comfortably against the wall beside my chair and chats. I learn that he lives in the condominium next door and teaches social studies and government at a nearby high school. He also teaches a class called Minority Studies, and I learn that he is not Hawaiian, but Japanese. He coaches football. *I was right about the athletics.* I bring up the subject of mainstreaming handicapped kids in the public school system. He doesn't seem to have very strong opinions about it. Perhaps he's being polite.

Finally, I say I should go; I need to get up early. Ken leaves, apparently to get his coat, and I wave good-by to Carol in the kitchen, thanking her for the party. Twila empties my bulging legbag. I have a long drive home by myself.

As the bag slowly drains into a bottle, Ken returns with his coat over his arm. As he swings it on, he says, "How about if we continue this conversation over dinner next Friday night?"

"I suppose so," I reply. "Sure. I'd like to go."

"Can I pick you up about six?"

"That would be fine."

On the way home, it suddenly occurs to me that I have actually accepted a date from a man—an attractive man. It was so casual, so natural. And while my legbag was draining—of all things! I think back over the scene in my friends' living room and chuckle to myself.

Oh, who cares. I learned the painful way long ago that there's no pretense possible with a handicap. You might as well be real.

"A BOUQUET OF roses? For me? Who are they from?" I ask.

Kerbe slips the tiny card out of its envelope and reads it to me. "Looking forward to Friday . . . Ken Tada."

I rub my nose against a soft yellow petal and sniff the delicate fragrance. "Um . . . nice gesture. They're really pretty."

"Is that all you can say?" Kerbe cries.

"Well, don't you think it's a bit much." I nod at the roses. "I mean, I hardly know him."

She places the vase on my bedroom dresser, fluffing and primping the buds and greenery. A garish satin bow tries to outdo the hothouse arrangement.

I feel slightly uneasy at the sight of the bouquet. Ken seems like a pleasant guy, but I don't want to make a big deal about this dinner date. I've had my share of distorting reality. And I had hoped he would approach it a bit more . . . more dispassionately.

Friday evening Ken arrives promptly, dressed up in a well-tailored blue suit. And with more flowers. I'm glad I dressed for the occasion in my white wool jacket and silk blouse. I just hope he doesn't pop a button in his dress shirt when he lifts me.

Judy and Kerbe give him a crash course in the essentials, explaining how to lift me single-handedly and straighten me in my wheelchair, how to tuck my jacket in the back so it won't wrinkle, and how to pull down the inseams of my slacks. He listens attentively and shows concern for details.

He wheels me outside to his car. I tell him, as graciously as possible, to be mindful of the steep ramp, cracks in the sidewalk, and turning sharp corners. He remarks that he never knew so much was involved in simply pushing a wheelchair. I hope I don't sound like a nag. "You should come to one of our workshops," I tease.

My housemates watch, arms folded, and somewhat amused, as Ken takes off his jacket, rolls up his sleeves, hikes up his pants, and squats by my chair to lift me. He slings my arm around his neck. I can tell from the way he gathers breath and strength that he has lifted weights before. With a mighty karate "hi-yah," he heaves me to his chest. I feel very heavy.

As Judy shows him how to fold my wheelchair and load it in the trunk, Kerbe leans into the car to straighten my jacket. "Have fun," she says with a coquettish smile and slams the door with a wave.

"You really aren't heavy at all," Ken says as he backs out of the driveway. "Light as a feather, in fact."

"Oh, really?" I say mockingly. "Judging from that weight-lifting exercise back there, I would never have known."

Ken steers with one hand while he slides a cassette into the tape deck. "Well, I *have* been working out . . . lifting weights and stuff." He's obviously missed my tongue-in-cheek joke.

"How much weight did you train with?"

"Oh, about 175 pounds."

"A hundred and what?!"

"I wanted to make sure I didn't drop you," he says with a smile. Perhaps the joke is on me.

"Just so you understand that I don't weigh 175 pounds."

"Oh, don't worry," he says with a mischievous grin. "I can tell how much you really weigh."

I return his smile. *So he know how much I weigh. So he's held me in his arms. So I hardly know him. So what!* I don't have the luxury of modesty most women would on a first date. Besides, none of that really matters. What matters is that there are no pretenses. It's a lovely twilight, and our drive on the freeway moves swiftly, as easily and as unencumbered as my conversation with this unassuming and delightfully ordinary guy.

We drive into Marina Del Rey, the flashy neon-lit city on the edge of the ocean. Rows of condominiums rise like giant cylinders of concrete, glass, and metal overlooking the bay and boats and crowded tennis courts. Disco music and siren-red Ferraris, California blonds with their bronzed boyfriends create a kaleidoscope of shiny street color and action everywhere I look. Ken takes several side streets to point out a certain dock on the marina. He looks for the tall mask of a boat belonging to someone he knows. We don't find the boat, but behind the glitter I notice silhouettes of solitary benches, framed by oleanders and palms, that invite couples to sit and gaze at the quiet canals and watch the shadows of dark and silent cabin cruisers putter by.

It's a wild place but not unfriendly.

Ken parks his Oldsmobile in front of a restaurant called The Warehouse. The name fits, I think, as I scan the weathered siding and tin shingles. Barrels with rusty rims, and massive ropes with block and tackle decorate the steps and boardwalk leading to the front door. Ken lifts me out of the car and situates me comfortably in my wheelchair. We look for a ramp but find none.

"You could ask the maître d' about a kitchen entrance," I offer.

"No, we don't have to worry about that." He dusts off his hands as though ready to do more lifting. "I can easily handle those steps." He wheels my chair backward, lodges the large wheels against the first wooden step, tilts me back, and pulls me one step at a time to the boardwalk level. "Easy." He commends himself.

I like his cool-headed approach to those steps. And to me. He's not trying to impress me with a lot of macho muscle-flexing. He just wants me to know he can handle my chair in an unflustered and unconcerned way. He wants to put me at ease. We amble down the boardwalk, stopping to look at the carp that swim in the brightly lit lagoon below.

Inside, the maître d' seats us at a window table. He presents a large, leather-bound menu to Ken. I ask him to place mine on the table. With a smile he flips open my linen napkin and places it on my lap. As the busboy fills our glasses with ice water and the waiter removes our wine glasses, I look out the window at the hundreds of different sailboats moored at the docks. The skyline of masts against the evening sky makes a beautiful seaside picture. *I should paint something like this.*

"You look nice tonight. I like that jacket," Ken says when the waiter leaves.

"Thank you." I inspect my cuffs. "I usually wear it when I'm speaking."

"Like at the Young Life dessert?"

"That's right . . . you were there."

"And I like what you said that night," he says as he leans on his elbow. "You talked about how we can relate to people whose circumstances are different than ours. Like your wheelchair. People don't have to be afraid of it." He picks up his menu and reaches over to open mine. "Or of you."

"What do you mean?" I say as I glance at the menu.

"Well, your wheelchair is one thing . . . people not knowing what to say or do. And the fact that you are well known is another. Some people think you have it all together. That you never struggle." He pauses a moment to study his menu, then closes it and continues. "But I don't need to be afraid just because you're different."

I admire so much confidence.

Ken orders steak and I order shrimp. He leans across the table to give me a forkful of his appetizer. I ask for a drink, and he stretches his arm across the table again and lifts the glass to my mouth. We chat about Joni and Friends, his school, Judy and Kerbe, Young Life, and our mutual friends from church. Our dinners arrive. Before I can ask the waiter to cut up my shrimp, Ken has my knife and fork poised over the plate. "May I?" he asks.

I cannot get over how comfortable, how happy I feel with this man. And I can't help comparing it with the dinner date with the gaffer when I was so nervous, so apprehensive about my handicap—were my inseams straight, was my catheter going to leak, would my make-up smear? I could hardly eat that night, my stomach was in such knots. With Ken, there is no stage fright.

"It seems you've been around disabled people before," I comment, scooping another bite of shrimp.

"Well, yes and no." Ken leans back from the table and dabs the napkin to the corner of his mouth. "Sometimes back I was switching channels on television and came across this program about Special Olympics. There were these great shots of mentally handicapped kids barreling down the track. Some stumbling. Some skipping. Others going flat out." He shakes his head with a grin as he folds his napkin and smooths it by his plate. "And there were these people at the finish line, cheering each one of those kids on. Everyone hugging each other. And then the announcer came on and said something about . . ." He searches for the exact words. "How in this world that seeks perfection, where is there room for those who aren't? Then they said, 'What really matters is not winning, but finishing.'" He is silent for a moment, stroking the folded napkin.

I admire so much physical strength mixed with such sensitivity.

He reaches for his water glass. "So, that's when I signed up at my school to get involved in Special Olympics. I've only worked with them, officiating and whatever, for a couple of years." He puts his glass down and leans on his elbow. "But dating someone in a wheelchair . . . no." He leans back shaking his head. "I've never done that before."

"Well, there's something else you're going to have to do that you've never done before," I say with a sly grin.

"What's that?" He reaches for his wallet to pay the bill.

"My legbag needs emptying."

"Okay," he says as he slips his credit card out of his wallet. "Just tell me what to do." Ken negotiates my wheelchair through the tables toward the door. We pause in front of the alcove that leads to the ladies room on the left and men's room on the right. "Uh . . . we have a problem here."

"Yes. Well, I hadn't thought about this one," I tease.

"Come on, Joni. No jokes," Ken whispers as several people walk around us, going in and out of the restrooms. "What do I do?"

I try to be serious but I can't resist saying, "Is this the part where you're not afraid even though I'm different?" I look at Ken with a Cheshire-cat grin. "Okay. Okay. Let's head outside and find a tree."

"A tree?!"

"Well, it *is* more classy than a fire hydrant, don't you think?"

K EN, DRESSED IN a T-shirt and warm-ups, holds his sport bag in one hand and opens the door with the other. "Can you make it through?" He flattens the glass door further.

I power my wheelchair into the lobby of the athletic club, slowing to let Ken catch up and lead the way. We head for the registration desk. A blonde in a club shirt with terry-cloth bands on her head and wrists greets Ken warmly and passes a clipboard across the counter for him to sign. He steps aside and introduces me. The girl, bubbly and effervescent, waves hello.

"Do I have to sign a guest registration?"

"Oh, no, don't worry about it," she says as she files the clipboard. "Any of Ken's friends are welcome here." She turns and slaps a key on the counter.

I follow Ken to another lobby, just off the main foyer, where tables and chairs in light wood and modern gray fabric are clustered in front of floor-to-ceiling Plexiglas panels through which we can view three racquetball courts. Track lighting illuminates two framed posters at the end of the lobby. A ceiling-mounted television is tuned to a football game, while the soft drumming of low-volume rock music pumps through overhead speakers. Men in sweaty shirts slouch in their chairs and sip juice drinks.

"How about sitting here?" Ken hikes his heavy sport bag onto a table.

I nod, and Ken shuffles a few chairs aside so I can maneuver my wheelchair close to the table. My legs don't fit underneath, and I stick out into the aisle a bit, but checking over my shoulder, I see that people are able to make their way by.

"This will be a nice place to sit," I tell Ken.

"Then you won't mind watching these things for me while I change?" Ken empties his pockets of keys and a wallet, rolls them in a sweat shirt, and slides the bundle across the table to me. "I'll only be a minute." He twirls his locker key on his finger.

As he crosses the room, he stops to slap the backs of a few racquetball buddies. Then he disappears behind a swinging door, and I turn my attention to a man and woman battling on one of the courts on the other side of the glass panel.

"You're a friend of Ken's?" someone says from behind me.

I turn my head as far to the side as possible, straining to see the speaker. "Yes, I am . . . but, uh—"

"Oh . . . I'm sorry . . . let me move around here," he says as he rearranges a chair or two to get by. "Good to see you." The man extends a hand of greeting.

"I'm a little slow in lifting my arm to his, but before the moment turns awkward he reaches forward and clasps his hand around my wrist.

"Yes, I'm a friend of Ken's, and I'm sure glad he brought me here. This is so fascinating." I nod my head in the direction of the two players on the court.

The man knots his hands around the ends of the towel draped over his neck and glances at the competitors. "Yeah, they're pretty good," he says. "That guy on the court is just warming up though." He leans toward the glass panel and slaps it hard to get the player's attention. He points to his watch and then thumbs in the direction of the locker room.

"He and Ken have a challenge game scheduled," he says as he flops into a chair and crosses his feet on the armrest of another.

Ken returns with his sport bag and shoes, greets the man beside me, and waves to the people on the court. His overstuffed bag is packed with towels and fresh folded T-shirts. A row of fifteen or more racquetball gloves dangles from the bag handle.

"Why so many?" I ask.

Ken unsnaps one and stretches it on his hand, securing it at his wrist. "When this one gets sweaty, I've always got more." He gestures at the row of gloves strung like scalps on the handle.

This guy means business, I think.

"Are you okay for a while?" Ken asks over his shoulder as he heads for the court, slapping his racquet against his shorts.

"Fine, just fine. Go for it," I call as he opens the court door.

Ken bounces the ball a few times, twists his body, backswings, and follows through, easily propelling the ball against the frontcourt wall. The ball bounces and returns to his racquet. He swings and hits, repeating the rhythm—hitting and striking and bouncing—over and over again.

His partner leans against the sidewall and wipes sweat from his forehead with his T-shirt. He grabs his racquet and stretches both arms over his head, waiting while Ken warms up.

Ken motions that he's ready and the game begins. His partner serves an easy ball and Ken, just as easily, hits it back. The pace quickens. The ball smacks against the wall with a loud hollow sound. Their shoes squeak, screeching as they stop and turn, each one jockeying for center-court position after he makes his hit. The partner finds his balance and slams the ball deep into the corner. Ken lunges forward but the ball is dead.

He positions himself for another serve. He's all concentration.

The game continues; the score flip-flops. I watch with wonder at the different styles of the two players. Ken's opponent bounces and jumps like a fly off the wall, smacking and swinging. Ken moves with grace; every swing of his arm is elegant. He shines on the court with style and symmetry.

A few passers-by idle near our table, watching the match. I eavesdrop on their comments, all racquetball jargon about style and form. I'm pleased they make so many good observations about Ken. I'm proud of him and feel special that he's sharing this part of his world with me.

The game ends and Ken reaches to shake the hand of his opponent. The man beside me slings his towel over his shoulder and rises to leave. "Not bad," he says. "Your friend's not bad."

I smile in return. I assume Ken has won.

The court door opens, and Ken comes out from behind the silence of the Plexiglas. Sweat pours from his face, and he reaches for a towel in his sport bag. "Are you okay?" he asks, pressing the towel to his neck and forehead.

"Am *I* okay?" I ask in amazement.

He unsnaps his glove. "Yeah . . . well, don't worry. I sweat pounds off like this all the time," he answers. He begins to grab the edges of his soaking T-shirt and then hesitates. "Mind if I change shirts?"

I smile, shrugging my shoulders. He tears off his shirt and throws it over one of the chairs. His dark skin glistens with sweat, highlighting each muscle. He leans near me as he reaches for a dry T-shirt from his bag. Suddenly, the moment seems very personal. Slightly embarrassed, I turn my eyes toward the television.

He rolls his wet shirt into a towel and stuffs it into the bag.

"Let's get something to drink," he suggests and leads the way to the juice bar. Gesturing with the Pepsi in his hand, he points out the locker rooms and clothes boutique, and explains where the sauna and Jacuzzis are.

"If we had time and if you were in your lighter chair," he says, glancing at my heavy power wheelchair, "I could show you the girls' aerobics room." He makes a motion above our heads. The ceiling shakes slightly, and we hear the muffled sound of rock music and screaming, clapping girls.

"No elevator?"

He shakes his head no and shrugs his shoulders as if to say he's sorry.

"That's okay," I comment as I watch a group of girls leave their locker room and head up the stairs. They wear slinky leotards cut high around the thighs.

Their tights, in high-fashion colors of hot pink, turquoise, and yellow, are made of some shiny slick fabric. Little belts and headbands, gold chains and fuzzy leg warmers complete what is obviously a certain "look." They giggle in a cluster and bounce up the steps. "Maybe we can go up there some other time. . . . I don't think I'd fit," I say with a knowing smile.

Ken and I head for my van. As I jab at a toggle switch to open the door, unfold the lift, and lower it to the ground, I applaud Ken on his game. "I don't want to sound gushy, but your coordination and athletic ability are tops."

My chair lurches onto the lift, and I jab at more buttons, which raise me to the floor level. The belts on my chair squeal and grind as I maneuver into the driver's position. My chair slams into the locked position. I am only slightly conscious of my own uncoordinated jerky movements.

Ken climbs in and I head for home.

The house is empty and dark. Judy and Kerbe are out for the evening, but everything is arranged. Judy has set things up as I asked. The cutting board and knives are on the kitchen counter. The table is set for two, with linen napkins, placemats, and candles. The coffee maker is ready on automatic. The meat, onions, mushrooms, and celery are in the refrigerator. Ken is going to show me how to fix stir-fry steak.

While he uses our shower, I wheel around the house and flick on lights. After jabbing at the stereo buttons, I wheel into the kitchen and wait.

When he returns to the kitchen, clean and relaxed in a fresh T-shirt and warm-ups, I explain where everything is. He gets the cooking oil and neatly piles the meat and vegetables next to the cutting board. Examining the edge of the knife, he reaches for the celery and angle cuts a stalk with precision, as though he were one of those Japanese chefs in a sushi bar.

"I learned all this from my mom." He beams proudly and reaches for another piece of celery.

I power closer to the kitchen counter to see how he does it.

"It's the angle that makes for better cooking," he explains. "Here, let me show you how you can do it . . . put your hand here . . . hold the celery like this." His voice falters. "Then . . . then you tilt the knife like so." He glances down at me. He has forgotten, just for the moment, that I cannot use my hands.

Neither of us mention his slip, and he continues to cut up the mushrooms and onions. After fifteen or twenty minutes of cutting, the novelty wears off.

Finally, he lays the knife beside the slabs of steak and leans, straight-armed and silent, against the kitchen counter. I look down at the useless hands folded on my lap, then at his hands, strong and muscled, now white-knuckled as he clenches the edge of the counter.

"I wish you could help me," he whispers, staring out the window above the sink.

"I wish I could too."

After several seconds our eyes meet. He smiles, leans back, and takes a deep breath. Then, picking up the knife, he reaches for a piece of steak and continues cutting and explaining.

JUDY, KERBE, AND I are flying East for Christmas 1980. I leave behind a cold locked house, a half-decorated tree that will dry out, a wreath that never made it to the front door, and greeting cards piled in disarray on the kitchen table. Ashes in the fireplace will make the closed-up house smell stale, I think, regretting that we didn't get it cleaned out before leaving.

Christmas is being divided between California and Maryland. But Christmas will be more like . . . like Christmas home on the farm. A year and a half in California hasn't allowed enough time to initiate new holiday habits and replace old ones, no matter how much I enjoy my life there.

Unlike any other holidays, Christmas draws me to the glow of homey images. Friends and family holding hands in prayer around a table of hot fragrant food. Creamy-skinned aunts who smell of lavender, fur, and silk. Distant cousins you haven't seen for years but greet like long-lost friends. Neighbors dropping by for a piece of pie and a few spirited carols around a cheery wood fire.

Nothing short of a Currier and Ives print can match the sight of the stone farmhouse with its candlelit windows and drifts of powdery snow shouldering the walls. Kathy, who has picked us up at the airport, drives by the barn where woolly horses stamp their feet and impatiently snort blasts of frosty breath as they wait for their bales of hay. We pull into the driveway, and old Charlie Cat, thick with winter fur, jumps up and makes his bed on the toasty hood of the car, tucking his head under his tail against the frigid night air. The thin sheet of ice covering the snow crackles and crunches underneath the weight of my chair as I wheel to the door. I breathe deep and my lungs sting.

"You're home!" Jay shouts with arms spread in welcome. "Just in time for hot chocolate." Cozy smells of vanilla candles and pine garlands invite us in. My arms are weighted and bulky under the heavy down jacket I've borrowed, but I lift them to show Jay I want a hug. She leans down and squeezes me, and the air hisses out of my jacket. "Where's Earecka?" I ask, eager to see my eight-month-old niece.

Jay points to where she sits in her pink pajamas underneath the gaily lit tree, eyeing the wrapped presents. She only half notices my entrance and the stuffed toy I picked up for her at the airport. The lights and tinsel fascinate her more.

"Earecka, come say hi to Aunt Joni," Jay insists.

She spreads her little hands on the floor, hikes her backside into the air, and crawls her way over to my wheelchair. She squats by the right wheel, plucks the wire spokes like strings on a harp, and at the twangy sound, beams me a toothy smile.

"No ordinary kid," I comment to Jay and Rob. "Most would just grab my tire and chew away."

That night I lay in bed and listen to gentle strains of Vivaldi waft through the farmhouse. All of this—the quiet, the music, the comfort of this old house—is mine for the moment. My mind wanders to other Christmases and pleasant memories often rehearsed. I recall one of the most familiar—the last Christmas I spent on my feet, just months before my accident. . . .

It has snowed heavily, and the afternoon has faded into a windy twilight. A high-school friend, Dick, and I decide to brave the unplowed roads in his tough little Volkswagen with chains. By the time we reach downtown Baltimore, the shoppers have left the streets. Dick and I exchange greetings with the smartly styled window mannequins as though they are in our private party. At the corner of Howard Street we pause, enchanted by the cathedral bells up on Mulberry Street ringing down the alley. The bells draw us to the church.

After climbing the slippery steps and stamping the slush from our boots, Dick and I quietly walk up the center aisle, rubbing our hands for warmth. The church is empty except for an old lady kneeling at the altar. We slide into one of the pews, and I lean back to look up into the vaulted silence of the cathedral ceiling, breathing in the scent of prayer candles and lemon-polished wood.

A roaring blast of wind startles me, and the logs of the cabin window creak. My memories fade like an old sepia photograph. As the wind dies, I wander further back to another Christmas. . . .

I am caroling on horseback with my family, clip-cloping down a wet street, stopping under a corner lamppost to sing in the falling snow.

My mind takes a sharp turn; this time toward a Christmas after my accident. . . .

My uncle and cousin have machined a pair of short, sturdy metal skis for my wheelchair. They push me to the top of the snow-packed street near my parents' house, clamp the wheels in place, and belt me in. We edge to the crest of the hill, and with a Geronimo yell, my cousin Eddie heaves my wheelchair forward and jumps on the back of the skis, steering with his weight. We reach the bottom, whooping and hollering, and in one piece.

Outside the frosted bedroom window of the present, bits of snow and ice spray against the glass. I wonder, burying my head underneath Jay's Norwegian comforter, if Charlie Cat has found refuge under the hay in the barn tonight.

The week slips by between parties, dinners, and midnight communion on Christmas Eve. Celebrating the birth of Christ has a wonderful sameness to it—singing in the little candlelit Episcopal church, hearing the familiar story from the book of Luke, and singing old carols. I am glad this has not changed.

Yet I can't help thinking how very different home is. Our family is larger. Jay is a new mother. New friends from Rob's film business drop by. Daddy's hearing and arthritis are getting worse. Kathy is teaching a different grade level. Linda has a new car.

Even my old friends have changed. Betsy is with Young Life in Dallas. Diana is a car-pooling mother, carting her two boys to school and soccer. Steve and Verna are expecting another baby. Dick is married with children of his own. Others have also married. Some have moved.

The pine trees by the farmhouse are taller than I remember. A housing development is taking over a neighboring field. Charlie Cat is no longer the family favorite; a dog named Grizz now rules the roost. It is home, but it is not quite home. Life in Maryland has changed as much as I have.

The night before I leave for California, I sit in the kitchen and talk with my mother and sisters as they do the supper dishes. Mother turns from her place at the sink, her arms immersed in suds, and our eyes meet. I can tell that she is already missing me.

The kitchen phone rings. Mother reaches for a dish towel, wipes her hands, and answers it.

"Yes, this is Mrs. Eareckson. Yes . . . oh, really?" She shoots a glance at me. "Uh-huh . . . it would be nice to meet you too. Just a moment, I'll let you speak to her."

Mother untangles the cord and stretches the receiver toward me. "It's a friend of yours from Los Angeles . . . a man," she adds, widening her eyes. Kathy takes the phone and presses it to my ear.

"Yes? . . . Ken?" I can barely contain the excitement in my voice. I glance at my family. The three of them are silent now, gingerly stacking plates in the cupboard.

"It's my new friend, Ken," I say in a hoarse whisper away from the receiver. "He's the one I told you about . . . remember?" Jay and Mother look at each other questioningly.

"Yes . . . yes, the weather's nice here . . . It is?" I lift my mouth away from the receiver again. "He says it's eighty degrees . . . sunny . . . he's been fishing," I whisper. Jay throws the dish towel over her shoulder, folds her arms, and leans against the sink. She smiles and cups her ear, pretending to be hard-of-hearing.

I close my eyes and lean into the phone. Ken tells me about a party he went to by himself, a racquetball match with a buddy, church on Sunday, and John MacArthur's sermon. He mentions that he met Rana and Vicky for the first time and that he stopped by Joni and Friends.

"How is Judy? . . . Is Kerbe with her parents?" he asks. "You're missing some beautiful, bright days. . . . When are you coming home?"

"Tomorrow. . . . Yes, I . . . I miss you too, Ken."

I watch as Kathy places the receiver back on the wall phone. Ken's voice, warm and close, instantly seems thousands of miles away. I do miss him. Yet as I look around, in a strange way I miss my family too, even though we congregate here in the kitchen to sip hot tea and nibble leftover pie. I don't want things to change, but they have.

Yet I am the one who made the first move, uprooting myself and, in a sense, everyone else. I am the one who chose to leave. And I am the one who probably has changed the most.

In the morning my mother helps Judy pack my suitcase, folding sweaters and filling the corners of the luggage with Christmas gifts. Inside, I sense a nervous knot tightening. I don't know if it's excitement over our return to California or fear of leaving Maryland.

Mother straightens from packing and rubs her forehead. "I don't believe all this stuff will fit." She runs her fingers over a small stack of presents on the bed next to the suitcase, then picks up a package in each hand. "Why don't you leave these gifts soaps here for the next time you come East? You don't have to take them home with you now."

"Did you hear what you just said?" I laugh.

"Yes, I did," she says, sitting on my suitcase lid to snap it shut. "I know exactly what I said." She grabs the luggage handle with both hands and slides the heavy suitcase off the bed and onto the floor. "I saw that look in your eyes when you were talking on the phone last night." She mockingly chides me with a shake of her finger.

"But Mom, I hardly—"

"Never you mind," she says as she smooths the bedspread. "Home, Joni, is where your heart is."

K EN CARRIES ME to the couch while Scruffy scrambles out of the way. It is good to be home in front of a crackling fire after spending a chilly afternoon down at the wharf in San Pedro with the wind whipping off the ocean.

"So you like going places?" I ask as Ken walks into the kitchen, picking up on the conversation we began as we warmed ourselves over Belgian waffles and tea in the corner window of a little café and watched the freighters from Europe and the Orient steam by.

"I do. But I haven't had the chance to travel that much," he calls from the kitchen. I hear a cupboard door open. "What makes you ask?"

"Nothing. I was just thinking of what you said about foreign places this afternoon." I am thinking about other things too. About how much I love being in my own living room with a cozy fire. With Scruffy curled at the end of the couch. With Ken.

"Maybe I'll get to go with you sometimes," he says, returning with a jar of cashews.

"Maybe." The idea of Ken traveling with me is appealing. Of course, visiting hospitals and rehabilitation centers and churches, whether in the States or abroad, doesn't have quite the romantic appeal of those colorful, exotic travel brochures. And anyway, how would it work? We're just friends.

"What do you talk about when you go to those places?" he asks as he plops next to me and munches on a handful of nuts.

I sling my arm up on the side of the couch to gain my balance. "Oh, you know—how God is in control of our lives . . . our disabilities. Lots of disabled people get lost in their questions. So Joni and Friends helps churches reach out to them. But many congregations are at a loss as to what to do. We try to make a dent through workshops, financial aid, counseling letters, materials, and stuff." I tilt my head as he cups his hand and slides some cashews into my mouth. I chew for a moment and then add, "Are you really interested?"

"Yes, I am. What you do is so much different than what I do at school or in Young Life." He pauses and tilts the jar of nuts toward me. "Want any more?"

"Uh-uh, no more for me," I say absently. "What exactly is your work like?"

"Well," Ken says emphatically as he rises to get another log for the fire, "I teach kids all day long at school, one class after the next. I talk to them in the hallways, see them after the last period. Coaching football every afternoon . . . Friday night games." He moves the fireplace screen aside. "And then at Young Life Club every Wednesday night." He throws a log into the back of the fire and nudges the andirons together with his palms.

With his back to me, he stands and brushes the soot off his hands. I admire the way he looks in his blue cotton tie pants, navy sweat shirt, and thongs, with his hair slightly mussed. He remains in front of the fire, warming his hands. The sun drops further from the afternoon sky, and the living room suddenly darkens. His features dim in the fading light, and with his legs slightly spread, he becomes a silhouette against the flames.

"I know how it is to feel lost in your questions, like you're going nowhere. I felt like that in high school." He looks down at his feet. "And I felt like that when I was in college.

"And then somebody asked me to go along on a Young Life weekend to help out . . . you know, more coaching and games with the kids. I wasn't a Christian then." He turns to face me and rubs his forehead. "But when I heard about Christ and all that He did for me . . . even when I could have cared less about Him, well, I knew I couldn't go away the same man."

Although I cannot see his face, I know he is looking at me and that his eyes reflect the wistfulness I hear in his voice. He is silent for a moment, and I wonder at his strength and tenderness. I have seen this gentleness in him before. It is part of the reason I am drawn to him. Like a moth to the flame before him, I am drawn.

"Listen . . . I don't know why God brought us together," he says abruptly, leaving the fire and returning to his place next to me on the couch, "but I do know that I like . . . really like being with you." His almond eyes glisten with the fire's reflection.

"I like you too, Ken."

"No . . . I mean . . ." He shakes his head and twists on the couch to face me better. "I mean that I've never . . . well, never felt so sure about—"

"Yes?" I think I know what he wants to say, and I am getting awfully nervous inside.

"Joni, I tell you things about myself that I don't tell just anybody. And I feel strong . . . not just emotionally, but spiritually too, when I'm with you." He reaches for the cashew jar on the coffee table and twists the lid back and forth. "But . . . but, I am afraid."

He looks up. "It's like this," he says, placing the jar back on the table. "When kids in Young Life come to me, all mixed up because they're dating somebody steadily and yet . . . yet going nowhere, they ask the most unbelievable questions. Like, 'How do I know if she is God's will for my life, Mr. Tada?'" He gestures with his hand in exasperation. "Or, there are kids who break up with their boyfriends and then cry on my desk because 'he won't talk to me anymore, Mr. Tada.'" He waves the other hand.

"And you know what I tell them?" He looks at me directly, the fire highlighting the side of his face. "I tell them that when they decide to date somebody seriously, it's going to end up one of two ways. Either they will marry that person . . . or they'll break up and never be really close again."

There is a gentle rap at the front door. Scruffy bounds off the couch. The handle turns and Kerbe peers around the corner. "Hi, guys," she says a little timidly. "Sorry to interrupt."

Ken takes a deep breath, greets her warmly, and goes to help her with her packages. I sigh deeply too, uncertain whether I am pleased or sorry we have been interrupted. "No bother at all, Kerbe. It's time I got off this couch anyway." I yawn, stretching out my stiff arms and giving them a spasm. "When you get through, could you help me up?"

They walk into the kitchen, flick on the light, and pile her sweater, packages, and purse on the table. Ken returns to the living room, shoves the coffee table aside, and angles the wheelchair for a transfer. They heave me into my chair and straighten my sweat shirt.

"I'll, uh, I'll be in my room," Kerbe says a bit awkwardly. "I've got a few things . . . um, drawers to straighten, you know." She backs out of the living room with a grin and a little wave. Down the hallway, her bedroom door clicks behind her.

Ken stands in front of me, holding Scruffy in his arms, gently rubbing her neck. I wait a moment for him to speak and then pick up the thread of conversation myself. "So you're afraid that if we keep spending time together . . . as friends or whatever—"

"That's just it, Joni. It's awfully hard for two people . . . a man and woman in their thirties, single . . . it's hard to be just friends. I want it that way, really. But then again, I don't," Ken says. "I'm afraid I'm going to have to swallow the same advice I give those high school kids. . . ." His voice drifts off.

He sets Scruffy on the floor and places his hands on the armrests of my wheelchair. "I cannot imagine not being close to you." He wraps his hand around the back of my neck and leans to kiss me.

The fire crackles.

"I'm afraid," I whisper.

"I know. So am I."

"OKAY, WHAT'S NEXT?" Ken strides alongside my wheelchair, juggling two boxes of popcorn, an ice cream bar, and Pepsis in his hands. His Mickey Mouse ears begin to slip off his head, and he wiggles a hand free just in time to grab them. This is the other side of the serious-minded teacher—the grown-up kid at Disneyland.

"Let's try that wild roller-coaster ride on the other side of the park," I decide. "I've never been on it before . . . but you look strong enough. I think we can handle it."

"Great, let's go!" Ken moves into high gear, plops his Mickey Mouse hat on my head, and begins unloading his armful on my lap. "If we want to make it, we've got to really move. The lines to that thing are blocks long." He wedges a box of popcorn between my knees.

I smile smugly and sashay my wheelchair down the walkway at slow speed.

"What's with you?" Ken runs behind the back of my chair and heaves his weight against it. "We haven't got all day."

"Aha . . . that's where I've got a secret," I say coyly.

"What are you talking about?"

"You'll see."

We arrive at the roller coaster and push through the thick lines snaking their way to the entrance of the ride. "Pardon me . . . excuse me please . . . watch your toes . . . sorry," I apologize as I inch through the crowd.

Ken, dumfounded, follows behind. After I nearly scrape somebody's shins, he leans down to my ear and hoarsely whispers, "What do you think you're doing? We just can't cut in front like this."

"I'm not cutting in front," I whisper. "I'm cutting in back."

We arrive at the exit where a cute boy in an Alpine suit welcomes us and swings the gate wide to let us enter.

"See?" I say matter-of-factly.

"Be careful," the boy warns as he ushers us in. We flatten ourselves against a wall as a flow of people stream toward the exit. We are salmon swimming upstream.

Amid the noise of the crowd and the clank of gears, Ken and our guide in the Alpine suit lift me into the waiting bobsled. Hurriedly the boy buckles me in while Ken lowers himself behind me. A car slams into the back of our sled, and Ken grips me with his arms and straddled legs as our toboggan lurches forward.

"I'm not ready, I'm not ready," I yell.

Our car slides easily down the track. "Am I in?" I shout.

The sled jerks to a halt and then with a "click-click" engages onto the chain that pulls us up the steep incline. "Yes, you're in . . . what else do you want me to do?" Ken yells back.

"I don't know. I think . . . I think I'm going to die!"

The roller coaster track climbs through a mountainous interior, an air-conditioned blast hits our faces, and darkness blankets our car just when we reach the top where our sled jerks again as the chain releases. We plunge off the crest. People scream into the downhill sweep, into the dark recesses of the mountain.

"Hold me . . . hold me!" I shriek in terror as my body slams from one side of the sled to the other, the car whipping and jolting down the track. "I don't have any balance!"

"What?" Ken hollers.

He releases his grip from his handholds and slips further down into the seat, pulling my body against his chest. With no way to hold on, both of us are at the mercy of the sled's racing twists and turns. Our bodies jam against the side as the sled snaps around a corner. He giggles hysterically.

After many long minutes, the sled begins to slow and then skids to a halt in front of the exit.

"How was it?" Our Alpine boy laughs as he sees us lying prone, exhausted, at the bottom of the sled. "Here, let me help." He offers a hand. "Oh, by the way, we occasionally let disabled people ride twice if they want . . . saves you the hassle of getting in and out again."

"You're kidding," I say with sarcasm. "You guys trying to get rid of us?"

"Hey, let's do it, Jon." Ken laughs with glee, scooting himself up behind me again. Another car slams into ours and jolts us forward.

"Wh-what? Hey, no," I say emphatically. "Not again. . . ." More cars hit us from behind and propel us down the track.

"Too late!" Ken laughs infectiously, squeezing my ribs.

Later, by the exit, we stop and catch our breath, puffing and wheezing. I fling my arm against him. "You jerk," I laugh, "I could have been killed. Seriously."

"Excuuuuuse me." He bows in jest. "I thought you were immortal."

"Youuuuu, you . . ." I power my wheels toward his toes.

As evening approaches, Disneyland become a sparkle of lights—truly a magic kingdom. A quartet sings under a glimmering streetlamp on the corner. Big Belgian horses plod along Main Street hauling old-fashioned streetcars. The strains of a Dixieland band playing Southern favorites drift our way. The aroma of hot buttered popcorn and roasted nuts fills the night air, and we head for a restaurant in the French Quarter.

For our dinner, Ken extravagantly orders every hors d'oeuvre on the menu.

"Being disabled has its advantages," Ken says, licking his fingers. "No standing in lines . . . going in the exits . . . getting on rides twice," he lists as he wipes his hands on his napkin. "Even your parking places are bigger."

He pushes away several dishes from between us and lightly touches the delicate folds of the single carnation centerpiece. "Knowing you is a real plus . . . in more ways than one." He smiles warmly. He rubs his hands together as though pleased with himself, with us. "This is great, Joni. Don't you sense it?"

I do sense it. But I also sense that the day has caught us up in a fairy-tale world of make-believe, where real life takes a back seat to daydreams and fantasies. A place where nobody frowns. A place where you can wish upon a star.

I'm having as much fun as he is, I confess to myself. But I also know that my wheelchair batteries can't last much longer and that I'm keeping an eye on a new pressure sore. That it's getting late and that it takes two hours to drive home. And that, once there, it will take another two hours for Kerbe to get me ready for bed. Somehow these mundane things that are so crucial to my existence and so out of my control have a way of bolting me to the earth.

But Ken is on cloud nine. "Did I say something wrong?" He leans forward.

"Oh . . . no, not at all." I shake my head. "I hate to spoil things, but it is getting late," I suggest.

During the long walk through the emptying parking lot, Ken recounts the times we've shared recently. The party at Carol and Twila's. Our first date at the marina. Dinners at my house. Restaurants. Church. Young Life Club. Over three months have passed since we started dating. Through it all, I've watched Ken's affections for me deepen—every time we pray, every time we talk on the phone, every time we sit together at church or ride in the car.

And every thing I sense his feelings increase, I double-check my own. What do I feel?

Our surreal day at Disneyland has frightened me in an odd way. The fantasy pushes me into a corner, makes me face what is happening in real life. Three months have passed and we have had no disagreements. No arguments. Nothing unpleasant. Everything is like the easy rides at Disneyland—no roller-coaster plunges. I yearn to probe deeper beneath the surface of what is going on between Ken and me. To find real substance, rock-bottom reality. *Where, oh where are we going?*

On the long drive home on the freeway I am quiet, and Ken asks me several times if I'm okay. I say, "Yes, I'm just thinking."

"About us?" he questions.

I turn to him and nod.

"I thought we had a great time."

"We did, Ken . . . Disneyland's always a good time."

"But it's more than that, Jon. We could have been anywhere today—the beach, a . . . a football game, a—"

It's clear his heart is ahead of mine. I feel guilty.

"You're right." I smile. "Just give me time to catch up with you."

He gives me a funny look. I can tell he doesn't know what I mean.

THIS IS THE first time I've seen Jack Fischer since he broke his neck. He sits across from Ken and me at the coffee shop and talks easily about his gymnastic buddies, smiling in honest pride for his friends who have gone on to National Championships or to the Olympics.

Ken likes Jack. That's understandable. They are both athletes. I lean on the armrest of my wheelchair and enjoy their conversation about sports and competition.

The parallel bars were Jack's favorite, and he describes his routines and his dismounts. He rambles on about his routine on the rings. The way he used to do an iron cross. Jack's year and a half of life as a quadriplegic hasn't rubbed away his spirit or the single-minded drive that made him a world-class gymnast. He is still world-class—even though he sits paralyzed in his wheelchair.

His boyish enthusiasm is charming. His eyes and smile flash like some clean-cut crystal—handsome, engaging. Although he can no longer snap his body into angular taut command, he is still muscular and sturdy; he adjusts himself, occasionally straightening his arms against his chair to shift his weight. Ken and I are impressed with his ability—*a super-quad*. I smile to myself.

Jack begins to ask me questions about adjusting and coping. I sense that he is not so much looking for answers as wanting to swap stepping-stone stories. We talk about courage and grace under pressure, about Christ and His gifts of endurance and patience, self-control and steadfastness. I can tell none of these gifts have been easily received. Instead of submitting with open palms, I picture

Jack tightly clasping his weak and disabled hands around promises from the Bible, pulling down from heaven what he knows is his in Christ.

It's Ken's turn to lean on his elbow, smile, and listen.

Now, Jack tells us, he is looking for an apartment near our end of the valley and wants to enroll in Sam Britten's Center of achievement at the university. He has plans to improve. Before we leave, we watch him manage a difficult transfer from his wheelchair to his car.

"You liked him, didn't you," I comment to Ken as we watch the car drive away.

"Yeah. He kind of reminds me of Vicky Olivas. You know . . . against all odds?" Ken pushes the toggle switch on the side of my van.

I shiver slightly in the night air, waiting for the mechanical lift to lower. "They're a lot alike in many ways, aren't they?" I propose as I power my chair toward the lift. "I mean . . ." I lodge my hand against the toggle switch that raises me to the van. "People like Vicky or Jack are easy . . . fun to be around. The models-of-inspiration type," I tease, swinging the lift into the van and ducking my head. Ken finishes clamping the spare seat in the driver's alcove.

"Don't you count yourself in the club?" Ken questions as he climbs into the seat and places his arm in my driving mechanism, preparing to take the controls for the long drive home. I position my chair behind him so I can see his face in the rear-view mirror.

"Do you think I'm an inspirational role model?"

"Sure you are." He tilts his head to catch my eye in the mirror. "Why? . . . Don't you like the idea?" Ken pokes buttons on the control box and starts the engine.

I smirk. "Well, I'm not even sure Jack or Vicky would relish the idea. I mean, it's neat to inspire others . . ." I pause to gather my words. "But I tend to think being typecast as an 'inspiration' puts you at a distance from people. You know, as though you were some plaster-of-Paris saint who doesn't live in the same world."

"Not so." He frowns. "Your example helps me to relate to a real world . . . to people like Jack."

"Ken," I say with emphasis, "Jack is the exception. Even Vicky, as tough as she has it, is an exception. Like I said earlier . . . they are easy, even fun to be around. You hardly notice their limitation. They make you feel good, they boost your—"

"I don't know what you're talking about," Ken interrupts, a bit miffed. Our discussion—almost our first healthy, solid disagreement—is cut short. Ken's words trail off, and he becomes preoccupied, or perhaps pretends to be, with the traffic as he steers onto the freeway. The topic is dropped.

The following Saturday Rana and I spend the afternoon at an aerobic Dance-A-Thon being sponsored by friends of Twila and Carol to raise money for a young man with severe cerebral palsy. In a wheelchair and unable to speak, Paul needs an expensive electronic communicator to replace his old wordboard. The funds from the Dance-A-Thon will be used to purchase the equipment through Joni and Friends.

Rana and I sit on the sidelines of the gymnasium watching the girls sweat through their jumping jacks, knee bends, and dance routines in pulsing time with the blaring cassette player. I look at my watch. They've been at it for hours, and hundreds of dollars have been raised. Besides that, I have a speaking engagement tonight at Los Angeles Baptist College.

"What time is Ken getting here with Paul?" Rana glances at her own watch and rubs the back of her neck. "I'm getting tired just looking at them." She motions toward the group.

I cast an anxious look toward the gymnasium entrance. "He should be here now." The dancers want to meet Paul and present the check to him in person.

While the music continues and the gymnasium resounds with bouncing, screaming girls, Sue, the aerobics leader, trots over to us, wiping her forehead with a towel. "We can't continue much longer, Joni," she sighs. "Do you know where your friend Paul might be?"

"No, but we'll find out," I resolve, putting my chair on high and speeding toward the gymnasium door. "Rana," I call, "telephone the nursing home, would you? And find out if anything's happened. I'll wait for Ken and Paul on the corner."

The clouds are darkening and the wind has picked up. I huddle in my coat and wheel up and down the sidewalk, watching for Ken's car. Finally, it skids to a halt at the curb.

"Where were you?" I challenge as soon as Ken opens the door.

"I'll explain later." He brushes off my question as he races to get Paul's wheelchair out of the trunk. "Are we too late?"

When the three of us get to the gym, the noise has diminished considerably. Most of the girls are sitting and talking in small groups or doing stretching exercises to cool down. They lightly applaud when they spot Paul being pushed by Ken.

Paul's hair is matted, shiny with grease in a few places. His shirt is stained and unevenly buttoned. Dried food is caked on his pants; smudges of the same are on his wheelchair. He sits with his legs drawn tightly in a stiff position and his gnarled and twisted hands clasp his wordboard. When he smiles, he shows yellowed teeth that need better care. I know the staff at his home are often overworked and underpaid, but I wish they would have made a better effort to get Paul ready today. Maybe Ken could have—should have—helped him.

After the presentation Paul grins at the girls and points to letters and words on his board. "Thank . . . you . . . very much . . . ," he communicates to them. His eyes glisten in gratitude.

By now I am late for my speaking engagement at the college. Outside, it is dark. A light drizzle begins to fall as Ken and Rana load Paul and me into my van.

I wait until we are on our way to ask, "Ken, what happened at Paul's place?" He doesn't answer me and I don't press it. Perhaps something happened that he doesn't want to mention in front of Paul.

"Good grief," Rana exclaims, leaning forward in the driver's seat. "It's really coming down. Do you know how far the college is up this road?" The windshield wipers slap away water, and through the window we can make out the smeary image of lights in the distance. "I see it!" She accelerates.

I'm late getting to the platform. I'm also wet and my wool sweater stinks. Even the notes I prepared have ink smears. I glance at Rana, sitting with Ken and Paul at the end of the front row of the field house. She shrugs her shoulders as if to say, "I wish I could help, but you're on your own." The place is packed; the weather hasn't put a damper on the students' enthusiasm. I wish I could say the same.

I'm relieved when the meeting is over, although it goes well. That in itself makes me ashamed of my irritation with Ken and Paul and the people at the nursing home. How can I harbor that attitude while talking about the grace of God?

On our way back to the nursing home, we stop at an all-night coffee shop for a snack. I hope it will dispel the difficulties of the day with a pleasant ending. Rana and Paul sit across from Ken and me. Paul points to a photo of a hamburger on the menu.

When our food arrives, I watch Paul grab at his hamburger with his spastic hands. He insists on feeding himself. His saliva mixes with the burger dressing and drools over his beard as he throws his head back and chews with his mouth open. He loses bits of his hamburger and bun this way, but I admire him for making the effort. Rana occasionally wipes his mouth. Ken is quiet and does not look up from his sandwich.

Before the meal ends, Paul motions toward the restroom. Rana and I look at Ken. No legbags this time. No trees, quick and convenient.

Ken shoots me a nervous glance before he pushes Paul into the men's room. He will have to lift Paul from his wheelchair, a man he only met today, and be his hands. "I hope they remember to use the wordboard . . . it's a first for Ken," I say to Rana with a weak smile.

It is later. Much later. Paul is home. Rana is gone. My wool sweater is drier. We close up the van and stand in my open garage. The storm has passed out of the valley and a slivered moon shines brighter than it should. Ken is still quiet, and I still want to end the evening on a nicer note.

"Did you . . . ah . . . manage okay with Paul?" I want to let him know that I understand his discomfort.

Ken shoves his hands in his pockets and shrugs his shoulders. "I suppose so. He explained how to, you know . . . do things . . . on his wordboard." He kicks an imaginary stone.

I picture the scene at the coffee shop: Paul's pride in feeding himself, refusing Rana's help, happily shaking his head no. The rest of us ignoring his mess. And Ken's absorption with his sandwich.

I imagine the scene in the bathroom. "It wasn't easy . . . was it?" I offer.

Ken doesn't respond.

"It . . . uh, wasn't any easier earlier at the nursing home. That's why you were so late. . . . Am I right?"

Ken slowly nods his head.

I continue, "I guess the place didn't—"

"The smell . . ." Ken looks up. "The place had this awful smell. I just didn't want to stay in there, Joni. They were getting Paul dressed, and I felt I couldn't help anyway. I waited outside, but they forgot to tell me when he was ready. That made us late." He waits for my reaction. "Joni, it was the smell. It was the drooling. It was . . . everything!"

I power my wheelchair toward the garage door, facing the night and the moon. "You know . . ." I breathe deeply. "Paul was in church the other week. He was watching me when you gave me that drink of water . . . remember, you held the cup to my mouth?" I look back at Ken. He nods.

"Well, you got involved in another conversation, but I noticed Paul motioning to me. I powered my wheelchair over to him, and he started pointing to his wordboard." Ken is looking directly at me now.

"You know what he said? He said, 'Joni, I am sorry you cannot use your hands.'"

We stand in the dark garage, our breath white and frosty in the moonlight flooding the concrete floor.

"Is what I'm saying making sense?" I feel a lump in my throat.

Ken still has his hands in his pockets, like a little boy caught in some mischief and about to be lectured—quiet, remorseful.

"Ken," I begin softly, "it's people like Paul, if anybody, who are the real inspirations. Not Jack. Not Vicky. Not me. It's like the last are the first, the foolish are the wise, and the weak are the strong." I stop to let my words sink in. "And . . . and I'm afraid you have me on some . . . some pedestal. Like one of those plaster-of-Paris saints." I turn my chair so I face Ken squarely, and in the moonlight I cast a long shadow over him. In the darkness I cannot see his face.

"I feel like I know the real you." He speaks, and his voice almost startles me.

"You don't know me," I chide. "You know a book. A movie. A record album. You take me to these speaking engagements. But there are things about me that would turn your stomach, just as surely as your stomach turned tonight at that coffee shop or in that bathroom," I insist. When he doesn't speak, I continue,

"And I'm not just talking about bathrooms and legbags and being paralyzed. There are things about me . . . times when I'm not very nice to be around."

"So what are you saying?" Ken steps out of my shadow.

"I don't know . . . I don't know," I reply. "It's been months, and our friendship doesn't seem like it's going anywhere. Not forward. Not deeper. I haven't met your family . . . uh . . ." I grab at straws. "You're emotional about me . . . my feelings nowhere match yours. Why," I laugh, "this is the closest we've ever come to having a real disagreement." I shake my head in disbelief.

"So?"

"So I think we should end it. Here. Now. While it doesn't hurt."

Ken's eyes reflect the moonlight and I think I see tears. My heart knots and I look away.

"OH. OH, NO, not again." The tone in Judy's voice alarms me.

"What? What's wrong?" I ask.

She removes the pillows stuffed behind me and slowly turns me from my side onto my back. "You know that red spot we've been watching? Well, it's open . . . your old pressure sore is open."

I wince and squirm my head into the pillow.

"I'm so sorry," she offers, placing her hands on my shoulders.

Judy scratches her head. "This time you'll be in bed for quite a while, I'm afraid."

"A week? A month? How bad is it?"

She presses her lips, afraid to prophesy. She rolls me on my side to examine the skin once more. "It's bad." Pulling up my covers, she adds, "Let's just take one week at a time."

In the silence of the next moments the implications begin to hit us: telling the office, bringing work home, arranging for different people to take care of me, canceling speaking engagements, curtailing painting, rearranging meals and bedroom furniture and housekeeping and . . .

"Onward and upward," Judy, the eternal optimist, sighs with a smile. "We'll do it."

"Yeah," I exhale. "We did it before. With God's grace I guess we'll do it again," I murmur, turning my head to the wall.

Drat it! Why didn't I watch this sore more closely. I remember my terrible times of depression last year when I spent three months in bed waiting for the same sore to heal. But this time I sense anger mounting.

Once again, I am not wrestling against the flesh and blood of a pressure sore, but against an unseen foe. It is a spiritual struggle with an enemy who uses my own attitudes and thoughts as weapons against me.

"Judy, call Rana and Vicky and Sam Britten and anybody else you can think of. Have them pray. . . . I need prayer." Even as I make the request, I feel my anger subside.

Judy scribbles names on a notepad by the television. "Do you want me to call Ken?"

Automatically I say, "Yes . . . please call Ken too." It's been days since I've seen him or talked to him. Yet deep inside, for some reason, I want . . . I long . . . for him to know. And to pray. At the same time I wonder if I am being fair to him and to his feelings.

Ken telephones the next day. He wants to come over after school. I say yes. Then I brood. What do we have to say to each other?

He arrives with flowers and a stuffed rabbit. I want to apologize for bothering him with my problems. I attempt to keep a friendly but obvious distance between us, weighing my words, playing the role of a casual friend.

"It's very nice of you to drive all the way out here," I say politely with a stiff smile.

Ken gives me a funny look and places the stuffed animal on my dresser. "What are you talking about? I've driven out here lots of times," he says, casually unwrapping the flowers. "Here. Let me put these in water. I'll be right back."

While he's gone, I decide I am being silly. I am the one who told Judy to call him. I am the one who told him it was fine to come over. So why am I playing this coy little game?

"So much for telling you we're through," I mumble when he walks back into my bedroom with the vase of flowers.

He stops midway between the door and my dresser. "Yeah, well . . . you never said we couldn't be friends."

His words remind me of the scene in front of the fireplace a few months earlier. *Most people either end up married or go their separate ways.* I was afraid then and I'm afraid now. Afraid I'll hurt him. Or myself. But perhaps he is afraid too, knowing it's a risk being with me. If so, he doesn't show it.

"Here." He pulls a bloom from the vase and extends it to me. "Smells nice, doesn't it?" I nod a little sheepishly. "How about if I do some shopping, then fix dinner for you and Judy? I'd be happy to feed you . . . maybe we'll read later." He reaches into his hip pocket and pulls out a paperback. "It's a book about friendship." He holds it up and grins.

Minutes later I hear the front door close behind him. When he returns with grocery bags, I listen to a mumbled conversation between him and Judy, to the cozy, comfortable sounds of clanging pots and running water. Familiar sounds, yet special.

Ken sets up a TV tray by my bedside. On it arranges a placemat and linen napkin, a candle, and little salt-and-pepper shakers. He raises the head of my bed and straightens the collar on my flannel pajama top. Situating a chair between my bed and the tray table, he announces, "Dinner is served, madam."

I feel so vulnerable, so powerless, lying here as he spoons soup into my mouth and wipes my chin. Flat on my back, the world—other people—take on a different posture. I seem so weak and dependent; they seem so strong and capable. Like Ken. He takes control tonight as though a crisis has hit and he has assumed command. He cleans away the dishes, folds the tray table, and wipes the crumbs off my blanket. He decides on creative ways to make the evening meaningful, even enjoyable, in spite of my bedridden condition. We play backgammon. He reads to me from his friendship book and from the Bible. He is the one who suggests that we pray together, and he does the praying. He tells me not to worry and that he'll be back tomorrow.

"Tomorrow," I lament. "It's only been a couple of days, and I feel like I've been in this bed forever. Maybe I'll forget how to write . . . or paint. Maybe I've done serious damage to this sore and—"

"Stop . . . just stop it." Ken has a fatherly look about him. "Remember what we read out of Lamentations 3 earlier? His compassions never cease or fail. They are new every morning."

I nod my head, yes.

"God gave you grace for today. Sufficient . . . just for today and this day only. There's no grace available yet for tomorrow's problems." He places his hand on my forehead and presses slightly, as if to press his point. "So quit worrying."

He folds his hands behind his head and arches in a stretch, laughing. "Besides, didn't I hear you say that very thing at a speaking deal recently?"

Unlike my last stint in bed, this time the weeks seem to fly by. Ken paints the floorboards in the living room. He hikes my bedroom door off its hinges, scrapes it, seals it, and gives it a new coat. Occasionally, he helps Judy and Kerbe with chores around the house.

"What in the world . . . ?" I'm surprised one day when he lugs my big, clumsy wooden art easel into my bedroom. "What are you going to do with that thing?"

"It's not what I'm going to do," he pants and leans the heavy easel against a wall, "it's what you're going to do." He wipes his forehead with the sleeve of his sweat shirt.

"Paint? You expect me to paint while lying on my back?"

"Sure," Ken says, surveying the width of my mattress with his hands. "We can spread-eagle the tripod right over your bed. I think with a few pillows propped here and there you'll be able to reach your canvas."

He holds up one of my brushes as if to measure its length, starts to place it in my mouth, thinks twice, and then leans down to kiss me instead.

My heart races, and I tilt my head to invite his kiss. I don't have time to examine my feelings. All I know is his compassion and tenderness, his warmth and acceptance of me—with my dirty hair, greasy face, and bad breath. Strangely, a verse— "We love . . . because He first loved us"[1]—keeps ringing in my ears, and I wonder as this new compulsion, this desire to submit and let him lead the way, takes hold. I hold on to his kiss with my lips, inviting him to linger. The moment is warm and tender, casting off fears and misgivings. He presses his cheek to mine and strokes my hair off my forehead.

"Just friends . . . right?" He smiles with mischief.

S UMMER COMES HOT and dry. The Santa Ana winds blow over the north ridge, sweeping the scent of gardenia and roses through the open sliding glass door of my bedroom. Summer 1981. It's been three years since the movie, two years since my move to California, and one year since Ken came into my life.

And today marks the end of my two-month stay in bed with this pressure sore. It is completely healed now and I can get up.

To celebrate, my mother and father have come for a visit. They are also here to meet Ken, of course. Mom has been curious about him ever since Christmas.

All this calls for a complete change of scenery. Fresh air breezing through the bedroom is not enough to sweep away the stale sameness of a bed and four walls. On an impulse, we decide to go camping, and Ken, Rana, and Vicky agree to go with us. Ken and Judy, Mom and Dad throw tents, sleeping bags, and fishing gear into the van.

Ken steers, Judy navigates, and Vicky, Rana, and I sit in the back with my parents. Hearts full and happy, we sing. Camping songs. Oldies but goodies. We are singing hymns as we climb out of the valley onto the plateau of the north desert, past the little town of Mojave—up out of the hot plains and into the back side of the cool Sierra mountains.

Out of bed at last, surrounded by family and friends, and out in the grandness of God's creation, I no longer need the special grace He has given me during the last two months. Yet I sense it lingering near, bright and powerful, like a sweet scent of charged air after a lightning storm. Grace lifts my spirits as high as the lofty peaks we pass. Grace makes me smile with gratitude, humbly thanking the

Father for giving me the chance to enjoy the beauty of ponderosa pines and sparkling lakes. Grace makes me feel as free as the wind that gusts through our open windows and ruffles my hair. *God, you are so good to me.* And I wonder at how powerful grace must be to overrule any residue of displeasure from pressure sores and months in bed.

It's joy, genuine joy, I feel. And yes, maybe Ken has something to do with it, I consider as I watch the wind toss his dark hair. Perhaps he too is a gift from God.

Tents are pitched and a fire is lit. My heart tugs a little, wishing I could help the others set up camp. But I'm not the only one who feels this way, I know. Vicky sits next to me in her wheelchair, and Daddy—the man who once pitched tents everywhere from Mexico to the Yukon—now stands and watches. But his arthritis and my disability don't deter our camping spirit. We decide to gather firewood, and my wheelchair makes a perfect truck for hauling the logs Daddy piles on my lap.

The sun settles behind the west side of the mountains, tinting the lake and trees a dusky mauve. The glow is eerie and golden, and for a moment we become almost as still as the surrounding rocks and trees as we watch the twilight phenomenon from our picnic table.

Ken and Rana set up the Coleman stove, and I turn to Vicky beside me. "What do you think of him?" I say out of the side of my mouth.

"He's a gift . . . a real gift," she says with a sly smile.

Despite my weariness with my confinement during the past months, I am happy when Judy and Mom tuck the heavy down comforter around me in my fold-out bed. How quickly I've forgotten the unpleasant nuisances linked with the idea of "bed." I fight off sleep to listen to the rushing wind in the tops of the ponderosas and watch the moonlight make dancing patterns on the sloping roof of the tent. Someone pumps hissing propane into a lantern, and I can hear Rana and Vicky murmuring in the tent next door. Ken slaps and punches the down of his sleeping bag outside by the fire. Snug, comforting sounds . . .

Ken takes my parents and me fishing on the high mountain lake while Rana and Vicky drive to Mammoth Mountain. He rents two boats—one for my parents and Judy, and one for us—and chains the two together. I'm comfortable in a beach chair wedged in the bow as we drift toward the shady lake edges where Ken tells us the fish are big and fat. We believe him.

He hooks and baits two rods and explains foreign words like "casting" and "reeling" to my mother and father. We laugh. Who cares if we catch anything— we're glad to be together.

Ken prepares a rod for me. "Here," he says, lodging it in my beach chair. "This is for your fish."

"But I didn't cast . . . you did," I protest lightly.

"Yeah, and you won't reel the fish in either. But you're still holding and watching and that makes it yours."

Our boats drift on the wind-rippled lake, and we chat idly and drink sodas. Mother shatters the silence of the lake with a sudden scream and turns her head away from the fighting fish on the end of her line. Ken tells her how to reel it in. She refuses to look but obediently cranks the line. Ken nets the trout, and we try to conceal our excitement so that some distant fishermen who occasionally look our way will not think we are novices.

I'm designated the official "keeper of the fish." Ken strings the trout by their gills through a metal clothespin that he then snaps to my armsplint. I dangle my hand in the water and watch the captive fish squirm and swim alongside our drifting boat. I feel sorry for them and name each of them, hoping to persuade Ken to release our tribe.

Ken and I notice that my father, who says little and sits with his back turned to us, seems preoccupied. Occasionally, he mumbles and shakes his head. Finally, Ken gingerly steps into the other boat to investigate. In dismay he holds up a tangle of knots looped around the reel. My left-handed father has reeled in his line backward.

Our loud and spontaneous laughter rings across the mountain lake. Poor Ken! Fishing is such a science to him. But he teasingly shakes his finger at Daddy and then proceeds to untangle the mess while the rest of us enjoy the sun and scenery, nearly forgetting our lines in the water.

I keep watching him as nearly an hour passes. He works steadily and patiently, pulling a bit here and looping a line there. Mother insists that he stop and relax, but he is committed to his slow and meticulous task. I'm impressed. I think about the verse, "being found faithful in a few things," only to be given charge over "greater things."[2] . . . Would he show such patience sharing a lifetime with me in a wheelchair?

Later in the morning, after we've caught a "mess" of fish, Ken reaches over me and unhooks the chains linking the two boats. We drift apart, but my parents and Judy hardly notice. They are talking and casting and reeling and already recounting their fish stories.

Ken sits near the stern, slides a paddle from its sleeve, and dips it into the water. His head eclipses the sun, and the rays shine out around him like a golden crown. In the shadows cast by the glow, I can't see his handsome features—only his dark glasses and the white of his smile against his tanned skin. I can tell he is staring at me. I stare back. He cuts an appealing figure in his fishing vest and khaki shorts, the red bandana knotted around his neck echoing the red trim on his gray wool socks and the red laces of his hiking boots.

"I love you, Joni," he says suddenly. He lays the oar across his knees and lets the boat find its own way.

I smile back at him but say nothing.

"Ever since that Young Life banquet a year ago—"

I raise my arm out of the water, dragging the line of fish for him to see.

"Don't change the subject," he says.

I plop my weak arm back into the water. "Well, you know what? . . . I love you too."

Now it's his turn to smile at me and say nothing.

"But it's crazy," I say, looking off into space. "I mean, I love you with no strings attached. Clean. With no conditions." I clumsily swing my arm back and forth and the fish follow obediently, wriggling and flipping their tails. "That's new for me," I say quietly. "I haven't let my heart go many times . . . except for wild and crazy feelings I drummed up toward a friend during the movie. But that was so self-centered.

"But with you, I don't have to feel all consumed, like you are my life and breath. The love I have for you is freer than that." I breathe deeply. "I guess I love you for the right reasons."

As our boat turns through the water, a spectacular view of lofty crags with their shadows in snow looms behind Ken.

"It could work, you know," he says.

I question him with a look.

"I've been watching Judy and Kerbe. I know I can do the things they do for you . . . even the private things I've never seen them help you with."

"You're talking marriage?" I am a little surprised, even alarmed.

"Our life together could be a real ministry for the Lord, Joni." He leans forward and reaches for the toes of my moccasins.

I shake my head cautiously. "I don't know. I need some time."

"You just said you loved me."

"Yes, but marriage is a big step. I've got to be sure. There's my disability and . . . and Joni and Friends and . . . I've been in bed for two months. Maybe I'm not thinking straight—"

"Oh, I get it. Now that you're sitting up, the old 'I'm calling the shots' side of you is coming out. I liked you better when you were flat on your back—less in command, more responsive," he chides.

I'm confused. This is the sort of conversation you dream about having all your life, and suddenly when it's here you stumble as though you've never given marriage a thought. I'm afraid again—that advice about either marrying or going separate ways. But I can't bear the idea of going separate ways. Must this happen so fast? Be so black and white?

"Look, there's no pressure." Ken reads my mind. "But I'll say this—I know the way you think, and I'm not about to be controlled. I love God and His Word. I can lead. I can make good decisions."

I find myself relaxing in his words. Perhaps it's because deep down I want him to be stronger than me. Maybe that is what irritated me months back—back when I wanted him to be more than just someone who admired me, looked up to me.

Over the next months we give ourselves time to think. I meet Ken's family—his parents, his sister, an aunt and uncle. They treat me a little cautiously at first, but that's understandable. They hardly know me—and I'm in a wheelchair and I'm not Japanese.

All the while I wonder how marriage would work. Our love now, I am finding, is restless by nature, continually searching and probing the depths of our relationship. And to be married would mean that we would not be taken off the front lines of love, but plunged further into the thick of things. Learning to become one. Sacrificing over and over again. Communicating, day in and day out. Not to mention housecleaning. Finding things we could really *do* together. Shopping. Menu planning and cooking. And we'd have to go to bed . . . sometime. And what about children.

Although these are good questions that need to be asked, I don't want a "yes" to Ken to be dependent on finding all the answers. In a way I want it to be a mystery. For how can our love prove to be sacrificial and committed unless it is separate, unattached from anything else that is like it or that has gone before? To have it any other way would be saying yes with strings attached.

Then, one rainy November afternoon he walks into my art studio. He admires the pot of red geraniums I am painting. Red is everywhere—tubes of it, stains on rags, tinted brushes, color tests tacked on the walls, the flowers on the canvas. And he asks me to marry him.

"Yes," I say, and the room glows, honestly glows, with the excitement and dazzle of red.

$\mathcal{L}\mathfrak{d}$

"ARE YOU NERVOUS?"

"Sure I'm nervous," Ken answers as he pulls the Scrabble game board out of its box. "The whole reason we've come East for Christmas is to get your parents' permission. They've probably been wondering what's been going on between us since summer."

"Isn't that funny?" I get sidetracked. "Here we are in our mid-thirties, asking our parents for permission."

"I hope it's easier with your folks than it was with mine," he says as he shakes the bag of letter tiles. I nod in agreement. "Don't worry though," Ken continues. "I can tell you already have a place in their hearts."

"If only I were Japanese," I joke and then grow serious. "But be prepared. My Mom and Dad think you're the greatest thing coming down the pike, but they're still going to have questions. I'm just glad we're doing this over Scrabble . . . believe me, it'll make the whole conversation, whatever turn it takes, go a lot smoother."

"I'll just let your mother win."

"Hah! You don't know my mother," I warn.

The four of us gather around the end of the dining-room table and draw our letter tiles. Mom goes first. She peers over her glasses, places her tiles on the board and scores high with a seven letter word. I grin, wondering where in this competitive arena Ken will introduce his big question of the evening.

"Ah . . . Mr. and Mrs. E.," he begins when it's his turn. "Joni and I want to ask you something important."

"Now?" my mother asks. "Aren't you going to put down a word?"

"Well, yes . . . eventually, but—"

"Good. Then let's keep it moving," she says, victory in sight. "I've got another good one here." Mother and Dad move their tiles in deep concentration. Ken and I just look at each other.

The evening passes quickly, and my mother, able to concentrate better than the rest, closes the game out easily with a win. But winning is not the only thing on her mind. Neither Mom nor Dad have forgotten the big question.

Ken tells them he would like to marry me. Just hearing him say those words again gives me butterflies. Mother says she knew all along. She can't wait to call Mrs. Tada. Dad has to lean forward and cup his ear, asking Ken to repeat his words.

"Wonderful, wonderful," my mother responds, folding her glasses into their case. ""But how do you intend to . . . uh . . . manage?"

"It won't be easy." Ken and I step on each other's lines.

"I've been thinking about a budget," Ken begins. "Medical costs are up there, but my school gives me good insurance coverage, a dental plan, ah . . ."

"Well, that's not what I really meant," Mom interrupts.

"Someone will help me keep house," I add hastily. "With my van, I can do a lot of my own food shopping . . . you know, with the help of a clerk or bag boy, whatever. I can use other people's hands to help me prepare and set the table. I've trained . . . let's see, four or five different girls to help me out with my morning routine—Ken leaves for work early. And he," I say, flopping my arm on top of Ken's shoulder, "can do my nighttime routine. Getting me undressed and washing my face, taking off legbags, stuff like that . . . it only takes a short while."

"You, ah . . .," Mother says hesitantly to Ken, "understand how all that's done?"

Ken blushes. "Not all of it, obviously . . . although I've washed Joni's face and brushed her teeth." He beams proudly. "She looks pretty good without make-up." He puts his arm around me and gives a playful squeeze.

My dad breaks in. "I can't speak for you, Ken, but I know that, ah, making, ah—" He nervously motions with his hands.

"Love? You mean making love?" I finish his sentence.

"Yes!" He raps the table. "That's the word."

"Daddy," I say with a wry grin, "you don't have trouble thinking of the word 'sex' when you need it in Scrabble."

"No, Mr. E.'s question is good." Ken gets to the point. "I know that Joni can't move. And she can't feel." He pats my knee. "But there's more to lovemaking than just an act. There's plenty of places that Joni can feel. We can be intimate, tender," he says as he reaches up and strokes the side of my neck with the back of his hand. I'm a little surprised that he's able to put it all into words so well. He's doing a better job than I could.

"I tell you, though . . ." Ken shakes his head and rubs his hands on his knees. "There have been some people—really well-meaning—who've suggested that we should go away for a weekend. Give it a try. Experiment," he says with a wave of his hand.

Mother taps her fingers on the table. Daddy leans even further forward to be sure he hears every word.

"But we can't . . . we wouldn't do that. Joni's disability doesn't give us an excuse to sin. Bend God's standards. Just because our circumstances are a little unusual doesn't mean we're the exception. God will only bless us if we obey Him, and we want—really want—that most of all."

This is the strength, the moral muscle that I've known all along was there in Ken. Upright in heart. Righteous and good. Wonderfully transparent. Clean clear through. Without guile. This is the depth, the intensity I've been looking for. It is a kind of magnetic power that is anything but animal and everything that is spiritual. And more than ever I realize how much I love him, really love him.

"I'm glad to hear that," Dad says softly.

"But Mr. E.," Ken teases and his eyes twinkle, "when honeymoon time comes, we won't have any trouble figuring out what to do. It's just going to take a little creativity," he says twirling his hand in the air, "a little . . . inventiveness." He grins.

ॐ

"I KNOW WHO did it," I lean to the right and whisper in Judy's ear.

"I bet you don't," she whispers back.

"Yes I do. It was that guy's mistress," I say, my voice getting a little louder.

"Uh-uh. You're wrong. She was nowhere around when the murder took place—"

"Shh!" Ken frowns and leans away from me on his side of the theater seat.

"I'm sorry," I hoarsely whisper, holding back a chuckle. I turn back to Judy. "Keep it down. . . . Now what were you saying about the murder? I think that the mistress knew all along that . . ."

The Agatha Christie movie concludes, and Judy and I break into an excited discussion before the credits barely start rolling. Ken doesn't join in but silently gathers his sweat shirt and box of popcorn.

"Excuse me, please," he states formally as he steps over our legs to retrieve the wheelchair at the front of the movie theater.

Something's wrong.

After the two of them transfer me into my chair, Judy leaves for the restroom.

"What's the matter?" I keep my voice low as a few people file past us in the aisle. He doesn't say anything but looks down to adjust my feet on the footpedals.

"What's wrong?" I insist again after they pass.

Still he doesn't answer.

Okay. This is it. We're going to have an argument, our first. And here he is—the silent type. I feel myself getting angry.

Judy meets us as we leave the theater, waves good-by and heads for her own car.

I'm relieved when she goes. Ken, I hope, is too. We need to get this resolved. We wheel toward the back lot where my van is parked.

I stop before we reach the lot. "I'm not going any further till you tell me what's wrong."

"Okay." Ken folds his arms across his chest. "You were talking during the movie . . . and you didn't stop even after I said something."

"Ken, first I wasn't talking, I was whispering," I say crisply. "Next, nobody could hear us."

"You were disturbing people," Ken accuses.

I look amazed. "That's ridiculous. Nobody could hear us 'cause nobody was around us. The place was nearly empty."

"Look, I had just gotten up to tell those teenagers down in front to put a lid on it, they were making so much noise. And then you and Judy . . ." He begins pacing. "You two go and do the same thing. How can I tell them to be quiet if you're not?"

"We weren't doing the same thing. We were whispering, not . . . not throwing popcorn and making a racket." My voice rises.

"Don't yell at me," Ken orders.

"Yelling? You think this is yelling?" I look at him wide-eyed. "You haven't heard anything yet—"

"Well, I don't yell."

"Well I do!" I wait and then add, "My whole family yells!"

"This is it," he mutters, pacing. "We get engaged and we become different people. I was afraid of this."

"Ken . . ." I try to control my voice. "I'm not a different person. This is who I am."

He stops and looks at me. "Haven't you ever heard of these verses about being angry and sinning not? Letting no unwholesome words come out of your mouth?"

Suddenly I feel trapped. Something ridiculously minor has become incredibly major, and he is pushing his expectations on me.

"Don't go throwing verses at me. Remember, love is supposed to cover a multitude of sins." My eyes narrow. "And I don't think I've even done anything 'multitudinous' here!"

I am ready to bare my fangs when a young couple gets out of their car at the edge of the parking lot.

"Excuse me," the young man says as they approach, smiling, hand-in-hand, "aren't you the lady who draws with her mouth . . . Joanie? We heard you speak at my mother's church once."

Shocked in midsentence, I glance at Ken, paste on a smile, and tell them yes. Before they can ask me questions, I introduce them to "Ken Tada, my fiancé." They look surprised and happy.

Ken weakly extends his hand, musters a smile, and mumbles a few words. His awkward, yet game way of handling the embarrassing encounter touches me. But at the same time I resent him for revealing my stubbornness, my lack of love. Suddenly it occurs to me that "wedded bliss" will be far more rigorous and demanding than I ever dreamed.

As Ken answers questions about our wedding, I meekly wonder if he is still all that excited.

The couple heads for the movie theater. Ken and I remain silent, watching them until they round the corner.

"So, Joni," he begins softly, "what *did* you talk about at his mother's church?"

"Huh?" I look directly at Ken. "Oh . . . yes . . . well, I probably talked about my paralysis helping me become Christlike. You know, being loving . . . self-controlled . . ." I lower my gaze. "Patient . . . without sin . . ."

"And?" he says, taking a step toward me.

"And I still want to get married," I say, smiling up at him, blinking back tears, ". . . if you do."

He gives me a big hug and we meander toward the van.

"You really though the mistress did it? Want to know something? I thought she did too," Ken says as he holds on to the armrest of my wheelchair.

❦

I 'VE SAT IN on bridal showers for so many others; it seems odd that it
should be my turn. In my wheelchair, with its dusty gears and squeaky belts, I am
slightly out-of-place among the delicately wrapped gifts, fancy paper doilies, and
dainty finger sandwiches. But I'm glad that the room is decorated with crepe
paper and ribbons, like any other shower.

The gifts are piled around my feet, and the daughters of two friends have the
proud honor of opening each one for me. The ladies gives me pots and pans, much
needed since Kerbe and Judy will be taking so many of their kitchen items with
them when they set up their own apartments. That makes me realize I will miss
them—a lonely but brief thought in the middle of such joy.

A coffee grinder and mugs. Casserole dishes and an ironing board. Dishtowels
and oven mitts.

My young friend struggles to lift a shiny steam iron out of its carton. She has
to use two hands to hold it high for everyone to see. "How can you use this, Joni?"
she asks honestly.

"The same way I will use those oven mitts."

"How's that?"

"By borrowing someone's hands. Just like I'm borrowing yours to open these
gifts."

Her curiosity satisfied, she continues on to the next box wrapped in lacy paper
with a huge white bow. Soon she is holding an exquisite, long black satin
negligee. As everyone gasps in admiration, I quickly read the card, "With all my

love, Vicky Olivas." I share a knowing smile with Vicky who is sitting at the back of the room with several others in wheelchairs.

After punch and cookies, it is time to say thank you. I gather some thoughts to close our afternoon together.

"When I was a teenager, pulling together my life from a wheelchair, I dreaded the idea of marriage. In fact," I laugh, "I once said in *People* magazine that if I ever loved a man enough to marry him, I hope I'd love him enough to say no."

"A little late for that, Jon," Rana calls from her seat next to Vicky. More laughter.

"Yes . . . well, as you see, perfect love casts out fears,"[3] I respond, building a bridge from light to serious. "Really . . . I think one of my biggest fears back then—this is going to sound silly—was having a bridal shower. I was so afraid of sitting in front of a roomful of girls and not being able to open my own gifts. Unable even to untie the ribbons."

Friends have stopped collecting punch glasses, and several wander in from the kitchen. The room is quiet.

I stare at the carton of crumpled wrapping paper at the foot of my wheelchair. "I was scared if I got an iron, everyone would know that I couldn't use it, not with hands that were paralyzed.

"But perfect love does cast out fear, and I can honestly say I feel that love. From each and every one of you." I glance at Mrs. Tada and Carol, my future sister-in-law. I smile at Vicky. If anyone can understand what I am feeling now, she can.

"And," I add, glancing at the black negligee, "I can love myself. God has made it so . . . whether my hands hold an iron or not. . . . Oh, and by the way, my housekeeper is going to *love* using that iron."

IN THE WEEKS before our July wedding, I paint more to quiet my nerves than to meet a publisher's deadline. But the paint and the brushes don't want to do ordinary compositions, and I find myself, in an almost mystical way, designing paintings that are light and airy, with lots of space. My eye enjoys an off-center balance on canvas. It is painting that is distinctly oriental. Japanese.

Ken's parents welcome me warmly into their home. Though very American, they hold on to a few of their Japanese traditions, and we get to know each other better over sukiyaki and sunomono. They tell me childhood stories of Ken and Carol and show me funny photos of Ken—chubby-cheeked and smiling.

They ask questions about my family and are glad to learn that my sister Kathy is flying out early to help me with wedding preparations.

"You and Kathy will really enjoy Grandpa's birthday party next weekend," Mrs. Tada says, clasping her hands together. "In Japan, to be eighty-eight is an honored occasion."

A few days later when Kathy wheels me into Grandpa's home, I am struck by the similarities between him and my own father—his silver white hair, his glasses, and his smile. And they've both short. Grandpa even paints—Japanese birds perched on plum blossom branches, willow trees and chrysanthemums, misty mountains and lakes. He proudly hangs his work for everyone to enjoy, just as my dad does with his paintings. As I wheel through the rooms admiring his work, Grandpa explains his art in Japanese while Mr. Tada translates.

Ken, Kathy, and Carol wheel me down the steps into Grandpa's backyard oriental garden. He walks ahead of us on the neat gravel path that winds through carefully groomed shrubs and exotic plants. Occasionally he stops to describe a certain herb. Although I cannot understand his language, I can understand his pride and joy.

That afternoon I learn more about Grandpa's talents in both calligraphy and poetry as he shows us pages of his beautifully scripted haiku. I smile, thinking of the many poems Daddy has written. I can't wait for the two of them to meet.

During the party I also see the serious side of Ken's family as I hear about the loss of homes, businesses, and property during their confinement in Japanese internment camps during World War II. Ken's father was the mayor of such a camp. He talks about it easily, the past of pain and loss far behind him. We discuss his import-export trade and how he still travels to the Orient to negotiate for other companies. I promise him that next time I will bring copies of my books translated into Japanese.

Mrs. Tada—I'm learning to call her "Mom T"—is a smiling outgoing lady with the same black hair and striking eyes as her son. She works as a bookkeeper for a large engineering firm but enjoys spending time in her kitchen and garden. I tell her I like to cook, and she promises to pick up some special Japanese staples and kitchen items the next time she drives to Little Tokyo in downtown Los Angeles. She wants to know how to give me a hug. I teach her, and when she embraces me, I realize that she is about the same height as I am in my wheelchair.

Carol, Ken's sister, is a college student, stylish and fun-loving like her brother, with the same dark, athletic good looks. During the party she flips through a fashion magazine, points out several photos of trendy dresses, and asks if we might go shopping together sometime. As she turns several more pages, I notice her glossy red nails against smooth tanned hands. I can tell I will enjoy having her as a sister-in-law.

At the close of the afternoon one of Ken's younger cousins performs a graceful dance dressed in a kimono and holding a fan. Grandpa makes a short speech in Japanese, thanking everyone for coming to celebrate this special traditional birthday. As we leave, I comment to Ken about how wonderfully different our backgrounds are.

That evening Kathy joins the two of us at a local sushi bar to outline last-minute plans for the wedding.

"H'm, tekkamaki . . . sashimi. Now *this* is a cultural experience for you two," Ken says as he rubs his chin, scanning the menu. "Ever tried raw fish, Kathy?"

"Ick! No. And I don't think I want to. . . . Let's see . . ." She examines the second page of her menu. "Aha! Oysters on the half shell. Now that's a Maryland dish for you. How about splitting a dozen with me, Joni?"

"Great. Ken," I say, nudging him, "want to share some?"

"Raw oysters?" He shakes his head in mock disgust. "You've got to be kidding!"

"And raw tuna is better?" I say as I sniff the air. "This place smells like whale breath."

"Maryland crab houses smell better?" Ken teases.

We laugh at the irony. Perhaps our two cultures are not that far apart after all.

꧁

"**I** CAN'T WAIT for you to see my wedding dress, Kathy. It's so simple and elegant." I talk excitedly as I drive my sister and Kerbe to the bridal shop to help me with the final fitting. "And I'm going to have a wreath of hand-crocheted daisies with lace. It really looks Scandinavian, and I think I should wear my hair up."

July 3, 1982, the date Ken and I have set, is only days away and I am a typical bride-to-be. Excited. Anxious. Nervous.

"Well, you said you wanted this to be like any other wedding," Kathy sighs and smiles. "I'm glad you decided on wearing a long bridal gown. Only how are you going to keep a long dress from getting tangled in your wheels as you move down the aisle?"

"Greg Barshaw's got an answer for that," Kerbe says. "A soft wire netting all around the sides and back of Joni's wheelchair. No way she'll roll over her gown or train."

To get me into the dress, Kathy and Kerbe have to lay me down on the only couch in the shop, near the front entrance. They position a standing screen around the couch for privacy. Moments later, sitting back up in my wheelchair, facing a mirror, I marvel at how beautiful, how elegant I feel in such a gown. It does, however, need to be altered.

The fitting lady, a short woman who speaks unclear English stands at a distance from me. She nervously winds a long yellow tape measure around her fingers. "I am so sorry. It is impossible." She shakes her head. "I am sorry."

I think she must mean that the gown just will not do. Perhaps, judging from her reaction, it is impossible to alter. Kerbe gathers material around the shoulder seam and asks if it can be taken in.

"No. I have never fitted someone like this." She flings out a hand in the same way one would cast off trash. "I am sorry," she says in a superior tone.

I am shocked and a little breathless. Kathy looks for our saleswoman. I can only stare at the fitting lady in stunned disbelief. The woman who sold me the dress approaches and asks if there is a problem.

"No, it is impossible," the fitting lady repeats. "I have never done anything like this before." She points in my direction, resolute, convinced, and immovable.

"Well, I've never done anything like this before either," I say in a desperate voice. "A wedding is a new thing for me, and you'll just have to try something new yourself," I insist, equally resolute and immovable.

This is not the way to handle the situation, I know. This is not the way we do it in those Joni and Friends worships. *For it is God's will that by doing good you should silence the ignorant talk of foolish men.*[4] The verse from 1 Peter flashes in my mind, and I know that I should be building a bridge rather than widening the gap. But this is my wedding, not a lecture in a seminar.

"Wait, please wait." The saleswoman steps in. Her voice is calm and soothing. "Let's work this out," she says gently. She quietly yet firmly addresses the fitting lady and then turns to me to apologize, placing her hand on my shoulder. With her fingers, she lightly lifts the lace on my headwreath and comments on how lovely I look. She kneels by my chair and gathers the extra material, folding the seam under.

"Where do you think we should pin it?" she looks up and asks the fitting lady.

The lady rubs her palms on the sides of her dress and reaches up to pull the tape measure from around her neck. Obediently, she kneels with the saleswoman and begins pulling pins from her wrist band. I watch in wonder as the fitting lady warms to the touch of the sweet, gentle spirit of the saleswoman. Within minutes the situation is defused and a confrontation avoided.

As I am about to leave, the saleswoman places her hand on the armrest of my wheelchair. "You will look charming on your wedding day," she says. "I am a Christian, and I will be praying for you and your bridegroom that morning."

"Blessed are the peacemakers for they shall be called the children of God."[5]

KATHY AND I lie in bed and watch the light of dawn shine on the splendid wedding gown that hangs in front of the bedroom window. Kathy holds my limp hand in hers, and together we softly sing to greet the day. My wedding day!

I have the "peace which passes all understanding." No doubts. No apprehensions. I feel . . . no, I am peacefully certain this is the right choice. Funny. I had the same conviction when I chose to do the movie. And move to California. And start a ministry to disabled people.

But love, pure and strong and deep, is far greater than convictions or decisions about a ministry or a move. Maybe this wonderful peace blooms from the assurance that our love has 20/20 vision. Our hearts haven't rushed ahead of reason.

"For marriage is the contemplation of the love of God in and through another human being" comes to mind—something I read recently, and I wonder what Ken is thinking this morning. I wonder how he slept. Is he nervous? No, probably not. I imagine he's enjoying this same glorious peace and quiet joy.

"Are you going to wear the necklace Ken gave you last night?" Kathy rolls over, leaning on her scrunched pillow, and fingers the delicate heart on the chain around my neck.

"Uh-huh . . . it'll look nice against the lace."

She smiles. "I don't get it. He gives you a dainty little necklace, and you give him a hunky Penn International 50-W fishing reel. Whatever possessed you to give him something so . . . so unromantic?"

I chuckle. "One of his friends in the wedding party gave me good advice: 'Encourage a husband to keep his dreams.' I guess the reel is a symbol of sorts that I want him to do just that." I pause and then make it a pronouncement: "May he always have plenty of time to enjoy fishing."

I am marrying a fisherman. A friend. A brother. A school-teacher. A racquetball player. I recall one of my earlier opinions of him: *A wonderfully ordinary guy.* But he is also extraordinary. And today he will be my husband.

"Yeah, some fishing reel. I hope you like cooking trout and tuna," Kathy laughs, throwing back her covers and jumping out of bed.

How odd to be discussing necklaces and fishing reels and tuna—such ordinary, unremarkable matters—on the morning of the biggest day in my life. But everything this morning seems at once ordinary and extraordinary. Breakfast with my parents, Jay and Rob, Kathy, and Kay, Jay's oldest daughter. Little Earecka, already in her long petticoat, bounds around the house. Jay washes my hair, helps me dress in casual clothes, hangs my gown in the back of the van, and sends me off with Judy while she oversees the rest of the family.

As I drive to the church amid the traffic on Ventura Freeway, I stay in my usual middle lane. But there's nothing usual about the day. "It's my wedding day," I happily shout to the cars speeding by. I wonder how the traffic is for Ken.

At the church my bridesmaids and friends help me dress. I watch in the mirror as they comb my hair and apply my make-up. I watch myself become a bride. I can't get over how calm I am. I don't chatter; I don't giggle. I sit and smile calmly, watching everyone else scurry around to get ready.

When my mother and sisters arrive, people begin taking photographs. Mother stands tall and proud by my chair as we pose for last-minute pictures. She is elegant with her blond hair swept back in a French roll. She lightly touches strands of hair at the back of my neck as she did when I was small.

I wonder how Ken's mom and dad are doing. I hope he's taking a lot of pictures too.

Then, an usher brings word that all the guests are seated and that it is time for us to line up. We move across the deserted grounds to the sanctuary entrance. I'm not wearing armsplints today so it's a little difficult to manage the bouquet of daisies on my lap and steer at the same time.

Jay and Kathy check the flowers in their hair in the reflection in the glass door at the entrance. They smooth their pale blue cotton gowns as they position themselves in line along with Kathy and Carol and my friend Betsy.

"I love you, Jon," Jay whispers as she steps into line.

Earecka, my flower girl, twirls in her first long dress, watching the skirt bell. Vicky Olivas sits at one side entrance, in her wheelchair, greeting latecomers who sign the guest book at her side. At the other side entrance, Debbie Stone does the same.

The door cracks open and the majestic organ music stirs us. I catch of glimpse of Steve Estes—my longtime friend now helping officiate at our wedding—standing at the front next to John MacArthur. Still, I sense such extraordinary calm. I've been more nervous speaking in front of churches half this size.

Daddy looks resplendent in a gray morning suit and a Windsor cravat. Usually he's in suspendered Levis and a flannel shirt; I've never seen him dressed so formally. But he seems to be enjoying the look and fit of his suit. He beams proudly at me. His youngest daughter. His namesake. I lean toward his ear and, above the organ music, tell him that I will wheel slowly so he can keep up with me. He gives Rana one of his crutches and holds on to the armrest of my chair for support.

"Nervous?" he asks.

I smile and shake my head no. I feel exquisitely at peace, remarkably calm.

As my last bridemaid begins her walk up the aisle, I inch my chair closer to the door and peer through the crack to catch a glimpse of Ken at the front. I see Diana. I see friends from the office.

Then, I see him. He waits at attention with hands clasped behind him, tall and stately in his morning suit. But he cranes his neck to look down the aisle. Looking for me.

My face grows hot and my heart pounds. Suddenly, everything is different. I have seen my beloved. The change is so dramatic I nearly step out of myself, wondering in amazement at my response. Joy. Anticipation. An overwhelming longing to be with him.

The music crescendos, and Daddy and I begin our arduous journey up the aisle, his cane clicking and my wheels turning slowly.

How we long for His appearing, I think, oblivious to the rows of family and friends. *When we see Him, we shall be like Him. . . .*[6] I have eyes only for Ken.

Marriage is the contemplation of God through another. . . .

This is how it will be when we see Jesus, I marvel, caught up in the music and the march, the candles, the flowers—all the symbols of two becoming one. There's no way—even with rehearsals and programs, even having attended scores of weddings—there's no way I could have prepared myself for this.

Nothing is like this moment.

Nothing will be like that moment.

꧁

K EN CARRIES ME over the threshold of the airplane door. The flight attendants direct us to the first row of seats, away from the view of the few other passengers in first class. Honeymooners. It's a silly word. And with all this special treatment—a surprise cake, Hawaiian leis, orange juice served in crystal glasses on a silver tray—everyone on board must know that this is our first full day as a married couple.

I love the privacy of our seats. We snuggle down into their high backs, rub noses, and snicker. Ken lifts the glass of juice to my mouth, sets it down, and twines my fingers in his. We share secrets and tell each other how wonderful last night was.

"We're about ready to begin the movie." A flight attendant bends over me and reaches for the window shade. Ken pushes our seats back, puts the earphones on me, stuffs a pillow between us, and we get ready for the film.

The cabin is darkened and the credits roll. *Whose Life Is It Anyway?* appears on the small screen directly in front of us. Immediately, I recognize it as the movie about a despondent quadriplegic who argues with his family and hospital to let him die. A depressing film, I've heard. Ken and I look at one another. What irony!

An embarrassed stewardess returns to apologize profusely. "And here it is your honeymoon!" she laments in a whisper, trying not to disturb the other passengers.

After she leaves, we grin at each other. Who's despondent about being paralyzed? It doesn't make any difference to us. We can handle it.

The five-hour flight to Hawaii on the 747 passes quickly. As soon as we arrive at the gate, Rana and Judy come down from their seats in the cabin above to help us off the plane. This is a honeymoon with "extras," but someone needs to teach Ken how to do everything from giving a bath to getting me dressed. Judy and Rana will stay at a hotel several blocks from ours and, when not serving as Ken's teachers, will enjoy their own vacation.

Outside the airport, we are hit with the heavy wet scent of jasmine and plumeria. The equatorial sun shines bright and hot, and we are glad for a fragrant breeze that lifts both the fronds of palms and our spirits.

Ken checks us into our hotel, tips the bellboy who will take care of our luggage, and immediately wheels me across the street to the white sandy beach. We'll worry about the room later.

What a breathtaking aquamarine the ocean is. The sun makes a highway of dazzling light on the water. Everything seems a collage of pink and aqua and green. Each wave curls perfectly in a crashing tube that stretches for miles down Waikiki Beach. An old pink terra-cotta hotel stands out from among the towering modern ones of steel and concrete. We decide we will eat dinner there.

Ken kicks off his thongs, runs his hands through his hair, claps them behind his head, yawns and stretches. The tails of his Hawaiian-print shirt flutter in the breeze. Here, more than ever, he looks more Hawaiian than Japanese.

While he strolls out onto the sand, I notice a family of three approaching on the sidewalk. The son wears a South Carolina football jersey, and his parents tote straw hats and bags. As they whisper and disguise their glances, I can tell I've been recognized. Oh, well. No matter.

"I don't believe it. George, look who it is," the woman says, lifting her sunglasses.

"Well, I'll be," George responds, reaching for his camera in his tote bag. "Martha, stand with her, and I'll get a snapshot."

"Well, uh . . . I'd rather . . ." I smile and extend my arm for an introduction, but it seems niceties such as learning names and asking courteous questions are to be overlooked. They probably don't mean to be rude. And I'm used to the scenario. So I make an effort to introduce myself and ask their names. The boy in the football jersey sticks his hands in his pockets and looks away, embarrassed by the hoo-hah his parents are making.

"Oh, honey!" The woman in the brightly colored muumuu reaches around my shoulder and pulls me toward her, squeezing my cheek against hers. "We are just so . . . so thrilled to meet you. I read your book and saw your movie, and my neighbors just aren't going to believe me when we get home," she squeals.

"Hold still," George says as he looks through the viewfinder and waves his hand. "And Junior, get in there."

"Ah . . . please, if you don't mind . . . I, uh, would rather we not take pictures. I'm on my honeymoon," I whisper. "Besides, talking is much nicer than an old photo," I say to soothe the disappointment in their faces.

"You're married?" The lady straightens her arms to hold me at a proud distance. "Why, isn't that wonderful. Who's the lucky fellow?" She looks around for someone who might be my husband. She ignores the dark Asian man who approaches in his Hawaiian-print shirt, shorts, and thongs, and continues to look behind and around him. It occurs to me that they must take Ken for either a local from the beach or my tour guide.

The man and woman appear startled when Ken stops behind me and leans over the back of my wheelchair to give me a hug.

"This is my husband, Ken Tada," I proudly announce.

"Oh . . . yes, well, hello." The woman hikes her tote bag on her shoulder and extends a hand of greeting. Her husband does the same, telling "Mr. Eareckson" that it is nice to meet him.

I quickly steer the conversation back to the family, asking them questions about their home and church. After a few minutes they seem relaxed again. So does Ken. We smile and say good-by.

"Mr. Eareckson!" Ken mutters as he pushes me back across the street to our hotel. "Tell me, do I look Swedish?"

Underneath his wisecrack I sense more hurt than Ken is willing to admit. As he pushes me to our room, I wonder how he will handle the other people who will say and do the same. As much as I'd like to deny it, I am a public person. And there will be others. Many others. Does Ken really understand that?

I feel protective, defensive of him. I know how people unintentionally put a spotlight on me that casts a long shadow over anyone who stands behind my wheelchair. Will the glare keep people from seeing reality, as it so often does? Will they know my husband has feelings? Will they care?

Like the lights on the movie set, that spotlight confuses the unreal with the real. And I want whatever becomes public about our life to be true and genuine. Yet more importantly, we need a life that is private and personal. Sane and balanced. I don't want Ken behind the chair. I want him next to me . . . out in front of me. And I want everyone to recognize him in that way too.

So the nagging question remains: How will we handle a life that is so public?

Ken unlocks our room and wedges a suitcase to hold the door open while he pushes me through. The bellboy has placed our hanging bags in the closet, our suitcases on the bed and dresser. A late afternoon breeze rustles the curtains by the open door to the balcony. Ken pushes me out on the balcony, and we silently watch the setting sun turn the aquamarine sea into pink glass. The fresh salty air pushes the disturbing thoughts out of my mind. We kiss and tell each other what a wonderful honeymoon this will be.

We go back into the room, and Ken checks out the bathroom, flicks the light on and off, and sees if the television works. I sit in the middle of the room and watch.

He takes off his shirt, throws it on the bed, unlocks his suitcase, and digs for a light sweater.

"Shall we unpack?" I ask after he finishes.

"Sure," Ken says, smacking his hands together. "Do you want your stuff put away?"

"Well . . . just take things out of the hanging bag so they won't wrinkle. I'll get Judy and Rana to unpack the rest when they come over."

Ken unzips the bag and lightly shakes the blouses on their hangers, smoothing any wrinkles. "Okay, I'm done," he says, folding the hanging bag and sticking it on the shelf of the closet. "What's next?"

"You mean . . . for me?"

He nods.

"Well, I'd rather help you unpack. Put things away. Decide what goes where," I say, shrugging my shoulders. "You know . . . like on the bathroom sink. You don't want my creams and cleansers all mixed up with your razor and after-shave."

He waves his hand flippantly. "Ah, I never unpack."

"You don't?" I say uneasily, eyeing the opened suitcase with socks and shorts half spilling out. "But I'd be glad to help . . . plan things out and all."

"Don't worry about it, Jon. It's not help I want," he says, stuffing his socks back in and clicking the suitcase shut. "I just prefer not to unpack when I travel."

Suddenly I want my hands. I want to unpack my husband's sweat shirts and shorts and push his suitcases under the bed and out of sight. I want to stand at the sink and neatly organize our bottles and jars. I want to hang up his shirts and line his shoes in a tidy row at the bottom of the closet.

I don't like the fact that he likes to live out of a suitcase while I like to unpack. And there's nothing I can do about it.

I conceal my frustration, but it bothers me. *Who's dependent about being paralyzed? It doesn't make any difference to us. We can handle it.*

And another nagging question remains: How will we handle our life that is private?

KEN AND I lie on the mattress in front of the fireplace with our heads together, the sheets kicked back, and the blanket half on the carpet. Usually our bedroom is the sanctuary we retreat to for idle talk, but tonight, Friday night, we are camped out on the living-room floor to welcome the weekend and celebrate our first fire of winter. My wheelchair is parked in the corner with my sweater and Levis hanging sloppily on its handles, shoes on the footpedals, and corset on the seat cushion. Scruffy makes herself a nest on the crumpled sheet at the foot of our mattress. The television, sound muted, plays images in the background.

Ken holds, straight-armed, an open Bible above us. The track lighting casts a glow as we lie in the shadow of Ephesians.

This is one of those nice rituals we're getting used to after several months of marriage—reading the Bible together before we go to sleep. And the book of Ephesians is becoming something of a ritual too. When single, I used to quickly leaf over the fifth chapter about being married. Now, commands about husbands and wives are searched and studied with newlywed enthusiasm. We are overly zealous, perhaps, wanting to live this new life the right way, fearful of making too many mistakes. So we make each word in each verse a priceless gem to be examined thoroughly, turning it over and over, scrutinizing it from every angle.

"For this reason a man will leave his father and mother and be united to his wife, and the two will become one flesh," Ken reads slowly, emphasizing the part where two become one. "This is a profound mystery,"[7] he concludes.

He plops the open Bible on his chest to give his arms a rest, then reaches behind his head to wad the pillow. "Two will become one," he muses and stares at the ceiling. "Do you feel like one yet?"

"Yes . . . and no," I say cautiously, wondering if this is some sort of test. "If you mean, like it says, in the flesh . . . yes, I do," I say lovingly. But my heart jumps a little, wondering what he means. "Why? Is there a problem with the way we—"

"No. No, it's not that," he says, scrunching the pillow tighter.

"Well, if you mean two people becoming one spiritually, emotionally . . . all those marriage books say it takes time." I pause, listening to the fire crackle. "Maybe that's part of the profound mystery."

Ken scoots up on the mattress and leans his back against the sofa. He closes the Bible and lays it on the cushion behind his shoulder. Reaching down, he pulls the covers over his knees and crosses and uncrosses his feet, making funny little hills and valleys with the blanket.

"I wonder if the wheelchair is supposed to be a help . . . or a hindrance," he says softly.

Startled, I look up at him. "Well, it's supposed to be a help. At least, that's what we figured before we got married," I say. When he doesn't reply, I add, "You know . . . all that stuff about God's power showing up best in weakness?"

He nods. The light from above our heads makes deep shadows on his face, and I have to squint to see his eyes.

"You're finding it hard, aren't you?" I say tenderly.

He shrugs his shoulders, then reaches over and places his palm on my forehead. I move my head back and forth under his hand, enjoying his caress.

"No, everything's fine. It's just . . ." His voice trails off as he kicks the blanket again. "It's just things like waking up to turn you in the middle of the night . . . every night. It's okay now, but I can see that it could get to me in years to come. And even this . . ." He points to our mattress and the fireplace. "We try and do fun things that normal couples do, but none of this can be impromptu . . . totally spontaneous . . . like it would be for everyone else."

I turn away from his eyes and look into the glowing embers. Biting my lip, I try hard not to take his words personally, try to separate myself from the wheelchair sitting in the dark corner.

Ken goes on. "And your nighttime routine is easy enough, but it's hard to think that I will be cleaning out legbags every night for the rest of our lives." He shakes his head.

I'm tempted to snap back at him. This is exactly the sort of ground we covered before we married. Talking over the commitment, the sacrifice. "But, Ken," I say meekly, "consider all those husbands who have to help with three or four children. That's tough too."

"Yes, but kids grow up."

In a way he's right. Who could say before our wedding what our marriage would really be like. And I know all too well that nothing can really prepare a person for dealing with paralysis. I sympathize with his struggle. I'm glad he's honest about it. Even after all these years I'm not totally used to legs and hands that don't work.

"I know," I sigh and look into his eyes pleadingly. "I've lived with it for years now, and I still struggle every once in a while. I wish . . . I really wish I could make it easier for you." This is one of those times when I long to be able to move so I could sit up next to him with my back against the same sofa—facing our problems in life together. But I lie still and paralyzed underneath my half of the blanket.

"And it would be nice if God healed me. Life sure would be easier," I sigh with a smile.

"Healing? I thought you put that to rest long ago."

"Oh, I did. But it's still helpful to voice that down-deep desire to God every once in a while. Let Him know I'm looking for that new body . . . whether in this life or the next."

"I can just picture you folding the laundry," Ken chides.

"Yes, and I'd even stack the towels so only the folds would show," I say proudly.

"Oh, you would?" he says with a sly grin. "Well, maybe you'd also take the trash out for the garbage man."

"No siree. *There* I would draw the line."

We laugh and then I add quietly, "But I really wish I could make it easier, Ken."

He replaces his hand on my forehead. "I know you do. . . . I know." He smiles. We linger that way, listening to the fire, me resting under the warmth of his palm. "Thanks for being strong . . . strong when I'm weak. Maybe what we're experiencing here is two becoming one," he concludes, the burden lifted.

He doesn't need or want answers; he wants me to listen. To say I understand. Ken knows as well as I that, for the meantime, the problems linked to my disability aren't going to go away. But for me to say and really mean that I understand—that seems to divide the burden and multiply the bond.

And that's what I must cling to. Somehow, God will multiply the bond and make us one. *It will take faith—simple faith—to make it happen,* I think as Ken kicks off the blanket and gathers my pillows to turn me on my side for the night. He punches and stuffs the pillow behind my back, coils my drainage tubing, and positions my legs until I am comfortable.

I will not allow myself to believe that our marriage is weakened by the presence of a wheelchair. Even though I cannot toss and turn to settle myself snugly into bed for the night. Even though I can't rub my husband's back when he's tired. Even though what used to be a tidy linen cabinet now serves as a place to stack medicines and catheters, drainage tubes and corsets. Even though I must use other people's hands to prepare dinner and set the table, to fold my husband's underwear and put away his T-shirts . . . The list grows, but I cling tenaciously to promises of God's power showing up best in weakness—and of two becoming one; I dream as I close my eyes against the heat of the fire.

The next day is Saturday, a damp and breezy gray morning. A day for sweat shirts and working in the backyard. Ken offers to lend me his hands for several hours so I can garden. Borrowing other people's hands is not new for me, and I watch as Ken prunes and clips each rosebush, asking me exactly how it should be done.

I find myself mesmerized after a while, gazing in a transfixed way at his hands. I watch the way he turns his wrist for a better angle at the rose stem. His fingers squeeze the clippers and the stem snaps. His knuckles whiten, and little veins furrowing between muscles in his hands bulge with strain as he clips a thicker branch closer to the root. He runs his thumb over the tiny jagged edge of a leaf. He fondles the angry point of a thorn.

A chilly breeze sends the dampness through my sweat shirt. I shiver and circle my wheelchair to the other side of Ken for protection. He straightens to stretch his back. Resting, he reaches out to feel the velvet of a petal between his forefinger and thumb. He stoops and digs in the dirt, getting his nails filthy, and seems to take pleasure in rubbing the soil in his palms, breaking up any clumps.

An odd feeling begins to envelop me. I have the strangest impression that his hands are mine. I can almost feel the dirt. The rubber-handled clippers. The touch of a thorn and rose. I want to tell Ken what I am experiencing but am afraid to break the spell. This is so . . . so vicarious. His abilities, right now, at this moment, are mine, and I have the wonderful sensation that we truly are one at last.

How odd that God should use my weakness, my inability, to bring us a greater sense of unity. Of oneness. This must be what faith does.

It is a profound mystery.

KEN PLACES HIS fork and knife on the plate and leans toward me to whisper, "Do you want me to put the coffee on now?"

"It's all taken care of," I whisper back, glancing around the dining-room table at our guests. "I had Rana put the coffee maker on automatic."

This is new for me. I've never had to organize quite like this before. Planning menus. Choosing table linens. Timing everything to go in and out of the oven or on and off the stove, might seem simple to some, but I've used the hands of three different people at three different times today.

"Great lamb, Joni," Greg comments.

"Yeah, didn't she do a super job?" Ken says as he reaches for the meat platter. "My wife's a good cook." He takes another slice of lamb and then ladles a spoonful of mint sauce on top.

"Really? I'm glad you like it. It's a favorite recipe." My cheeks feel a little flushed. Not with embarrassment, but with pride. Although every person at the table knows that I didn't slice the garlic or rub the spices into the meat or place it on a rack in the oven, they all acknowledge that I cooked the meal.

And most importantly, Ken is proud. *"My wife's a good cook."* I savor the taste of his words.

After dinner our guests join in to clear the table and stack the dishes. I don't mind. In fact, I'm glad they feel comfortable enough to make themselves at home. And it gives Ken some help that I can't give.

Oh, I do so love being his wife. And this whole journey of two becoming one is what I enjoy most. It's an adventure. The path that we travel in a wheelchair, though, is sometimes covered with thin ice. But so far we haven't fallen flat. My disability hasn't made the journey arduous. I not only love Ken, I'm in love with him.

We sit around the table, lingering over custard pie, coffee, and small talk. Ken leans on his elbow and pokes his crust with a fork, telling Greg and Nancy some of his favorite stories about our new life together. Finally, though, Greg rises and stretches, saying that it's late and they should leave.

The front door clicks shut behind Ken as he walks out to the car with Greg and Nancy. I wheel to the kitchen to flick on the outside lights for them. Then I turn my wheelchair in a tight circle away from the wall switch and carefully bulldoze aside one of the dining-room chairs so I can reach the table. In a clumsy effort to help Ken with cleaning up, I lean forward, straining to wedge my arm behind several coffee cups and dessert plates. As I gingerly slide the dishes toward the edge of the table, my arm suddenly spasms. The dishes crash to the floor, and the forks clatter, the coffee and cream spilling on our oriental rug.

"Drat!" I grimace. My pants leg is soaked and a puddle of cream pools on my footpedal and drips on the rug. I cannot even wheel away from the mess for fear of picking up splinters and slivers of shattered china in my wheels and tracking the debris over the floor. So I sit. Frustrated and near tears, I make stupid wishes about being a paraplegic. Then, at least, I could use my hands.

I knew this evening was too good to be true, I bemoan. Our friends are barely out of the driveway and I've ruined everything. And poor Ken. He'll not only have to clean dishes, but me and this mess too. And I can't even help.

I will not allow myself to believe that our marriage is weakened by the presence of a wheelchair. My thoughts come back to haunt me. I know—I've reminded Ken—that God's power shows up best in weakness, but now I'm too weak to even pray for emotional strength.

The front door jars open. "Hey, wasn't this fun?" Ken calls from the hallway. He enters the room and abruptly stops. "Wh-what?"

I wait, my stomach knotting.

He laughs. "What in the world . . . ?" He bends and picks up a broken dish. "Here," he says, rising, "let me get a dishcloth."

"I . . . I thought I'd be able to help," I stammer.

"Help?" he says, standing at the kitchen sink, waiting for the water to warm up. He adds, "It's not your job to clean up, Jon. You did enough making dinner."

I watch him in silence as he stoops to wipe the rug and floor. He refolds the cloth and swipes the crumbs off my pants leg, lifting my foot to dab the cream off the footpedal.

"It means a lot that you liked tonight . . . you know, the dinner and all," I say quietly.

He looks up. "Joni, I told you, it was great."

"No, I mean that I'm glad that you really thought . . . uh, thought that—"

"—that you actually made the meal?" he asks, his hand on my knee.

I smile.

He laughs again, and a wave of relief washes over me. I am weak but he is strong. He has lifted the burden, and I suddenly remember another time when I had done the same for him. With just a word, a smile . . . we bear each other's burdens and multiply more of those bonds.

HERE I AM, just like any other homemaker, I think to myself while watching the box boy load my groceries into the van. I move my wheelchair aside to allow a woman with a brimming supermarket cart to go to her car. She smiles as she passes. She carries a baby strapped to her chest in a kangaroo pouch. With one hand she handles the cart and with the other a toddler who insists on grabbing for grapes that spill over the bag. I smile. She and I have something in common: people might ask us both, "How do you ever manage?"

I notice a slogan on the license-plate holder of her station wagon. *Love is a daily decision.* I tell Ken about it when I get home.

He shrugs his shoulders and continues rummaging through the bags, asking if I got his favorite cookies.

I say not and ask if he brought in the mail. He mumbles and thumbs in the direction of the living room. I wheel to the sofa table, push a few letters around, and spot a third notice on a bill. I call back into the kitchen, asking if he's taken care of it yet.

"No," he says, as he walks to the living-room door with an opened box of crackers in his hands. He suddenly remembers that a letter came today from my mother. "It was a nice note," he says and walks over to the pile of mail and begins to sort through it one by one. No letter. He murmurs that it must be somewhere.

I wheel back into the kitchen to take a look at the casserole in the oven. No casserole. My voice has an edge when I ask why he didn't put dinner in the oven.

"What dinner?" he asks. There was no casserole thawing on the kitchen sink when he came home. Oh, bother. I forgot to remind my attendant to take it out of the freezer this morning. I sound exasperated when I ask if he'd mind leftovers. He sighs, says that's fine, and grabs another handful of crackers from the box tucked under his arm. He opens the dry-goods cupboard and shuffles cans and jars around looking for peanuts.

He'll have to prepare dinner, I think to myself and decide that I better not push the point of crackers and peanuts.

He opens the refrigerator door and places several bowls of food on the counter. I suggest some ideas of warming up the leftovers, but he sends out a silent signal that he would rather do it himself. I leave him alone and head back toward the living room to look further for my mother's letter. As I pass, I spy it open on one of the kitchen chairs under the table.

"What's it doing *here!*" I mutter. I know Ken hears me.

"What's that?" he says with a hint of challenge.

"The mail. I wish we could decide on one place to put it."

The refrigerator door slams. "It's *always* on the sofa table, Joni."

"Well I *always* find it slopped on a chair or thrown on top of the medical cupboard or . . ." My words fade away. I've made my point.

"Are you in a bad mood or something?"

"No. Why, are you?" I snap.

Suddenly we are reading a bad script, speaking words that are poised, ready to strike and hurt. Why, he asks, don't I use my own razors. Why, I ask, does he use my good eyebrow tweezers to pick fleas off Scruffy. Each of us checks off a list of negatives, and the quarrel grows loud and grotesque, out of proportion and a little insane. I slam my wheelchair on fast forward and skim his toes as I pass him.

Dinner is forgotten, at least for a while. Fuming, I wish I could get out of the house and into my van, but I'd have to ask him to open the door to the garage. I don't want to ask him to do anything for me.

Instead, I park my wheelchair by the sliding glass door in the living room and stare blankly out at the backyard. Pots clunk on the counter and cupboard doors bang shut. Scruffy sits by the footpedal of my wheelchair, looking up at me with bewildered eyes. I feel my face losing the glowing red heat of the quarrel, and numb feelings of hopelessness fill the moments. I don't think. I just feel . . . despondent.

And paralyzed. I have never felt so paralyzed.

I drop my gaze to my motionless legs. I imagine myself stomping out the front door or standing up to him with an accusing finger for every pointed word I have to say. I picture myself gathering up the mail and throwing it defiantly in the waste can or banging pots and kicking cupboard doors shut, all in the name of leftovers.

But I cannot do any of these things—will never be able to do them.

I feel trapped. By Ken. And by God.

An hour passes, and the tactical satisfaction of sitting silently in front of the glass door also passes. I sense Ken enter the living room behind me. I decide that I shall speak soon if he doesn't, but he breaks the silence first.

"I think this is a lot more than we figured on."

"So what do you want to do about it?" When he doesn't answer, I turn my wheelchair around to face him. He sits slumped on the couch, arms folded, his gaze frozen on the empty fireplace as if wishing he were elsewhere too.

"I don't know. I don't know if it's me or you or your wheelchair. I just know I can't live like this. I can't stand it when you come on with that strong-willed tone of yours." I try to interrupt, but he continues. "And I know . . . I know," he says, holding his hand out like a cop stopping traffic, "it's because you're a survivor, a . . . a fighter. The wheelchair has made you that way." He pauses. "But I just can't handle you like that."

Since we're being honest, I peel back a layer of my heart and tell him the truth for the moment. "Well, I don't mean this to sound hurtful, but . . . I don't like you either. I feel like every time the slightest little conflict surfaces, you back off, and I'm the one who's supposed to walk on eggshells around the house. I can't live like that."

He looks up, not at all surprised with my confession. "Well, so we don't like each other," he says in a matter-of-fact way. We sit there in stubborn silence. I am out in deep and unknown waters, far beyond the shallows of my own security. We are in the dangerous and unpredictable depths of a real marital conflict.

"Maybe the only thing to do now is pray," he offers after a while.

I know he's right, but I don't want to pray for him. I'm ashamed I feel that way.

"I don't know what to pray for," he adds. "Let's pray about . . . oh, what the heck, I don't know . . . whatever." He lowers his voice as well as his head, sliding his hands through his hair.

He mumbles a few well-worn phrases, mechanically saying things about God and His greatness and goodness and holiness and mercy. But as I listen, I hear his heart begin to soften through his words. The pace of his prayer slows, and his quiet voice wrenches and pleads as he finishes.

My prayer begins just as hollow sounding as his—I'm reluctant to give way any more than is necessary, mouthing phrases I don't feel and pulling back from the full intensity of the moment. But I know prayer is the right way, and I have faith enough to doubt and yet still believe. After several moments, I too sense my heart beginning to melt. In a broken way I ask for mercy. Mercy for me, a sinner who jealously guards against the irresponsible use of my eyebrow tweezers. And mercy for Ken, who's just doing his best, just trying to make his way.

Ken prays again, and I find myself listening in as if hiding behind a confessional curtain, wondering at the way he exposes his heart, naked and bleeding, in prayer. Tears begin to well. It seems such a private, sacred moment. And as Ken continues to labor in his prayer, his hands tightly clasped, I have an overwhelming desire to quit praying and reach out to embrace him.

Within moments he abruptly stops, looks up and takes a deep breath with his hands on his chest. "I can't believe this. A load of concrete is off of me. I feel so . . . so light."

"'That's amazing," I tell him. "And just seconds ago I felt the same peace. And contentment." I look at him with understanding eyes. Without thinking I utter those words, "I love you."

Ken rises and steps around the coffee table, his arms outstretched. He leans down and embraces me, burying his head into my shoulder. He holds me tightly. I'm nearly breathless.

We remember a verse: "No temptation has seized you except what is common to man. And God is faithful; he will not let you be tempted beyond what you can bear. But when you are tempted, he will also provide a way out so that you can stand up under it."[8] Our problems are not all that extraordinary, even with a severe disability. And our problems won't go away. But once again, grace and prayer—words that can sound so ethereal and esoteric—find substance and meaning through those very problems.

And we feel a sense of wonder at how strong Ken is when I am weak. At how weak Ken is when I am strong.

And how God, with His strength, keeps us both from falling from grace.

J ESUS LEARNED OBEDIENCE from the things that He suffered. And Ken and I, servants no greater than our Master, learn to do the same. This is the gristmill of our marriage. And yet what peaceful fruit it yields. Ken and I are growing. Individually, yes. Together, so much more.

The heavy hand of heartache lays us low when we disobey. But we learn from suffering. My . . . that is, *our* wheelchair, this strange and oftentimes unwelcomed addition to our life together, makes us trust. Teaches us to obey. And we find joy, fresh and invigorating, each day.

We also find we have a message. Joni and Friends sends us to Poland where we speak before churches and give Christ's gospel to disabled people at rehabilitation centers. My books are read there. The film in Polish is shown there. But who am I . . . who are we . . . to inspire or encourage others who must suffer so much more than we do? Ken and I carefully study maps, learning the names of strange-sounding places like Katowice or Wroclaw. We also carefully study what we should say.

Behind a flimsy wooden screen that separates us from a noisy and packed church, Ken, with his strong and dark hands, grasps my lifeless fingers. We plead together in prayer that the Spirit will speak through us, empty vessels for His use.

I peek out from around the screen and peer into the faces of the people of Poland. Farmers with their families. Steelworkers and miners. Little boys who tug at each other and bump one another's shoulders. Young women with brightly colored kerchiefs, spots of blue and red and yellow dotted throughout a crowd dressed mostly in heavy dark coats and sweaters.

Two old women squeeze together on the front pew, their heads thinly framed in tight black scarves. Their faces are lined and tired, yet full rosy cheeks and blue eyes that sparkle tell us they enjoy their lives, hard though they may be. They look expectantly, yet subserviently, at their pastor as do so many others who are standing, crowded in the middle or side aisles. Everyone is listening to him make introductory remarks.

I can't understand why the church is so noisy, observing that no one is talking. Then it occurs to me that the din is from hundreds of coats and scarves and shoes and canes and crutches crowding and rustling against one another. The cold paster walls of the church echo sounds off the high wooden ceiling. It is a chilly night, yet the air is tight and hot and humid—and charged.

A young man, who I guess has multiple sclerosis, sits humped over in his pea jacket, his hands twisting a handkerchief. His wheelchair is old, the drab green leather torn. Its wheels are different sizes, as though he has pieced together mismatching parts, perhaps cannibalizing footpedals and armrests from other, older wheelchairs. My heart goes out to him, and I wonder if he will ask me about some rumors he has heard of wondrous medical cures in the West. Perhaps that's why he twists his scarf, anxious for hope and a chance to talk with someone who might hold some secret answers.

The bright scrubbed face of a young girl whose lips, full and naturally pink, are parted in a mild and gentle smile. Her eyes glow. I'm sure she knows Jesus. She sits in a molded orange plastic chair someone has provided at the end of the first pew and leans on a black cane. Spindly thin calves encased in old leg braces and 1940s shoes tell me she may have had polio.

I look down at my own wheelchair, each aluminum spoke of my wheels polished and clean. I look at my black seat cushion, a $250 price tag in the West. I have already met many disabled people in Poland who sit on couch cushions or doubled-up feather pillows. Or no cushions at all. I'm glad that I have worn a very plain wool sweater and that my hair is styled simply. I vigorously rub my cheek on my sweater sleeve to scrub off any trace of blusher. Ken guesses what I am thinking, reaches around my neck and tilts my head back and kisses me reassuringly.

He wheels me onto the platform and parks my chair next to the woman who will translate our message. The noise in the church increases as people slide forward in their seats or shoulder in front of one another to get a better view. Ken and I trade shy, nervous smiles with the congregation.

My message is about trusting and obeying. I had planned to share the story of the thoroughbred hunter I trained in show jumping as a teenager. Through my horse I have often drawn parallels between the absolute trust and confidence he showed me, his master, and the sort of unchallenged and abandoned trust and obedience God expects from us. But that story won't work here. The only horses I've seen in Poland are plowing fields or pulling carts. So I make up a story about their horses, obediently plowing the straight and narrow, plodding steadily under a heavy yoke. The farmers seem happy, surprised even, that I know the language of their earth. But I'm more happy that they so readily grasp the point—to trust and obey. The farmers, who handle harnesses and horses every day, also learn something new from a girl in a wheelchair.

"So then, those of you who suffer according to the will of God, commit yourself to your faithful Creator and continue to do good,"[9] I sum up. "Committing yourself to God is trusting Him . . . continuing to do good is obeying Him," I say, my eyes making contact with the wizened old women who sit nodding in the front pew and with the black liquid eyes of the young handicapped girl who smiles back at me with confidence and hope. As I speak, I think about the struggles she must face here in Eastern Europe and how her faith, a gentle and fragrant offering to God, contrasts with the oppression all around her. In many ways she is a prisoner. Yet her confident gaze, her hopeful smile, even the way she leans forward on her cane tell me she is far more free than many I know in the West.

Ken comes back and joins me on the platform, and we talk about trusting and obeying in our marriage. We explain how the disability has become a weakness about which to boast, for then God's power rests on us.

Oh, but they mustn't think I am extraordinary or heroic. Me, this Westerner with wings on her wheelchair, able to smile and speak and write and paint and sing. We are by no means heroic, Ken and I. Marriage has made us face up to every hidden, disguised little weakness, and we know too well who we really are. We are sinners—thankfully, saved by grace. And that, appropriately, closes our message.

Nothing extraordinary or heroic happens this evening in church. But what does happen is a very ordinary, miraculous work of the Holy Spirit. The meeting ends, but people stay to pray and talk. The young man with multiple sclerosis seeks more of a cure for his despondency than his disability.

Ken kneels beside the wheelchair of a boy and draws him out with simple questions through the aid of a friend who speaks Polish. My strong husband touches the boy's fragile, thin arm, and he throws back his head and grins. This is so like Ken, taking time to open himself to another who hurts, sharing healing through his words and his smile.

The young girl with the cane hobbles up to me and says that she always knew, always felt that we were very much alike, very much one in the Spirit of Christ. I clumsily lift my arm in a welcoming gesture. She props her cane against my chair, and we embrace, two believers from different worlds.

As the girl holds me tightly in her arms, I watch Ken move to the next boy in a wheelchair. I picture moments when he and I have touched and embraced. I think about lavishing my life on him—pouring myself into him, just one other person. Yes, perhaps I would like to think of myself as having a great impact on the world, touching and influencing thousands of lives. But that thought is balanced by the realization that there are times when I do not even adequately touch Ken's life, the person closest to me. It is a humbling thought, and I feel tremendous gratitude for my husband as I watch him turn and greet some of the farmers.

The young girl straightens and dabs her eyes with her kerchief. She tells me how much my book has meant to her and then steps back to allow others to come forward. As her eyes continue to hold mine, I remember that it is not a movie or a ministry that makes my mark in eternity. It is not a book—or many books. It is not even the chance to travel so many thousands of miles from home to talk about Jesus. For this girl—living within limits I can hardly imagine, coming from a culture so strange and different—this girl and I approach God's throne in the same manner. Jesus asks the same of both of us.

Whether single or married, in plenty or in want, we must both trust. We must obey.

E VERYWHERE WE GO in Poland people give us flowers—fresh, thick bouquets of friesians and sweet pea, tulips and gladiola in full bloom in our drab hotel rooms.

But how odd it is to see these same flowers swishing in the wind. Here. Here in Auschwitz. Even though the grounds of this death camp are so very tidy, delicate wisps of wildflowers crop up here and there, around the bases of brick buildings and trunks of trees. We wonder if the government, which operates a museum here, has sown wildflower seeds to brighten this horrible, depressing place.

I notice a row of lovely rose bushes planted just yards away from the gruesome gas chambers. I ask our guide about the roses, and he is quick to point out that where flowers are now was once hard, naked clay, every blade of grass picked clean by starving prisoners.

Bare bricks and barbed wire . . . storehouses of eyeglasses and hair and gold teeth, canes and crutches, shoes, hearing aids . . . stacks of yellowed and dusty record books, neatly tabulated numberless names . . . gallows and guard towers . . . even the ominous chimneys and the ovens—all these things I've always associated with Nazi death camps are here. And I shiver, not so much from the cold as from the thought that people handicapped like me were the first to be exterminated, labeled as "useless bread gobblers."

But even this thought is not entirely new.

It's the flowers. The flowers are something I didn't expect. And for that reason, their out-of-placeness touches me as nothing else.

We journey the short distance from Auschwitz to Birkenau. Here, trainloads of Jews and dissidents were emptied out into the freezing night to face the machine guns of powerful and insane men. Children were gun-butted one way; their mothers herded the other. Men were separated into groups of the old and young. But virtually all of them, millions of them, ended up in one place—the incinerator, now crumbled and overgrown at the end of the camp.

Nothing stands in this camp. Our guide explains that what appear to be orderly rows of heaps of brick were once the smoke stacks of wooden barracks. Nothing remains of the guard towers. Even the train tracks and railroad ties are rotted and uprooted.

But light, airy little field daisies carpet the acres, swaying in wave upon wave.

"What are you thinking?" Ken asks, stooping to pluck a wildflower.

"I was thinking of Tante Corrie . . . Corrie ten Boom," I finally answer. "She was in a place not unlike this." I nod toward the field of ghosts. "By all accounts, she should have died forty years ago in that concentration camp," I sigh.

Ken shakes his head in wonder. "Who would have thought she would leave that awful place. At fifty years of age," he marvels, his eyes fastened on the crumbled incinerators just yards away. "And then to start a whole new ministry."

I recall Tante Corrie's recent funeral at a small suburban cemetery a few miles south of Los Angeles. It was the flowers that impressed me that day too. No hothouse blooms stuck in styrofoam cut-out shapes of hearts or crosses or doves. No white satin banners with gold-sprinkled messages of sympathy. Instead, there were vases—tens of vases—of freshly cut tulips of yellow and red. Bouquets of dewy white carnations and bunches of heavy red roses someone had clipped from Corrie's backyard.

The casket was closed. The music was Bach. The eulogies were glowing but understated. The only extravagance was the profusion of flowers, and the little stone chapel was filled with a sweet fragrance.

Now I sit in silence in this vast field, memories of Corrie stirring my thoughts. The only things that move are the wind and the daisies. It is at once striking and poignant. For Corrie, who came out of the pit of this hell, would be the first to say that the suffering in this place confronted her with the reality of the love or hate in her own heart. The confinement of her lonely cell attacked her own vanity and lonely pride. The crushing needs of her fellow prisoners constantly exposed her own need to give and share. She could not blame. She could only forgive.

I drop my gaze to the daisies Ken has tucked into the straps of my arm splints. A knowing smile crosses my lips. I would be the first to say that my wheelchair confronts me daily with the love or hate in my own heart. It attacks my pride and constantly exposes my need to give to others who suffer. I have no one to blame for my circumstances.

I glance at Ken who sits beside me in the grass. God has placed us together to have and to hold. To build up. To encourage. To love. Our marriage tirelessly exposes my need . . . our need to give and share and to cast aside blame.

I recall another memory of Corrie and flowers: the evening at that convention when, amid the applause of thousands, she lifted her bouquet of roses toward heaven. She would be the first to say that books on a bestseller list mean nothing—except that lives are changed through them. She would say that a first-run major motion picture of her life was not worth the accolades—except that people were helped through it. Even a ministry that took her all over the world with opportunities to speak and meet headlining names in evangelical circles—even that, she would say, only counts in the Kingdom as far as it serves Christ.

And I would say the same. In both my public ministry and my private life with Ken, God constantly asks me to uncover my face. But that is my joyous choice: to ask Him to chasten and purify and melt any resistance to change I might secretly hold on to.

I smile. In fact, I throw my head back and laugh out loud. And I tell Ken of the time I first met that remarkable woman years ago when we were both attending a convention where our new books were being presented. Corrie approached from down the long red-carpeted hallway of a hotel. People were all about and many sought her attention. But she strode directly toward me, hiked her cane on her elbow, reached for my hand with those strong hands that all survivors have, and announced in her thick Dutch accent, "One day, my friend, we will be dancing together in heaven because of the Lord Jesus."

And today I can laugh and rejoice because Corrie is dancing now. Over the Devil and over this place.

And once changed, we shall join her.

Epilogue

"Whoever tries to keep his life will lose it, and whoever loses his life will preserve it."

Luke 17:33

᭞

I T IS ANOTHER month, another year. Ten years since the movie. If asked, I would say that I have found who I am. A prisoner of Christ. Free in Christ. I know where I'm going.

The changes in my journey keep unfolding like the petals of one of those huge pink roses from the bush near our bedroom window. Every once in a while that line from the song in the movie rings true for me: "Each mile I put between the past and the future in Your hand, I learn more of Your providence and I find out who I am."

Who I am—really am—keeps changing. But in a nice sort of way. A movie and a marriage, not to mention a ministry to disabled people, have taught me that in losing my life—trusting, obeying, submitting—I am finding it. Like that rose, I am a bud being "transformed from glory to glory."

It hits me especially this evening how much everything has changed. We sit in the back of a crowded school auditorium in Montreal, Canada. My mother has joined Judy and me on this trip, and the three of us watch, without the benefit of a translator, a French version of the movie *Joni*.

The movie. I have nearly forgotten those wrenching times of fits and starts in my walk with Christ. Putting on masks and painfully ripping them off as though they were stuck to me with adhesive. My discontent and restlessness during that film taught me never to be surprised by my sin. And there will always be new and painful adjustments, even though by the grace of God I have fully accepted my wheelchair.

The movie went on to grow in its own way. We still hear—years later—reports on showings around the world and how through its message tens of thousands of people have stepped into the Kingdom of Christ. I feel humbled and warmed at that. This strip of celluloid with its transparent images has a life of its own.

As I watch, I hear the familiar actors and actresses saying words that make no sense to my American ears. But the images are intimate, and I study the pretty actress in the blue bathing suit as her brown hands grasp the edge of the raft, and in one graceful motion she fluidly lifts her body out of the water. Her knees bend, and she pitches forward in an awkward dive, her body slicing into the surface of the water. She is under.

But I have come up and out. I can tell. Nothing about this scene jars me. It is, after all, a movie about a seventeen-year-old girl who long ago and far away fell into the water. And fell into a whole new life.

I look at my mother who still is gripped by these scenes. Yet she has changed. Tears no longer stain her face when she thinks of my wheelchair. My dear dad, too old and frail to make this special trip to Montreal with us, has changed also. We will telephone him in Maryland tonight from our motel-room phone, but I know how bad his hearing has gotten—he will barely understand us. Mom and I will call Jay and Rob and talk to Earecka—she is learning so many new grown-up words. Then we will call Ken back in California. Oh, how I miss him when he is not able to travel with me.

"Each mile I put between the past and the . . . future . . ."

The future. Nothing about the future jars me either. I used to have this idea that God was leading me to some particular end in this life, some desired goal. I'd get to excited, so anxious, I would barely pay attention to the present moment.

But I'm finding out more and more that reaching a particular earthly goal is merely incidental. It is trusting and obeying the Lord Jesus Christ in the mile of the journey right now that counts.

I close my eyes and think about this moment around me. There is a girl in a wheelchair at the end of the row in front of us. There is a teenager sitting directly ahead, her boyfriend sensuously rubbing her back and neck as she squirms. I must make certain to talk with them. An elderly couple sits in folded chairs at the other end of our row. I hope they don't rush away. This is the moment—and perhaps these are the people who, by the Spirit of Christ, will be changed tonight.

I keep my eyes closed and listen to the movie in French. If I were to open them I could tell, line for line, what the characters are saying. They represent a family and a small group of friends just trying, with God's grace, to get on with their lives. To find out who they are and where they fit in the Kingdom.

It is just an old, old story of people losing their lives only to find them. New characters have been added—Ken and the Tada family, Vicky and Rana, Judy and

Sam, and many others. There are some different locations besides the Maryland farm—places like California and Poland and Montreal.

But the journey continues. And it is still a drama of choices and changes for us all.

NOTES

Notes

The Movie

1. 1 Corinthians 10:12 NASB.
2. Ephesians 4:17-19.
3. Romans 12:3.
4. "Journey's End" by Rob Tregenza. Used by permission.
5. Isaiah 40:31 KJV.
6. The quotes are from Dr. Martyn Lloyd-Jones, *Studies in the Sermon on the Mount* (Grand Rapids, Mich.: Wm. B. Eerdmans, 1971), 62.
7. 1 Corinthians 15:39-40, 48, 50.
8. James 4:8-10.
9. Arthur Bennet, *Valley of Vision* (Glasgow: Banner of Truth, 1983), 187.

The Ministry

1. John 19:28, paraphrased.
2. Matthew 25:35, 40.
3. 2 Corinthians 1:9.
4. James 2:15.
5. Mark 2:3-5.
6. Matthew 16:17 RSV.
7. 1 Corinthians 1:27.
8. Ephesians 6:13.
9. Ephesians 6:13, 16.

10. Ephesians 6:12.
11. "When Pretty Things Get Broken" by Joni Eareckson Tada. Used by permission.
12. Colossians 2:6-7.
13. "Joni's Waltz" by Nancy Honeytree. Used by permission.
14. 2 Corinthians 10:5.

Our Marriage

1. 1 John 4:19.
2. Matthew 25:21, paraphrased.
3. 1 John 4:19 RSV.
4. 1 Peter 2:15.
5. Matthew 5:9 KJV.
6. 2 Timothy 4:8 and 1 John 3:2, paraphrased.
7. Ephesians 3:31-32.
8. 1 Corinthians 10:13.
9. 1 Peter 4:19, paraphrased.

JONI EARECKSON TADA is the founder and president of JAF Ministries, an organization accelerating Christian ministry in the disability community. Mrs. Tada's role as an advocate for disabled persons led to a presidential appointment on the National Council on Disability for three and a half years, during which time the Americans with Disabilities Act became law.

Through her work with JAF Ministries, she records a five-minute radio program, "Joni and Friends," which is heard daily on over 900 broadcast outlets worldwide, providing information and encouragement to those with disabilities as well as raising disability awareness. Other JAF ministries include The Christian Fund for the Disabled (a financial assistance program), Family Retreats, Field Ministry, and Wheels For The World, which collects and refurbishes used wheelchairs and medical equipment to distribute around the world. Mrs. Tada is a sought-after conference speaker both in the U.S. and internationally, and she writes a column for *Moody Monthly* magazine.

Mrs. Tada's first name is recognized in many countries due to her bestselling books, especially *Joni*, and the full-length feature film of the same name which has been translated into numerous languages and shown in scores of countries around the world. She is also an internationally known mouth artist as a result of long hours during her rehabilitation learning how to paint, holding a brush between her teeth. She is the author of 18 books, ranging from autobiography, children's books and disability outreach to the issue of euthanasia and assisted suicide. She has received the American Academy of Achievement's Golden Plate Award, the Courage Award of the Courage Rehabilitation Center, the Award of Excellence from the Patricia Neal Rehabilitation Center, and the Victory Award from the National Rehabilitation Hospital.

1/16